POLITICS IN THE REPUBLIC OF IRELAND

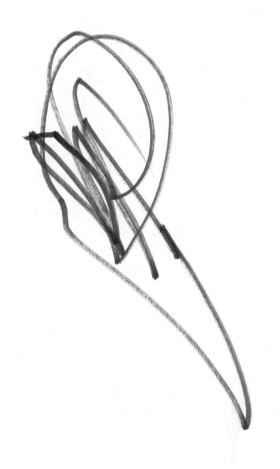

Politics in the Republic of Ireland

**second edition
reprinted with minor amendments**

Edited by

John Coakley
and
Michael Gallagher

PSAI Press

A paperback original

© PSAI Press 1992, 1993, 1996

ISBN 0 9519748 3 1

Origination by the editors
Cover design by Michael Laver
Printed by SciPrint, Shannon

PSAI Press, College of Humanities, University of Limerick
Fax: +353-61-202569

Contents

List of Tables

List of Figures

Preface to the first edition

This book arose out of a shared feeling among a number of teachers of courses on Irish Politics at universities and other third-level institutions in Ireland and further afield that there was no book that matched satisfactorily the course they taught. Existing texts were either out of date or did not give adequate coverage of some central elements in the Irish Politics courses that were actually offered. The problem was becoming particularly acute given the steady growth of interest among students and the rapidly expanding numbers taking such courses.

Ironically, this shortage of material coincided with an increase both in the output of research into many aspects of Irish politics and government and in the number of academics who had built up an expertise in particular areas of the subject. It was only a matter of time before the logical solution was arrived at: a collaborative effort that would draw on the wide range of expertise among Irish political scientists to produce the book that we, as teachers of Irish politics and government, have been looking for.

The emergence of the book owes a lot to the existence of the Political Studies Association of Ireland (PSAI), the body that draws together and represents those engaged in the professional study of politics in and of Ireland. Its meetings and conferences have provided the opportunity for the establishment of informal networks between those teaching at different institutions, for comparing notes on our experience with existing textbooks and for discussing alternatives. It is fitting that the book is published by the Association's publishing house, the PSAI Press, with any profits being ploughed back into financing further publications and activities of the Association.

Planning for the book began in 1991 and the final outline was sent to contributors in November of that year. The target of having the book ready by September 1992 was thus highly ambitious, even with the benefits of desktop publishing and the fast turnaround guaranteed by our printers, and there were those who doubted whether the schedule was realistic. The fact that the book has appeared by the target date is due primarily to the 13 contributors, who accepted with equanimity the news that they would not receive any royalties for their efforts, applied themselves enthusiastically to the task, and did not protest too vigorously at the constant harassment to which they were subjected by the editors.

As well as writing their own chapters, several contributors have been especially helpful to the project by suggesting improvements to the overall plan or to individual chapters. In particular, Brian Farrell has been an enthusiastic backer of the project from the start—as has Michael Laver, who can also take credit for the cover design, for producing the financial projections that convinced first the committee and then the 1991 annual general meeting of the PSAI that paying for the start-up costs of a book such as this was likely to be a sound investment, and for his energetic pre-publication efforts to ensure that it would be. Others who have helped by commenting on one or more chapters include Brian Keary, John Logan, Brian Mercer Walker and Bernadette Whelan.

The aim throughout has been to produce a book that combined real substance and a readable style. It is aimed particularly at undergraduates at third-level institutions, but we hope that it will also meet the needs of the wider public interested in the politics and government of Ireland. In addition, since no coun-try's politics can be understood in isolation, the authors have written their chap-ters with a comparative (especially a western European) dimension very much in mind. The venerable generalisation that "Ireland is different", so that there is no need to make the effort to compare its politics with those of other countries, is no longer adequate. It is a well-worn observation that Ireland has become a more outward-looking country since the 1950s, and its academic community has not been unaffected by this development. *Politics in the Republic of Ireland* is among the fruits of these broader horizons.

John Coakley and Michael Gallagher
Limerick and Dublin, August 1992

Preface to the reprinted second edition

When the first edition of *Politics in the Republic of Ireland* was published in 1992, the expectation of authors and editors alike was that only after a period of several years would a second edition need to be contemplated. However, the positive reception accorded to the book, whose entire print run sold out in less than a year, meant that either a reprint or a second edition would be needed by September 1993 at the latest. The incidence of a number of significant political events between mid 1992 and autumn 1993 tipped the scales in favour of producing a fresh edition of the book. The general election of November 1992, the formation of the Fianna Fáil-Labour "Partnership" government with new ideas on maximising the effectiveness of the machinery of government, and the three abortion-related referendums of November 1992 are perhaps the most notable of these, but developments in virtually every field of the governmental and political systems have required amendment to and updating of every chapter in this book. In addition, suggestions for improvement from a number of quarters have been taken into account in the production of this edition. As with the first edition, a number of people have helped by giving their comments on one or more chapters or in other ways, and we should like to thank particularly John Baird, Gerard Hogan, Jack Jones, Darragh Murphy, Bernadette Whelan and members of the staff of the Houses of the Oireachtas.

This volume is a reprinted version of the second edition, which was originally published in 1993. The opportunity has been taken to correct a few minor errors, but otherwise the book is the same as the 1993 edition. Like the first edition of *Politics in the Republic of Ireland*, this reprinted second edition is published by PSAI Press, the publishing house of the Political Studies Association of Ireland, and profits from the book will be ploughed back into financing further publication and other activities of the Association.

John Coakley and Michael Gallagher
Dublin, September 1996

1 / THE FOUNDATIONS OF STATEHOOD

John Coakley

In attempting to understand contemporary politics in any country, familiarity with its past provides not merely a useful explanation of certain unusual patterns of behaviour but also an essential key in grasping many of the central realities of political life. The study of Ireland's past is particularly important to an understanding of its present. Although political histories of Ireland often start at 1922 and conventional wisdom stresses the "new era" that then began, significant elements of continuity underlay the sharp political break that took place at the time that the state was founded. Before looking at the establishment of the state itself and at subsequent developments, then, we must examine the legacy of the old regime. In the first section of this chapter, particular emphasis is placed on institutional developments and political processes of the pre-independence period that were to prove of enduring significance; the third section takes up these themes for the post-independence period. In between these two sections is sandwiched a discussion of the political background to the establishment of the independent Irish state (for more general histories of the period see Lyons, 1973; Foster, 1988; Lee, 1989).

THE PRELUDE TO STATEHOOD

The apparatus of the modern state first developed in Ireland under the tutelage of the English monarchy. Prior to this, Gaelic Irish society, though attaining a very considerable degree of cultural, artistic and literary development in the early medieval period, had shown few signs of following the path of contemporary European political development. The Norman invasions that began in 1169 and the establishment of the Lordship of Ireland that followed after 1171 (with the Norman King of England exercising the functions of Lord of Ireland) marked the beginning of rudimentary statehood. Although Norman or English control was little more than nominal for several centuries, the vigorous Tudor dynasty subjugated the island in the sixteenth century, a process whose beginning was marked by the promotion in 1541 of the Lord of Ireland to the status of King. The Kingdom of Ireland continued thereafter to have its own political institutions, though a much more profound degree of British influence followed on the passing of the Act of Union in 1800, which created a new state, the United Kingdom of Great Britain and Ireland (UK).

In looking at the legacy of this system of government to independent Ireland, we may identify three areas in which spillover effects were important. First, at the *constitutional* level, certain roles and offices that had evolved over the centuries provided an important stepping stone for the builders of the new state. Second, at the *administrative* level, the development of a large civil service bequeathed to the new state a body of trained professional staff. Third, at the *political* level, Irish voters and politicians had for some decades before 1922 been accustomed to increasingly democratic political practices and had been part of a political culture whose assumptions bore some similarity to those of today.

The constitution of the old regime

In an era when travel was slow, difficult and dangerous, it was neither sensible nor practical for expanding dynasties to seek to govern all of their territories from a fixed centre or capital. In common with the peripheral areas of other medieval states, then, Norman Ireland acquired a set of political institutions that were gradually to evolve into modern ones. The hub around which political life revolved, at least in theory, was the King's personal representative in Ireland, the Lord Lieutenant. The Lord Lieutenant was advised on everyday affairs of government by a "Privy Council" made up of his chief officials, and on longer-term matters by a "Great Council" or Parliament that met irregularly.

The evolution of the Irish Parliament followed a path similar to that of its English counterpart (see Farrell, 1973). It first met in Castledermot, Co Kildare, in 1264, and for the next four centuries it continued to assemble from time to time in various Irish towns, with Dublin increasingly becoming dominant. By 1692 it had acquired the shape that it was to retain up to 1800. Its House of Commons consisted of 300 members (two each from 32 counties, from 117 cities, towns or boroughs and from Trinity College, Dublin), and its House of Lords of a small but variable number: archbishops and bishops of the established (Protestant) Church of Ireland and lay members of the Irish peerage. The Irish parliament thus resembled its English counterpart closely, despite the earlier existence of a third house (of the clergy; such a house was common in continental Europe).

By accepting the Act of Union of 1800, this parliament voted itself out of existence, opting instead for a merged or "united" parliament for all of Great Britain and Ireland. In the new House of Commons there were to be 100 Irish MPs (about 15 per cent of the total), while the House of Lords would receive 32 additional members: the Irish peerage would elect 28 of its number for life, and four members of the Irish Protestant episcopate would sit in the House of Lords in rotation.

Although the legislative branch of government thus disappeared completely from Ireland, the executive branch did not. Throughout the entire period of the union, the existence of a "Government of Ireland" was recognised. The Lord Lieutenant, as representative of the sovereign, was formal head of this government. This post was always filled by a leading nobleman who, in addition to his governmental functions, was "the embodiment of the 'dignified' aspects of the state, the official leader of Irish social life" (McDowell, 1964, p. 52). He left the actual day-to-day running of the process of government, however, to his principal assistant, the Chief Secretary. This official had responsibility for the management of Irish affairs in the House of Commons and, although he was not always a member of the cabinet, he was at least a prominent member of the governing party. Increasingly, effective power passed from the Lord Lieutenant to the Chief Secretary, following the pattern of a similar shift in power in Britain from the King to the Prime Minister. (Significantly, the Lord Lieutenant's official residence, the Viceregal Lodge in the Phoenix Park, has now become the President's residence, Áras an Uachtaráin, while the Chief Secretary's Office in Dublin Castle went on to become the core of the Department of the Taoiseach.)

Even after the union, Ireland remained constitutionally distinct from the rest of the UK. Although all legislation was now enacted through the UK parliament, in many policy areas (including education, agriculture, land reform, policing, health and local government) separate legislation was enacted for the different components of the United Kingdom. For example, the parliament of 1880-85 passed 71 Acts whose application was exclusively Irish (out of a total of 422 Acts, the rest being "English", "Scottish", "United Kingdom" or other). Electoral reforms illustrate the extent to which Ireland was treated in a distinctive way even in the matter of representation at Westminster: it was only in 1884 that a uniform electoral law was adopted for all parts of the UK.

The question of electoral reform indeed has a central place in the process of constitutional evolution. This is important not only in itself but also, as we shall see, as an illustration of the constitutional distinctiveness of Ireland. It has been assumed since the late nineteenth century that democratic elections have four characteristics, and these are frequently written into modern constitutions: voting is *direct*, the process is *secret*, all votes are of *equal* weight and suffrage is *universal*. Elections to the old Irish House of Commons and to its post-union successor always operated on the basis of direct voting: electors selected their members of parliament without the intervention of any intermediate electoral college, so the first of the four conditions was met.

The second condition was met rather later. Traditionally, voting was open: a public poll was conducted at a central place in the constituency, and voters declared orally the names of the candidates for whom they wished their votes to be recorded. This obviously permitted intimidation by opinion leaders such as landlords and clergy, but the Ballot Act (1872) abruptly and permanently changed these practices: in future voting was to be carried out by secret ballot, except in the case of illiterates and other incapacitated persons.

Third, in the old Irish House of Commons voters' voices were of unequal weight; large counties (such as Cork) and small boroughs (such as Tulsk, Bannow and Ardfert) were all represented by two MPs each, with complete disregard for their greatly varying populations. This position was rectified in three principal stages. In 1800 the smaller boroughs were abolished; in 1885 all seats were redistributed to conform more closely to the distribution of the population; and in 1922 the new constitution guaranteed that all votes would be equal.

Fourth, although in many countries extension of the right to vote was characterised by a number of major reforms and the proportion enfranchised increased in stages, the process in Ireland was more complex. This may be seen in Table 1.1. The most sweeping early changes were the extension of the right to vote to Catholics (1793) and the abolition of the county "forty-shilling freehold" (1829), one greatly extending, the other greatly reducing the electorate. The reforms of 1832, 1850 and 1868 (unlike the English reforms of 1832 and 1867) had an incremental effect only. The major reforms were those of 1884, associated with the birth of modern politics in Ireland, 1918, linked with another episode of electoral revolution, and 1923, which completed the process (for an illustration of the impact of these reforms on the proportion of the population entitled to vote, see Figure 1.1 and discussion below).

Table 1.1: Extension of voting rights, 1793-1973

Act	Major effect
Catholic Relief Act, 1793	Extension of vote to Catholics
Parliamentary Elections (Ireland) Act, 1829	Raising of county qualification from £2 to £10
Representation of the People (Ireland) Act, 1832	Minor extension of borough franchise
Representation of the People (Ireland) Act, 1850	Lowering of county qualification
Representation of the People (Ireland) Act, 1868	Lowering of borough qualification
Representation of the People Act, 1884	Uniform householder and lodger franchise
Representation of the People Act, 1918	Universal male and limited female suffrage
Electoral Act, 1923	Universal suffrage
Electoral (Amendment) Act, 1973	Reduction of voting age from 21 to 18

Emergence of state bureaucracy

Underneath the political superstructure of the Irish government, the modern Irish civil service developed gradually. This consisted of a number of departments, offices and other bodies employing considerable numbers of officials and established from time to time as the need was seen to arise. Formal control of these bodies was normally collegial rather than individual: they were directed by "Boards" or "Commissions" or groups of "Commissioners", generally overseen by the Chief Secretary. The extent of the Chief Secretary's influence was not uniform; it was decisive in the case of the Local Government Board (founded in 1872), for instance, but indirect in the case of others, such as the Board of National Education (1831). There were 29 of these bodies by 1911, employing a staff of 4,000; examples of the more important include the Department of Agriculture and Technical Instruction (1899), the Land Commission (1881) and the Congested Districts Board (1891).

In addition to these "Irish" departments answerable to the Chief Secretary, a number of departments of the "Imperial" civil service also had branches in Ireland. These were controlled ultimately by the relevant British cabinet ministers, and in some cases employed very large staffs in Ireland. The pre-union Post Office (1785) was merged with its British counterpart (1831), and underwent rapid expansion in the late nineteenth century. The old Irish revenue boards also survived the union, but were merged with their British counterparts following the Anglo-Irish customs amalgamation of 1823; they also developed considerable staffs (see Meghen, 1962; McDowell 1964). By 1911 these bodies, 11 in all, had some 23,000 employees in Ireland, of whom 20,000 worked in the Post Office.

By the beginning of the twentieth century, then, Ireland already had a very sizeable civil service, with more than 27,000 employees spread over 29 Irish and 11 UK departments. In addition, there were large field staffs in certain other areas: two police forces, the Dublin Metropolitan Police (1787) with about 1,200 and the Royal Irish Constabulary (1836) with about 10,700, and the body of national teachers, numbering some 15,600. Together, these amounted in 1911-13 to about 55,000 state employees, not including the large numbers of army and naval personnel stationed in Ireland.

Finally, it is necessary to consider the system of local government. In urban areas this had consisted of 68 cities, towns and boroughs whose local administrations survived the Act of Union, each governed by a council or corporation headed by a mayor, "sovereign", "portreeve" or "provost". Although some of these bodies were open to limited forms of election, most were not; a report in 1835 showed that most were oligarchic and self-perpetuating, that almost all were exclusively Protestant, and that only one (Tuam) had a Catholic majority. Comprehensive reform took place with the Municipal Corporations (Ireland) Act, 1840, which abolished all of these bodies and replaced those in the ten largest cities by corporations elected on a limited franchise. A second set of urban elective bodies was set up under acts of 1828 and 1854: towns with a certain minimum population were to be allowed to elect Town Commissioners to make provision for lighting of streets, paving and other local infrastructural purposes.

In rural areas the principal authority was the county grand jury, made up of large property owners selected by the county sheriff (an official appointed, in turn, by the Lord Lieutenant) and responsible for most of the activities that we associate with county councils today. As public intervention grew in the nineteenth century, however, most notably in the areas of poor relief and health, responsibilities were delegated to other bodies. In 1838 the country was divided into 130 Poor Law Unions, each governed by a Board of "Guardians", of whom some were elected and some held office *ex officio*. The "union workhouses" through which they administered poor relief continue to form a prominent feature of the local urban landscape (though they have been converted to serve a variety of other uses today); the dispensaries through which they attended to public health survive to the present; and the rating system by which they were funded formed a lasting basis for local taxation.

The final stage in the modernisation of the local government system came with the Local Government (Ireland) Act, 1898. This drew up the basis of the system of local government that has survived with some changes to the present by transferring the administrative functions of the county grand juries to new, elected county councils. It also further democratised the franchise for elections to the Boards of Guardians of Poor Law Unions, and introduced a new, lower tier of local government, consisting of rural district councils (corresponding to the rural portions of poor law unions, except when these crossed county boundaries, in which case the portions of the unions in different counties became separate rural districts) and urban district councils in the larger towns; in the smaller towns, the town commissioners continued. The only significant change in this system before independence was the introduction of proportional representation in 1920 (see Roche, 1982).

The birth of modern party politics

It is sometimes said that modern party politics began in Ireland in 1922, with only the small Labour Party being in existence before that date. In fact, there is little truth in any part of this: modern party politics began in the 1880s, and the Labour

Party dates only from 1922 as an actual political party. The growth of party politics in nineteenth century Ireland indeed follows closely a pattern of evolution identified elsewhere (Sartori, 1976, pp. 18-24). Three phases in this growth may be identified; the transition between them was marked by significant changes in levels of electoral mobilisation.

In the first phase, political life was dominated by *parliamentary parties*, defined as groups of MPs without any kind of regular electoral organisation to provide support at election time. Insofar as parties existed before the 1830s, they fell into this category. These were not parties in any recognisably modern sense; instead, Irish MPs allied themselves after 1800 to one or other of the two great English groupings, the Tories and the Whigs. Already during this period, however, the linkage between the Tory party and the Protestant establishment was beginning to find expression in geographical terms, as Tories achieved a much stronger position in the north than in the south. This may be seen in appendix 2a, which summarises the results of the 31 elections that took place under the Act of Union (because of the large number of uncontested elections, we have to rely on distribution of seats rather than of votes for an indication of party strengths). This point emerges even more clearly from Table 1.2, which is based on this appendix: in the ten elections before 1832, Tories already controlled 74 per cent of the seats in the present territory of Northern Ireland, but only 45 per cent of those in the south.

In the second phase we see the appearance of *electoral parties*, consisting not merely of loosely linked sets of MPs but rather of groups standing for some more or less coherent policy positions and supported by constituency organisations that enjoyed a degree of continuity over time. This phase began around 1830 and lasted for approximately five decades. It was characterised by the metamorphosis of the Whigs into the Liberal Party, which increasingly became the party of Catholic Ireland, and of the Tories into the Conservative Party, which quickly became the party of Protestants. The members of these parties in parliament were supported by organisations at constituency level. These support groups used such names as "Independent Clubs" on the Liberal side and "Constitutional Clubs" on the Conservative side. From a comparative perspective, this was unusual in two respects. First, constituency organisations developed at a remarkably early stage in the Irish case. Second, the content of the liberal-conservative polarisation, with its sectarian overtones, contrasted sharply with the issues at stake behind similarly named instances of polarisation elsewhere in Europe, where constitutional issues (such as conflict between the monarchy and parliament) were to the fore. In particular, the association between Catholicism and liberalism appears strange in a European context where liberalism was associated with anticlericalism.

In the context of an electorate restricted to the wealthy (who were disproportionately Protestant), Irish Conservatives, though reduced from their position of overall dominance (especially in the south, where they now controlled only 24 per cent of the seats), enjoyed solid support throughout most of this period. The relationship between the Liberals and the Catholic vote was, however, much less secure, and was open to challenge from parties representing specifically Irish interests. The most significant of these were O'Connell's Repeal Party in the 1830s and 1840s, the Independent Irish Party in the 1850s, the rather amorphous National

Table 1.2: Irish parliamentary representation, 1801-1918

Group (Number of elections)	1801-31 (10)	1832-80 (12)	1885-1910 (8)	1918 (1)
North:				
Tories/Unionists	73.6	78.6	69.5	80.0
Whigs/Liberals	14.1	18.5	2.5	0.0
Nationalists, etc.	-	0.0	28.0	10.0
Others	12.3	2.9	0.0	10.0
(Number)	(220)	(276)	(200)	(30)
South:				
Tories/Unionists	44.5	24.4	3.7	4.0
Whigs/Liberals	41.4	39.6	0.0	0.0
Nationalists, etc.	-	35.3	96.3	2.7
Others	14.1	0.7	0.0	93.3
(Number)	(780)	(980)	(624)	(75)
All Ireland:				
Tories/Unionists	50.9	36.3	19.7	25.7
Whigs/Liberals	35.4	35.0	0.6	0.0
Nationalists, etc.	-	27.5	79.7	4.8
Others	13.7	1.2	0.0	69.5
(Number)	(1,000)	(1,256)	(824)	(105)

Note: Party strengths are indicated as percentages of seats won. Before 1832 party affiliations are approximate only. "Tories/Unionists" includes Liberal Unionists; "Nationalists, etc." includes independent nationalists; in 1918, "others" refers to Sinn Féin MPs. The north is defined as the present area of Northern Ireland, the south as the Republic. The number of MPs returned by constituencies in the north was 22, 23 and 25 in the first three periods; in the south it was 78 in the first and third periods and 82 in the second period, except for the last two elections, in 1874 and 1880, when the number was 80.
Source: Calculated from appendix 2.

Association in the 1860s and, most importantly, the Home Rule Party from 1874 onwards.

The third phase was marked by the birth of modern *mass parties*. These took the form of tightly disciplined parliamentary groups resting on the support of a permanent party secretariat and a well-oiled party machine: thousands of members were organised into branches at local level, with provision for constituency conventions to select candidates and for an annual convention to elect an executive and, at least in theory, to determine policy. This development took place first on the Catholic side, with the formation of the Irish National League (1882) as constituency organisation of the Home Rule or Nationalist Party. This was modelled on an earlier agrarian organisation, the Land League (1879); another organisational predecessor, the Home Rule League, founded in 1873, had followed the model of the electoral party. On the Protestant side a similar development took place in 1885 with the formation of the Irish Loyal Patriotic Union (from 1891, the Irish Unionist Alliance), to represent southern Unionists, and a range of similar organisations, eventually brought together under the Ulster Unionist Council in 1905, to represent northern Unionists. These parties were prototypes of the party organisations that appeared after 1922 in the south (see chapter 6), and, indeed, the Ulster Unionist Council continues to the present to constitute the organisational apex of the Ulster Unionist Party in Northern Ireland.

The 1885 election marks the birth of modern Irish party politics. It was characterised by a strict polarisation between Protestant and Catholic Ireland, in which the Liberals were completely eliminated, being decisively defeated by the Nationalist Party in competing for Catholic votes. In the territory that was to become the Republic of Ireland, Nationalists won virtually all of the seats. In the north, a geographical balance between Nationalists and Unionists was established that was to persist to 1969, a phenomenon of electoral continuity without parallel in Europe (after 1969, the Nationalists were replaced by the Social Democratic and Labour Party and the Unionists were seriously challenged, most notably by the Democratic Unionist Party).

Nationalist domination of the south lasted for more than 30 years, for most of this period in single-party form (the most important exceptions were the deep divisions within the party in 1890-1900 precipitated by the issue of the leadership of Charles Stewart Parnell and the creation of a small breakaway party, largely confined to Co Cork, by William O'Brien in 1910). The Irish National League indeed suffered serious consequences from the Parnellite split (the more electorally successful anti-Parnellites setting up their own rival Irish National Federation); but when the two wings of the party reunited in 1900 they adopted a new organisation, the United Irish League, as their constituency body. Nationalist Party dominance in the south was consolidated at local level by the 1898 reforms.

Figure 1.1: Electorate as percentage of population, 1828-1973

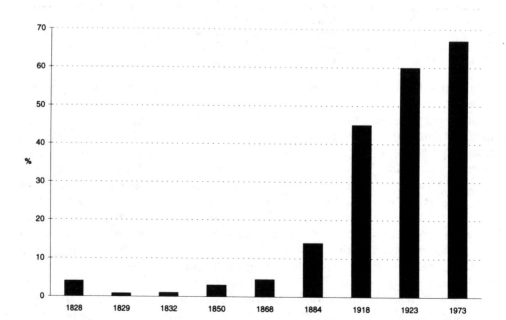

Note: The data refer to all of Ireland up to 1918, but only to the south in 1923 and 1973.
Source: Coakley, 1986.

Two important points need to be made about the background to the emerging Irish party system. The first is the relationship between electoral reform and political mobilisation. The appearance of major new political forces has often been associated with major waves of franchise extension; indeed, it is obvious that new groups that target unenfranchised sections of the population can win their electoral support only if these groups are actually given the vote. Franchise extension alone, however, does not necessarily bring about electoral mobilisation, as the Irish experience vividly illustrates. This may be seen by looking at political mobilisation in the context of changes in the proportion of the population actually entitled to vote, as summarised in Figure 1.1. Thus, the enormous expansion of voting strength that followed from the Catholic Relief Act of 1793 had a negligible political effect; instead, landowners simply had more voters to manage at election time. By contrast, the first appearance of modern electoral parties began in 1830, *after* the huge disenfranchisement of 1829 and before the reform of 1832. Again, the wave of electoral rebellion that began in the late 1870s and that marked the birth of modern mass politics took place a few years *before* the 1884 reform; it was to be seen vividly at the level not only of parliamentary but also of local elections (Feingold, 1975). The major reforms of 1884 and 1918 may, in fact, be seen as permitting the consummation of new voter-party alliances rather than as making the match in the first place.

Second, divisions between the main Irish parties corresponded closely to social divisions. Irish political life was dominated by three principal relationships in the 120 years after the Act of Union came into effect: between Ireland and the United Kingdom, between Catholics and Protestants and between tenants and landlords. By the 1880s the two major parties had adopted fairly unambiguous positions on these issues: the Nationalist Party stood for Home Rule for Ireland, for defence of Catholic rights and for the principle of state intervention to promote the interests of tenant farmers. The Unionist Party adopted a contrary position on each of these issues. The two parties were supported by two clearly defined communities, the line of division coinciding with the religious cleavage. As an instance of early electoral mobilisation behind monolithic ethnic blocs, this development was without parallel in the Europe of the time.

THE ESTABLISHMENT OF STATEHOOD

To the extent that the agenda of the principal forces in Irish politics was dominated by the issue of Ireland's relationship with the United Kingdom, election results made it clear that most voters endorsed the policy of "Home Rule" or devolved government for Ireland. It was not, however, this constitutional nationalist movement but rather a more militant alternative that was responsible for the chain of events that led to the establishment of the new state. We must turn now to this more militant tradition and examine the British response to its demands and activities.

1916 and the republican ideal
For an important section of Irish public opinion, the efforts of the Nationalist Party to win Home Rule for Ireland were not merely futile but rested on a flawed interpretation of the nature of Irish-British relations. This more radical strand

shared with mainstream nationalism an interpretation of Irish history that cast the neighbouring island in a negative light: the British presence in Ireland was based on a process of conquest in which foul means had overshadowed fair ones; the lands of Irish Catholics had been confiscated and the Catholic religion had been suppressed; British trade policy had sought to stifle nascent Irish industrialisation in the eighteenth century; the Act of Union had been procured by bribery and corruption; and Britain's indifference to the terrible problems of Irish poverty had been highlighted most vividly in a failure to intervene effectively in the catastrophic famine of 1845-49, in the course of which a million people died and a million emigrated. While there was some substance to these charges, of greater importance than their objective truth or falsity is the fact that they were generally believed: there was a widespread acceptance among Irish Catholics of a version of Irish history that associated British rule with evil, and that largely ignored such material benefits as it had brought. This ideological package was disseminated in the oral tradition and in popular literature and, in a bizarre development, especially after 1900, through the national schools, which themselves were subject of British government control.

While Irish Catholic opinion in general drew the conclusion from this version of history that some form of self-government for Ireland was a necessary antidote, the more radical strand referred to above went further. Since British rule in Ireland had been achieved by military force, the argument ran, it could only be reversed by the same means: by armed rebellion, not by parliamentary or constitutional means. Furthermore, since Britain's presence in Ireland was seen as entirely illegitimate, the ultimate goal became a complete break and the establishment of a separate Irish republic. This argument was reinforced by powerful cultural ones: among other organisations, the Gaelic Athletic Association (1884) and the Gaelic League (1893) emphasised, respectively, the distinctiveness of Ireland's sporting traditions and its language, and sought to cultivate these to combat English influence.

The most obvious representative of political separatism was the Irish Republican Brotherhood (IRB), established in 1858 and committed to setting up an independent republic by force of arms. In this it followed a tradition of revolutionary activism that could be traced back to the Young Ireland movement that had attempted a rebellion in 1848; it also claimed the United Irishmen of the 1790s as its ancestors, even though their movement and their rebellion in 1798 were Protestant led and were influenced by the values of French radical democracy, not Irish ethnic nationalism. Although the IRB's attempted insurrection in 1867 was a failure, it was not without sympathy in prominent places: many members and supporters of the parliamentary Nationalist Party may well have seen Home Rule as a half-way house to complete separation of Ireland from Great Britain, and MPs with IRB associations were elected on occasion. Nevertheless, extreme nationalist organisations were unable to challenge the electoral machine of the Nationalist Party. This is clear from the experience of Sinn Féin, a radical nationalist group founded in 1905 by a journalist, Arthur Griffith. Its object was to establish a separate Irish state linked to Great Britain only through a shared head of state, the King; but it had little electoral success, and this was confined to local level.

A spiral of paramilitary developments began in the years immediately before the first world war. The first stage was the formation in 1912 of the Ulster Volunteers, committed to opposing Home Rule for Ireland. The National Volunteers were founded the following year to support Home Rule, and they quickly came under the control of the Nationalist Party. Although members of both forces joined the British Army in their thousands in the course of the first world war, a breakaway section of the latter, the Irish Volunteers, engaged in rebellion in Dublin in April 1916 (the Easter Rising) under IRB leadership, declaring Ireland to be an independent republic with the IRB Military Council as its provisional government. The rebellion was crushed within days and appears to have had little popular support, but the circumstances of the execution of its leaders and the harsh treatment of other suspects alienated public opinion. This alienation was reinforced by the government's threat to introduce conscription in 1918 and by a pan-European climate of political radicalism in the closing months of the war. The main beneficiary was Sinn Féin, reconstituted in 1917 as a broad nationalist front under the leadership of Eamon de Valera, the senior surviving commander of the 1916 rebels. Despite military defeat, the 1916 rebels were elevated to the pantheon of Irish nationalism, and Patrick Pearse and the other executed leaders were for long to be regarded as the spiritual fathers of independent Ireland.

As Table 1.2 shows, Sinn Féin gained an overwhelming electoral victory in the 1918 general election, when it won 73 of Ireland's 105 seats. Although it is true that a significant number of voters supported the Nationalist Party, demoralisation within the party itself and the fact that the electoral system caused minorities to be under-represented left it with only two seats in the south and four in the north. Sinn Féin won almost all of the remaining seats in the south.

Hardly surprisingly, Sinn Féin took this result as a mandate to pursue a separatist policy. Its members abstained from attendance at the British Parliament, and instead established their own revolutionary assembly, Dáil Éireann, in January 1919. The Dáil ratified the 1916 rebels' proclamation of Ireland as an independent republic, set up its own government under de Valera and in 1919-21 accepted responsibility for a guerrilla war against the security forces fought by the Irish Republican Army (IRA), reconstituted from the Irish Volunteers. These efforts were reinforced by an attempt, which inevitably had strictly limited success, to set up a separate state and to obtain international recognition for it, especially by bringing American pressure to bear on the British. Since the Dáil could not hope to control the official Irish government agencies, its efforts to secure the running of its writ were confined by the size of its own tiny civil service, and by the fact that this could not operate openly. Nevertheless, after the local elections of 1920 it was able to detach the loyalty of most local authorities from the Local Government Board, and it enjoyed some success in establishing a network of local courts.

From Home Rule to partition

One of the reasons advanced to explain the rapid electoral advances of the militants is the failure of the British to make sufficient concessions to constitutional nationalists. It is true that the British had brought forward Home Rule proposals for Ireland. The first such bill had, however, been defeated in the House of Commons in 1886. A second Home Rule Bill passed the House of Commons but was blocked by the House of Lords in 1893. The third Home Rule Bill had to wait until the Nationalist Party again held the balance of power after the 1910 election. Introduced in 1912, it eventually became law in 1914. It proposed to establish a bicameral parliament in Dublin that would legislate in areas of domestic concern (essentially, those covered by the "Irish" government departments described above), with a separate Irish executive or cabinet. Ireland would continue to send MPs to Westminster, but their numbers would be greatly reduced.

The implementation of the Home Rule Act was postponed because of the out-break of war but also for a more fundamental reason: opposition in Ulster. The Protestant population of Ireland did not share the view of Irish history described above, perceiving itself as being connected by a network of historical ties to Britain, from where many Irish Protestants had come as colonists in the seven-teenth century. In addition to seeing the British link as a guarantee of civil and re-ligious liberties in a Catholic island, many Protestants, especially in the north east, regarded the Act of Union as having brought significant economic benefits and as having assisted the industrialisation of Belfast and its hinterland; these benefits, they believed, would be threatened by Irish autonomy (see Laffan, 1983).

Determined political pressure and threatened paramilitary resistance in Ulster, together with support from within the British Conservative party, was sufficient to ensure that the terms of the Home Rule Act would have to be changed. The re-sult was the partition of Ireland by the Government of Ireland Act (1920). This broadly reproduced the 1914 Act but instead of concentrating power in a single capital it made provision for parallel institutions in Belfast (to govern six north-eastern counties that contained 71 per cent of the Irish Protestant population) and Dublin (to govern the remaining 26 counties). The Act came into effect in 1921, and was successfully implemented in one of the new states that it created, Northern Ireland, where it formed the basic constitutional document until 1972.

Although the Act proved largely ineffective in the south, its provisions for the government of "Southern Ireland" formed an important precedent for constituti-onal development. Alongside the Irish government there was to be a parliament of two houses. The House of Commons was to consist of 128 members elected by proportional representation by means of the single transferable vote. The Senate was to consist of 64 members, of whom three were *ex officio* members (the Lord Chancellor and the Lord Mayors of Dublin and Cork), 17 were to be nominated by the Lord Lieutenant to represent commerce, labour and the scientific and learned professions and 44 were to be elected by five other groups (four Catholic bishops, two Protestant bishops, 16 southern Irish peers, eight privy councillors and 14 county councillors). In the first election to the House of Commons in 1921, Sinn Féin won 124 seats, all uncontested, and interpreted this election and that to the Northern Ireland House of Commons as elections to the "second Dáil". Since only four MPs turned up for the first meeting of the legally constituted House (all from Trinity College, Dublin) and two for the second, it adjourned *sine die*. Although attendance at the Senate was better (18 senators attended at least one of its two meetings) it suffered the same fate, and, in the absence of support from any significant group, the Act ceased to have real effect in the south.

It is worth noting that although it has been called the "partition act", the Gov-ernment of Ireland Act also sought to make provision for all-Irish institutions. Irish unity would continue to be symbolised by the continuance of certain offices, including that of the Lord Lieutenant, and provision was made for a 40-member inter-parliamentary Council of Ireland, with 13 members from each House of Commons and seven from each Senate. The responsibility of the Council was confined to a small range of matters initially, but provision was made for it to become an embryonic Irish parliament.

The Treaty and the new state

The deadlock between the Dáil and the British government was finally broken following the conclusion of a military truce in July 1921. In the subsequent negotiations between the two sides, a "Treaty" was agreed in December 1921. This went much further than conceding Home Rule, but stopped well short of permitting complete separation. Instead, a state would be established that would be almost fully independent, but which would be a member of the British Commonwealth and would recognise the King as its head. The King would be represented in Ireland by a Governor-General, and constitutional provision would be made for a parliamentary oath of allegiance to the King. Partition would remain, but the location of the boundary line would be determined by an intergovernmental commission; the British would also retain naval facilities in certain seaports. Since two of the six counties and other border areas had Catholic majorities, the Irish negotiators believed that this would result in a major revision of the line of the border, and that this in turn might undermine the viability of the northern state.

Although the Treaty was narrowly ratified by the Dáil in January 1922, the division that it generated was bitter and saw the resignation of de Valera as head of government and the departure of his anti-Treaty supporters from the Dáil. The constitutional position that followed was complex. First, the second Dáil continued to exist, though only pro-Treaty Sinn Féin members now attended. On 10 January 1922 Arthur Griffith was elected President of the Dáil government in succession to de Valera and a new Dáil government was appointed; on Griffith's death on 12 August 1922 he was succeeded as President by William T. Cosgrave. Second, the Treaty made provision for a meeting of "members of parliament elected for constituencies in Southern Ireland", who duly came together on 14 January for their one and only meeting; at this they formally approved the Treaty and elected a Provisional Government with Michael Collins, guiding force of the IRA campaign and head of the IRB, as its Chairman. On Collins's death on 22 August 1922 he was succeeded as Chairman by Cosgrave. Although Cosgrave's succession to both of these posts helped to disguise the anomalous existence of two governments, both pro-Treaty, the reality was that there was not complete overlap in the membership of the two. A general election took place in June 1922, however, and when the new (third) Dáil eventually met on 9 September 1922, again in the absence of the anti-Treaty deputies, it removed this anomaly by electing Cosgrave to the single post of President. The Dáil also approved the new constitution on 25 October 1922, and when this came into force Cosgrave became President of the Executive Council (yet another title for the prime minister) on 6 December 1922.

THE CONSOLIDATION OF STATEHOOD

The new state, then, did not have a particularly easy birth. The remaining chapters in this volume look at the kinds of political structures and patterns of behaviour that have evolved in Ireland since independence. Since the authors have where appropriate set their examinations of contemporary politics in historical context, a detailed overview of post-1922 politics is not needed here. It is nevertheless necessary to review a number of themes that link contemporary politics with the events and institutions already discussed. First, the nature of the independence struggle left the new state with a series of challenges to its legitimacy. Second, a steady evolution took place in the content of political conflict. Third, however, the administrative structures inherited by the new state provided an important bedrock of stability.

Problems of legitimacy

The new state was faced with the difficult task of attempting to work within the framework of the Treaty while at the same time presenting itself as legitimate heir to the republican past. This was reflected in the curious anomaly described above: the coexistence for several months in 1922 of a President of the Dáil Government (Griffith) and a Chairman of the Provisional Government (Collins). This was a deliberate attempt by the new regime to claim legitimacy in the eyes both of Irish republicans and British politicians and to fudge the essential incompatibility between these positions; the post-1922 President of the Executive Council could claim continuity with the republican tradition. Partial symbolic success in this is reflected in the fact that, to the present, each Dáil is numbered on the basis of a recognition of the Dáil of 1919 as the first one (the Dáil elected in 1992, for instance, is designated the 27th Dáil even in official circles, though it is only the 25th since the state came into existence in 1922).

This attempt to turn two ways at once presented the state with fundamental challenges from both directions. At one extreme, its birth upset those who remained loyal to the United Kingdom: the sizeable unionist population, which had wished to maintain the political integrity of the British Isles, and the significant population that had supported the Nationalist Party in the 1918 election and which would have been happy with devolved government for Ireland within the United Kingdom. Since the union appeared irretrievably dissolved, however, and the spectre of de Valera and the Republicans appeared to be the main alternative to the Free State, many former Unionists and Nationalists switched to a position of neutrality towards (or even support for) the new regime.

At the other extreme, and more seriously, the new regime also offended those Republicans who took the view that the proclamation of a republic in 1916 and its confirmation by the Dáil in 1919 were irreversible. They regarded the Irish Free State as a hideously deformed alternative to "the Republic", deficient not only because it represented a truncation of the "national territory" but also because it retained important links of subordination to the United Kingdom, at least at a symbolic level. This issue split the IRA, whose pro-Treaty wing became the core of the new national army; it eventually spilled over into open armed conflict, during a civil war that lasted from June 1922 to May 1923. In the course of this, many hundreds died as a consequence of armed clashes, executions and assassinations. In the early stages of the civil war, the anti-Treaty Sinn Féin members sought to undermine the constitutional position of the pro-Treaty side. They asserted that the 1922 general election was not legitimate since the second Dáil (elected in 1921) had not dissolved itself, declared themselves to be the "second Dáil" and met on 25 October 1922 to elect de Valera once more as "President of the Republic". Even after the civil war, this group (now known simply as Sinn Féin) continued to abstain from the Dáil. This fundamental challenge to a new state was not unique to Ireland: in the emerging postwar states of Finland, Estonia, Latvia and Lithuania similar civil wars were fought, though these had a more obviously social content, pitting left against right (see Coakley, 1987).

The building of the new state and its institutions was in the hands of a group of people who supported the political and economic status quo either through conviction or out of political realism. Their cornerstone was the constitution of 1922, which, ironically, they designed and amended in such a way that their rivals could dismantle it after 1932 (by deferring the requirement for a referendum on constitutional change, they ensured that it could easily be amended; see chapter 3). The core of the new political elite was made up of pro-Treaty members of Sinn Féin, who reorganised under the label Cumann na nGaedheal in 1923 (this had been the name of a precursor of the old Sinn Féin, organised by Arthur Griffith in 1900). Led by Cosgrave, its character was shaped by other strong political figures of a broadly conservative disposition, a conservatism that was reflected in a new, close relationship with the Catholic church. Although the 1922 constitution was an entirely secular document, the new government quickly moved to show its deference to Catholic moral values. Thus divorce was prohibited, restrictions were placed on the sale of alcohol and censorship of films and publications was greatly intensified. Yet not all policy areas were dominated by conservatism: state intervention in the energy production sector was represented by the initiation in 1925 of the Shannon hydro-electric scheme, for instance, and, in a rather different area, the new government sought vigorously to promote the Irish language.

Although Cumann na nGaedheal struggled to protect the autonomy of the new state and even to extend it in a Commonwealth context, its conservatism in the constitutional arena and its increasingly unreserved defence of the Treaty had two kinds of consequence for political realignment in the 1920s. First, those who had accepted Collins's argument that the Treaty was "a stepping stone to the Republic" became disillusioned, and broke with the party. This issue was used as a pretext in the "Army Mutiny" of 1924, when a group of senior officers demanded action from the government to end partition (though other motivations were also present; see Lee, 1989, pp. 96-105). Another division took place on the leaking of the report of the Boundary Commission in 1925 (set up under the terms of the Treaty, the commission recommended that only marginal changes be made to the line of the border). The latter occasion, incidentally, resulted in an agreement between the Irish, British and Northern Irish governments to "freeze" the border as it stood, and to shelve the idea of a Council of Ireland. Second, however, former supporters of the now-defunct Nationalist and Unionist parties increasingly came to identify with Cumann na nGaedheal, especially after 1927. Many of the former had briefly given their support to a short-lived party, the National League, in 1927; the latter had either remained detached, voted for independent candidates, or, in the 1920s, supported two smaller parties, the Farmers' Party and the Business Men's Party.

One of the most significant developments in the normalisation of the new state occurred following a major split within Sinn Féin in 1926. Support for the party had been dropping off in the mid-1920s, as it continued its policy of abstention from the Dáil, and de Valera resolved on an alternative strategy. At the party's 1926 ard-fheis (convention), he proposed a resolution to the effect that, in the event of the removal of the oath of allegiance, abstention from the Dáil would become a matter "not of principle but of policy". The resolution was defeated, and de Valera and his supporters broke with Sinn Féin and immediately founded an alternative republican party, Fianna Fáil. The popularity of this move became obvious in June 1927, when a general election gave Fianna Fáil 44 seats, to Sinn Féin's five.

There were two further stages in this process of political normalisation. On 10 July 1927 a leading minister, Kevin O'Higgins, was assassinated. Among the measures adopted in response by the government was a bill requiring all future parliamentary candidates to declare that, if elected, they would take the oath of allegiance. This left abstentionist parties with a difficult choice: either to enter parliament or to be wiped out. Fianna Fáil decided on the former course, and de Valera and his supporters took the oath in August 1927 in what they described as an empty gesture. Ironically, by thus forcing Fianna Fáil into the Dáil, the government changed the balance of political forces there and, facing defeat, called a second general election in 1927 at which both Cumann na nGaedheal and Fianna Fáil gained, at the expense of smaller parties (see appendices 2b and 2c).

The ultimate stage in political normalisation followed the next election, in 1932. Fianna Fáil became the largest party and, although it did not have an overall majority, it was able to form a government with Labour Party support. This peaceful transfer of power by the victors in the civil war to the vanquished was an important milestone in the consolidation of democracy in Ireland. Within a year, a new general election gave Fianna Fáil an overall majority, and it was to remain in power without interruption until 1948.

The early years of the new Fianna Fáil government were characterised, not surprisingly, by vigorous moves to dismantle some of those elements in the constitution that republicans found objectionable. Thus, the oath of allegiance, the right of appeal to the Privy Council in London (a limited but symbolically important restriction on the sovereignty of the Irish judicial system) and the Governor-General's right to veto legislation were abolished in 1933. Although these amendments were strongly opposed by the British on the grounds that they violated certain provisions of the Treaty, the context within which they took place had changed considerably since 1922. A series of Commonwealth Conferences in the 1920s had been moving in the direction of giving Commonwealth states greater independence from London, and these culminated in the Statute of Westminster (1931), which authorised any Commonwealth state to amend or repeal British legislation that affected it.

The character of the constitution was even more fundamentally altered in 1936, when the Senate was abolished and the sudden abdication of King Edward VIII was used as an opportunity to remove almost all references to the Governor-General from the constitution. This left the way open for the adoption of a new constitution, which, although it stopped short of declaring Ireland a republic, made no mention of the Commonwealth and was intended to symbolise the completion of the process of Irish independence, at least for part of Ireland (see chapter 3).

Opposition to a British role in Ireland also extended to the issue of "land annuities", payments due to the British exchequer from Irish farmers as a consequence of loans taken by them to purchase their holdings under the provisions of the Land Acts of the pre-1922 period. On coming to power in 1932, de Valera simply retained the repayments for the Irish exchequer. An Anglo-Irish trade war followed, with each side imposing import duties on selected goods from the other; it was concluded by a trade agreement in 1938 and British acceptance of a once-off lump sum payment. The second issue was that of the naval facilities that the British had been allowed to retain under the terms of the Treaty. This issue was settled more amicably, also in 1938: the British ceded control of the ports, thus laying the ground for the policy of neutrality that the Irish government was able to follow during the war.

As these changes proceeded, the original pro-Treaty forces found themselves increasingly impotent. The spectre of extreme republicanism raised by the Fianna Fáil victory in 1932 and the polarised climate of the 1930s formed the background for the formation of a fascist-type movement in Ireland. This was born as the Army Comrades' Association (1931), transformed in 1933 into the National Guard (popularly known as the Blueshirts) led by the former head of the police, General Eoin O'Duffy. The parallels with continental European fascist movements were close: the fascist salute, the wearing of a distinctive shirt as a uniform, anti-communist rhetoric and, most importantly, an authoritarian nationalist ideology that was suspicious of parliamentary government and sympathetic towards a re-organisation of the state along corporatist lines, where the primary divisions would not be between parties but rather between different socio-economic segments, such as agriculture, industry and the professions (see Manning, 1987; Bew, Hazelkorn and Patterson, 1989, pp. 48-67). This development was followed by a further realignment of anti-Fianna Fáil forces. In 1933 a demoralised Cumann na nGaedheal merged with the Blueshirts and another small party, the National Centre Party, to form the United Ireland Party, which quickly became better known by its Irish name, Fine Gael. Led initially by O'Duffy, the party came increasingly to resemble the old Cumann na nGaedheal party, especially after William Cosgrave replaced O'Duffy as leader in 1935. Fine Gael, however, was no match for Fianna Fáil in electoral terms, and its share of the vote dropped until 1948. Then, in an ironic development, its worst-ever electoral performance was followed by its entry into a coalition government; and, even more ironically, this government moved to break the last remaining links between Ireland and the Commonwealth, with the decision in 1948 to declare the state a Republic.

By this stage, then, the anti-Treaty side no longer objected to the terms of the Treaty with its old vehemency, and the pro-Treaty side had actually declared the country a republic. While one might have expected this to copper-fasten the legitimacy of the state, a problem remained. The rump of Sinn Féin and the IRA that survived after 1926 remained adamant in their hostility to the state, which they continued to reject as an illegitimate, British-imposed institution. Instead they continued to give their allegiance to the "Second Dáil", and then to the Army Council of the IRA, to which the remnants of the "Second Dáil" transferred their authority in 1938. While this might appear to be of importance only in the world of myth, myths can be of powerful political significance. It is precisely in terms of this myth that the re-born IRA and Sinn Féin were able after 1970 to claim legitimacy for their struggle to oust the British from Northern Ireland (see chapter 2 for a discussion of the concept of legitimacy).

Political issues in the new Ireland

The most visible political conflicts in the new Irish state have already been discussed above; during the 1920s and the 1930s these focused largely on constitutional matters, or on matters pertaining to Anglo-Irish relations. On these issues, the principal line of division was between the pro- and anti-Treaty splinters from Sinn Féin. Other political interests also sought, however, to force alternative issues onto the political agenda, and the proportional representation electoral system permitted them to gain significant Dáil representation (see chapter 4 on the electoral system; for an overview of the parties' electoral strengths, see appendix 2b).

The most significant of these in the long term was the Labour Party, which had been conceived by the Irish Trades Union Congress in 1912 and was finally born in 1922 as a party committed to a moderate policy of defence of workers' rights. The party was marginalised by debates on the national question, on which it was unable to adopt a distinctive position, and moved quickly into the role that it has retained ever since: that of third party in a three-party system. In the absence also of a significant classical revolutionary left, the consistent weakness of Labour has been remarkable in a European context (see chapter 5).

A second important issue was that of agriculture. In 1922 a Farmers' Party appeared, drawing its strength from the large farmers of the south and east. The Farmers' Party found it difficult to maintain an identity separate from that of Cumann na nGaedheal, and it faded away after 1927. A successor party with a similar support base, the National Centre Party (founded in 1932 as the National Farmers' and Ratepayers' League), was one of the parties that, as we have seen, merged to form Fine Gael. In 1939 a farmers' party of a rather different kind appeared. This was Clann na Talmhan, originating among the small farmers of the west, which won significant support in the elections of the 1940s and even participated in two governments but which was unable to prevent its voters from drifting back to the two large parties subsequently.

Three other types of political force also fought for Dáil seats. First, especially in the 1920s and the 1930s a considerable number of independent deputies represented diverse opinions, including those of former unionists and nationalists. Increasingly, however, the support base of deputies of this kind was mopped up by the larger parties. Second, former nationalists made a more determined attempt to re-group through the National League (founded in 1926), which won eight seats in the June 1927 general election. In fact, following Fianna Fáil's entry to the Dáil, the prospect of a minority Labour-National League coalition government, with Fianna Fáil support, appeared to be a realistic possibility. The calling of a snap second election in 1927 put paid to the prospects of this party, however; it lost all but two of its seats. Third, there have been dissident republican parties caused by divisions within Cumann na nGaedheal in the 1920s (the National Group in 1924 and Clann Éireann in 1925) and within Fianna Fáil in the 1970s (Aontacht Éireann in 1971 and Independent Fianna Fáil in Donegal from 1973). By contrast to these small groups, another republican party, Clann na Poblachta, founded in 1946 by Seán McBride, a former IRA chief of staff, appeared destined for greater things. This party was able to capitalise on post-war disillusion with Fianna Fáil and win ten seats in the 1948 election. But following bitter internal disputes, most notably over the "Mother and Child" scheme for the provision of comprehensive postnatal care in the social welfare system (on which the party's health minister, Noel Browne, had clashed with the church), its support collapsed in the 1951 election and never subsequently recovered (for minor parties generally, see Gallagher, 1985, pp. 93-120; Coakley, 1990).

It was, indeed, precisely the intervention of Clann na Poblachta in the 1948 general election that ushered in a new era in Irish politics. Fianna Fáil was unable to form a government after the election, and was replaced in office by a five-party coalition supported also by independent deputies, the first "Inter-Party" government. In this Clann na Poblachta sat alongside its principal enemy, Fine Gael, together with Clann na Talmhan, Labour and the National Labour Party (a group of deputies that had broken with Labour and maintained a separate party in the years 1944-50). Headed by Fine Gael's John A. Costello, this coalition broke up in disarray in 1951, to be replaced by a Fianna Fáil government. Costello was nevertheless back in 1954, this time heading a three-party coalition of Fine Gael, Labour and Clann na Talmhan. Following the 1957 election, however, Fianna Fáil returned for a second 16-year period in office.

The fact that a single party was in power for this lengthy period disguises the extent of change that took place between 1957 and 1973. The period began under de Valera's leadership with a cabinet still made up largely of activists of the 1919-23 period; after a transition under Seán Lemass (1959-66), one of the youngest of those involved in the independence movement, it ended with a younger cabinet led by Jack Lynch and consisting of ministers without direct experience of the civil war (see chapter 9 for an assessment of recent government leaders). The ghosts of the civil war were, however, disturbed by the outbreak of the Northern Ireland "troubles" in 1969. In a dramatic incident in May 1970, Lynch dismissed two ministers, Neil Blaney and Charles Haughey, for alleged involvement in the illegal purchase and supply of arms to Northern Ireland nationalists, and, in related developments, he accepted the resignations of two more. Together with the ensuing trial, this incident was to haunt Fianna Fáil for over two decades.

Although the Northern Ireland problem thus ensured that certain traditional issues would remain on the agenda, the post-war period was in general characterised to an increasing extent by conflict over economic rather than constitutional matters. Protests over high rates of unemployment and inflation in the 1950s forced these issues into the political arena, though without translating them into votes for the left. The principal policy shifts were, indeed, a consequence of civil service decisions rather than of public debates (see chapter 10 on policy making). These followed the direction especially of relying on foreign investment rather than on traditional Sinn Féin-type policies of encouragement of indigenous industry. The most notable landmarks were the announcement of the first Programme for Economic Expansion (1958), the signing of the Anglo-Irish Free Trade Agreement (1965) and the decision to join the European Communities (1972).

The 16 unbroken years of Fianna Fáil rule that ended in 1973 were succeeded by 16 years of alternation between Fine Gael-Labour coalitions and single-party Fianna Fáil governments; the pattern was broken in 1989, when Fianna Fáil entered a coalition for the first time (for a list of governments, see appendix 3). Some election results of the period were decisive, such as that of 1977, in which Fianna Fáil emulated its 1938 performance by winning a majority not only of Dáil seats but also of popular votes (though ironically party leader Lynch's popularity ebbed quickly afterwards, and he was replaced in 1979 after an intense internal campaign by Charles Haughey). All subsequent election results were less decisive, however, and brought a new element of unpredictability to electoral competition.

Although the old political issues continued on into the 1980s and 1990s, new ones arose. In particular, moral issues acquired increased prominence. Despite the weakness of the secular tradition in Irish society, politicians were increasingly forced to take positions that might place them at odds with the Catholic church. In the 1970s the sale of contraceptives was finally permitted; in the 1980s abortion and divorce found their way into the public forum, though in both cases referendum results came up with conservative verdicts; both of these issues returned to the political agenda in the 1990s, while in 1993 the sale of contraceptives was further liberalised and homosexual activity was decriminalised. Not all of these issues acquired political salience as a consequence of pressure group activity or initiatives by politicians; Irish and European courts played a considerable role. The issue of women's rights and women's representation in the political domain also reached a new prominence in the 1980s and 1990s (see chapter 11). These developments found expression not only in policy changes within the traditional parties but also in the appearance of new parties.

On the left, the Labour Party was challenged by a form of transformed republicanism. The remnants of the Sinn Féin movement that had survived the 1926 split had been reactivated in the 1950s and the 1960s; in 1970 this small party again split, with a more activist wing breaking away as "Provisional Sinn Féin" and becoming a major political force in Northern Ireland in the 1980s. The remaining "official" Sinn Féin was gradually transformed into a radical left party of secular and, strangely, anti-nationalist orientation, and was renamed the Workers' Party in 1982. After steadily building up its Dáil strength to seven deputies in 1989, this party split in turn in 1992, six of its seven Dáil deputies breaking away to form the Democratic Left. This development resembled in many ways the reconstitution of the Italian Communist Party in 1991 as the Democratic Party of the Left and the secession of its traditionalist elements, and it had a similar outcome: the combined vote of the two parties fell significantly in the 1992 general election.

On the right, a new liberal-type party, the Progressive Democrats, appeared in 1985. Although the immediate cause of the party's appearance was a deep division within Fianna Fáil on Northern Ireland policy and on the issue of Charles Haughey's leadership of the party, the new party managed quickly to establish a distinctive niche for itself: conservative on economic policy, liberal on social policy and moderate on Northern Ireland. The party won 14 seats in the 1987 general election; although this dropped back to six in 1989, it became the first party to form a coalition with Fianna Fáil after that election; and although its share of the poll dropped further in 1992, it managed to climb back to ten seats.

The new flexibility within Fianna Fáil marks a decisive shift in the dynamics of Irish party competition (see chapter 5). The decision of Charles Haughey in 1989 to enter coalition caused enormous strains in the party and undermined his leadership; but Albert Reynolds, who succeeded him in 1992, managed to survive an even more momentous reorientation by negotiating a coalition with the Labour Party in 1993. Although the more open attitudes to coalition formation and the new issues in Irish politics echo those in continental Europe, however, the kind of political forces that we find elsewhere in Europe have been weak or absent. In a political system dominated by two successors of a nationalist party and with only a weak Labour Party, there has been little room for the appearance of alternative political forces. It is true that farmers' parties have appeared from time to time, but these proved ephemeral. It remains to be seen whether the secular, liberal tradition represented by the Progressive Democrats is to be a lasting force or yet another temporary electoral rebellion. The impact of the deepening of Ireland's relationship with the EC on domestic political structures will also, no doubt, increase over time (see chapter 12).

The administrative infrastructure

If the pattern of politics in post-1922 Ireland shows strands of continuity beneath seemingly dramatic political changes, stability is even more strikingly a characteristic of the administrative system that has lain underneath. As we have seen, the old regime had built up a formidable administrative infrastructure already before 1922, and this was to serve the new state well.

First, the central bureaucracy continued with little change. Officials transferred from the old regime constituted the core of the new civil service, which for many years consisted of about 20,000 employees. The small number of members of the Dáil civil service (of whom 131 were transferred) made little impact on this, and the character of this body changed very slowly as new staff were recruited. Thus, in 1922 98.9 per cent of civil servants had been recruited under the old regime; by 1927-28 this figure had dropped to 64.3 per cent, and as late as 1934 a majority (50.1 per cent) of civil servants had been recruited to the pre-1922 service (calculated from Commission of Inquiry into the Civil Service, 1935, pp. 3, 9, 138). The fact that so large a body of civil servants could adapt to working in an entirely different state structure owes much to the "greening" of the Irish civil service that had been taking place steadily since the advent of open competition for recruitment to lower ranks of the civil service in 1876 and a deliberate policy of appointing or promoting nationalist-oriented civil servants to senior ranks from 1892 onwards, at least under Liberal administrations (McBride, 1991).

The external staff associated with certain departments posed particular problems. Surprisingly, the Department of Education had little difficulty with its body of teachers and inspectors, even though these had been recruited and trained under the old regime. The shift towards ideals of Irish nationalism was not difficult for teachers, since they had allegedly been spreading such ideas even before 1922; the main problem lay in raising their proficiency in the Irish language to a level that would allow them to become effective agents in the state's language revival policy. Matters were different in the area of security. Although the Dublin Metropolitan Police continued until 1925, the more politicised, paramilitary Royal Irish Constabulary (RIC) was disbanded in the south and renamed the Royal Ulster Constabulary (RUC) in the north. The new, unarmed Civic Guard (Garda Síochána) was an entirely new force established in 1922, though it used the administrative structures, buildings and other property of the RIC. It eventually settled into a force of more than 6,000. There was a similarly complete break in the military domain: the withdrawing British Army was replaced by an Irish Army built up around a nucleus of the pro-Treaty members of the IRA. It expanded rapidly in response to civil war needs, and by the end of March 1923 had some 50,000 soldiers. This number had dropped to 16,000 by the following year, and after 1926 further rapid reduction brought this figure to 6,700 by 1932. Apart from temporary expansion during the second world war, the army was to remain at this size until the end of the 1960s. Then, following the outbreak of the Northern Ireland troubles and with increased crime in the south, the size of both the defence forces and the police was increased by about 50 per cent in the 1970s.

In terms of its structure, the new civil service was a rationalisation of the old one. The 29 "Irish" departments were reorganised into a smaller number of new departments; but in areas associated with "imperial" departments the state, while it inherited thousands of civil servants, had to create new structures on the British model (in foreign affairs, defence and finance, for instance). The formal organisation of the new system was defined in the Ministers and Secretaries Act, 1924; subsequent changes (such as the transfer of areas from one department to another, or the creation of new departments) were on a smaller scale, but their cumulative effect was to increase the number of departments from 10 in 1922 to 16 in 1993.

The evolution of the civil service tells much about the changing nature of the process of government. An over-simplified picture is as follows. Six core departments have continued with little change other than in name: those of the President of the Executive Council (renamed Taoiseach, 1937), Finance, External Affairs (renamed Foreign Affairs, 1971), Home Affairs (renamed Justice, 1924), Defence, and Education. The post-war expansion of the welfare state was reflected in a division of the Department of Local Government, with Departments of Health and Social Welfare branching off in 1946 (the original department was renamed Environment in 1977). Areas relating to economic and commercial development were managed for many decades by a single Department of Industry and Commerce, but, after a series of complex changes and developments, by 1993 there were four departments in this area: Enterprise and Employment (as the old Industry and Commerce department was renamed in 1993); Transport, Energy and Communications (the latter absorbing the old Department of Posts and Telegraphs); Tourism and Trade; and Equality and Law Reform. Finally, the strange mixture of functions performed by the old Department of Agriculture is now carried out by three departments: Agriculture and Food; the Marine; and, in part, Arts, Culture and the Gaeltacht (responsibility for arts and culture was detached from other departments and linked with responsibility for the Irish language).

At the level of local government, continuity was also obvious. The old system continued on after 1922, still governed by the principles of the 1898 Act, with only incremental change. In terms of formal structures, the most significant changes were the abolition of poor law unions and their boards of guardians (1923) and of rural district councils (1925) and the transfer of their functions to county councils (in Co Dublin this process was deferred until 1930). This left the state with a system of local government sharply different from the European norm, where local government has typically been two-tiered: an upper level consisting of a small number of counties or provinces, modelled on the French *départements* and acting largely as agencies of the central government, and a lower level consisting of a very large number of communes or municipalities of greatly varying sizes, each one with a local council and considerable administrative powers. Especially after 1925, the latter level was largely missing from Ireland, and the main focus of local representative government was centred on county level. While a restructuring of local government was being discussed up to the 1990s, only minor changes were actually implemented.

Post-independence governments have also been disposed to exercise central control to a much greater degree than their predecessors. This may be seen in the first place in a willingness to suspend local authorities and replace them by appointed commissioners (especially in earlier years, allegations of corruption against local authorities were often used as a justification for this). This was the fate of several councils in the 1920s (including those of the cities of Dublin and Cork); Dublin city council was again suspended in 1969. Second, from 1942 a system of "county management", implemented earlier in the cities, gave considerable executive power at local level to an official appointed by the Local Appointments Commissions, itself a central body. Third, the term of office of all councils was extended in 1953 from three to five years, but the elections are regularly postponed by the government. Thus the elections due in 1965 were postponed until 1967, the next elections were again deferred for two years, and the two most recent sets of local elections (in 1985 and 1991) each took place one year late.

One of the most significant changes in the area of state intervention lay in the creation of "state-sponsored bodies" to carry out certain functions. The number of such bodies, over which government control is only indirect, increased steadily from an initial four in 1927 to well over 100 in the 1990s. They have accounted for a great deal of the expansion of public service employment, though it must be noted that much of the increase in the labour force of the state-sponsored bodies arises from a redefinition of bodies originally belonging to other sectors. Examples are the health boards, which were administered by the local authorities until 1971, and An Post and Telecom Éireann, part of the civil service (Department of Posts and Telegraphs) until 1984.

CONCLUSION

While the birth of the new Irish state marked a decisive political shift, we should not ignore the extent to which its political institutions built on pre-1922 roots. Although there was a sharp break in constitutional theory and at the level of the political elite, narrowly defined, there was little change in much of the administrative infrastructure. While local government was radically restructured, the civil service, the judicial system and the educational system were merely overhauled; but all continued to be staffed by much the same personnel after 1922 as before.

In this, of course, the Irish experience is not greatly different from that in other post-revolutionary societies. Radical though some strands in the independence movement may have been, it was the more cautious, conservative wing that ultimately won power in the new state and shaped its character during the early, formative years. Although Fianna Fáil's victory in 1932 led to some far-reaching changes, the most obvious, long-term effects of independence on the system of government were superficial: the faces and accents in Dublin Castle were different, but the business of government itself was little changed.

REFERENCES AND FURTHER READING

Bew, Paul, Ellen Hazelkorn and Henry Patterson, 1989. *The Dynamics of Irish Politics*. London: Lawrence and Wishart.

Coakley, John, 1986. "The evolution of Irish party politics", pp. 29-54 in Brian Girvin and Roland Sturm (eds), *Politics and Society in Contemporary Ireland*. London: Gower.

Coakley, John, 1987. "Political succession during the transition to independence: evidence from Europe", pp. 161-70 in Peter Calvert (ed.), *The Process of Political Succession*. London: Macmillan.

Coakley, John, 1990. "Minor parties in Irish political life, 1922-1989", *Economic and Social Review* 21:3, pp. 269-97.

Commission of Inquiry into the Civil Service, 1935. *Final Report with Appendices*. Dublin: Stationery Office.

Delany, V. T. H., 1975. *The Administration of Justice in Ireland*, 4th ed, edited by Charles Lysaght. Dublin: Institute of Public Administration.

Farrell, Brian (ed.), 1973. *The Irish Parliamentary Tradition*. Dublin: Gill and Macmillan.

Feingold, W. F., 1975. "The tenants' movement to capture the Irish poor law boards, 1877-1886", *Albion* 7, pp. 216-31.

Foster, Roy, 1988. *Modern Ireland 1600-1972*. London: Allen Lane.

Gallagher, Michael, 1985. *Political Parties in the Republic of Ireland*. Dublin: Gill and Macmillan.

Girvin, Brian, 1989. *Between Two Worlds: Politics and Economics in Independent Ireland*. Dublin: Gill and Macmillan.

Hoppen, K. T., 1984. *Elections, Politics and Society in Ireland 1832-1885*. Oxford: Clarendon Press.

Laffan, Michael, 1983. *The Partition of Ireland, 1911-25*. Dundalk: Dundalgan Press, for the Dublin Historical Association.

Lee, J. J., 1989. *Ireland 1912-1985: Politics and Society*. Cambridge: Cambridge University Press.

Lyons, F. S. L., 1973. *Ireland Since the Famine*. London: Fontana.

McBride, Lawrence W. 1991. *The Greening of Dublin Castle: The Transformation of Bureaucratic and Judicial Personnel in Ireland, 1892-1922*. Washington, DC: Catholic University of America Press.

McDowell, R. B., 1964. *The Irish Administration 1801-1914*. London: Routledge and Kegan Paul.

MacMillan, Gretchen, 1993. *State, Society and Authority in Ireland: The Foundation of the Modern State*. Dublin: Gill and Macmillan.

Manning, Maurice, 1987. *The Blueshirts*, new ed. Dublin: Gill and Macmillan.

Meghen, P. J., 1962. *A Short History of the Public Service in Ireland*. Dublin: Institute of Public Administration.

O'Halpin, Eunan, 1987. *The Decline of the Union: British Government in Ireland 1892-1920*. Dublin: Gill and Macmillan.

Prager, Jeffrey, 1986. *Building Democracy in Ireland: Political Order and Cultural Integration in a Newly Independent Nation*. Cambridge: Cambridge University Press.

Roche, Desmond, 1982. *Local Government in Ireland*. Dublin: Institute of Public Administration.

Sartori, Giovanni, 1976. *Parties and Party Systems: a Framework for Analysis*. Cambridge: Cambridge University Press.

Smith, Henry Stooks, 1973. *The Parliaments of England from 1715 to 1847*, 2nd ed, edited by F. W. S. Craig. Chichester: Political Reference Publications.

Walker, Brian M., 1978. *Parliamentary Election Results in Ireland, 1801-1922*. Dublin: Royal Irish Academy.

2 / SOCIETY AND POLITICAL CULTURE

John Coakley

It was once commonly thought that politics could be fully understood by reference to the constitution and to the political institutions for which it made provision. It is true that in most societies what the constitution says has an important effect on political life; but the constitution does not operate in a vacuum. It is given substance by the set of political values and expectations that are dominant in the society within which it operates. The term *political culture* has been coined to describe this set of attitudes; it refers to fundamental, deeply held views on the state itself, on the rules of the political game and on the kind of principles that should underlie political decision making.

This chapter begins with a discussion of the concept of political culture and an examination of its importance in political life. This discussion will show that political cultural values do not exist in isolation; they are influenced by the social backgrounds and life experiences of those who hold them. We continue, therefore, by looking at the context within which Irish political cultural values have been acquired: we examine the evolution of certain aspects of Irish society. We go on to examine the extent to which this pattern of evolution has generated a characteristic set of political cultural values. Finally, we need to consider the prospects for change in Irish political culture and the divisions within it that have been brought on by the rapid pace of social evolution over recent decades.

POLITICAL CULTURE AND ITS IMPORTANCE

It is now taken for granted that political stability depends on compatibility between political culture and political institutions: the way in which a society is governed must not deviate too far from the system of government favoured by the politically conscious public. The political culture of a particular society need not, of course, be supportive of democratic institutions; idealistic attempts to impose liberal democratic constitutions in societies that do not share the kind of thinking that underlies them may well end in failure. This was what happened in many of the new states that appeared in central and eastern Europe after the first world war, and in areas outside Europe (for instance, in the British Commonwealth) after the second world war. What is important is that there be a match of some kind between political institutions and political culture; even authoritarian government presupposes a supportive political culture unless it is to rely entirely on rule by force, as the collapse of the Communist regimes in central and eastern Europe in 1989 showed.

The widespread use of the term "political culture" and the creation of a more systematic theory arguing its central importance in the political process dates from the publication in 1963 of *The Civic Culture* by two American scholars, Gabriel Almond and Sydney Verba (see Almond and Verba, 1989a). Although their work has been subjected to extensive criticism on methodological grounds and certain of its theoretical assumptions have been undermined (see the essays in Almond and Verba, 1989b), the term "political culture" has been assimilated into the everyday vocabulary of political science. It is therefore appropriate to look at the kinds of area in which political cultural values have most importance.

A useful starting point is the suggestion by Almond, Powell and Mundt (1993, pp. 9-11, 55-59) that the political system has three principal levels and that these offer a good framework for mapping the contours of its political culture. The *system* level refers to the state itself and to people's attitudes towards it. The *process* level refers to the rules of the political game—the basic constitutional principles that determine how decisions are taken—and the public's view of these. The *policy* level refers to the actual outcomes of the decision making process—the pattern of public policy that is followed by the state—and the extent to which it matches citizens' expectations. This division corresponds closely with another approach that distinguishes between macro-, meso- and micropolitical culture (Girvin, 1989, pp. 34-36).

To use yet another terminology, we may distinguish between three layers of values that an individual acquires through the process of political socialisation—*core* values, absorbed during childhood and early adolescence, relating to such matters as national identity; an *inner layer* of values, acquired during adolescence and early adulthood, relating to fundamental principles of government; and an *outer layer* of values, acquired for the most part in adult life, relating to day-to-day political issues. Research on political socialisation (which examines the processes and agencies by which the individual arrives at these values—through the influence of the family, school or peers, for instance) suggests that core values are almost unalterable, inner layer values are extremely difficult to dislodge and even outer layer values (such as a commitment to a particular political tradition, party or ideology) tend to remain relatively unchanged within the individual.

While it might be possible to confine ourselves to describing Ireland's political culture in terms of this framework, it is important to remember that no political cultural pattern comes about simply by accident. The same kinds of forces help to shape it as influence political life more generally. We may group these into three broad dimensions. First, the shape of a country's path of *socio-economic development* is of great importance: the extent to which society has industrialised, the nature of this industrialisation and its effects on social structure. The second dimension is the pattern of *cultural evolution*: the degree to which particular values (such as religious ones) have come to be dominant and the extent to which these are challenged by alternative values (such as loyalty to distinctive ethnic or linguistic groups). Third, a country's long-term *political experience* needs to be considered: external influences, patterns of past domination by distinctive groups and other consequences of the course of history may be of great significance.

The relationship between these background societal factors and political cultural values is illustrated in Figure 2.1. A free interpretation of the three dimensions of political culture identified by Almond, Powell and Mundt allows us to highlight examples of the kinds of issues that arise when the influence of societal factors on particular aspects of political culture is assessed. Thus, people's perceptions of the legitimacy of the state, especially with reference to their satisfaction with the way in which it reflects their feelings of national identity, are strongly influenced by variations in the pattern of socio-economic development; cultural (and, above all, linguistic) homogeneity is of great importance if people are to be loyal to the state; and particular aspects of political experience (such as a period of colonial rule) may also affect this. Second, the level of socio-economic development has a major bearing on the form of government adopted in the constitution (more specifically, liberal democracy is said to require a relatively advanced level of development); this is also related to cultural factors (such as religious denominational membership or, more clearly, level of literacy); and, once again, political experience may cause certain systems of government to be regarded as more "normal" than others. Third, attitudes towards more concrete public policy issues are also obviously related to social background factors—rapid economic development may promote interclass tensions and therefore conflicting views on public policy, for instance; religious fragmentation may promote conflict over moral issues; and diverging perceptions of history may cause divisions over other policy areas, such as foreign relations.

Figure 2.1: The effect of societal factors on political culture: a typology

Societal factors	Political cultural characteristics affected		
	Core values: legitimacy of state	*Inner layer values: acceptability of constitutional principles*	*Outer layer values: agreement with public policy outcomes*
Socio-economic development	National identity	Authoritarian versus democratic values	Conflict over resource allocation
Cultural evolution	As above	As above	Religious versus secular values
Political experience	As above	As above	Foreign policy issues

Note: Each element in the cells of this figure is an example of the kind of political cultural issue that is influenced by the corresponding societal factor.

The pattern of political activity in any society is, then, in large measure a product of the political culture of that society; and political culture is, in turn, a product of a complex interplay of more fundamental societal factors. It should not be assumed from this, however, that causation is entirely in one direction. It is true that political culture gives substance to the institutions of state; but the direction of causation may sometimes be reversed. Few states are merely passive victims of their political cultures; most attempt—some with exceptional vigour—also to shape their citizens' political values. This may be done through speeches and other direct cues from political leaders, through central control or manipulation of the mass media or, most powerfully of all, through the education system. The teaching of such subjects as history and civics, in particular, may be a very effective mechanism for attempting to influence or even remould a political culture. Debates about the manner in which Irish history should be taught in schools constitute a good example. Even more fundamentally, a state may in the long term seek to transform its own socio-economic infrastructure or to convert its citizens from one religion to another (and, indeed, sociologists since Max Weber have been conscious of the mutual influence of these two underlying dimensions, socio-economic development and religion).

The Irish state, as we have seen in chapter 1, came into existence in difficult circumstances at the same time as certain short-lived democracies in central and eastern Europe. Since it also shared many structural and historical characteristics with these states, it is important to ask why democratic institutions were apparently able to flourish here. We may find at least part of the answer in Ireland's political culture: in the set of deeply ingrained attitudes that caused Irish people to see democratic institutions and practices as normal and legitimate. This set of attitudes has had a double effect. On the one hand, the close conformity between political culture and political institutions reinforced the structures of the state. On the other hand, precisely because political cultural values normally change slowly, it is likely that these very values will act as an obstacle to future political evolution and that they will have an essentially conservative effect.

In the two sections that follow we look in turn at the two axes of Figure 2.1 to describe the position in Ireland: first at the set of long-term societal trends that have been relevant for Irish political culture, and then at the nature of this political culture itself. We concentrate in these sections on those aspects of Irish political culture that have traditionally been identified. This approach oversimplifies the position by assuming, first, that Irish political culture is stable and, second, that it is homogeneous. The two last sections of the chapter compensate by turning to the issues of change and fragmentation.

THE EVOLUTION OF IRISH SOCIETY

In looking at the complex set of changes in Irish society over the past century or so, we follow up the three-point framework in Figure 2.1. The three dimensions listed there (socio-economic development, cultural evolution and political experience) indeed overlap with the "source elements in Irish political culture" identified by Brian Farrell (1971, p. xv).

Socio-economic development
The outstanding characteristic of socio-economic development in Ireland, viewed over the long term, has been a radical change in socio-economic structure. In this Ireland has not been unique; researchers from different disciplines and ideological perspectives have pointed to the central importance of the revolutionary socio-economic transition through which all western societies have progressed, whether this is described as a transition from agrarian (or preindustrial) to industrial society, from feudal (or precapitalist) to capitalist society, or, to use more value-laden terms, from traditional to modern society. This change may best be appreciated by considering "ideal types" (theoretical descriptions that do not necessarily exist in reality) of the two kinds of society. It should be noted that these types refer to more or less integrated packages of characteristics spanning a wide range of areas rather than being confined exclusively to economic change as implied in the narrow sense of the word "industrial".

Agrarian society has been typified as one in which the population, by definition, is overwhelmingly agrarian (with peasants relying on mixed subsistence agriculture, and the minuscule industrial sector being confined to small-scale cottage industries and crafts); with predominantly rural settlement patterns; mainly illiterate, and with an oral tradition dominated by village-based or regional dialects; with only a restricted transport network; and with poorly devel-

oped communications media. In industrial society these characteristics are reversed. The population is overwhelmingly involved in the industrial or services
sectors (with large-scale, machine dependent industry and a small, surviving agricultural sector of specialised commercial farmers); with predominantly urban
settlement patterns; mainly or even universally literate in a modern, standardised
language; and with a high degree of mobility—of people and goods, and of ideas.

A yet more profound difference between the two types of society takes place in
the area of social relations. In agrarian society the individual is born into a particular rank in society, kinship group and village, and faces a fixed set of occupational options. Mobility prospects are restricted not just by society itself but also
by the individual's own acceptance of his or her existing role as inevitable and
natural. In industrial society, by contrast, regardless of the position into which an
individual is born the prospects for spatial and occupational mobility are much
greater not just because society is open to this, but because the individual's own
perspective allows him or her freely to contemplate such roles. By contrast to
agrarian society, where the existing order and the individual's role within it are
accepted, in industrial society the typical individual has a capacity to envisage
himself or herself occupying an unlimited range of roles.

**Figure 2.2: Urban population, non-agrarian population, literacy and
language, 1841-1991**

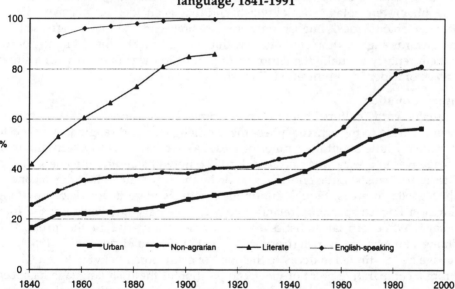

Where does Ireland fit between the poles of agrarian and industrial society defined above? The data on occupational structure and urbanisation in appendix 1
are summarised in Figure 2.2, which also considers two other variables, language
and literacy. If economic development was relatively slow, with Irish society long
remaining rural and agrarian, the pace of other aspects of social change was
relatively rapid. Although secondary education, in Ireland as elsewhere, was left
to private interests or to the church until recent decades and third level education
was of negligible impact until recently, the state intervened at an early stage in
primary education. After 1831 an ambitious network of "national schools" was
established throughout the country, and by the end of the nineteenth century the

great bulk of children of school-going age were attending these schools. The impact of this system and of the efforts of other agencies on levels of literacy was dramatic, as Figure 2.2 shows. Furthermore, between the 1880s and 1920s the stark cleavage between landlords and tenants (a common feature of agrarian societies) was overcome as the process of state sponsored land purchase established and consolidated the principle of peasant proprietorship and led to the disappearance of traditional landlords as a class.

The level of educational development in Ireland and the growth of literacy, then, proceeded much more quickly than the more retarded pace of economic development would have suggested. This anomaly draws attention to one of the hazards of viewing socio-economic development in isolation from external relationships and influences, especially those of dependence. Although Ireland (or at least the south) was an economically backward periphery, it formed until 1922 part of one of the world's most advanced industrial states. The British government was prepared to promote a separate agenda for Ireland, overseeing the establishment there of an advanced primary education system and of a developed transport infrastructure that included thousands of miles of roads and railways.

British educational policy in Ireland was not disinterested: it also contributed to the anglicisation of the country. The earliest reliable information on the linguistic structure of the population dates from 1851, and shows that already at that time almost all of the population (94 per cent of those in the present territory of the Republic) were able to speak English, and that a considerable majority (61 per cent) were able to speak English only. As the nineteenth century progressed the trend towards anglicisation continued, with the result that by the beginning of the twentieth century virtually the entire adult population was familiar with a single language of wider communication, English.

Cultural evolution

We use the word "culture" here not in its normal broad sense but as a shorthand way of referring to the concrete phenomena of language and religion. We need to say relatively little about the former of these. As we have already seen, the Irish language was in a very weak position by 1922, notwithstanding the energetic activities of revivalists. Little effort was made by the new state to halt the decline of Irish in gaeltacht areas, though enormous resources were devoted to providing children in English-speaking Ireland with a rudimentary knowledge of the Irish language. While official statistics thus show a steady rise in the proportion claiming a knowledge of Irish (from 18 per cent in 1911 to 31 per cent in 1986), the language has continued to decay to the point of extinction as a living language.

From a comparative point of view, the position of the Irish language has been unique and extraordinary. It has been given a powerful constitutional and legal position because of its status as the perceived ancestral language, yet most of the population fail to understand it and very few speak it on a daily basis. Although the language issue was used by the early nationalist movement, it was important as a symbol of Irish identity rather than as a medium of communication. The language revival movement was, strangely, made up overwhelmingly of people whose home language was English, and, by sharp contrast to the position in central and eastern Europe, the language boundary in Ireland did not separate two ethnic groups—speakers of the two languages felt equally Irish.

When we turn to the question of religion, the position is rather different. In terms of religious affiliation, a great majority of the population has belonged to the Catholic church (see appendix 1a). The Protestant population, which in the nineteenth century constituted 25 per cent of the population of the island, amounted to a minority of only 10 per cent in the south after partition. Furthermore, many members of this community had been killed during the first world war; many had been strongly associated with the old regime, and left after 1922; many were landlords who lost their estates or who were subjected to intimidation at around the same period, and who also left; while the remaining population had shrunk to less than four per cent by 1981. This was a consequence of continued emigration, a low rate of natural increase (in fact, for many decades Protestant deaths outnumbered births) and assimilation to the Catholic community especially through mixed marriages (the children of which have typically been brought up as Catholics).

From a comparative point of view, the position of the Catholic religion within Irish society has been as unique and extraordinary as that of the Irish language. Unlike the position in comparable societies in eastern Europe, it was along religious denominational rather than along linguistic lines that political mobilisation took place in the nineteenth century. This arose in part from the perceived (but, in reality, imperfect) coincidence between the two main religions and two ethnic traditions—Catholic Irish natives, and Protestant British settlers. It was also related to the fact that the institutional Catholic church in Ireland up to the nineteenth century was not a major landowner, was not linked with the old regime, and was neutral or sympathetic on the issues of democratisation and nationalism, rather than being suspicious or hostile, as in continental Europe.

In any case, Irish history offers many illustrations of the grip of the Catholic church on the people. Even before the famine of 1845-49, when evidence suggests that only a minority of Catholics attended weekly mass, the church had become intimately involved in political movements—first in the movement for Catholic emancipation, then in that for repeal of the Act of Union, both led by Daniel O'Connell. This involvement continued and intensified in post-famine Ireland. In what has been described as a "devotional revolution", weekly mass attendance rates began to approach 100 per cent. Already before the new state was founded, Ireland was noted for the remarkable loyalty of Catholics to the church and for the absence of a tradition of anticlericalism (Whyte, 1980, pp. 3-8). This relationship was cemented through the educational system, in which the Catholic church has had an unchallenged role. Catholic identity—the self-perception of Catholics as an oppressed group, with both clergy and laity discriminated against by the state—became an important element of Irish national identity. Like all processes of collective mobilisation, of course, the political integration of the Catholic population had a negative aspect, its differentiation from others; in this case, the excluded group was the Protestant population.

For all the intensity of Irish Catholicism, its character did not remain unaltered. Change may be seen in terms of a three-fold classification of ethical behaviour that has been identified as existing within Christianity: *magical*, in which material goals are pursued through traditional prescriptions and formulas, *legalistic*, in which the emphasis is on adherence to traditional rules and regulations, and *principled*, in which an individually reasoned set of ethical guidelines is followed (Inglis, 1987, pp. 14-17). Until the nineteenth century, Inglis argued, the magical type was predominant in Irish Catholicism, and elements of this survive; but religious legalistic behaviour became dominant at the beginning of the twentieth century (Inglis, 1987, pp. 221-4).

Finally, the significance of interdenominational differences for an important aspect of development that has already been discussed, education, needs to be underscored. Historically, a preoccupation with education was characteristic of Protestant, not Catholic, societies; in the former, particular emphasis was placed on the need of every individual to be able to read the Bible and, hence, it was seen as imperative for all to be provided with rudimentary schooling. Evidence abounds from Europe of the enormous differences in Catholic and Protestant literacy levels, and the same trends are apparent in nineteenth century Ireland. In 1861 in the present territory of the Republic, for instance, 47 per cent of Catholics were illiterate, as against only 12 per cent of Protestants. While these figures must be treated with some caution since Protestants were also, in general, of a higher social status than Catholics, they do draw attention to an important aspect of the interplay between cultural evolution and socio-economic development.

Political experience

The dominant element in Ireland's political experience, viewed over a long time span, has been the legacy of British rule, which appears to have left a lasting impact on the Irish political mentality. This is not surprising, given the centuries-long British presence on the island. Whether or not Ireland was a willing recipient, Britain bequeathed to its neighbouring island its dominant language, much of its culture, many of its social practices and, most importantly for present purposes, its political vocabulary, concepts, institutions and patterns of behaviour. A large volume of Irish emigration to (and a smaller volume of reverse migration from) Britain has been characteristic of Irish population movement patterns. For long after independence a close economic relationship also remained, with the two countries sharing a common currency until 1979 and with a remarkably high degree of Irish trade dependence on the British market: for several decades after 1922 the greater part of Ireland's imports came from Great Britain, and approximately three quarters of Irish exports were destined for Britain.

This influence was determined not only by history but also by geography. Not only goods and people but also ideas travelled freely to Ireland from the neighbouring island. British newspapers circulated widely in Ireland and continue to do so. They accounted for at least 10 per cent of daily newspaper circulation in Ireland in 1968, and 21 per cent in 1992 (not including the Irish edition of the *Star*, with 14 per cent); of Sunday newspapers, British titles accounted for at least 40 per cent in 1968, though this figure had dropped to 31 per cent by 1992 (calculated from Chubb, 1970, pp. 124-5; Wilson Hartnell, 1992, pp. 17-18). Irish people's first familiarity with radio and with the powerful medium of television came from Britain, and even with the development of Irish services competition from Britain has been intense, especially on the east coast.

Nor has British influence been balanced by countervailing influences from elsewhere. The enormous Irish diaspora in the United States and in other English-speaking countries has had only occasional impact on attitudes at home. Links with the nearer countries of continental Europe, intense by contemporary standards until the eighteenth century, were rather weak in the nineteenth and early twentieth centuries; it is clear from data on the destinations of Irish emigrants that they were oriented almost entirely to the English-speaking world rather than to continental Europe.

THE POLITICAL CULTURE OF INDEPENDENT IRELAND

The long-term economic and social processes discussed above have produced a society in which particular patterns of political cultural values are likely to flourish. The first overview of Irish political culture identified seven main features: the British influence, nationalism, the dying peasant society, Irish Catholicism, authoritarianism, loyalty and anti-intellectualism (Chubb, 1970, pp. 43-60; Chubb 1992, pp. 3-20). In general, other authors have agreed in identifying authoritarianism as a feature, but some have emphasised other traits, such as personalism (Schmitt, 1973, pp. 55-64), individualism and conformism (Gallagher, 1982, pp. 16-20) or nationalism and Catholic values (Girvin, 1986, pp. 5-6, 15-16).

Certain of these features (the British influence and Catholicism) have been discussed in the last section as underlying societal factors. In turning to the characteristics that have been dominant in Irish political culture since independence, we return to the framework of Figure 2.1 and seek to relate the features identified above to this. We begin with the most fundamental issue, the legitimacy of the state itself, an issue on which, as we have seen, individual beliefs are likely to be least flexible. This is followed by a discussion of attitudes towards the constitutional principles that govern decision making in Ireland. A short concluding subsection looks at attitudes towards public policy outputs.

Attitudes towards the state

In most societies, potential threats to political stability are directed at political structures and decision making mechanisms, rather than at the territorial identity of the state itself. In Ireland, however, the very legitimacy of the state was an issue. By the *legitimacy* of a state we mean its capacity to attract the committed support of its citizens; they may not always like particular government decisions, but they accept the right of central state institutions to carry out their functions and they recognise these as valid. The United Kingdom for a few years before 1922 was an example of a state whose legitimacy was in question. Although Irish people might not have objected to the actual *content* of the laws being enacted at Westminster, in large numbers they rejected the *right* of Westminster to legislate for them. A majority of their representatives refused to attend parliament after 1918, symbolic of their rejection of its legitimacy, and attempted to establish a separate state, as we have seen in chapter 1.

If Irish nationalism rejected the legitimacy of the United Kingdom, it did not follow that this automatically conferred legitimacy on the new Irish Free State. In fact, broad sections of the population questioned the identity of a state that was unable to assert its sovereignty over all of the island; those who had thought of Ireland as an indivisible island found the truncated "Free State" difficult to accept. Furthermore, the new state was too independent of Great Britain for some, and insufficiently so for others. The latter group in particular, because of the intensity with which they rejected the state and because of their numbers, initially constituted a potentially very serious threat. Defeated in the civil war of 1922-23, most of them left the fundamentalist republican movement to join Fianna Fáil in 1926, reached an accommodation with the state in 1927 and began to transform the state into a shape that they found more acceptable after 1932.

Yet a small fundamentalist republican group survived. Support for or sympathy with its objectives extends outside its central group of active supporters, and it continues to reject the legitimacy not only of Northern Ireland but also of the

Republic (a term that it refuses to apply to the southern state, which it still refers to as "the Free State"). This ideology was summarised by the President of (Provisional) Sinn Féin on the occasion of the 60th anniversary of the 1916 rising. The "republic" of 1916 was endowed with an eternal significance, but

> that Republic proclaimed in 1916 and set functioning in all 32 counties from 1919 to 1921, was overthrown by force and suppressed by a British Dominion for 26 counties and a Crown Colony for Six Counties. ... While that British Dominion, known as the Irish Free State, changed its name and its constitution, over the years, it remains manifestly what it was designed to be by the English government which created it 55 years ago—a colonial state destined to rule the greatest part of Ireland in the interests of Britain (Ó Brádaigh, 1976, p. 2).

While elements of this kind of language are to be found in left-wing movements in many western societies since the late 1960s, the great significance of the extract cited above is that it is underlain by deep historical roots, by passionate commitment (extending to a willingness to engage in an armed struggle or to die on hunger strike) and by extensive public support, at least in Northern Ireland.

How extensive and committed has public support been for this ideology in the south? If measured in terms of support for Sinn Féin in national or local elections, the answer appears to be "not much". Although the party won four Dáil seats in 1957, that election may have been its last significant intervention in the south. Two candidates were elected to the Dáil in 1981 on a "H-Block" ticket during hunger strikes in Northern Ireland, but Sinn Féin was unable to hold their seats subsequently. In any case, the motivations of those who vote for Sinn Féin in the south are complex; in those areas of Dublin where Sinn Féin has done well in local elections, for instance, local issues rather than metaphysical discussion of "the Republic" are likely to have been crucial. The traditional argument that the Dáil is an illegitimate, British-imposed institution, though attractive to the purists, is likely to have won few votes. Nevertheless, it is clear that nationalism has been an important ingredient in Irish political culture; although Irish people might not have supported Sinn Féin, few would question the intensity with which they supported autonomy and rejected partition of the island for many decades into the life of the new state.

These nationalist values may well have had the effect of undermining the legitimacy of the state in its early years; but, as the formal British influence diminished and the issue of partition receded from public consciousness, nationalism became a factor in enhancing the state's legitimacy, and, as elsewhere, it was used to this end by the state. The cultivation of pride in Irish achievements in sports, literature, the arts and other areas of international comparison or competition helped in the long term to displace grievances of the past in stimulating Irish nationalism and in boosting the legitimacy of the regime.

This "normalisation" of the values of Irish nationalism is reflected in survey evidence. It is true that in surveys in 1981 and 1990 the Irish were significantly more likely than other Europeans to claim that they would be willing to fight for their country in the event of war, and that a much higher proportion (76 per cent in 1990) declared themselves to be "very proud" of their nationality; the average for other European countries was 37 per cent (Ashford and Timms, 1992, p. 90). The survival of traditional nationalist attitudes was also indicated by the fact that a clear majority of Irish respondents in a 1993 survey (71 per cent) wanted decision making in the sensitive areas of security and defence to remain at national level, but this position was supported by only 42 per cent of Europeans

(*Eurobarometer* no. 39, 1993, pp. A26-27). On the other hand, a 1990 survey showed the Irish to have a more tolerant attitude towards immigrants than the typical European one (Ashford and Timms, 1992, p. 14). (The very low proportion of immigrants in Ireland should be borne in mind, though; intolerance tends to increase as the proportion of immigrants increases.) This was confirmed in a 1993 survey in respect of attitudes towards non-EC immigrants as well as people from other EC countries (*Eurobarometer* no. 39, 1993, pp. A51-54). The latter survey also showed (p. A50) that traditional hostility towards the British was breaking down: Irish respondents trusted the British more than many other European nationalities, though they did give the Belgians, Danes, Dutch and French a higher rating.

Historical explanations of Irish nationalism have generally referred to the factors considered in the first section of this chapter: Ireland's slow pace of economic and social development was juxtaposed with a much more developed Britain in a relationship of dependency; Catholics resented their heritage of oppression, and the church could see in self-government for Ireland a buttress against "godless" ideas from across the Irish Sea; and Britain may be said to have governed Ireland with insufficient wisdom to secure Irish loyalty to the united state established in 1800. While these factors have had an obvious and lasting impact on attitudes in Northern Ireland, elements of them appear also to have survived, if in less acute form, in the south; "normalisation" of nationalist attitudes has proceeded only to the extent that consciousness of these factors has faded away.

Attitudes towards the political system

We move out now from core values to the inner layer of political culture: attitudes to the constitutional principles by which the state is governed. Observers of Irish political culture are agreed that a basic commitment to *democratic values* is a central feature. The very fact that the state and its constitutional system managed to survive a difficult birth (see Prager, 1986) and that it has persisted for so long is itself evidence of this. Irish voters adopted the country's democratic basic law, the constitution, in 1937, at a time when democracy was collapsing elsewhere in Europe. No significant voice has been raised against democratic institutions and practices, though certain fringe groups and personalities in the 1930s and the 1940s did advocate alternative forms of political organisation incompatible with democracy as we know it. Data relating to voting turnout confirm the similarity between the pattern in Ireland and that in other democracies. While a larger proportion of Irish people typically abstain from voting than is the case in continental Europe, Ireland compares favourably with other English-speaking countries, with an average turnout rate of 72.7 per cent in the 24 general elections over the period 1923-92.

Survey evidence bears out the view that the Irish are relatively supportive of liberal democratic government. The most useful evidence of this kind comes from polls that allow us to look at Ireland in comparative context. The first such survey, carried out in 1970 but reported much later, replicated questions from the classic study of political culture published originally in 1963 (Almond and Verba, 1989a). The researchers found that in certain areas Ireland was to be grouped with countries that had a political culture said to be conducive to democracy (Great Britain, the USA and, to a lesser extent, Germany), though the evidence covered very limited areas: perceptions of the impact of national and local government on everyday life, and expectations of fair treatment by the police (Raven and Whelan, 1976, pp. 22, 24, 46). In other areas, however, the same body of evidence suggested that Irish people have a more relaxed attitude to democracy. In a comparative context, their level of "subjective competence" (sense of having the capacity to influence the political process at local and national levels) was found to be low (Raven and Whelan, 1976, p. 26).

More recent survey evidence confirms the similarity between Irish attitudes and those in other European states; indeed, in most important respects the Irish are significantly more favourably disposed towards major institutions than their European counterparts. Thus, a 1981 survey showed that the Irish were more likely than the "average" European to express confidence in the police, the civil service, parliament and the press (Fogarty, Ryan and Lee, 1984, pp. 179, 243). These findings were confirmed from the opposite perspective in a 1990 survey: the Irish were much less likely than the "average" European to express lack of confidence in these same institutions, except the press; furthermore, Irish people's sense of subjective competence appeared now to be higher (Ashford and Timms, 1992, pp. 16, 98). A series of surveys carried out regularly since 1973 has shown that a clear majority of those questioned has been consistently satisfied with "the way democracy works" (*Eurobarometer trends 1974-1990*, March 1991, pp. 18-31).

The results of a more recent survey from this series are reported in Table 2.1. This shows that the Irish tend to rank higher than Europeans in general in knowledge about political matters, and very much higher in their satisfaction with the political process. Reported interest in politics was slightly lower than the European average, however, being challenged by religion, which Europeans regarded as being of lesser importance (the Irish, and Europeans generally, regarded work, the family, friends and leisure as much more important than politics).

Table 2.1: Knowledge of and attitudes towards politics, Ireland and EC, 1993

Area	Ireland	EC	Irish-EC difference
Political knowledge			
Can identify correctly:			
- the national capital	99	94	+5
- the name of the prime minister	95	94	+1
· the role of the head of state	84	81	+3
- the capital of the EC	78	72	+6
- the number of countries in the EC	49	53	-4
- the name of the President of the EC Commission	44	38	+6
Political attitudes			
Satisfied with the way democracy works in own country	62	42	+20
Satisfied with the way democracy works in the EC	62	41	+21
Considers politics to be generally important	29	35	-6

Note: All figures are percentages.
Source: Eurobarometer no. 39, June 1993, pp. A14, A32-34, A48.

Survey evidence of this kind is notoriously difficult to interpret. The meaning of words changes between cultures, and responses must be assessed in the context of the political environment within which questions are asked. Italians strongly committed to democracy, for instance, might be expected to express dissatisfaction with the way democracy works in Italy in the wake of the political scandals of 1992-93, but this does not make them any less democratically inclined. We need, therefore, also to take account of more intuitively based descriptions of Irish political culture.

While observers are agreed that Irish people by and large accept the principles of liberal democratic government, they have also pointed to certain features of Irish political culture that are of questionable compatibility with democracy. These have been mentioned above, and they may be grouped here for further analysis. First, *authoritarianism, conformism, anti-intellectualism* and *loyalty* have been identified as distinctive elements in Irish political culture. These terms belong to a common category to the extent that each of them implies commitment to opinions received from above, and a suspicion of those who are not prepared to accept these. (The term *authoritarianism* is used here in a very specific and, perhaps, unusual sense, and we will adopt it in the rest of this chapter; it is taken to refer not to a particular system of government but rather to a distinctive type of attitude that combines *deference* to the views of established leaders with *intolerance* of those who dissent from these views. The source of authority is not necessarily the will of the majority but some principle held to be objective and absolute, transcending individual preferences.)

There are thus two areas where we may look for evidence about this aspect of Irish political culture. First, a preoccupation with a "strong leader" has long been characteristic of authoritarian attitudes. A survey in 1966 found that 71 per cent of Dubliners agreed that "a few strong leaders would do more for the country than all the laws and talk" (Hart, 1970, p. 386). A survey in 1970 found that 93 per cent considered "a good strong leader" to be one of the most important factors for the future of the country (Raven and Whelan, 1976, p. 40).

The second area concerns attitudes towards and tolerance of minorities. A survey in 1970 found that 61 per cent believed that they would be justified in imposing on others "something which one believes to be good and right" and 78 per cent agreed that "certain political groups must be curbed when they abuse freedom of speech" (Raven and Whelan, 1976, pp. 47-48). A large survey in Dublin in 1972-73 led to the conclusion that there was a "relatively high level of dormant or latent racialism, and a moderately high degree of intolerance against political and social outgroups", as well as "a considerable degree of general intolerance and authoritarianism" (Mac Gréil, 1977, p. 530). If this was the case in Dublin, it may well be that such attitudes were even more common in rural Ireland. The flavour of Dublin attitudes may be conveyed by some examples. The percentages agreeing with the following statements were (Mac Gréil, 1977, p. 424):

Communism should be outlawed in Ireland	54
A thing is either right or wrong and none of this ambiguous woolly thinking	48
Men whose doctrines are false should not be allowed to preach in this country	44
Skinheads should be locked up	39
Gardaí should be armed always	32
There should be very strict control of RTE	29
Student protest should be outlawed	25

There is other evidence of Irish people's deference to authority. Observers have commented on the high degree of public acquiescence in decisions by governments to postpone local elections, or even to suspend local councils and replace them by appointed commissioners, and one observer has commented that "the public is relatively unconcerned about local democracy" (Collins, 1987, p. 51). A book-length analysis of Irish political culture identified authoritarianism as one of its central characteristics (Schmitt, 1973, pp. 43-54); a strong pressure towards political conformism, especially in rural areas, has been noted (Gallagher, 1982, pp. 19-20); and loyalty (to leaders in church and state) and anti-intellectualism (in which a consensus on religious and political values was able for long to continue virtually unchallenged) have been seen as key elements, especially in the past (Chubb, 1992, pp. 18-20).

Since authoritarianism can rest on nondemocratic processes of decision making, it is often accompanied by a willingness to rely on mechanisms other than the ballot box to give effect to political decisions. The cult of political violence has, indeed, played a significant role in Irish history, but the evidence suggests that the Irish have buried the rifle. A 1970 survey showed that while a majority clearly opposed the use of force, a large minority (20 per cent) agreed that the use of force was at least sometimes the only way to advance an ideal (Raven and Whelan, 1976, p. 49), while a survey carried out in 1978 suggested that 21 per cent supported IRA activities (Davis and Sinnott, 1979, pp. 97-9). On the other hand, despite the long tradition of revolutionary violence in Ireland, regular surveys since 1976 have shown that Irish people's attitudes to political change are not greatly different from those in other parts of the EC: only tiny minorities are prepared to endorse attempts to change society by revolutionary means (*Eurobarometer trends 1974-1990*, March 1991, pp. 32-49).

The second set of political cultural features whose implications for democracy are questionable appears at first sight to be incompatible with the set just discussed: *personalism* (Schmitt, 1973, pp. 55-64) and *individualism* (Gallagher, 1982, pp. 16-20). Personalism has been defined as "a pattern of social relations in which people are valued for who they are and whom they know—not solely for what technical qualifications they possess" (Schmitt, 1973, p. 55). This is a more general articulation of the traditional maxim about recruitment: "it's not what you know that matters, it's whom you know". It also implies a tendency to evaluate and respond to persons in positions of power (such as the President, the Taoiseach or a local Dáil deputy) in terms of their personal character rather than in terms of the authority associated with their office. Its principal aspects include a closely integrated pattern of social and political relationships, and brokerage politics (see chapter 8). It is entirely compatible with the broader concept of individualism, defined as "a preference for individual action as opposed to cooperation" (Gallagher, 1982, p. 16), and has the same political consequences. This characteristic is similar to the "amoral familism" detected by Edward Banfield (1967) in village life in southern Italy—a suspicion of and sense of competition with all those outside the immediate family, attributable to a low level of economic development and a legacy of foreign rule—features also of the Irish experience.

Despite appearances, these two sets of attitudes are not mutually incompatible. For all their deference to strong leaders, the Irish are not noted for their compliance with laws and regulations; and, while the state is to be obeyed, the rationale for obedience may be a fear of coercion rather than a sense of duty. Thus many aspects of deviant behaviour, such as traffic violations or tax evasion, enjoy a considerable degree of public tolerance and are seen as legitimate contests between the individual and agents of the state, the police officer or tax inspector. The argument may then be rephrased: Irish people defer to authority collectively in principle, while reserving the right individually to frustrate it.

We should not be surprised at the curious blend of apparently incompatible values in Irish political culture. Authoritarian and democratic values clearly clash, but their coexistence within western cultures has been noted for some time. Indeed, it has even been suggested that democracy can survive only provided a significant strain of authoritarianism runs through society—in other words, it is important that people be disposed to accept decisions from above, but it is equally important that most people should be prepared to leave the making of these decisions to others. (It is not possible here to explore the peculiar implications of this viewpoint for democratic theory.) More specifically, Schmitt (1973, pp. 77-80) has concluded that authoritarianism and personalism have actually contributed to the successful development of a democratic society in Ireland.

Finally, we need to account for these characteristics of Irish political culture. The discussion earlier in this chapter of the impact of socio-economic development implies that the dissemination of democratic values depends on the coming of industrial society. To the extent that this process was developed, it "explains" the openness of Irish society to democratic values; to the extent that this process had not been completed, it "explains" the persistence of authoritarian values, with their peculiar overtones of individualism. In pre-industrial society peasants regarded the state as something external and hostile. For instance, French peasants in the nineteenth century were said to regard the state and government as "given to mischief-making, hard on little people, that demands taxes, prevents contraband and dwells in Paris" (Weber, 1977, pp. 242-3). The tendency towards individualism in Irish society may well represent the survival of such attitudes.

Second, the dominance of the Catholic church and its influence through the educational system are likely to have strengthened authoritarianism. This influence was probably both direct (through the teaching of the value of obedience) and indirect (through a transfer from religious into political life of authoritarian values). Unlike the Protestant churches, the Catholic church is strikingly undemocratic and hierarchical in structure, with instructions issuing from the pope through bishops and priests to the laity. The source of these precepts is itself sharply different from that in the Protestant churches, with their emphasis on the individual's discovery of the truth in the Bible and decision on action in accordance with conscience; in the Catholic tradition the emphasis is on an objective morality, on which the church is authoritative arbiter, and on collective compliance with rules. One comparative study of the political cultural implications of Catholicism, Islam, Hinduism and Buddhism concluded that it was remarkable that "the one Western religion among the four is the least conducive to an open, democratic political culture" (Smith, 1970, p. 178). The "carry-over" effect of religion on other aspects of behaviour helps to explain not only authoritarianism but also individualistic behaviour: it is possible on the one hand to subscribe to a general ethical principle but, on the other, to act in breach of this principle occasionally, or even frequently, in everyday life. The contrast between the religious legalism of Irish Catholicism and the individually principled ethics said to be characteristic of Protestantism has been described as follows:

> Individually principled ethics do not appear to be very common among Irish Catholics. The majority seem to follow the church's interpretation of Christ's teachings. Even though they may be disobedient, most Irish Catholics rarely seem to disagree with the Church's teachings. ... Such is the acceptance of the Church's interpretation of Christ's teachings and what constitutes good Christian behaviour that most Irish Catholics do not bother to read the Bible or gospels (Inglis, 1987, pp. 30-1).

Third, the British influence was paradoxical. On the one hand, much of Irish political history was dominated by an Irish nationalist struggle against the British; on the other, this was accompanied by a strong (and in some areas uncritical) admiration for the British way of life and for British political models. It is possible that Ireland's relationship of dependence on Great Britain indeed left a deep mark: nationalist political mobilisation took place at an extremely early stage in the nineteenth century, and it was characterised by passionate loyalty to "strong leaders" such as O'Connell and Parnell, a tradition that may well have survived. We should also recall that some of the most authoritarian attitudes and most slavish patterns of leadership adulation have developed in "modern" industrial societies.

Attitudes towards public policy
While an individual's sense of national identity tends to be immutable and his or her attitude to the rules of the political game tends to be relatively inflexible, the prospect of an individual switching opinions on matters of day-to-day public policy is considerable. Indeed, flexibility in responding to changing circumstances is a requirement for the political actor. Nevertheless, behind the ebb and flow of popular attitudes on the principal political issues of the moment we may detect certain patterns of values that give some predictability to public opinion. While these values may not be carved in stone as far as the individual is concerned, they are relatively stable, and form part of the "outer layer" of the political culture. Without seeking to provide a comprehensive overview of underlying Irish values on public policy matters, we may discuss three labels that have been pinned on the Irish: conservatism, clericalism and isolationism.

At first sight, there is an abundance of evidence for the *conservatism* of the Irish on matters of economic policy. Support for parties of the left has consistently been much weaker than in any other European democracy, legislation has been of a relatively conservative character and survey evidence has shown that when Irish respondents are asked to identify where they are located on the left-right spectrum they place themselves much further to the right, on average, than other Europeans (see Gallagher, 1982, pp. 8-11). On the other hand, there is little evidence of commitment to ideologies of the extreme right. Indeed, survey data from 1979-83 placed the Irish in clear second position after the Greeks among EC peoples in their willingness to endorse classic economic policies of the left—many more of them were in favour of reducing income inequality (90 per cent), of more government management of the economy (72 per cent) and of more nationalisation of industry (64 per cent) than was the case in other west European states (Inglehart, 1990, p. 255). There appears also to be considerable support for the kind of interventionist policies that have created a big public sector in Ireland. While the political conservatism of the Irish is, then, undoubted, it coexists ambiguously with a rather pragmatic attitude towards economic development and an egalitarian attitude towards the distribution of resources.

Second, *clericalism* in Irish political life and its impact on social policy is so well documented that it needs little further comment (see Gallagher, 1982, pp. 12-16 and Girvin, 1986, for short discussions, and Whyte, 1980, for a more extended analysis). For many decades into the life of the new state public policy was firmly guided by Roman Catholic principles. The Labour Party dropped the expression "Workers' Republic" from its constitution in 1940 and the government refused to support Noel Browne, Minister for Health, in his ambitious welfare programme in the so-called "Mother and Child" controversy in 1951, in response to pressure from the Catholic bishops. More significant than the effect of episcopal intervention, however, is the fact that it has had to be used so rarely. On other occasions public opinion was sufficiently supportive of the Catholic position to make clerical intervention unnecessary, and when the bishops did intervene in the two cases mentioned their position was compatible with dominant lay opinion. Although the authority of the church to express its views in political areas could no longer be said to be unquestioned, there remain significant differences between the perceptions of Irish people and of other Europeans on areas in which it is appropriate for the church to speak out, as may be seen from Table 2.2. While merely speaking out on an issue falls well short of effective intervention and most Irish respondents did not endorse the right of the church to speak out on government policy, the fact that clericalism is significantly stronger in Ireland than elsewhere in Europe is clear.

Table 2.2: Support for public voice for church, Ireland and EC, 1990

Area	Ireland	EC	Irish-EC difference
Consider it proper for the church to speak out on:			
- third world problems	92	76	16
- abortion	81	52	29
- euthanasia	77	54	23
- unemployment	77	45	32
- extra-marital affairs	71	41	30
- homosexuality	59	35	24
- government policy	34	22	12

Note: All figures are percentages. The EC data exclude Denmark, Greece and Luxembourg.
Source: Ashford and Timms, 1992, pp. 34-5.

Third, *isolationism* has been an underlying feature of Irish attitudes towards foreign policy. This is essentially the concrete expression of a much more profound value, nationalism, which has already been discussed. It refers specifically to support for a policy of neutrality in international relations of a kind that has been demonstrated consistently in surveys. Irish respondents want control over security and military matters to be retained at national level, as we have seen, and political leaders have hesitated to point out to voters the long-term implications for Irish neutrality of joining the EC and subsequently of supporting the accelerated pace of European integration. There also appears to be significant support for an independent Irish voice in world affairs, though this is not necessarily reflected at elite level. The frequency with which politicians call for a "debate" on neutrality but stop short of indicating their own views suggests a distinct nervousness on the issue, and possibly a perception that people's commitment to the principle is deeply rooted.

These three characteristics of the outer layer of Irish political culture may be related with superficial ease to the three underlying societal factors listed in Figure 2.1. In an obvious sense, conservatism may be related to the Irish path of socio-economic evolution, with the early disappearance of the traditional landed class, the installation of a strong farming class, late industrialisation and retarded development of class consciousness; clericalism arises from the high proportion of

Catholics in the population and from the intensity of their beliefs; and isolationism arises from the country's "colonial" and "post-colonial" experience. In reality, the picture is more complex: Ireland's path of economic development has influenced clericalist and isolationist values, the Catholic church has reinforced conservatism and, in certain respects, isolationism, and historical experience and British models have affected both Irish conservatism and Irish clericalism.

A CHANGING POLITICAL CULTURE?

In the two preceding sections we presented Irish political culture and the societal factors that underlie it in oversimplified terms; apart from some incidental remarks to the contrary, we took it that these phenomena were both stable and uniform. This is, of course, incorrect, so it is appropriate now to rectify the picture by looking at the issues of change and fragmentation in Irish political culture. To begin with, much recent writing on Irish society has drawn attention to large-scale social changes, which may eventually bring political cultural change in their wake. We look now at these changes (in the three dimensions already identified—socio-economic, cultural and politico-historical) and at their impact on Irish political culture.

Change in Irish society
Appendix 1 and Figure 2.2 show clearly that, after many decades of relative stability, the period since 1960 has been characterised by social change that is almost revolutionary in scope. The proportion of the workforce engaged in agriculture has been plummeting and the urban population has expanded. Qualitative changes have also been taking place, with the transformation of agriculture from a way of life into a business. A communications revolution has occurred, with an explosion in access to a new, powerful medium, television, and greatly enhanced geographical mobility as a consequence of the increased availability of cars. The extent of these changes is indicated in Table 2.3, which covers the period 1960-90. The most useful yardstick for interpreting these data is the number of households per hundred people. In 1986, there were 27.3 households for every 100 people, a relatively stable figure; by 1990 the proportion of telephones had reached this figure, and the proportion of television licenses and cars had almost reached it. Similar changes took place in other areas, such as education (with increased numbers attending schools, and a trebling of the third-level population).

Second, although the great bulk of the population remains Catholic, the character of Catholicism has changed. This has been reflected most superficially in a drop-off in church attendance rates. Surveys show that Irish church attendance rates remain extraordinarily high by European standards—for example, in 1990 81 per cent of Irish respondents reported that they attended church at least weekly, much higher than the average European figure of 29 per cent (Ashford and Timms, 1992, p. 46). However, surveys also show significant differences between age groups, with younger people recording lower attendance rates than older ones. More profoundly, it could also be argued that religious attitudes are themselves changing, with an increasing number of Catholics prepared to take a more analytical, "principled ethical" approach, as described above, entailing a greater degree of independence from clerical guidance (see Inglis, 1987, pp. 221-

Table 2.3: Telephones, televisions and private cars, 1960-90

Year	Telephones		Television licences		Private cars	
	Number	per 100 population	Number	per 100 population	Number	per 100 population
1960	148,818	5.3	(92,675)	(3.3)	169,681	6.0
1970	291,478	9.8	415,918	14.0	440,185	14.8
1980	650,000	18.9	642,751	18.9	735,760	21.4
1990	967,000	27.4	806,055	22.8	796,408	22.6

Note: The earliest data on television licences refer to 1962.
Source: Computed from *Statistical Abstract of Ireland*, 1963-1991.

2). Agreement with the monolithic package of beliefs enshrined in the Catholic catechism appears also to be breaking down; while 96 per cent of Irish respondents in 1990 stated that they believed in God, only 77 per cent believed in life after death and 50 per cent in Hell (Ashford and Timms, 1992, p. 40), figures that would have been inconceivable 30 years earlier.

Third, the long-dominant British influence has been challenged by other sources. While the signing of the Anglo-Irish Free Trade Agreement in 1965 represented a further rapprochement between the two countries and might have been expected to lead to closer bilateral economic ties, Ireland's accession to the EC in 1973 acted as a counterbalance. There was a great increase in travel in general, and especially, insofar as we can measure it, in travel between Ireland and the continent. In 1960 a little more than a million passenger movements out of Ireland took place by ship and aeroplane, 7 per cent of them to destinations other than Great Britain; by 1990 this figure had increased fivefold, and the proportion travelling directly to non-British destinations had increased to 24 per cent (calculated from *Statistical Abstract of Ireland*, 1961 and 1991). In addition, Ireland's trade relationships changed dramatically. In 1960, 46 per cent of Irish imports and 61 per cent of Irish exports were from or to Great Britain; by 1990 these proportions had dropped to 38 and 28 per cent, respectively (calculated from *Statistical Abstract of Ireland*, 1961 and 1991). Ironically, although in the long term the significance of the UK-Irish border is likely to diminish, over recent decades it has actually increased: different VAT rates, excise duties and the impact of the break in parity between the Irish and British currencies reinforced the border. The Northern Ireland civil unrest that began in 1968, and in particular the increasingly detached southern attitude towards it, also drew attention to the extent of the gap that had grown between north and south after two generations of partition.

Change in Irish political culture
Survey-based research has suggested that a "silent revolution" has been taking place in western political culture in recent decades as a response to societal changes of the kind discussed above. In particular, one leading analyst of survey data has pointed to a steady value shift between generations, a shift from "materialist" to "postmaterialist" values (Inglehart, 1990). This shift, he further states, has had an impact on people's values at a number of levels. To put it in terms of the terminology used in this chapter, people's core values of national identity are being broken down, with increased support for European integration; in terms of the inner layer of values, people expect to have a greater say in the

decision making process; and, in terms of outer values, there has been a shift from concern with material issues to such issues as protection of civil liberties and of the environment.

Inglehart's enormous database indeed shows that these changed attitudes are characteristic of people that he defines as postmaterialists, and that the proportion of postmaterialists is increasing steadily. However, the significance of his findings is undermined by the small absolute number of postmaterialists: in 1986-87 they amounted to only 15 per cent of EC respondents, and to a mere 9 per cent of Irish respondents (Inglehart, 1990, p. 93). Even though there are significant inter-generational differences, with the proportion of postmaterialists increasing in the younger age groups, it is too early to evaluate the long-term significance of Inglehart's findings.

This is not to say, however, that there are no significant changes. Irish people's commitment to *nationalism* appears certainly to have weakened. Surveys since 1973 have shown consistently high levels of support in Ireland for EC membership and for the process of European integration, which implies a diminution of the proclamation of sovereignty in the constitution, and the referendums in 1972, 1987 and 1992 confirmed this. There appears even to have been a rapprochement with the "ancient enemy"; the closer diplomatic ties since the early 1980s were crowned by the creation of an Anglo-Irish Inter-Parliamentary Council, which the suspicious could see as symbolising the unity of the British Isles, with few signs of public disquiet or even interest. By contrast, especially over the past two decades the psychological gap between the south and Northern Ireland appears to have grown. Although majorities in public opinion surveys still claim to desire a united Ireland, at least in the long term, support for this appears to lack the intensity it once possessed, and suggested measures that might bring a degree of unity to the island (such as the creation of an all-Ireland police force) have evoked a hostile reaction in the south. Public reaction in the Republic to violence in Northern Ireland and to its overspill into Great Britain suggests that the former sympathy with the Catholic population of Northern Ireland is dead or dying, and that many southern Irish find it easier to empathise with victims of paramilitary violence in Warrington than in Belfast.

Survey evidence from 1988-89 confirms this pattern of re-orientation, though comparison with an earlier survey in Dublin in 1972-73 suggests that this re-orientation pre-dated the 1970s; there were few differences between the two sets of data. Irish people, it appears, felt considerably closer to English (or British) people than to the Northern Irish of both communities, in terms of willingness to contemplate marriage relationships, close friendship or neighbourliness. Indeed, large numbers felt that Northern Ireland and the Republic were two separate nations (49 per cent agreed, 42 per cent disagreed) and that "Northerners on all sides tend to be extreme and unreasonable" (35 per cent agreed, 46 per cent disagreed) (Mac Gréil, 1992, pp. 4, 23, 29).

As regards attitudes to the *democratic process*, it is to be expected that in the emerging postindustrial society Irish political culture will accept formal mechanisms of participant decision making and be less authoritarian, personalist and individualist—in other words, that people will expect formal rules to be followed, will be less deferential to traditional power groups, and have an enhanced evaluation of the "common good". The contrast between recent survey evidence on Irish attitudes towards democracy (which appears to show the Irish to be typical of advanced industrial societies) and earlier remarks of observers (referring to the survival of certain traditional, pre-democratic values), as discussed in the last section (pp. 35-9), are compatible with the view that in this respect Irish political cultural values are, indeed, changing slowly. The greater willingness of people to mobilise behind "cause" groups, such as environmentalist ones, and their insistence that their voices be heeded, is further evidence of this. Furthermore, active participation by women—for long relegated to a subordinate role in the political process—at all levels of political life has also increasingly been seen as valid.

In terms of attitudes towards *public policy outcomes* there are also signs of change. It is true that the upsurge in support for the Labour Party in 1992 is insufficient evidence of a decline in conservatism, and the fact that policy makers are now contemplating a more activist, peace-enforcement role for Irish troops abroad (as opposed to their traditional peace-keeping role) is only limited evidence of a less isolationist position on foreign policy. However, the phenomenon of Irish clericalism appears to be seriously under threat. Signs of this are to be seen in the large numbers of people who, at least in public opinion polls, hold positions of which the church has traditionally been critical, notably in the areas of divorce, abortion and availability of contraceptives. Although the 1983 and 1986 referendums on abortion and divorce respectively resulted in conservative decisions, the very fact that these matters were subjected to a constitutional poll and the size of the minority vote were themselves indicators of change. The liberalisation in 1993 of the laws relating to the sale of contraceptives and to homosexual practices would have been inconceivable in 1973, or, perhaps, even in 1983. The authority of the Catholic bishops in speaking on matters of public morality was undermined by a pattern of social change linked with a climate of public opinion in which the press felt free to reveal that a prominent bishop had fathered a child in the course of an affair with an American divorcee.

A FRAGMENTED POLITICAL CULTURE?

The discussion up to now has focused on the "typical" Irish person's political cultural values. Society, of course, is made up of individuals holding a great range of values; while the opinion poll data discussed so far in this chapter have drawn attention to areas where certain values are dominant or where the Irish adopt distinctive positions, we need to turn now to look at those who do not subscribe to these values and examine the extent of *fragmentation* in Irish society and in its political culture.

Social cleavages
Clearly, economic and social development did not proceed at a uniform pace in Ireland or in any other society; some groups always lagged behind others, and the process itself created some divisions while perhaps rendering others irrelevant. In the Irish case, this process, at least in its later stages, appears to have been associated with elements of a rural-urban and agrarian-industrial clash. It has also promoted divisions within each of these sectors, though many of these remain latent. On the agrarian side, although agricultural labourers, small subsistence farmers and large, commercially oriented farmers have conflicting interests, these are now rarely articulated. On the industrial side, an urban proletariat developed

slowly, but levels of politicised class conflict remained low by European standards (though the level of industrial disputes was high).

In the religious domain, the most obvious historical division was that between Catholics and Protestants, and this survives, even though the Protestant minority is now of negligible size. Within the Catholic community recent decades have seen the growth of secular values; although there is nothing corresponding to the secular subcultures of continental Catholic Europe, tensions between traditional Catholics and those with more liberal beliefs are likely to grow.

Contrasting perceptions of the past were also strongly held by different groups, with unionist, moderate nationalist and republican versions of history coexisting. Similarly, the degree of exposure to British, European and other influences tends to vary with region, class, occupation and level of education. We might expect these features, like the ones discussed in the last two paragraphs, to promote conflicting currents within Irish political culture; to what extent is there evidence for this?

Political cultural cleavages

The most fundamental political cultural cleavage faced by the new state related to the question of *national identity*. In the early years, a strong "republican" subculture struggled against the dominant values of the ruling group but, as we have seen, these two sets of values were largely accommodated to each other by 1948 at the latest. In any case, as the example of Northern Ireland shows, the cleavage between constitutional nationalism and Irish republicanism pales into insignificance beside the Catholic-Protestant cleavage over national identity. The history of Northern Ireland provides a good example of the force of this cleavage; why has conflict of this kind been so strikingly absent in the south?

A number of contrasts between the northern and southern minorities help to explain this divergence between the two parts of Ireland. In demographic terms, the southern Protestant minority is much smaller and is shrinking rather than increasing as a proportion of the total population. In the socio-economic domain, this minority has traditionally been associated with a position of relative advantage, and has occupied more prestigious positions in a type of cultural division of labour. Politically, it was associated with a programme (maintenance of the union with Great Britain) that was quickly seen to be entirely unrealistic after 1922. Most significantly of all, however, it appears to have been ethnically assimilated to the dominant group. Whereas at the beginning of the twentieth century southern Protestants were a national minority with their own ethnic symbols, myth of history and political programme, today they are essentially a denominational minority, distinguished from the majority mainly in terms of religious practice and belief. In all of these respects, the position of the Catholic minority in Northern Ireland has been the reverse of this.

On the matter of *democratic values*, there appears to be a considerable degree of consensus, and challenges from groups adhering to sources of authority other than "the people's will" have been few and weak. Nationalist authoritarianism—the belief that "the nation" has a collective destiny which must be protected by an elite, if necessary against the wishes of a majority—largely disappeared in the south after the 1930s. Religious authoritarianism—the belief that no electoral or political majority has a right to contravene the "natural law", as defined, in an Irish context, by the Catholic church—may, however, come to the fore as Catholic values are subjected to increasing challenge. Ironically, though, up to the early

1990s Catholic activists have relied on public opinion and referendum results to defend their position, whereas their more "progressive" rivals have sought to by-pass these and to use the courts and parliament to bring about change. The ease with which the will of the majority may be translated into the dictatorship of the majority has not yet become the subject of public debate.

In terms of attitudes towards *public policy*, there are predictable divisions within Irish society. First, there is clearly a division between left and right, one side supporting interventionist economic policies, the other advocating privatisation and the free market. While the boundary between the two sides is not very precise, and does not correspond entirely with social class or with party political divisions, the two tendencies are nonetheless real. Second, there is an emerging division between secular and clerical forces, ranging Protestants and liberal Catholics against those disposed to accept church teaching more fully. Third, there are elements of a division between cosmopolitan and isolationist views, the former arguing for a redefinition of Ireland's relationship with Europe and a reassessment of its policy of military neutrality, the latter defending the traditional position in these respects.

CONCLUSION

While political culture is an elusive concept and our instruments for measuring it are poor, the survey evidence reported in this chapter is sufficiently compatible with the perceptions of observers to allow us to make some generalisations about the nature of Irish political culture. First, there appears to be a consensus among the population in terms of core values relating to national identity: there is virtually universal agreement on one of the cardinal principles of Irish *nationalism* (the need for a separate Irish state), and the legitimacy of the Republic of Ireland is therefore now virtually unchallengeable. Second, commitment to *democratic values* appears to be solidly rooted within people's inner values. The challenge from *authoritarianism* is weak—nationalist authoritarianism has receded in recent decades, and religious authoritarianism has yet to be articulated in such a way that it constitutes a serious challenge to democratic principles. Third, in terms of people's outer layer of values relating to principles of public policy, we can detect elements both of stability and of conflict. On socio-economic issues, *conservatism* appears to be dominant, even if the manner in which it is articulated has changed. On foreign policy issues, there may well be an emerging tension between positions that may be labelled *isolationism* and *cosmopolitanism*. Most obviously of all, however, on social and moral issues there is an emerging basis for conflict between *clericalism* and *secularism*.

Political culture in Ireland, then, resembles that in other west European states rather closely, despite a significant lag in socio-economic development in this country. While the legacy of history and preoccupation with British dominance may have been a particular influence in the past, it is probably the pattern of underlying religious values in a slowly secularising society that will be responsible for the most distinctive elements in Irish political culture in the future.

REFERENCES AND FURTHER READING

Almond, Gabriel A, G. Bingham Powell and Robert J. Mundt, 1993. *Comparative Politics: a Theoretical Approach.* New York: HarperCollins College Publishers.

Almond, Gabriel A. and Sidney Verba, 1989a. *The Civic Culture: Political Attitudes and Democracy in Five Nations,* new ed. London: Sage.

Almond, Gabriel A. and Sidney Verba (eds), 1989b. *The Civic Culture Revisited,* new ed. London: Sage.

Ashford, Sheena and Noel Timms, 1992. *What Europe Thinks: a Study of West European Values.* Aldershot: Dartmouth.

Banfield, Edward, 1967. *The Moral Basis of a Backward Society,* new ed. London: Collier-Macmillan.

Breen, Richard, Damien F. Hannan, David B. Rottman and Christopher T. Whelan, 1990. *Understanding Contemporary Ireland: State, Class and Development in the Republic of Ireland.* Dublin: Gill and Macmillan.

Chubb, Basil, 1970. *The Government and Politics of Ireland.* Stanford: Stanford University Press.

Chubb, Basil, 1992. *The Government and Politics of Ireland,* 3rd ed. London: Longman.

Clancy, Patrick, Sheelagh Drudy, Kathleen Lynch and Liam O'Dowd (eds), 1986. *Ireland: A Sociological Profile.* Dublin: Institute of Public Administration.

Collins, Neil, 1987. *Local Government Managers at Work: the City and County Management System of Local Government in the Republic of Ireland.* Dublin: Institute of Public Administration.

Davis, E. E. and Richard Sinnott, 1979. *Attitudes in the Republic of Ireland Relevant to the Northern Ireland Problem.* Dublin: Economic and Social Research Institute.

Farrell, Brian, 1971. *The Founding of Dáil Éireann: Parliament and Nation-Building.* Dublin: Gill and Macmillan.

Fogarty, Michael, Liam Ryan and Joseph Lee, 1984. *Irish Values and Attitudes: the Irish Report of the European Value Systems Study.* Dublin: Dominican Publications.

Gallagher, Michael, 1982. *The Irish Labour Party in Transition, 1957-82.* Dublin: Gill and Macmillan, and Manchester: Manchester University Press.

Girvin, Brian, 1986. "Nationalism, democracy, and Irish political culture", pp. 3-28 in Brian Girvin and Roland Sturm (eds), *Politics and Society in Contemporary Ireland.* Aldershot: Gower.

Girvin, Brian, 1989. "Change and continuity in liberal democratic political culture", pp. 31-51 in John Gibbins (ed.), *Contemporary Political Culture: Politics in a Postmodern Age.* London: Sage.

Hart, Ian, 1970. "Public opinion on civil servants and the role and power of the individual in the local community", *Administration* 18:4, pp. 375-91.

Inglehart, Ronald, 1990. *Culture Shift in Advanced Industrial Society.* Princeton, NJ: Princeton University Press.

Inglis, Tom, 1987. *Moral Monopoly: the Catholic Church in Modern Irish Society.* Dublin: Gill and Macmillan.

Mac Gréil, Mícheál, 1977. *Prejudice and Tolerance in Ireland.* Dublin: Research Section, College of Industrial Relations.

Mac Gréil, Mícheál, 1992. *Irish Political Attitudes and Opinions.* Maynooth: Survey and Research Unit, St Patrick's College.

Ó Brádaigh, Ruairí, 1976. "Introduction", in *Aisling 1916-1976.* Dublin: Sinn Féin.

Prager, Jeffrey, 1986. *Building Democracy in Ireland: Political Order and Cultural Integration in a Newly Independent Nation.* Cambridge: Cambridge University Press.

Raven, John and C. T. Whelan; Paul A. Pfretzschner and Donald M. Borock, 1976. *Political Culture in Ireland: the Views of Two Generations.* Dublin: Institute of Public Administration.

Schmitt, David E., 1973. *The Irony of Irish Democracy: the Impact of Political Culture on Administrative and Democratic Political Development in Ireland.* Lexington: Lexington Books.

Smith, Donald Eugene, 1970. *Religion and Political Development: an Analytic Study.* Boston, MA: Little, Brown.

Weber, Eugen, 1977. *Peasants into Frenchmen: the Modernization of Rural France 1870-1914.* London: Chatto and Windus.

Whyte, J. H., 1980. *Church and State in Modern Ireland 1923-1979,* 2nd ed. Dublin: Gill and Macmillan.

Wilson Hartnell, 1992. *The Irish Market: Facts and Figures,* 8th ed. Dublin: Wilson Hartnell Advertising.

3 / THE CONSTITUTION

Michael Gallagher

Constitutions are important documents in liberal democracies. They lay down the ground rules about how political power is attained and how it can be exercised, about what governments can do and what they cannot do. We cannot expect to get a full picture of the way in which a country's politics operate just by studying its constitution, because constitutions often take little or no cognisance of central features of modern politics such as large and disciplined political parties. They tend, rather, to define the perimeter of the area within which politics must operate, without specifying exactly what must take place within the permitted area. In addition, they often specify certain values, held to be central to the country's political culture, and deem it the duty of the state to aim to promote or defend them.

THE BACKGROUND: THE IRISH FREE STATE CONSTITUTION

Ireland's current constitution (Bunreacht na hÉireann) dates from 1937, but despite its significant innovations it marked a development of previous constitutional experience rather than a decisive break with it. Its precursor, the 1922 Irish Free State constitution, was drawn up under the terms of the Anglo-Irish Treaty, and so the British government insisted on modifications to the version agreed by the Provisional Government so as to ensure that it contained nothing that conflicted with the Treaty. As a result, the final document was rather different from what the Irish government would have wanted (for an overview, see Farrell, 1988b). This British pressure manifested itself particularly in those articles that provided for a Governor-General, representing the Crown, and for the terms of an oath that all members of the Oireachtas (parliament) had to take, swearing to "be faithful to HM King George V, his heirs and successors". The Free State was declared to be a member of the British Commonwealth, and the constitution provided for an upper house that was designed to give strong representation to Protestants. Moreover, the introductory section of the Act establishing the constitution stated that if any provision of the constitution was, even after the British government's legal officers had scrutinised the document with a fine toothcomb, in conflict with the Anglo-Irish Treaty, that provision was "absolutely void and inoperative".

Apart from these articles representing the result of arm-twisting by the British, the broad outlines of the governmental system also showed a strong British influence, as the constitution provided for government by a cabinet (the Executive Council), chaired by a prime minister (the President of the Executive Council). There were none of the rhetorical flourishes to be found in the 1937 constitution, and, unlike that document, the Irish Free State constitution was explicitly neutral as between religious denominations and, despite pressure from some quarters to make it so, could not have been described as a "Catholic constitution".

But although in some ways the constitution marked an attempt to codify some central aspects of the Westminster model of government, it by no means represented a slavish acceptance of British practice. The very decision to have a written constitution made this clear. In addition, mainly due to a desire to avoid an over-centralisation of power in the cabinet, the constitution contained some features designed to make the parliament more accountable to the people and the government more accountable to the parliament than was the case in the United Kingdom.

One of these was a proportional representation (PR) electoral system. There was also provision for referendums on both laws and constitutional amendments, for the legislative initiative (under which, if enough voters signed a petition calling for a particular change in the law, the Oireachtas would have either to make the change or to submit the issue to a referendum), and for judicial review of the constitution. In addition, the constitution allowed for the appointment of ministers who were not required to be members of the Dáil, an option that, had it been availed of, would have brought Ireland into line with the mainstream in western Europe, where ministers are not usually obliged to be parliamentarians. These "extern ministers", as they were termed, would be appointed by the Dáil and answerable directly to it. However, apart from PR, most of these devices proved to be of little significance. No extern ministers were appointed after 1927, and even those who were appointed before then were all TDs. In 1928, the government used its parliamentary majority to abolish both the legislative referendum and the initiative, after Fianna Fáil took the first steps towards forcing a referendum on the oath of allegiance. It was characteristic of the Cumann na nGaedheal government's decidedly non-populist style that it abolished articles that might have enjoyed some support in the electorate while doggedly defending the most unpopular ones, such as those relating to the oath and the Governor-General.

The provision for judicial review did not prove much of a check on the government. For one thing, the Oireachtas itself could amend the constitution at will. The original version allowed it to do this (provided that any amendment came within the terms of the Treaty) for a period of eight years after 1922, after which amendment would require a referendum. But since this article itself could be amended, a simple extension of the period from eight to 16 years in 1929 ensured that the document was under the control of the Oireachtas throughout its unhappy life. Moreover, although constitutions are usually more powerful than ordinary legislation, so that if the two conflict it is the constitution that prevails, the Irish Free State constitution was a weak document. Laws that contradicted the constitution, far from being thereby invalid, could simply declare themselves to have amended the constitution to the extent necessary to render them constitutional (Casey, 1992, p. 13; Kelly, 1984, pp. 717-19; Macmillan, 1993, p. 196).

When Fianna Fáil came to power in 1932, it moved rapidly to remove those parts of the constitution that offended it most. In 1932 it abolished the oath, and in 1936 the Seanad and the office of Governor-General went the same way (Sexton, 1989, pp. 165-6). By this time, it might have been imagined that the resulting document was to Fianna Fáil's liking. Instead, it satisfied no-one.

Fianna Fáil had always viewed it with distaste, while even those who had clung so faithfully to it during the 1920s could not have felt much affection for it by 1937. Apart from the substance of the changes made by Fianna Fáil, the very fact that the document had been amended so many times (41 of the 83 articles had been changed) gave it a moth-eaten look. In any case, for Fianna Fáil the Irish Free State constitution was inherently illegitimate no matter how it read. Eamon de Valera in particular felt the need for the state to have an entirely new constitution, and to this end he began drafting one in 1935 (Fanning, 1988; Keogh, 1988a). The resulting document was debated and finally passed by the Dáil in June 1937 (the vote on the final stage was 62 to 48). Although legally and constitutionally this new constitution could have been enacted by the Oireachtas as one long amendment to the existing constitution, this would have defeated the whole point of the exercise—it was vital symbolically to seem to make a new beginning, and to have the Irish people confer the new constitution on themselves. Accordingly, it was put to the people in a referendum (termed a plebiscite) on 1 July 1937, the same day as a general election. It was passed by 57 per cent to 43 per cent and came into effect on 29 December 1937 (see Appendix 2h on results of referendums).

THE MAIN FEATURES OF THE CONSTITUTION

The promulgation of a new constitution was not purely symbolic, for despite the high degree of continuity, the 1937 constitution was in some respects significantly different from its predecessor in terms of both its scope and its substance. We shall now examine some of its main features, without going in any depth into areas that are covered in other chapters of this book.

Nation and state

Articles 1 to 3 relate to "The Nation" and Articles 4 to 11 to "The State". These articles emphasise the importance attached to the constitution's role as a statement of the independence of the Irish state. Articles 1 and 5 both contain affirmations of sovereignty, and Article 6 says that all powers of government derive from the Irish people, emphasising that the institutions of the state should not be seen as having been in any way bestowed on the people by the British in 1922. Among this group of articles, Articles 2 and 3 have caused most controversy. Article 2 defines "the national territory" as "the whole island of Ireland, its islands and the territorial seas". Article 3 declares that, notwithstanding this, the laws enacted by the state shall, "pending the re-integration of the national territory", apply only to the 26 counties, but by referring to the "right" of the state's parliament and government to exercise jurisdiction over the whole of the national territory it affirms a clear claim to Northern Ireland. These articles were once seen as purely aspirational, but in delivering a judgment in March 1990 (in the McGimpsey case) the Supreme Court declared that Article 2 was "a declaration of the extent of the national territory as a claim of legal right".

The state was described as sovereign, independent and democratic. It also had a President, and yet it was not explicitly described as a republic. The reasons for this coyness seem to have been partly a naive belief on de Valera's part that Ulster unionists would be more willing to join an all-Ireland state if it did not declare itself a republic, and partly a reluctance to issue a challenge to the British government that might lead to unwanted consequences (Fanning, 1983, pp. 118-19). The name of the state remains an enigma to many. Article 4 reads "The name of the State is Éire, or in the English language, *Ireland*". The 1948 Republic of Ireland Act refrained from giving a name to the state, so as not to violate this article; instead, its formulation is that "the description of the State shall be the Republic of Ireland". In different contexts, the state is now known as "Éire", "Ireland" and "the Republic of Ireland", a confusion that the constitution does not entirely resolve.

Political institutions

Articles 12 to 33 deal with political institutions. As far as the operation of government was concerned, there was little major change from the Irish Free State constitution. There was to be an Oireachtas, consisting of a President and two houses. The lower house, Dáil Éireann, was to be directly elected by proportional representation, using the single transferable vote (see chapter 4) as before. The re-emergence of the upper house, the Seanad, which de Valera had abolished only a year earlier, was surprising; given the nominally vocational basis of the Seanad (see pp. 143-4 below), this may have been an adroit move to make a token concession to the transient clamour for the introduction of a vocationalist system of government (Lee, 1989, p. 272). The prime minister was now termed the Taoiseach (see glossary), and his or her dominance within the government was strengthened in a number of ways—for example, the power to call a general election belonged now to the Taoiseach alone rather than to the government as a whole as before (see chapter 9). It is clear, though, that the constitution was merely codifying what had become existing practice rather than enforcing a change in that practice.

The office of the presidency (Articles 12 to 14), however, did mark a major innovation. The President is to be directly elected for a seven-year term in a nationwide vote, but the nomination procedure is such that the major parties can, if they collude, prevent a contest. An outgoing or former President can nominate himself or herself for a second term, but any other aspirant needs to be proposed either by 20 members of the Houses of the Oireachtas (TDs or senators) or by the councils of four counties or county boroughs. Given that the local authorities are composed on party lines, it is clear that anyone without party backing faces an uphill struggle to get onto the ballot paper. Since the office was instituted, in fact, it has fallen vacant on 10 occasions, but there have been only five contests. On the other five occasions (in 1938, 1952, 1974, 1976 and 1983), only one candidate was nominated. Moreover, even the five contested elections (in 1945, 1959, 1966, 1973 and 1990) have been fought by a total of only 12 candidates between them (see appendix 2g for a list of presidential elections).

The President is not expected to play an active part in the day-to-day affairs of government, but is given six discretionary powers for use in specific situations. Of these, three give him or her an adjudicatory role in disputes, of a sort that have never arisen to date, between Dáil and Seanad. A fourth (Article 13.2.3) gives the President the power to convene a meeting of either or both of the Houses of the Oireachtas. Fifth (Article 26), the President, when presented with a bill passed by the Houses of the Oireachtas, can, instead of taking the usual course of signing it into law, instead refer it to the Supreme Court for a judgment on its compatibility with the constitution. Before exercising any of these five powers, the President must listen to (but is not bound by) the advice of the Council of State, which contains a number of past and present senior political figures together with up to seven people whom she or he has personally appointed. The sixth power, which relates to the dissolution of the Dáil, requires no consultation. Under normal circumstances, when a Taoiseach requests the President to dissolve the Dáil and thereby bring about a general election, the President is bound to accede to the request. However, the President, in the words of Article 13.2.2, "may in his absolute discretion refuse to dissolve Dáil Éireann on the advice of a Taoiseach who has ceased to retain the support of a majority in Dáil Éireann". A Taoiseach whose administration has lost a vote on a confidence motion is clearly covered by this article, but there is room for uncertainty as to whether there are any other circumstances in which a President could turn down a Taoiseach's request for a dissolution—for example, what about a Taoiseach whose Dáil base has patently disappeared but who has not actually been beaten there in a formal vote (for discussion, see Casey, 1992, pp. 72-4; Gallagher, 1988, pp. 83-7; Hogan, 1989, pp. 165-8; Kelly, 1984, p. 62)? Perhaps more to the point, no President has ever exercised this power, and some think that it would be politically unwise, even if it were constitutionally acceptable, for any future President to do so.

In fact, of the six presidential powers, only the fifth has so far been employed. On eight occasions since 1937, a President has referred a bill to the Supreme Court for a decision on its constitutionality. The exercise of this power can be controversial. In 1976, when President Ó Dálaigh quite reasonably referred the Emergency Powers Bill to the Supreme Court, his action led to open criticism from the Minister for Defence, Paddy Donegan, who reportedly called Ó Dálaigh a "thundering disgrace". This set in motion a sequence of events that led to the resignation of Ó Dálaigh, who took the view that the apology he received from Donegan was inadequate and felt that the minister should have been dismissed from the government.

More seriously, the Supreme Court itself made clear its unhappiness when in 1983 President Hillery referred to it a bill dealing with rent control. The problem with this presidential power lies in the fact that Article 34.3.3 gives a dreadful finality to a positive verdict of the Supreme Court in such cases; it states that the validity of a bill (or any part thereof) that is cleared by the Supreme Court after referral by the President may never again be questioned by any court. Even if the views of Supreme Court judges change over time, as of course they do, or if operation of the Act reveals aspects that no-one had detected when the bill was argued about in abstract form, the Act is immune from all further challenge. This particular presidential power, then, seems best confined to bills raising, as Casey (1992, p. 270) puts it, "a pure question of constitutional interpretation".

In many ways the role of the presidency has resembled that of a particularly powerless constitutional monarch. Most Presidents up to 1990 were elderly men when they entered office: Douglas Hyde was 78, Eamon de Valera 76, Erskine Childers 67, Seán T. O'Kelly 63 and Cearbhall Ó Dálaigh 62, with Patrick Hillery a relatively youthful 53 (see Appendix 4 for further details of Presidents). All of them except Hyde, moreover, were current or former Fianna Fáil members. The position was not an active political role in its own right but one to which politicians might retire. The election of Mary Robinson in 1990 raised expectations of an expansion of the role of the office. At 46, Robinson was the youngest person and the first woman to become President, and her victory over Brian Lenihan was the first time that a Fianna Fáil presidential candidate had been beaten (Gallagher and Marsh, 1993). During her campaign she had occasionally spoken of confronting the government if elected, but once elected she made it clear that she accepted the limitations of the office and that she would not intervene in matters that were the prerogative of the government. Even so, she was determined to be more active than her predecessors: she made many visits to various parts of the country, convened and addressed a meeting of the Oireachtas in July 1992, and paid a controversial visit to west Belfast (during the course of which she shook hands with Sinn Féin president Gerry Adams) in June 1993 even though the government had expressed to her its "concern" about the visit.

The rights of citizens
The articles of the 1937 constitution that deal with citizens' rights (40-45) differed significantly from those of its predecessor. Like the earlier document, the new constitution guaranteed the usual liberal democratic rights—habeas corpus, free association, free speech, inviolability of dwellings, and so on—though (as is the case in most constitutions, and in the European Convention of Human Rights) almost invariably the ringing enunciation of a right is followed by a qualifying clause or paragraph asserting the power of the legislature to curtail it if, for example, "public order" or "morality" justifies that. The main difference was that the rights articles were now strongly influenced by Catholic social thought (Whyte, 1980, pp. 51-6; Keogh, 1988b). In some cases, admittedly, there is nothing visibly Catholic about the phraseology to the uninformed eye—only those familiar with Catholic social thought of the period would be able to identify the genesis of the expressions used. In other cases, though, the Catholic flavour is obvious, such as the prohibition, in Article 41.3.2, of the legalisation of divorce. In addition, two clauses of Article 44 gave Roman Catholicism a unique status. Article 44.1.2 read "The State recognises the special position of the Holy Catholic Apostolic and Roman Church as the guardian of the Faith professed by the great majority of the citizens", while, in Article 44.1.3, the State merely "recognised" a list of other and presumably less significant religions.

At the end of the century, the impact of Catholic thought on the constitution has led to its sometimes being branded a narrowly confessional document. However, in the context of its time it could even be seen as liberal. The final formulation of Article 44 met with the approval of all the non-Catholic religions, while many in the Catholic church were clearly disappointed, since they had hoped that theirs would be recognised as "the one true church" and were reluctant even to accept that the word "church" could validly be claimed by other religions (Keogh, 1988b, pp. 111-17). The first large scale protests against the religious articles came, 12 years later, not from non-Catholics but from the ultra-Catholic Maria Duce group, which wanted Article 44 amended to recognise the Catholic church as the one true church (Whyte, 1980, pp. 163-5). Whyte also points out (p. 50) that since 1922 the law had fallen steadily more into line with Catholic teaching, and the 1937 constitution was merely the "coping-stone" of a trend. De Valera, far from imposing a sectarian constitution on a pluralistic society, was steering a middle course between non-Catholics on the one hand and triumphalist Catholics on the other, and he displeased the latter more than the former.

Moreover, as Lee (1989, p. 203) observes, the explicit recognition given to the Jewish congregations was "a gesture not without dignity in the Europe of 1937".

DEVELOPMENT OF THE CONSTITUTION

Since 1937 the constitution has been developed in three ways. First, the Oireachtas made a number of amendments; second, the people effected some amendments by referendum; third, it has been developed by judicial interpretation.

Amendment by parliament

The constitution contained, in Articles 51-63, transitory provisions to cover an interim period. These articles are no longer included in official texts of the constitution (they can be found in Kelly, 1984, pp. 716-30) but continue to have the force of law. Article 51 permitted the Oireachtas to amend the constitution for a period of three years after the first President entered office, which meant up to 25 June 1941. Any subsequent amendment would require the consent of the people. The loophole left in the Irish Free State constitution was addressed: Article 51 prevented the three-year transition period from being extended by the Oireachtas.

Two packages of amendments were made in this way. The first, made in September 1939, altered only one article (28.3.3, the "emergency" article), while the second, in May 1941, amended 16 different articles simultaneously. Some of the changes made in 1941 were minor "housekeeping" changes, merely ironing out defects that had been detected in the articles affected. Other changes were more significant, especially those relating to Articles 26 and 34, which we discuss on pp. 63-4 below, and to Article 28.3.3, which now looked quite different from the version approved by the people in 1937. In its original form, this article had stated that nothing in the constitution could be invoked to invalidate legislation designed to secure public safety and the preservation of the state in time of war or armed rebellion. The two amendments widened the scope of the article in circumstances where each House of the Oireachtas passes a resolution declaring that a national emergency exists affecting the vital interests of the state. After amendment, the article now says that "time of war or armed rebellion" can include a time when an armed conflict is taking place that affects the vital interests of the state, even if the state is not directly involved, and a time after the war or armed rebellion has ceased but during which the Oireachtas takes the view that the emergency created by the conflict still exists. The Oireachtas declared a state of emergency after the outbreak of the second world war in 1939, and this emergency remained in existence up to 1976, being lifted only by a resolution that simultaneously declared a fresh emergency arising "out of the armed conflict now taking place in Northern Ireland", an emergency that remains in force.

While it could plausibly be argued that the state's vital interests were indeed affected by the second world war, in a way that persisted for some time after that war formally ended, it is easy to see that this article could potentially set at nothing all the rights guaranteed elsewhere in the constitution. At least at first sight, it appears that in order to pass any legislation it chooses, a government that has effective majority support in the Oireachtas, as most governments have, need only have the Oireachtas pass a resolution declaring that an emergency exists and then secure the passage of the legislation by declaring it to have the purpose of securing the public safety and preserving the state. In this way, it seems, legislation that, for example, proscribed opposition parties, outlawed elections or prescribed euthanasia rather than a pension for those reaching the age of 65 would be immune from scrutiny by the courts.

However, a significant judgment of the Supreme Court in 1976, when it pronounced the Emergency Powers Bill constitutional, tempered the potential effect of Article 28.3.3. While not disputing the right of the Oireachtas to enact any legislation it saw fit in order to preserve public safety and the state once an emergency had been declared, the court said that it "expressly reserves for future consideration" the question of whether it had the right to consider whether the Oireachtas was justified in declaring that a national emergency existed. No case has arisen subsequently to test the extent to which the courts' thinking on this issue has developed, but the warning shot sounded in 1976 may have counterbalanced to some extent the action of the Oireachtas in 1939 and 1941 in widening the scope of Article 28.3.3.

Amendment by the people

Most constitutions are more rigid—that is, less easily amended—than ordinary legislation. In most countries, altering the constitution entails either the consent of more than just a bare majority in parliament (a figure of two-thirds or higher may be stipulated), or the direct approval of the people. Ireland is among those countries requiring the consent of the people: Article 46 lays down that a proposal to amend the constitution must be passed by the Oireachtas and then be put to a referendum. Up to September 1993, 16 proposed amendments had been put to the people, of which 11 had been approved (see table in appendix 2h). Of the 16, six related to voting, six to moral or religious issues and three to the European Community (EC), while the sixteenth (an amendment to Article 37 to place the legality of adoptions above question) was a minor and technical matter.

Of the six proposals concerning voting, two were unsuccessful attempts by Fianna Fáil to replace the PR-STV electoral system by the single-member constituency system (these referendums are described at pp. 76-7 below). On the second occasion, in 1968, this proposal was coupled with one that was designed to permit rural voters to be over-represented at the expense of urban voters. The other three referendums caused little controversy between the parties. In 1972, there was all-party backing for lowering the voting age, and in 1979 an amendment to allow the university seats in Seanad Éireann to be reorganised got strong support among those sufficiently motivated to vote on the issue. In 1984 a proposal to permit the Oireachtas to extend the vote to non-citizens received general endorsement.

Of the six referendums on moral or religious issues, the first proposal was passed comfortably, with the backing of all the parties and the opposition only of conservative Catholic groups (Cardinal Conway, the Catholic primate, had already given his blessing to the amendment). It removed from Article 44.1 the two subsections, already referred to, that recognised the "special position" of the Catholic church and the mere existence of a number of other churches. It was ironic, and an indication of the change in attitudes, that the article amended was the very one that all the churches had approved in 1937 (Keogh, 1988b, p. 118). The two referendums of the 1980s were much more heated affairs, with deep divisions apparent within as well as between the parties. The first, in 1983, inserted what its proponents termed a "pro-life" amendment, to the effect that the state "acknowledges the right to life of the unborn" and undertakes "by its laws to defend and vindicate that right" (Article 40.3.3). The second, in 1986, would have made it possible for the Oireachtas to legalise divorce in restricted circumstances (Girvin, 1987). Voting on the two occasions was very similar (the statistical correlation between the vote for the 1983 "pro-life" amendment by constituency and the 1986 anti-divorce vote was 0.97), indicating that both proposals brought the liberal-conservative cleavage in Irish society to the fore, as discussed in chapter 2. The other three "moral" referendums were held in November 1992 in response to the Supreme Court decision in the "X" case (see p. 59 below). Amendments stating that Article 40.3.3 does not limit either freedom to travel outside the state or freedom to obtain information about services lawfully available in another state were passed with the support of both "liberal" and "centrist" voters and of all the political parties (Kennelly and Ward, 1993). A third proposal, which would have permitted abortions only in cases where a continued pregnancy would have meant a risk to "the life, as distinct from the health, of the mother" (except where the risk to life arose from the possibility of suicide), was defeated, as both liberal and conservative voters opposed it, along with all the political parties except Fianna Fáil.

EC membership, and the progressively greater degree of integration entailed by developments within the Community, has been responsible for three referendums (which are discussed further in chapter 12 below). Joining the EC in the first place required a referendum because the obligations of membership would otherwise have been in conflict with the constitution. As well as the symbolic declaration of sovereignty, the constitution gives the Oireachtas a legislative monopoly, declaring that "no other legislative authority has power to make laws for the State" (Article 15.2.1); it makes a similar assertion in the judicial area, stating that "the decision of the Supreme Court shall in all cases be final and conclusive" (Article 34.4.6). These articles are incompatible with belonging to the EC, since the Community's institutions have the power to make laws for the state and the EC's Court of Justice has the power in certain circumstances to overturn decisions of the Supreme Court. However, the decision was taken in 1972 not to amend every article over which EC membership might cast a shadow but instead to introduce a catchall amendment, by adding a new subsection (Article 29.4.3) allowing the state to join the EC and adding that "No provision of this constitution invalidates laws enacted, acts done or measures adopted by the State necessitated by the obligations of membership of the Communities or prevents laws enacted, acts done or measures adopted by the Communities, or institutions thereof, from having the force of law in the State". The 1987 amendment to allow the state to ratify the Single European Act (for which see McCutcheon, 1992) dealt only with that specific issue, but the 1992 referendum, which followed the Maastricht agreement of December 1991, was again broader (Holmes, 1993). It allowed the state to ratify the European Union treaty and a 1989 patents agreement, and also replaced the sentence in Article 29.4.3 quoted above, with its reference to the obligations of membership of the Communities, by a new subsection (29.4.5) that refers to the obligations of membership of the European Union or the Communities or bodies competent under the treaties establishing the Communities.

The referendum requirement in Article 46 has been a powerful check on governments wanting to make changes that do not have broad support across the political spectrum. On only one occasion (the plebiscite to approve the constitution in 1937) have the people approved a proposal not backed by the major opposition party—and even then the third party, Labour, adopted a neutral position. Since 1937, when governments have put forward proposals not supported by the main opposition party—Fianna Fáil's attempts to change the electoral system in 1959 and 1968 and to restrict the circumstances under which abortion could be legal in 1992, and the Fine Gael-Labour coalition's proposed legalisation of divorce in 1986—the people have rejected them.

Judicial interpretation
Given that a constitution lays down rules about what government and parliament can and cannot do, someone clearly has to keep an eye on them to make sure that they are obeying the rules. In some European countries, such as France, Germany and Italy, there is a special constitutional court, but in Ireland this function is assigned by the constitution to the regular courts. If the constitutionality of a law passed by the Oireachtas is challenged, it is the responsibility of the High Court or, if an appeal is made against its decision, of the Supreme Court to decide whether the law is valid or whether it must be struck down. In addition, any other act of the government (such as the signing of an agreement with another government) may be challenged in the courts as a violation of the constitution. In order to take a constitutional case, citizens must show that they have *locus standi*—that is, that they are in some way affected by the action or statute they are complaining about and are not merely busybodies.

The judges cannot alter the text of the constitution, but they decide what the text means. This power to interpret the constitution is considerable, since judges can, if they are so minded, "discover" meanings that were never envisaged or intended by anyone initially. In the United States of America, where judicial interpretation has reached a unique pitch, the judges of the Supreme Court must be counted among the policy makers; a Chief Justice once bluntly declared that "the constitution is what the judges say it is". In Ireland, judicial review has proved to be the main method by which the constitution has been developed.

Until the mid-1960s, the courts tended to interpret the constitution in a "positivist" or literal manner, sticking closely to the letter of the document and taking the view that there was no more to it than the words it contained. The position then began to change, reflecting a "general rise in the level of judicial activism observed in the western democracies since the 1960s" (Holland, 1991, p. 10). In Ireland, this development was due partly to the accession of a new generation of judges and partly to the general changes taking place in society and political culture at that time, and a more "creative" approach was adopted (see Casey, 1992, pp. 300-49; Chubb, 1991, pp. 60-78; Hogan, 1988; Kelly, 1984, pp. 473-90; Tóibín, 1985). Judges began to speak of the general tenor or spirit of the constitution and of the rights that those living under such a constitution must by definition, in their view, enjoy. The key article in this process turned out to be Article 40.3.1: "The State guarantees in its laws to respect, and, as far as practicable, by its laws to defend and vindicate the personal rights of the citizen." Although this may appear to be merely a pious declaration without any substance (as may, indeed, have been the intention), it has proved to be of great significance. Until the 1960s, it was assumed that the "rights" referred to in Article 40.3.1 were those listed in Articles 40-44, but a landmark judgment in 1963 changed that. The plaintiff in the case of Ryan v Attorney General argued that the fluoridation of water violated her right to bodily integrity, a right not mentioned anywhere in the constitution. In his judgment, Mr Justice Kenny accepted her contention that she—and by extension every other citizen—did indeed have such a right (unfortunately for her, he did not accept that putting fluoride in the water violated it), and said: "The personal rights which may be invoked to invalidate legislation are not confined to those specified in Article 40 but include all those rights which result from the Christian and democratic nature of the State".

In subsequent cases judges "discovered" many more "undisclosed human rights" lurking within the constitution—in recent years, indeed, the number of constitutional cases brought to the courts has increased greatly. One of the most dramatic judgments came in 1973, when the Supreme Court (in the case of McGee v Attorney General) accepted the plaintiff's claim that she had a right to marital privacy, and accordingly it struck down the 1935 legislation banning the importation of contraceptives. Given de Valera's strongly Catholic views, and since it was his government's legislation that was now being declared unconstitutional, we can say that from this moment the 1937 constitution visibly ceased to be "de Valera's constitution", a term sometimes applied to it. His creation now had a life of its own, and it was for the courts, not for any politician, to decide what its words meant. (It is generally believed, incidentally, that de Valera did not anticipate judicial review being anything like as significant or extensive as it has proved.)

Since 1973 the courts have made a number of decisions that have had major political implications (details of the main cases can be found in Doolan, 1988). They have defined and seemingly redefined the circumstances when the "political offence" argument can be used by a defendant to avoid extradition (most notably in the McGlinchey case in 1982, the Shannon case of 1984 and the Carron, Clarke and Finucane cases of 1990). In 1987, the Supreme Court, by its decision in the Crotty case, prevented the state from ratifying the Single European Act until the constitution was amended to permit this (see McCutcheon, 1992; Thompson, 1991). In March 1992, in the "X" case (which concerned a 14-year-old girl who had become pregnant, allegedly as a result of being raped), it interpreted the 1983 "pro-life" amendment as conferring a right to have an abortion on women whose lives would be threatened by continuing with a pregnancy. This interpretation shocked supporters of the 1983 amendment, which they had intended to have the effect of preventing either the legislature or the judiciary from legalising abortion in any circumstances, but was less surprising to opponents of the amendment, who had warned that the wording of the "pro-life" amendment could lead to precisely the outcome that occurred in 1992. In August 1992, it decided that the constitutional reference to collective cabinet responsibility (Article 28.4) entailed an absolute ban on all disclosure of discussions at cabinet meetings (Hogan, 1993).

Furthermore, in addition to high-profile judgments such as these, there have been many less spectacular but nonetheless significant judgments in which the courts, relying on their power to interpret the constitution, have effectively changed the law. To give one from many possible examples: in the McKinley v Ireland case of 1992, the plaintiff claimed that injuries (for which she held the defendants responsible) to her husband had deprived her of certain conjugal rights. Under common law, only a husband could claim compensation for the loss of these rights, but in July 1992 the Supreme Court decided that this did not prevent it from "developing" the rights in question so as to vest them in a wife as well. The cumulative effect of such judgments in invalidating old and unreformed statute and common law embodying anomalies or injustices should not be underestimated.

Clearly, provision for judicial review carries potential dangers in a democratic state, because it puts significant power into the hands of unelected individuals who are not accountable or answerable to anyone. (Under Article 35.4, judges can be dismissed by majority vote of the Dáil and Seanad for "stated misbehaviour or incapacity", but there has never been any move to dismiss a judge.) Mr Justice Kenny once said that "judges have become legislators, and have the advantage that they do not have to face an opposition" (Kelly, 1984, p. 475)—he might have added that neither do they have to face the people, as politicians do. This power raises the questions of who the judges are, how they came to be judges and what values they hold. In the United Kingdom, judges have been called part of "the secret state", as they are not elected, they enjoy substantial autonomy from control or scrutiny by elected representatives, and they are closed and secretive as to how they work. These points would also apply to Irish judges, who enjoy even more power than their British counterparts since Britain does not have a written constitution.

By law, Irish judges must be barristers of at least 12 years' standing. They are appointed by the government, with the Taoiseach usually having the decisive voice, so, not surprisingly, a record of sympathy with the government of the day is an important factor in appointment. The first detailed study of judges' backgrounds was made over 20 years ago by an American, Paul Bartholomew, who found that three-quarters of all Irish judges to hold office under the 1937 constitution had been active in party politics at some time. Fianna Fáil had been in power for 31 of the previous 37 years when he conducted his research, and in interviews 73 per cent of the judges said that they had been Fianna Fáil supporters when first appointed, with 50 per cent saying that they remained supporters of the party (Bartholomew, 1971, p. 48). None of the judges was of "humble social background"—about two-thirds were from upper middle class backgrounds, over a quarter were sons of lawyers, many had attended expensive private schools, and about two-thirds had been educated at University College Dublin. All the judges were men—indeed, even up to 1993 only one women has been appointed to the Supreme Court and only two have become High Court judges (see p. 213 below). A later study of judicial appointments confirmed that governments not only look for appointees of the right political background but have also taken into account the views of those under consideration. In the mid to late 1960s the government, and especially the Department of Justice, was disturbed at the flurry of creative decisions being made by the courts, and the Department "decided to ensure that no more liberal judges were appointed" (Tóibín, 1985, pp. 17-20). Across western Europe generally, "there is a tendency toward greater politicisation in the judicial appointment process" (Volcansek, 1992, p. 5).

What impact does this have on the judgments the courts deliver? In Britain, judges have been described as "a body of elderly upper-class men who have lived unadventurous lives ... [they] tend to be old-fashioned and conservative in their views and out of step with social, cultural and ethical change, for they have no first-hand knowledge of how the great majority of people live their lives" (Dearlove and Saunders, 1984, p. 136). Some studies have maintained that there is evidence of judicial sympathy for the political views of the Conservative Party, especially in cases involving trade unions or race relations. There have been no comparable studies of decisions of the Irish judiciary, although one writer goes so far as to state that "there are few in Ireland and none in the law profession who think for one moment that ... judges ... are politically biased in their professional activities" (Chubb, 1992, p. 295). But even if Fianna Fáil (or Fine Gael) supporters appointed to the bench do not see themselves as Fianna Fáil (or Fine Gael) judges, with a mission to use their positions to continue their political activities, it might still be true that the values that led judges to join one or other of the parties in the first place will inform the decisions they make. This has sometimes seemed to characterise judgments in cases involving extradition to Northern Ireland; judges with a background in Fine Gael tend to be less sympathetic to a "political offence" line of defence than do those whose background is in Fianna Fáil. In any case, it is obvious that quite apart from their party allegiances, the personal values of judges will play a large part in affecting the judgments they make. Although judges conventionally avoid comment on politically sensitive topics, this practice was breached on a number of occasions in 1992 by High Court judge Rory O'Hanlon, who, in the wake of the Supreme Court decision in the "X" case, described abortion as "one of the greatest evils of our time", and later expressed concern that any interpretation of Article 40.3.3 that construed it as permitting abortion under any circumstances could be in conflict with "the Divine Law and the Natural Law which formed the bedrock on which the entire constitution was founded and to which all the provisions of the constitution and any amendment thereof must conform" (*Sunday Tribune* 5 April 1992; *Irish Times* 23 November 1992). Reviewing the decisions made by the judiciary in constitutional cases, Hogan (1988, p. 187; see also Chubb, 1991, pp. 71-3) points to the absence of any consistent approach on the part of the judges, with a strong suspicion that they utilise "whatever method might seem to be most convenient or to offer adventitious support for conclusions they had already reached."

The dilemma of judicial review is inherently unresolvable. It places a lot of power in the hands of a non-elected, unrepresentative, elite answerable to no-one. But if judges were somehow made genuinely accountable to the government or the Oireachtas, they would cease to be an independent judiciary, one of the checks and balances of a liberal democracy. Judicial review has allowed judges to make important quasi-political decisions in areas like extradition without reference to the people or their elected representatives. However, Irish judges have not come in for the type of criticism levelled against their British counterparts (see above), perhaps because their decisions have often shown them to be more liberal and protective of citizens' rights than the Oireachtas. For example, governments had shown no inclination to grasp the nettle of reforming the restrictive contraception laws until the courts forced their hand by the McGee judgment of 1973. Significantly, the strongest objections were voiced after the Supreme Court delivered its verdict in the "X" case in March 1992, when anti-abortionists criticised both the specific judgments delivered (arguing that the judges had "lost their way") and, it seemed, the principle of judicial review. Fianna Fáil Senator Des Hanafin, chairman of the "Pro-Life Trust", declared that "it is wholly unacceptable and indeed a deep affront to the people of Ireland that four judges who are preserved by the constitution from accountability can radically alter the constitution and place in peril the most vulnerable section of our society" (*Irish Times*, 6 March 1992). However, this seems to be a minority viewpoint. Calls for reform of the system of judicial appointment, for example by the introduction of US-style Oireachtas assessments of proposed appointees, have up to now been voices in the wilderness, as the consensus among insiders appears to be that the present system, whatever its theoretical drawbacks, operates quite satisfactorily in practice.

A NEED FOR FURTHER MODIFICATION?

Up until the mid-1960s there was remarkably little criticism of the constitution. The first systematic assessment was made in 1966-67, when an all-party Oireachtas committee, which included former Taoiseach Seán Lemass, examined it article by article and issued a report recommending certain changes and assessing the merits of other possible amendments. The bipartisan approach adopted by this committee was brought to an abrupt end when Fianna Fáil went ahead the following year with its second attempt to change the electoral system, and it has never been resurrected. Of the committee's suggestions, only the (unanimous) recommendation that the two subsections of Article 44 relating to the churches be deleted was acted upon, five years later. Since the early 1970s, attacks on the constitution have multiplied. Change is advocated on any of a number of grounds, and some favour the adoption of a completely new constitution.

There are a few areas of the constitution where it seems likely that modification would cause little controversy. The most obvious example is Article 41.2 on the position of women; it seems to incorporate the view that women's place is in the home, saying that the state will "endeavour to ensure that mothers shall not be obliged by economic necessity to engage in labour to the neglect of their duties in the home" (see chapter 11, especially p. 218, for a fuller discussion). Even if this is only symbolic, it would find few contemporary defenders. Article 41 also refers to the family based on marriage, making no mention of single-parent families. In practice this does not mean that legislation recognising the existence of single parents is unconstitutional—for example, maternity grants and allowances go to all mothers, married or single (Casey, 1992, pp. 495). But, as with Article 41.2, it might be generally objected to even if it is only symbolic. There has also been widespread criticism of Article 43, whose protection of property rights is alleged to be an impediment to a more redistributive government policy (for a discussion see Keane, 1988).

More frequently, the argument for change is based on pluralism rather than majority demand—some articles are criticised on the ground that even if they do have majority backing, they infringe the rights of minorities. The most cited article here is 41.3.2, preventing the Oireachtas from legalising divorce. The 1986 referendum showed a clear majority in favour of retaining the article, but this left many people in a very difficult position, unable to remarry even though their first marriage has irretrievably broken down. The "pro-life" amendment of 1983, preventing the legislature from decriminalising abortion, also reflected only the majority ethos, having been backed by the Catholic church but opposed by all the other churches—as in 1986, the liberal camp deployed pluralist arguments, but to equally little avail. Many of the other rights articles, as we have seen, were strongly influenced by Catholic social thought. In July 1993, a visiting delegation from the United Nations Committee on Human Rights "expressed disquiet" about Articles 12.8 and 34.5.1, which provide that the President and Supreme Court judges respectively must take an oath "in the presence of Almighty God" before entering office, which the delegation suggested could exclude nonbelievers from these offices and might conflict with provisions in the UN Covenant on Civil and Political Rights guaranteeing freedom of conscience.

Article 8.1, declaring that "The Irish language as the national language is the first official language", has also been cited as selectively valuing, if only in aspiration, one ethos above another. Murphy (1975, p. 91) says that this article "made a large contribution to the double-think and hypocrisy which always characterised the state's policy on language restoration". This attitude towards Irish carries through into the constitution itself, since, in the event of a conflict between the Irish- and English-language texts, the former prevails (Article 25.5.4), even though any discrepancy between the two could have come about only during the process of translation from English to Irish.

Since the early 1970s, the Northern Ireland dimension has also been used to back up calls for amendment. Most of the articles already mentioned surface again here: they are attacked as embodying a Catholic, nationalist, Gaelic ethos and therefore implying that the Protestant unionist tradition is not part of the Irish nation envisaged by the constitution. Although Longford and O'Neill (1974, p. 296) say that de Valera's "aim throughout was to produce a constitution which would not require any fundamental change when the unity of Ireland was accomplished", it is now often argued that these articles in particular are a barrier to better relations between north and south, heightening northern unionist suspicion of the southern state. The preamble especially seems to exclude unionists from membership of "the people of Éire", as it conveys a view of history in which unionists could not recognise themselves: "We the people of Éire, humbly acknowledging all our obligations to our divine lord Jesus Christ, who sustained our fathers through centuries of trial, gratefully remembering their heroic and unremitting struggle to regain the rightful independence of our nation ...". In addition, Articles 2 and 3, which claim sovereignty over Northern Ireland, are often cited by northern unionists themselves as offensive, and can hardly fail to reinforce unionists' siege mentality. The 1966-67 constitutional review committee recommended rephrasing these articles to replace the claim by an aspiration (Committee on the Constitution, 1967, pp. 5-6), but Fianna Fáil has always expressed opposition to the idea of amending them, although all the other parties in the Dáil would now favour a change.

Other changes suggested are of a less political and more narrowly constitutional nature. The 1967 committee recommended modification of Article 34.3.3, which at present freezes for all time a verdict that a bill referred to the Supreme Court by the President is constitutional (see p. 53 above). It suggested (1967, p. 36) that such Acts should become open to challenge like any other legislation after a period of, say, seven years, an eminently reasonable proposal that has not been followed up. A similarly sensible recommendation, that an emergency declared by the Oireachtas for the purpose of enacting legislation under Article 28.3.3 should automatically lapse after a certain period (such as three years), rather

than being allowed to remain in force indefinitely, has also been ignored. There
has been criticism of Article 34.4.5, which prevents the Supreme Court from giving more than one opinion when pronouncing on the constitutionality of post-1937
Acts of the Oireachtas, or even disclosing the existence of opinions other than
the one delivered (Article 26.2.2 makes exactly the same stipulation concerning
bills referred to the Supreme Court by the President for a decision on their constitutionality). This means not only that dissenting judgments are suppressed; it
also poses problems if judges have reached the same conclusion but for different
reasons. There seems no good reason for this restriction, which has been criticised
by senior judges such as Brian Walsh and Donal Barrington; the former maintains
that it "seriously hampers the development of our constitutional jurisprudence"
(in the foreword to Casey, 1992, p. xi). It is perhaps significant that each of the
four articles mentioned in this paragraph owes its final form to amendments
made by the Oireachtas in 1941—the versions put to and approved by the people
in 1937 were less restrictive.

The question of making it easier to amend the constitution has also been raised.
While a constitution should clearly be more rigid than ordinary legislation, the
need to hold a referendum to make even minor changes may have a conservative
effect. Given the expense of referendums (that on the Single European Act in 1987
was said to have cost over £2 million, as was the 1992 Maastricht referendum), it
is not practical to make changes even when these would cause no controversy; the
uncontentious changes made in 1979, it is argued, should not have required a referendum. If change were easier, many improvements could be made: the removal
of Article 41.2 on the home-making "duties" of women, the clarification of im-
precisions in phraseology, the deletion of what the 1967 Report termed "spent
matter", and the resolution of what some see as ambiguities and even inconsistencies. Two methods of enabling amendments to be made more readily have been
discussed (Committee on the Constitution, 1967, pp. 49-51; Redmond, 1978, pp. 49-
52). One would enable the Oireachtas to amend the constitution provided the
majority in favour reached some fixed level, such as two-thirds or four-fifths.
The second would try to divide the constitution into fundamental and non-funda-
mental sections and, while preserving the requirement that only the people could
amend the former, would allow the Oireachtas, perhaps by qualified majority,
to alter the latter. However, any change of the rules governing amendment would
of course itself require a referendum, and given that the people have had control
over the wording of the constitution for over 50 years, it is unlikely that they
would agree to forfeit even a part of this control to the politicians.

CONCLUSION: A NEW CONSTITUTION?

Some would argue that the constitution now needs so many amendments that it
would not be worth trying to make them all, just as it makes more sense to buy a
new bicycle tube than to put dozens of patches on an old one. There should be a
new constitution, it is said, shorn of the rhetoric and theatricality of the present
one and preferably confined to basics like the American constitution.

However, there would be at least two dangers in taking this course. First, to
scrap the existing constitution would in some respects be to throw the baby out
with the bathwater. It might mean losing all the unenunciated rights "discov-

ered" by judges in it, most of which have had the effect of enhancing the civic rights of citizens. There is no guarantee that a new constitution would contain them all, especially as some have been inconvenient to the government of the day, and a new constitution might be worded so as to restrict the courts' ability to "discover" undisclosed rights. The second is the opposite possibility: keeping the constitution very short and simple might be to give even more power to judges, in that they would have to fill the gaps and use their own discretion in areas where the constitution was silent, as has happened in the USA, where it has been said that "the Supreme Court is well aware that its functions and powers lie in the gaps of the constitution" (Foley, 1989, p. 119). Besides, Ireland's constitution is by no means verbose by worldwide standards; its length of about 14,000 words (in each language) compares with an estimated 15,900-word average length for 142 national constitutions examined by van Maarseveen and van der Tang (1978, p. 177).

As things stand, the adoption of a new constitution seems unlikely. The Progressive Democrats published one in January 1988, which among other things entailed the abolition of the Seanad, but they did not succeed in placing the issue of constitutional reform anywhere near the top of the political agenda. Deciding what a new constitution should look like would require a degree of consensus among the parties that would be very difficult to achieve. Despite the criticisms that can be made of some specific articles, the present constitution as a whole seems to retain the kind of widespread acceptance and legitimacy that the Irish Free State constitution never attracted. Moreover, in terms of political realities, many would criticise a government that spent its time and resources during a period of high unemployment and emigration on a topic that few see as a priority. The 1937 constitution is likely to remain the fundamental law of the state for some time to come.

REFERENCES AND FURTHER READING

Bartholomew, Paul C., 1971. *The Irish Judiciary*. Dublin: Institute of Public Administration.

Bunreacht na hÉireann (Constitution of Ireland). Dublin: Stationery Office.

Casey, James, 1992. *Constitutional Law in Ireland*, 2nd ed. London: Sweet and Maxwell.

Chubb, Basil, 1991. *The Politics of the Irish Constitution*. Dublin: Institute of Public Administration.

Chubb, Basil, 1992. *The Government and Politics of Ireland*, 3rd ed. Harlow: Longman.

Committee on the Constitution, 1967. *Report* (Pr. 9817). Dublin: Stationery Office.

Constitution of the Irish Free State. Dublin: Stationery Office.

Dearlove, John and Peter Saunders, 1984. *Introduction to British Politics: Analysing a Capitalist Democracy*. Cambridge: Polity Press.

Doolan, Brian, 1988. *Constitutional Law and Constitutional Rights in Ireland*, 2nd ed. Dublin: Gill and Macmillan.

Fanning, Ronan, 1983. *Independent Ireland*. Dublin: Helicon.

Fanning, Ronan, 1988. "Mr de Valera drafts a constitution", pp. 33-45 in Farrell (1988a).

Farrell, Brian, 1971. *The Founding of Dáil Éireann: Parliament and Nation-Building*. Dublin: Gill and Macmillan.

Farrell, Brian (ed.), 1988a. *De Valera's Constitution and Ours*. Dublin: Gill and Macmillan.

Farrell, Brian, 1988b. "From first Dáil through Irish Free State", pp. 18-32 in Farrell (1988a).

Foley, Michael, 1989. *The Silence of Constitutions: Gaps, "Abeyances" and Political Temperament in the Maintenance of Government*. London and New York: Routledge.

Gallagher, Michael, 1988. "The people, the President and the constitution", pp. 75-92 in Farrell (1988a).

Gallagher, Michael and Michael Marsh, 1993. "The 1990 presidential election: implications for the future", pp. 62-81 in Ronald J. Hill and Michael Marsh (eds), *Modern Irish Democracy: Essays in Honour of Basil Chubb*. Dublin: Irish Academic Press.

Girvin, Brian, 1987. "The divorce referendum in the Republic, June 1986", *Irish Political Studies* 2, pp. 93-9.

Hogan, Gerard, 1988. "Constitutional interpretation", pp. 173-91 in Litton (1988).

Hogan, Gerard, 1989. "Legal and constitutional issues arising from the 1989 general election", *Irish Jurist* (new series) 24:2, pp. 157-81.

Hogan, Gerard, 1993. "The cabinet confidentiality case of 1992", *Irish Political Studies* 8, pp. 131-7.

Holland, Kenneth M., 1991. "Introduction", pp. 1-11 in Kenneth M. Holland (ed.), *Judicial Activism in Comparative Perspective*. Basingstoke: Macmillan.

Holmes, Michael, 1993. "The Maastricht Treaty referendum of June 1992", *Irish Political Studies* 8, pp. 105-10.

Keane, Ronan, 1988. "Property in the constitution and in the courts", pp. 137-51 in Farrell (1988).

Kelly, J. M., 1984. *The Irish Constitution*, 2nd ed. Dublin: Jurist Publishing Company.

Kelly, J. M., with G. W. Hogan and G. Whyte, 1987. *The Irish Constitution: Supplement to the Second Edition*. Dublin: Jurist Publishing Company.

Kennelly, Brendan and Eilís Ward, 1993. "The abortion referendums", pp. 115-34 in Michael Gallagher and Michael Laver (eds), *How Ireland Voted 1992*. Dublin: Folens and Limerick: PSAI Press.

Keogh, Dermot, 1988a. "The constitutional revolution: an analysis of the making of the constitution", pp. 4-84 in Litton (1988).

Keogh, Dermot, 1988b. "Church, state and society", pp. 103-22 in Farrell (1988a).

Lee, J. J., 1989. *Ireland 1912-1985: Politics and Society*. Cambridge: Cambridge University Press.

Litton, Frank (ed.), 1988. *The Constitution of Ireland 1937-1987*. Dublin: Institute of Public Administration.

Longford, Earl of and Thomas P. O'Neill, 1974. *Eamon de Valera*. London: Arrow.

McCutcheon, Paul, 1992. "The Irish constitution and the ratification of the Single European Act", *L'Irlande Politique et Sociale* 4, pp. 19-41.

Macmillan, Gretchen M., 1993. *State, Society and Authority in Ireland: the Foundations of the Modern State*. Dublin: Gill and Macmillan.

Morgan, David Gwynn, 1990. *Constitutional Law of Ireland: the Law of the Executive, Legislature and Judicature*, 2nd ed. Blackrock: Round Hall Press.

Murphy, John A., 1975. *Ireland in the Twentieth Century*. Dublin: Gill and Macmillan.

Redmond, Mary, 1978. "Constitutional aspects of pluralism", *Studies* 67:1, pp. 40-58.

Sexton, Brendan, 1989. *Ireland and the Crown, 1922-1936: the Governor-Generalship of the Irish Free State*. Dublin: Irish Academic Press.

Thompson, Brian, 1991. "Living with a Supreme Court in Ireland", *Parliamentary Affairs* 44:1, pp. 33-49.

Tóibín, Colm, 1985. "Inside the Supreme Court", *Magill* 8:7, February, pp. 8-35.

Van Maarseveen, Henc and Ger van der Tang, 1978. *Written Constitutions: a Computerized Comparative Study*. Dobbs Ferry, NY: Oceana Publications.

Volcansek, Mary L., 1992. "Judges, courts and policy-making in western Europe", *West European Politics* 15:3, pp. 1-8.

Whyte, J. H., 1980. *Church and State in Modern Ireland 1923-1979*. Dublin: Gill and Macmillan.

4 / THE ELECTORAL SYSTEM

Richard Sinnott

Ireland has had two referendums in which the government of the day sought to change the electoral system. Both attempts were rejected. This illustrates the point that electoral systems (the rules governing how votes are cast and seats are allocated on the basis of those votes) are a matter of political choice. They are also a matter of design; they have more or less identifiable political consequences and a system can be selected or rejected with a view to achieving or avoiding certain outcomes. Before considering this aspect, we ask: why proportional representation (PR) in the first place? We then look at why Ireland has the particular form of PR it has (i.e. proportional representation by means of the single transferable vote, or PR-STV) and at how that system works, before examining the consequences of PR-STV in Ireland.

WHY PR IN IRELAND?

Proportional representation is widely used in modern democracies because the main alternative—dividing the country up into single-member constituencies and giving the seat in each constituency to the candidate with the most votes—can lead to egregiously unfair outcomes at national level. This latter system, usually known as the plurality or "first past the post" system, is used for elections to the House of Commons in the United Kingdom (it is also used in Canada, India and the United States). The 1992 British general election illustrates its capacity to permit an "unfair" outcome: the Conservatives won 42 per cent of the vote and 51 per cent of the seats, whereas the Liberal Democrats won 18 per cent of the vote and 2 per cent of the seats. Such an outcome can occur because, within each constituency, the winning party takes 100 per cent of the representation (i.e., the one and only seat) while all the other parties or candidates receive zero representation. The winner thus receives what may be a sizeable "bonus" (the difference between share of the seats and share of the votes). The imbalances within each constituency may even themselves out across the country or they may be cumulative, in which case a party with considerably less than a majority of the votes may obtain a majority of the seats in parliament and take 100 per cent of the seats in cabinet and all the power and patronage that goes with control of government. The unfairness is compounded by the fact that the bonus usually goes to the largest party or parties while the smallest suffer.

Arguments in defence of this system stress the notion of elections as "devices to choose viable governments and give them legitimacy" (Butler, 1981, p. 22) and maintain that the bonus given to the winning party, with all the consequences that entails, is the best way of doing that. However, in the nineteenth century, as the franchise was being democratised, alternatives were sought because of the non-proportional outcomes that the plurality method can produce. Proponents of

PR came up with a wide range of ideas, the main distinction being between list systems on the one hand and PR-STV on the other. The former were generally favoured in continental Europe and PR-STV was the preferred alternative to the plurality system in Britain.

In a list system, each party presents a list of its candidates in each multi-member constituency, and the voter chooses between the various lists; the primary decision to be made by the voter is the choice of party. Seats are then allocated to parties on the basis of their share of the vote. In theory, a party obtaining, say, 35 per cent of the vote is entitled to 35 per cent of the seats, though how closely the outcome approaches this varies from system to system (for an overview see Gallagher, Laver and Mair, 1992, pp. 145-72). These list systems vary in the methods they use to award seats to individual candidates within parties: in some, the matter is decided by the party organisation, while in others the voters can express preferences for specific candidates on their chosen party's list. Even in the latter systems, the fact remains that the vote cast is primarily a vote for the party and may end up assisting the election of a candidate to whom the voter is actually opposed (Bogdanor, 1983, p. 15).

In contrast, the primary focus of PR-STV is on the choice of individual representatives. Indeed, the originators of PR-STV in Britain were highly critical of political parties and of the role they played (Carstairs, 1980, p. 194). Reservations about the role of parties were also quite widespread in Ireland when PR-STV was adopted, and the party affiliation of candidates was not listed on ballot papers in Ireland until the 1965 election. PR-STV, therefore, involves a notion of the connection between the individual representative and his or her constituency that is much closer to the notion of representation implicit in the first past the post system than to the notion of the representation of parties underlying list systems.

PR-STV is not widely used, Malta being the only other country that employs it to elect the lower house of its national parliament (it is also used, with modifications, in elections to the Australian Senate and in elections in Tasmania and Northern Ireland). How did this relatively uncommon system come to be adopted in Ireland? Developed simultaneously by Carl Andrae in Denmark and by Thomas Hare in England in the late 1850s, PR-STV became the favoured option of electoral system reformers in Britain. In the early years of this century, the problem of minority representation in the event of Home Rule seemed to make PR particularly relevant in Ireland. A Proportional Representation Society of Ireland was formed, with Arthur Griffith, founder of Sinn Féin, among its first members. An element of PR-STV was inserted in the abortive Home Rule Bill of 1912 and, in 1918, PR-STV was enacted for a single local council (Sligo Corporation); an election was held there under the new provisions in January 1919. The next step was the decision by the British government to introduce PR-STV for the 1920 local elections in Ireland and then for the 1921 election to be held under the Government of Ireland Act.

Thus, by 1921, PR-STV had not only been endorsed by a significant section of the nationalist movement but had actually reached the statute books. It is not surprising, therefore, that when independence negotiations were under way and the issue of representation of minorities was being considered, the desirability of PR was common ground. The result was that PR was included in the 1922 Free State constitution. The constitution did not specify the precise form, but it was automatically assumed that this would be PR-STV and this was the system specified in the Electoral Act of 1923.

HOW PR-STV WORKS

There are three distinct senses in which one can have an understanding of PR-STV: in terms of what is involved in the act of voting, in terms of the basic logic of the system and in terms of the mechanics of the count. The first is quite simple and the instructions are self-explanatory. Upon entering the polling station, voters are given a ballot paper that lists the candidates in alphabetical order and bears the instruction: "Write 1 beside the name of the candidate of your first choice, 2 beside your second choice, and so on". The simplicity of PR-STV from the voter's perspective is worth emphasising because a frequent objection to the system is the claim that voters will not be able to understand it. If one had in mind the second or third kind of understanding of the system mentioned above, this might well be so. The bulk of the voters probably have, at best, a hazy notion of the logic of the system and certainly do not understand its "mechanics". On this very issue, Seán Lemass argued in the Dáil debate on PR prior to the 1959 referendum: "There are not half the Deputies in this House, much less half the electorate of the country, who can give an intelligent explanation of what happens a No. 3 preference on a ballot paper. Is it not far better to give the people of the country a system of election they can understand?" (quoted in FitzGerald, 1959, p. 7). This criticism misses the point. The point is that PR-STV is easily understood in the sense in which the voter needs to understand it, and this does not include knowing what happens to a No. 3 preference. All that is needed in order to use the system to the full is an understanding of the notion of ranking a set of candidates according to one's preferences. This level of understanding is sufficient to enable loyal party voters to participate in the vote management strategies adopted by some parties in some constituencies (see Gallagher, 1993, pp. 70-1). For such strategies to work, the party managers need to know the subtleties of the system; the party voter simply needs to know that the party wants him or her to express a particular order of preferences.

In the case of the first past the post system, the logic is clear: give the seat to the candidate with most votes regardless of what proportion of the total vote this is. The majority or two-ballot system, as used in French presidential elections, introduces a refinement on this rule—in order to win a seat a candidate must cross a certain threshold, namely 50 per cent plus one, that is, an absolute majority. Again, the logic is clear. What is the logic of PR-STV?

Understanding the logic of PR-STV is best approached by first considering how the system works when there is only a single seat to be filled, as in presidential elections and by-elections in Ireland. Because multi-seat constituencies are an essential feature of PR—since a single seat cannot, obviously, be shared out proportionally—this is not, strictly speaking, PR-STV.[1] However, starting with this

---

1. Technically, the single transferable vote in a single-seat contest is known as the alternative vote (AV). It is important to emphasise that this is not PR because, in debate about electoral reform in Ireland, the option of "PR in single-seat constituencies" is sometimes put forward. What is being referred to is in fact the alternative vote, which, for reasons that will become clear in a moment, is not a form of PR.

simpler situation allows us to examine the logic of the system by isolating the STV element, elaborating on the significance of the quota and then going on to see the effect of the introduction of multi-seat constituencies.

Whatever the number of seats, PR-STV entails a quota—the number of votes that guarantees election. Once a candidate reaches this quota, he or she is declared elected.[2] The quota is calculated as follows:

$$\text{Quota} = \frac{\text{Total number of valid votes}}{\text{Number of seats} + 1} + 1$$

Any fractional remainder is disregarded. When there is only one seat available, the above formula yields a quota that is identical to that used in the French presidential election system, i.e. one more than half the number of votes. STV in a single-seat contest is in fact simply a sophisticated version of the majority system. The sophistication lies in how it deals with the problem of no candidate reaching the quota, something that may well happen if there are more than two candidates. When this arises in a French presidential election, all but the top two candidates are eliminated and the voters troop back a second time two weeks later to choose between the remaining two. This amounts to asking those who voted for eliminated candidates to register a second preference. STV does not, as it were, waste the voters' time by asking them to come back later to register their second choice. Instead, it collects this information, and information on third, fourth, fifth and further choices, all in one economical operation. Then, rather than disposing of all but the leading two candidates in one fell swoop, STV eliminates them one by one, reassigning the votes of the eliminated candidate according to the next preferences they contain. This has the advantage of including information on the preferences of the voters across the full range of candidates rather than, as in the two-ballot system, merely as between the two candidates who are in the lead after the first round of voting.

PR-STV is not, however, merely a refined version of the majority rule procedure—it has the all-important additional feature of multi-seat constituencies. The multi-seat constituency introduces two new elements into the logic of the system. The first is a lowering of the quota as a percentage of the votes cast. We have seen that in the single-seat situation the quota is half the votes plus one. A quick look at the formula shows that this principle can be easily extended as follows: in a two-seat constituency, the quota is a third plus one, in a three-seater it is a quarter plus one, in a four-seater it is a fifth plus one, and so on (see Table 4.1). Thus, as the number of seats is increased, the proportion of votes carrying an entitlement to a seat is progressively lowered—a nine-seat constituency produces a quota of only 10 per cent.

The second feature introduced by moving to multi-seat constituencies is the transfer of the surplus votes of elected candidates—these being the votes of an elected candidate over and above the quota, i.e. in excess of the number needed to guarantee a seat. If no such transfer were made, those who voted for such a candidate would not get the full share of representation to which, as a group, they are

2.   The quota is not the same as a "threshold", since a candidate can be declared elected on the last count without reaching the quota (as in the Galway West example described later). It is therefore a sufficient but not a necessary condition, and is to be distinguished from the kind of threshold imposed by, for example, the rule in the German electoral system that parties may participate in the proportional distribution of seats only if they have won a minimum of 5 per cent of the list vote (or three constituency seats).

entitled. For example, suppose that in a three-seat constituency just over 50 per cent of the voters vote for candidate A, and that A's supporters represent a particular point of view. Since the quota in a three-seater is 25 per cent plus one, and since this is sufficient to elect A, without a redistribution of A's surplus the second 25 per cent would achieve no representation and would be, as it were, wasted. The problem is solved by transferring the surplus votes to continuing candidates according to the second preferences of the supporters of the elected candidate. This is the point at which the mechanics of the counting procedure become somewhat complex, and we shall describe them later, but the complexities are not strictly relevant to grasping the logic of the system.

Table 4.1: Quota by district magnitude in PR-STV

District magnitude (TDs per constituency)	Quota, in per cent
1	50.0
2	33.3
3	25.0
4	20.0
5	16.7

To summarise: the logic of PR-STV is that it ensures proportionality by (a) lowering the cost of a seat by reducing the size of the quota that obtains in a single-seat contest (50 per cent + 1) by the addition of extra seats per constituency, by (b) eliciting and using extra information on the voter's choice, i.e. his or her order of preference among the competing candidates, and by (c) using this information not just in a process of elimination of the lowest candidates but also in dealing with the problem of what would otherwise be the wasted votes of a portion of the voters who supported candidates who have exceeded the quota.

Understanding the mechanics of the system is best achieved by working through an actual count. Again we begin with the simple situation—a single-seat contest and the transfer of the votes of an eliminated candidate. The presidential election of November 1990 provides a good illustration (see Figure 4.1). Valid votes amounted to 1,574,651, which, when divided by the number of seats +

Figure 4.1: The Irish presidential election, 1990

Candidate	First preferences	Transfer of Currie's votes	Second count result
Currie, Austin	267,902	- 267,902	
Lenihan, Brian	694,484	+ 36,789	731,273
Robinson, Mary	612,265	+ 205,565	817,830
Non-transferable papers		+ 25,548	25,548

Valid votes: 1,574,651.   Quota: 787,326.

1 (i.e., by 2) yields 787,325.5. Disregarding the fraction and adding 1 to this number gives a quota of 787,326 votes. After the first preference votes had been counted Brian Lenihan was leading, but since no candidate had reached the quota, the returning officer proceeded to eliminate the candidate with the lowest number of votes (Currie) and to distribute his votes in accordance with the second preferences indicated. On the second count about three-quarters (205,565) of Currie's votes were found to carry a second preference for Robinson. This gave Robinson a total of 817,830, well in excess of the quota, and so she was declared elected. Lenihan received only 13.7 per cent of Currie's second preferences, while 9.5 per cent of those who supported Currie did not specify a second preference and their ballots appear in the "non-transferable papers" row (for another example, see the presidential election result of 1945 in Appendix 2g).

As we have said, counting the votes in general elections is a more complicated process because PR-STV is based on the use of multi-seat constituencies. We can illustrate the counting process by looking at the Galway West constituency in the 1989 election, a case that illustrates several aspects of the vote-counting process without involving the need to go through a large number of counts. Galway West was a five-seat constituency and there was a valid poll of 49,339 votes. When this is divided by the number of seats + 1 (i.e., by 6) and, disregarding the fraction, 1 is added to the result, the quota is 8,224 votes, i.e. one sixth of the votes plus one (see Figure 4.2). One candidate (Bobby Molloy) exceeded the quota on the first count by a margin of 693 votes. He was therefore declared elected, and the next task was the distribution of his surplus.

The destination of that surplus is determined by re-examining the entire set of 8,917 votes for Molloy. These votes are arranged in "sub-parcels" according to the second preferences indicated on them, with votes indicating no further preference being set to one side. The total number of transferable votes is then used as the base for calculating each continuing candidate's share of the transferable vote.[3] These proportions are then applied to the 693 votes that are actually available for transfer. Thus, if candidate X obtains 60 per cent of the transferable vote in the original 8,917 votes examined, he or she is entitled to 60 per cent of the 693 surplus votes. Molloy had no party running mate to whom transfers could be passed by loyal PD voters; 48 per cent was divided between the two Fine Gael candidates, 26 per cent went to Michael D. Higgins of Labour, and only 20 per cent went to the three Fianna Fáil candidates.

Once the number of surplus votes going to each candidate has been ascertained, the votes must be physically transferred and the question arises: which actual ballot papers should be transferred and which should remain with the elected candidate? The choice could make a difference to the outcome since the papers transferred may subsequently be examined for their third or lower preference. The rules state: "The particular papers to be transferred from each sub-parcel shall be those last filed in the sub-parcel". The defence of this procedure is that the counting process requires that the papers be thoroughly mixed and that, therefore, the set of papers chosen comes close to being a random sample of the entire sub-parcel. However, it has been argued that it would be worth the extra

---

3.   The fact that the non-transferable votes are set aside before the ratio that is to be applied to the surplus is calculated has considerable implications for the interpretation of transfer patterns. These are discussed in Sinnott (1994).

Figure 4.2: Counting and transfer of votes in Galway West, 1989 general election

Electorate: 77,178;   Valid votes: 49,339;   Number of seats: 5;   Quota: 8,224

	First count	Second count Transfer of Molloy's surplus		Third count Transfer of O'Connor's & Shanley's votes		Fourth count Transfer of Brick's votes		Fifth count Transfer of Higgins's surplus		Sixth count Transfer of Ó Cuív's votes		Seventh count Transfer of Fahey's surplus	
Brick, Jimmy (WP)	1555	+ 30	1585	+ 38	1623	-1623							
Coogan, Fintan (FG)	5297	+ 204	5501	+ 18	5519	+ 204	5723	+ 352	6075	+ 253	6328	+ 229	6557
Fahey, Frank (FF)	8010	+ 44	8054	+ 7	8061	+ 68	8129	+ 48	8177	+ 2152	10329	-2105	8224
Geoghegan-Quinn, Máire (FF)	5902	+ 39	5941	+ 8	5949	+ 47	5996	+ 47	6043	+ 2272	8315		8315
Higgins, Michael Daniel (Lab)	7727	+ 181	7908	+ 67	7975	+1155	9130	- 906	8224		8224		8224
McCormack, Pádraic (FG)	5987	+ 131	6118	+ 12	6130	+ 49	6179	+ 152	6331	+ 380	6711	+ 211	6922
Molloy, Bobby (PD)	8917	- 693	8224		8224		8224		8224		8224		8224
O'Connor, Paul Ollie (PD)	84	+ 3	87	- 87									
Ó Cuív, Eamon (FF)	5733	+ 59	5792	+ 25	5817	+ 36	5853	+ 63	5916	- 5916			
Shanley, Dermot (Non-Party)	127	+ 2	129	- 129									
Non-transferable papers		+ 0	0	+ 41	41	+ 64	105	+ 244	349	+ 859	1208	+1665	2783
TOTAL	49339		49339		49339		49339		49339		49339		49339

Elected: Molloy, Bobby (PD); Higgins, Michael D. (Lab); Fahey, Frank (FF); Geoghegan-Quinn, Máire (FF); McCormack, Pádraic (FG)

cost in time to transfer all the papers in the sub-parcel at the appropriate fraction of their value, thereby avoiding all risk of bias or distortion, as is done in the counting of votes at Seanad elections (for discussion see Coakley and O'Neill, 1984; Gallagher and Unwin, 1986).[4]

The next step in the process of counting the votes in Galway West (the third count) was the transfer of the votes of the lowest candidate. In fact, on this count, two candidates were eliminated in one operation. This is because the difference between the second last and third last candidates (Shanley and Brick respectively) was greater than the total vote of the last candidate (O'Connor), so, even if all of O'Connor's votes went to Shanley, Shanley would still be the next to be eliminated. Accordingly, it makes sense to carry out both eliminations in a single count. Note that what is being examined at this stage is what the rules call "the next available preference". For example, if some of O'Connor's votes had a second preference for Molloy, then, because Molloy has already been elected, it would be the third preference that becomes operative for that particular vote. If that third preference happened to be for Shanley, then, because he has been eliminated, the fourth preference would be the "next available preference". The third count did not take any candidate over the quota, though Fahey and Higgins were getting close to it. On the fourth count, therefore, the next lowest candidate (Brick) was eliminated, and over 60 per cent of his votes transferred to the other left-wing candidate, Higgins, taking him over the quota with 906 votes to spare.

The fifth count involved the distribution of this surplus. The approach to the distribution of a surplus that arises at this stage of the count is the same as that described above, except that the proportions are determined not on the basis of a re-examination of the entire 9,130 votes of Higgins but on the basis of the "last parcel received", that is, on the basis of the 1,155 votes he received from Brick. This procedure does involve substantial savings in time and effort. Its rationale is that the "last parcel received" is what put the elected candidate over the quota and in this way created the surplus. It could equally well be argued, however, that the procedure involves a potential distortion of the process in that the distribution of next available preferences in Brick's vote may not correspond to the distribution of such preferences in the entire vote of Higgins and that the logic of the system requires that all of the voters for an elected candidate should have a say in the destination of his or her surplus.[5] The distribution of Higgins's surplus differed from Molloy's in another way. This is because the number of transferable votes in the last parcel received by Higgins was less than the sur-

---

4. While on the subject of anomalies in the system it is worth mentioning the alphabetical voting phenomenon. This arises because the candidates are listed on the ballot paper in alphabetical order of their surnames and some voters, presumably indifferent as to the individual candidates put forward by their preferred party, simply vote 1, 2, 3 for candidates of the party in the order in which they appear on the ballot paper. The result of this is an over-representation in the Dáil of individuals whose surnames begin with the letters A, B or C. The problem could easily be eliminated by arranging the names in a varied and randomised order on the ballot paper (see Robson and Walsh, 1974).

5. Sykes, in a robust polemic against PR-STV, argues that, faced with the daunting complexity of the task of re-examining the entire vote of all candidates elected at later counts, "the system quails and adopts an easier but illogical alternative" (Sykes, 1990, p. 12). The overall tone of the Sykes book is typified in a statement in the introduction (p. xii): "In the following pages I shall argue that [STV] is not just cranky, but bad: irrational, insufferably complex, prone to lapses into absurdity, unreliable as a guarantee of proportionality, and potentially detrimental to the authority and the effectiveness of Parliament".

plus to be transferred. When this happens, all the votes that can be transferred are transferred (i.e. there is no need for the calculation of transfer ratios). Since the number of transferable votes is less than the surplus, the difference is reported as "non-transferable papers" (in this case 244).

The sixth count consisted of a straightforward elimination of the next lowest candidate (Ó Cuív). Seventy-three per cent of his vote transferred to his two Fianna Fáil running mates. The fairly even distribution of the transfers between the two Fianna Fáil candidates was sufficient to put both over the quota, Fahey by a substantial margin of 2,205 votes and Geoghegan-Quinn by 91 votes.

At this stage of the count there were two candidates, both Fine Gael, still in contention and just one seat to be filled. The final step in the count was the distribution of Fahey's surplus which, like that of Higgins's surplus in the fifth count, was done on the basis of examining the distribution of next available preferences in the last parcel of votes received by Fahey (from Ó Cuív on the sixth count). As in the case of Higgins's surplus, the number of transferable votes was less than the surplus to be transferred, so all the transferable votes were passed on. The result was the allocation of 229 votes to Coogan and 211 votes to McCormack with 1,665 votes being reported as non-transferable. McCormack maintained his lead and, since these were the last two candidates in contention and since Geoghegan-Quinn's surplus of 91 was less than the difference between them, McCormack was declared elected without reaching the quota. Given that the difference between McCormack and Coogan going into the seventh count was only 383 votes and the surplus was 2,105, the outcome could well have been different had those voters who plumped for Fianna Fáil (four-fifths of the Ó Cuív voters who transferred to Fahey) expressed a further preference. The fact that McCormack fell short of the quota by 1,302 while there were 1,665 non-transferable votes in Fahey's surplus also illustrates why the last candidate elected is frequently returned without reaching the quota.

RECONSIDERATIONS

The decision to have PR-STV as the electoral system in Ireland has been reconsidered three times. Each time the choice has been reaffirmed, though with varying degrees of commitment. The first occasion was the writing of the new constitution in 1937. De Valera opted not just to include PR, as the 1922 constitution had done, but to specify PR by means of the single transferable vote. The matter did not give rise to extensive debate. Fine Gael had at one stage expressed some reservations regarding PR-STV (O'Leary, 1979, pp. 25-6). However, in the debate John A. Costello of Fine Gael merely questioned why the details of the electoral system should go into the constitution rather than be left to the greater flexibility of ordinary legislation, to which de Valera replied that the matter was too important to be left to the vagaries of party warfare. Pointing to some evidence that even at that time de Valera may have had reservations regarding PR, O'Leary speculates that the reason for putting PR in the constitution may have been a fear that its omission might have mobilised the opposition and led to the rejection of the constitution as a whole (O'Leary, 1979, p. 33). De Valera may then have taken the view that if PR had to be in the constitution, it was better from a Fianna Fáil point of view that it be PR-STV, which had at least offered some bonus to the largest party (see below). In any event, Article 16.2.5 of the constitution, referring to the members of Dáil Éireann, states: "The members shall be elected on the system of proportional representation by means of the single transferable vote". Article 16.2.6 stipulates that "No law shall be enacted whereby the number of members to be returned for any constituency shall be less than three". Since any change to the constitution requires a referendum, further consideration of the issue of the electoral system would involve reference to the people.

Twenty years later, shortly before retiring as Taoiseach, de Valera initiated just such a referral by proposing the abolition of PR-STV and its replacement by the plurality system. Although Fianna Fáil had been in power for 21 of the previous 27 years, it had won an overall majority on only four occasions, and, unless PR were abolished, might be less likely to do so in future without his leadership. Needless to say, the government did not put the case for change in such partisan terms but in terms of two other arguments (for a useful summary of the Dáil debate, see FitzGerald, 1959). The first argument was that PR has a disintegrating effect, creating a multiplicity of parties and increasing the probability of governmental instability. The second was that, whereas the plurality system enables the electorate to make a clear choice between two competing alternative governments, PR makes the formation of government a matter for post-election bargaining among parties, depriving the electorate of a direct say.

Fine Gael stifled whatever doubts it may have had about PR-STV and led the opposition to change. As a small party, Labour had even fewer doubts. The opposition counter-argument emphasised the issues of proportionality and fairness, particularly the question of the representation of minorities. Opposition speakers also attacked the proposal on the grounds that it would perpetuate Fianna Fáil rule indefinitely and undermine the parliamentary opposition. The debate in the Dáil on the enabling legislation extended from mid-November 1958 to the end of January 1959 and ran to some 600,000 words in the official report (FitzGerald, 1959, p. 1). And that was not the end of it. The bill was then debated in the Seanad, where the surprise outcome was a defeat for the government—the first defeat of a government bill in the Seanad since the reconstitution of that body in 1937—requiring the Dáil to use its power to override the Seanad (for which, see p. 144 below). The government also faced an array of opposition outside parliament, including all the national newspapers (except the Fianna Fáil-aligned *Irish Press*) and large sections of the trade union movement.

A controversial aspect of the contest was de Valera's decision to run for election to the presidency and to hold the presidential election on the same day as the referendum. The defenders of PR argued that holding both contests on the same day was loading the dice in favour of the proposed change. In the event, whatever effect the coincidence may have had, it was not sufficient. De Valera was elected to the presidency, but his proposal to abolish PR was narrowly defeated, with 48 per cent in favour and 52 per cent against (see appendix 2h).

Obviously Fianna Fáil took some encouragement from the fact that it had lost by a narrow margin (33,667 votes). Otherwise it would be difficult to explain the party's decision to put the very same proposal to the people again just nine years later. The underlying problem for Fianna Fáil—that of securing a single-party majority—remained. Seán Lemass had had to form a minority government in 1961 and secured exactly half the seats in 1965. Lemass himself appeared to toy with the possibility of reforms other than a simple move to the first past the post system, but he retired as Taoiseach shortly thereafter, and an all-party Oireachtas committee established in 1966 to review the constitution failed to reach agreement on the question of the electoral system and simply set out the arguments for and against (Committee on the Constitution, 1967).

In the event the government opted in 1968 for the same proposal as in 1959, i.e. to replace PR-STV by the plurality system. A second amendment proposed at the same time related to a constitutional requirement that the ratio of members of the Dáil to population in each constituency "shall, so far as it is practicable, be the same throughout the country" (Article 16.2.3). The new proposal would allow a deviation of up to one sixth from the national average. The purpose of the change was to enable rural areas with declining populations to maintain their level of parliamentary representation. It did not, however, go unnoticed that the areas that would benefit from such a change tended to be areas in which Fianna Fáil had strong and stable support.

Essentially the same forces were ranged against the government on this occasion, the only difference being that the defenders of the status quo campaigned with more confidence and conviction (for a summary of the debate see O'Leary, 1979, pp. 66-70). The outcome was also more decisive: the result on the question of PR was 39 per cent in favour of abolition, 61 per cent in favour of retention, and the voting on the other proposed amendment was virtually identical (see the table on referendum results in appendix 2h). The position of PR-STV was undoubtedly greatly strengthened by this decisive popular reaffirmation. Certainly, nothing more is likely to be heard about moving to the plurality system. However, plurality voting is not the only alternative and there have recently been signs of a renewal of debate about the consequences of the system and about the possibility of altering it.

THE POLITICAL CONSEQUENCES OF PR-STV

We said at the outset that electoral systems have a more or less identifiable political impact. The qualification "more or less identifiable" is necessary because there is considerable debate about what the consequences are and it is possible to be more precise and confident in identifying some of them than others. With a view to evaluating PR-STV, we shall examine its impact in three areas: the proportionality of the relationship between votes and seats, the stability of government, and the role of the elected representative.

Consequences for proportionality

Proportionality is usually measured by comparing parties' shares of the votes with their shares of the seats. There is a complication under STV, given the system's focus on individual candidates rather than parties and the way in which transfers as well as first preferences determine who wins the seats. This means that any index of proportionality in PR-STV is only approximate, so we need not be excessively concerned about subtle differences between the various ways of measuring proportionality (on these variations see Gallagher, 1991b). The most widely used index is that devised by Loosemore and Hanby (Lijphart, 1990, p. 483). It takes the sum of the absolute differences between vote and seat shares for all parties and divides by two. Mackie and Rose subtract this result from 100 to give an index in which 100 would represent perfect proportionality (that is, a complete correspondence between every party's share of the votes and its share of the seats). On the basis of the most recent election prior to 1991, PR-STV in Ireland produces a relatively proportional outcome (95), a score that placed Ireland in joint seventh place out of 25 in a proportionality league table calculated by Mackie and Rose (1991, pp. 509-11). In some ways this is a surprisingly high position, given that district magnitude (the number of deputies per constituency) in Ireland, on average only 4 over the years, is lower than in most countries that use PR. Larger district magnitudes are associated with greater proportionality since, with a smaller quota (see Table 4.1), fewer votes are wasted.

Over the years, the overall proportionality of the Irish system has been fairly consistent—the average for the period 1923-92 has been 94.9, with a range running from 97.6 (1933) to 90.9 (1987). Fianna Fáil has consistently obtained a bonus in seats over votes—on average, its bonus (percentage of the seats minus percentage of the votes) has been 3.1. Although this bonus has varied considerably in size, it has, as we shall see in a moment, often been enough to put the party over the crucial threshold of 50 per cent of the seats. Fine Gael has generally benefited from the system (its average bonus has been 1.5), though not to the same extent as Fianna Fáil, either in terms of the consistency of obtaining a bonus or of the average size of the bonus obtained. Labour, on the other hand, has obtained a share of the seats smaller than its share of first preference votes in 17 of the 24 elections of the 1923-92 period (with an average "bonus" of -0.9), and the minor parties and independents are even more consistent losers. Only once (in 1938) did the latter as a group obtain a greater share of votes than seats, and that was by a tiny amount, while their deficit has at times been very substantial, the highest being -8.8 in 1987.

Proportionality is crucially affected by the actual preferences and behaviour of the voters. Thus Fianna Fáil's bonus was minimal in 1951, 1954, 1973 and in the three elections of 1981-82—elections that were all marked by relatively high levels of transfers of preference votes between its main opponents.[6] On the other hand, there was quite a high level of transfers between Fine Gael and Labour in 1977, yet Fianna Fáil ended up with its highest ever bonus in seats over votes. This election and that of 1969 illustrate the disproportionality that can arise when constituency boundaries are gerrymandered. In the Irish case, this is more a matter of arranging an advantageous number of seats in areas with certain levels of support for the party or parties doing the gerrymandering and less a matter of including or excluding groups of supporters as in the classic "gerrymander" from which the term derives (Coakley, 1980, pp. 316-17). Such arrangements are no longer possible following the establishment of an independent boundary commission in 1980, but before then the rule of thumb was to create three-seat constituencies in areas in which the governing party or parties were presumed to be strong (say around 50 per cent of the votes) and four-seaters where support for the government was only moderate (say 40 per cent). Since the quota is 25 per cent in a three-seater and 20 per cent in a four-seater, the expected outcome of such an arrangement was two out of three (or 67 per cent of the representation) in a three-

---

6.   For an analysis of transfer patterns between 1922 and 1977 see Gallagher (1978). For analysis of more recent patterns see Sinnott (1994).

seater and two out of four (or 50 per cent of the representation) in a four-seater, thus maximising the representation gained. Of course, if the assumptions on which such a scheme was based did not prove accurate, it would backfire. This is precisely what happened in 1977, when an arrangement of constituencies design-ed to suit the presumed strength of Fine Gael and Labour combined was upended by a major swing in votes to Fianna Fáil, making Fianna Fáil the beneficiary of the carefully crafted "tullymander".[7] In the 1969 election the high Fianna Fáil bonus was a product of a combination of low transfers between Fine Gael and Labour and the advantage gained from an effective assignment of three- and four-seat constituencies to suit Fianna Fáil.

Consequences for the party system and government stability

The classic case against proportional representation, argued mainly on the basis of case histories of Weimar Germany and of France and Italy in the 1950s, was that it leads to a proliferation of parties and thus to political instability or at least stalemate. The alleged effects of PR have been the subject of endless debate and altercation over the years. The 1980s saw a renewal of this debate with more assiduous attention to systematic evidence and generally with the use of more sophisticated methodologies. In so far as the effect of PR on the number of parties is concerned, a consensus has emerged from recent research. It is summed up in Sar-tori's rewriting of one of the "laws" of the French political scientist Maurice Duverger: "PR formulas facilitate multi-partyism and are, conversely, hardly conducive to two-partyism" (Sartori, 1986, p. 64).

Has the electoral system caused a proliferation of parties in Ireland? Has multipartyism in Ireland led to governmental instability? Both these questions raise the issue of how to decide how many parties there have been at any partic-ular time. Simple as it may seem, this is not an easy question to decide. Just adding up all the parties that win votes or, if the focus is on the number of leg-islative parties, seats, is not enough, because parties differ enormously in size. For example, take two party systems, each with three parties. If the vote or seat shares of the three parties are in the range 30 to 40 per cent, then the system is clearly a three-party system. Suppose, however, that the parties have vote or seat shares in the region of 55, 25 and 20 per cent respectively. One still has three parties but the party system is radically different. In particular, the dynamics of government formation and the factors that make for government stability or in-stability will be quite different. One attempt to solve the counting problem is that of Laakso and Taagepera (1979), who propose an index that they call the "effective number of parties". This is not the place to go into the rationale for and the method of calculating the index; it is sufficient to note that it is a way of taking account of both the number and the relative size of the parties in a system. It is particularly useful for comparing the number of parties in different countries, or in the same country at different points in time.

After the 1989 election Ireland had an effective party score of 3 (after the 1992 election this rose to 3.5), while the average for 19 western European democracies at around the same time was 3.8. Thus Ireland had one of the less fragmented

---

7. Given that the term gerrymander is itself derived from the name of a politician, it has been sug-gested that the incident has contributed a new term to the political lexicon. The minister respon-sible was James Tully, and a tullymander is a gerrymander that has an effect opposite to that intended.

party systems, ranking joint seventh from the bottom together with Austria and France. Examples of countries with a high number of parties as measured in this way are Switzerland (7.5) and Belgium (7.1); the lowest are Malta (2.0) and the United Kingdom (2.2) (figures from Gallagher, Laver and Mair, 1992, p. 163).

In an attempt to provide evidence relevant to the questions raised above, Figure 4.3 presents (a) the effective number of parties in the Dáil over the period 1923-92 (b) the duration of governments (obviously, at the time of writing, this cannot be entered for the government formed after the 1992 election) and (c) the size of each government's majority (for ease of interpretation of the latter, the graph includes a horizontal line at zero on the right hand axis indicating exact equality of seats between government and opposition). The effective number of Dáil parties declined from a peak in June 1927 and remained low throughout the 1930s. It rose sharply twice in the 1940s, but then fell back and settled down at a low level from 1965 to 1982. In 1987, it began a rise that continued over the next two elections, being particularly pronounced in 1992. The number for 1992 reflects the very strong showing by the Labour Party. It is clear from this that the number of parties is not simply a function of the electoral system. Ireland has had the same electoral system since the foundation of the state but the number of parties has fluctuated considerably. At most, in the Irish context, PR has, in Sartori's terms, facilitated multi-partyism when other factors were leading in that direction.

It is also clear that government duration is quite unrelated to the number of parties. Government duration fluctuated dramatically from one inter-election period to the next between 1927 and 1944. All but one of the short governmental terms in those years were brought about by de Valera's snap election tactics and two of these occurred between 1932 and 1938, when the number of parties in the system was at its lowest. Similarly, the shortness of governments' lives in 1981-82 was not related to a sudden jump in the number of parties; rather, this was related to the closeness of the result in terms of the major groups of parties, to the existence of a small number of ideologically-inclined independents, and to particular strategies of government formation pursued by the major parties. In short, the number of parties in the Dáil at any given time is not what determines how stable the government of the day will be.

The third line in the graph reinforces the point. It shows that the simple and obvious fact of the presence or absence of a government majority is the key to government duration and that this is not necessarily a function of the number of parties. In so far as PR-STV deprives the large parties of regular and very substantial bonuses and therefore makes majorities more difficult to attain and in so far as it facilitates minor party representation, it can be said to be a source of governmental instability. On the other hand, it does both of these things only to a limited extent, because it does give some bonus to the larger parties and it does penalise small parties. In any event, whether or not instability ensues depends on a number of other factors. In sum, PR-STV cannot be held responsible for the (limited) instability the system has experienced.

Consequences for the role of the TD: does PR-STV lead to clientelism?

This issue hardly figured at all in the debates of 1959 and 1968. For example, a pamphlet by a civic-minded study group that aimed to provide an objective assessment of the arguments in 1959 devoted a page and a half to the issue of the

Figure 4.3: Effective number of Dáil parties, government majority, and government duration, 1923-92

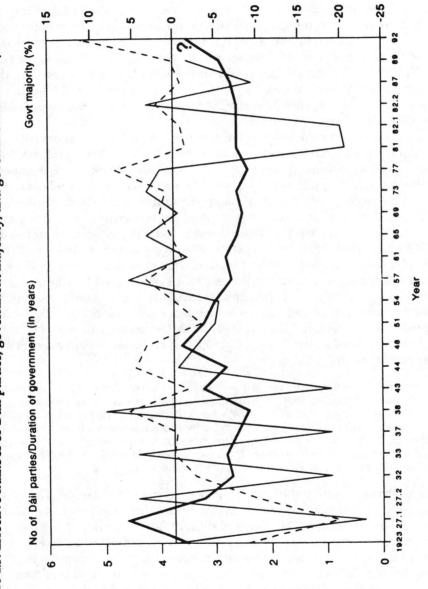

Effective no. parties — Government majority — Government duration

quality of TDs, but only five lines of this dealt with the problem of constituency service (Tuairim, 1959, pp. 19-20). In contrast, the subsequent increase in the burden of constituency work led Farrell (1985, p. 14) to note in the mid-1980s that "there is an evident consensus among deputies that the competition in constituency service has got out of hand". The debate now emerging focuses on the question of how far the electoral system is a cause of this. The fact that the expressions of concern are coming from present or former politicians from both major parties (see Boland, 1991; FitzGerald, 1991; Martin, 1991) suggests that there is a prima facie case to be examined. The impetus for change is not limited to the personal reflections of individual TDs on the problems of their role. Change in the electoral system was mooted by Charles Haughey as Taoiseach and "favoured" by his successor, Albert Reynolds, in his first press conference on becoming leader of Fianna Fáil (*Irish Times*, 29 November 1991 and 7 February 1992).

Academic support for the proposition that the Irish electoral system leads to excessive emphasis on constituency work is not hard to find. Katz (1984, pp. 143-4) argues that interpersonal competition tends to supersede interparty competition with the result that, ultimately, "competition between parties tends to be on the basis of services rendered, rather than policy differences". Carty emphasises the fact that PR-STV allows the voter to combine two criteria at once—party and personal service. He sees the electoral system as an independent contributory factor that adds to the cultural impetus to brokerage that is already there: "This dimension of electoral politics—local brokers competing for a party vote—has been institutionalised in Ireland by the electoral system ... With little to distinguish themselves from their opponents (particularly party colleagues), politicians are driven to emphasise their brokerage services to constituents, thus reinforcing cultural expectations" (Carty, 1981, p. 134). Even the balanced and measured view of the New Zealand Royal Commission on the Electoral System (1986, p. 60) contains some strong language:

> We have some concern, however that the fierce intra-party competition over constituency service experienced under STV in some countries overseas would, if introduced in New Zealand, seriously undermine MPs' work in Parliament ... [We refer] to the situation in Ireland where intra-party constituency competition has resulted in many members of the Dáil doing little else but attend to the demands of their constituents. While this might result in a higher level of service for the constituents concerned, to the extent that it occurs, policy and parliamentary functions of MPs must suffer.

The hypothesis underlying the above views is certainly plausible. The argument goes like this: the main competition for seats is between candidates of the same party. Since such candidates cannot differentiate themselves from one another on the basis of party policy, party record in government or party leadership, they compete on the basis of record of service to their constituents. This involves handling a large volume of casework relating to individual benefits ranging from welfare allowances to cattle headage payments. It means holding regular clinics throughout the constituency, attending meetings of residents' associations and local pressure groups of all sorts and being seen at social gatherings and functions from local sports events to funerals.

Of the various possible political consequences of PR-STV this is the most difficult to draw definite conclusions about. For one thing, there are clearly other causes of the constituency service role, as discussed in chapter 8: aspects of political culture, the small size of the society, and the nature of the administrative system. The key issue here is: what is the impact of the electoral system? There are four possibilities. PR-STV could be a sufficient condition of brokerage, it could be a necessary but not sufficient condition, it could be a contributory factor among others or, finally, it could play no role at all. Comparative evidence from Denmark and Switzerland cited by Gallagher (1987, pp. 31-2) suggests that the combination of preferential voting and intra-party competition does not automatically lead to a brokerage role. Similarly, the proposition that it is a necessary condition seems to be refuted by the widespread occurrence of brokerage in countries with all sorts of different electoral systems (Gallagher, 1987, p. 33). On the other hand, it would be hazardous to conclude that the electoral system plays no role at all. It is arguable that, in attacking the conventional wisdom that a primary cause of brokerage is PR-STV, Gallagher goes too far when he says "What can be disputed is that any of this is due to STV" (Gallagher, 1986, p. 267). This leaves us with the third proposition: PR-STV is a contributory factor among a considerable number of others. However, the question of what weight should be attached to the electoral system as a cause remains. This is probably unanswerable, at least with either sufficient precision or certitude to be useful in coming to a conclusion on the underlying issue of whether the abandonment of PR-STV would significantly reduce the incidence of brokerage and thus justify changing the electoral system on these grounds.

CONCLUSION

PR-STV is a highly distinctive electoral system. It differs fundamentally from both the other main variants of electoral systems—from the plurality system by virtue of its proportionality and from list systems by virtue of putting the emphasis on individual candidates rather than political parties. Both these differences are seen as weaknesses by its critics. The first criticism—that it produces results that are too proportional—is easily dealt with. First, STV produces moderate rather than extreme proportionality and second, high degrees of disproportionality are indefensible. The second criticism—that it devalues parties—raises a much more fundamental issue. Katz (1984, p. 145) argues that "the choice offered by PR [by which he means a list system] ... is a choice *within* party, while the choice offered under STV is a choice without regard to party. The effect has been to offer voters under STV a wider choice, but one which, in terms of the arguments used by its advocates, is less meaningful". Katz opts for a small-district PR list system, in part on the grounds that it provides "the kind of parties needed for effective implementation of the public will".

It may be that the party versus non-party dilemma is overstated by Katz in the phrase "choice without regard to party". It is true that the choice in PR-STV is not tied to party. Rather, it is open and flexible, because it elicits more information from the voter and places less constraint on the kind of information that can be transmitted. But this means that voters can vote on a party basis if they wish, and much of the evidence from the analysis of transfer patterns suggests that they do (for references on transfer analysis see footnote 6; see also Bowler and Farrell (1991) for a development of the argument that the system actually encourages an emphasis on party rather than individual candidacy). Even accepting this qualification, however, still leaves a dilemma—should the structuring of electoral choice put the main emphasis on parties or should the emphasis be determined by the voter? It has been argued that reform modelled on the German system—that is, a system that combines individual constituency-based representation by means of plurality voting with party list representation to achieve proportionality—would overcome the dilemma. The danger in the Irish case is that such a system might exacerbate the two-tier character of the Dáil and do so in a way that would reduce the legitimacy of the policy-making and legislative elite in the eyes of the electorate.

In order to achieve their objective, those who wish to reduce the brokerage burden and foster a legislative role for TDs would have to make many changes to the governmental system in addition to changing the electoral system. All of these changes—fundamental Dáil reform, the improvement of the provision of welfare and other services, the provision of more information centres, simplification of the rules and regulations relating to benefits, real devolution of powers to local level, improved funding to provide better research and secretarial services for TDs, public financing of political parties with the proviso that the finance be used for policy research and development, a comprehensive civics curriculum in the schools—are unambiguously desirable in their own right. There is insufficient evidence that the impact of such changes on the role of the elected representative and on the performance of the Dáil would be contingent on changing the electoral system. In any event, they should be implemented for their own sake. If it then appears that TDs cannot be got out of their clinics and into committees, there would be evidence that PR-STV is a powerful and independent cause of brokerage and there might be a case for change.

REFERENCES AND FURTHER READING

Bogdanor, Vernon, 1983. "Introduction", pp. 1-19 in Vernon Bogdanor and David Butler (eds), *Democracy and Elections: Electoral Systems and their Political Consequences*. Cambridge: Cambridge University Press.

Boland, John, 1991. "Dáil can only be reformed if TDs are liberated from multi-seat constituencies", *Representation* 30:111, December, pp. 42-3.

Bowler, Shaun and David M. Farrell, 1991. "Voter behaviour under STV-PR: solving the puzzle of the Irish party system", *Political Behaviour* 13:4, pp. 303-20.

Butler, David, 1981. "Electoral systems", pp. 7-25 in David Butler, Howard R. Penniman and Austin Ranney (eds), *Democracy at the Polls: a Comparative Study of Competitive National Elections*. Washington DC: American Enterprise Institute for Public Policy Research.

Carstairs, Andrew McLaren, 1980. *A Short History of Electoral Systems in Western Europe*. London: George Allen and Unwin.

Carty, R. K., 1981. *Party and Parish Pump: Electoral Politics in Ireland*. Waterloo, Ontario: Wilfrid Laurier University Press.

Committee on the Constitution, 1967. *Report* (Pr. 9817). Dublin: Stationery Office.

Coakley, John, 1980. "Constituency boundary revision and seat redistribution in the Irish parliamentary tradition", *Administration* 28:3, pp. 291-328.

Coakley, John, 1991. "The single transferable vote in Ireland: an historical assessment", *Representation* 30:111, December, pp. 46-8.

Coakley, John and Gerald O'Neill, 1984. "Chance in preferential voting systems: an unacceptable element in Irish electoral law?", *Economic and Social Review* 16:1, pp. 1-18.

Farrell, Brian, 1985. "Ireland: from friends and neighbours to clients and partisans: some dimensions of parliamentary representation under PR-STV", pp. 237-64 in Vernon Bogdanor (ed.), *Representatives of the People? Parliaments and Constituents in Western Democracies*. Aldershot: Gower.

FitzGerald, Garret, 1959. "PR—The great debate", *Studies* 48, pp. 1-20.

FitzGerald, Garret, 1991. "The Irish electoral system: defects and possible reforms", *Representation* 30:111, December, pp. 49-53.

Gallagher, Michael, 1978. "Party solidarity, exclusivity and inter-party relationships in Ireland, 1922-1977: the evidence of transfers", *Economic and Social Review* 10:1, pp. 1-22.

Gallagher, Michael, 1986. "The political consequences of the electoral system in the Republic of Ireland", *Electoral Studies* 5:3, pp. 253-75.

Gallagher, Michael, 1987. "Does Ireland need a new electoral system?", *Irish Political Studies* 2, pp. 27-48.

Gallagher, Michael, 1991a. "The single transferable vote and constituency representation", *Representation* 30:111, December, pp. 44-6.

Gallagher, Michael, 1991b. "Proportionality, disproportionality and electoral systems", *Electoral Studies* 10:1, pp. 33-51.

Gallagher, Michael, 1993. "The election of the 27th Dáil", pp. 57-78 in Michael Gallagher and Michael Laver (eds), *How Ireland Voted 1992*. Dublin: Folens and Limerick: PSAI Press.

Gallagher, Michael and A. R. Unwin, 1986. "Electoral distortion under STV random sampling procedures", *British Journal of Political Science* 16:2, pp. 243-53.

Gallagher, Michael, Michael Laver and Peter Mair, 1992. *Representative Government in Western Europe*. New York: McGraw-Hill.

Katz, Richard, 1984. "The single transferable vote and proportional representation", pp. 135-45 in Lijphart and Grofman (1984).

Laakso, Markku and Rein Taagepera, 1979. "'Effective' number of parties: a measure with application to West Europe", *Comparative Political Studies* 12:1, pp. 3-27.

Lijphart, Arend, 1990. "The political consequences of electoral laws", *American Political Science Review* 84:2, pp. 481-96.

Lijphart, Arend and Bernard Grofman (eds), 1984. *Choosing an Electoral System: Issues and Alternatives*. New York: Praeger.

Mackie, Thomas T. and Richard Rose, 1991. *The International Almanac of Electoral History*, 3rd ed. Basingstoke: Macmillan.

Martin, Micheál, 1991. "Fianna Fáil has a problem—it's time to deal with it", *Sunday Tribune* 4 August, p. 12.

O'Donoghue, John, 1991. "Multi-seat system keeps TDs on their toes", *Representation* 30:111, December, p. 43.

O'Leary, Cornelius, 1979. *Irish Elections 1918-1977: Parties, Voters and Proportional Representation*. Dublin: Gill and Macmillan.

Robson, Christopher and Brendan Walsh, 1974. "The importance of positional voting in the Irish general election of 1973", *Political Studies* 22:2, pp. 191-203.

Royal Commission on the [New Zealand] Electoral System, 1986. *Report: Towards a Better Democracy*. Wellington: Government Printer.

Sartori, Giovanni, 1986. "The influence of electoral systems: faulty laws or faulty method?", pp. 43-68 in Bernard Grofman and Arend Lijphart (eds), *Electoral Laws and their Political Consequences*. New York: Agathon Press.

Sinnott, Richard, 1994. *Irish Voters Decide: Voting Behaviour in Elections and Referendums, 1918-92*. Manchester: Manchester University Press, forthcoming.

Sykes, Leslie, 1990. *Proportional Representation: Which System?* Leicester: Hornbeam Press.

Tuairim Research Group, 1959. *P.R.—For or Against?* Dublin: Tuairim.

5 / THE PARTY SYSTEM AND PARTY COMPETITION

Peter Mair

Although the constitution and electoral law define the formal framework within which political parties compete, they tell us little about the content of politics or about the behaviour of politicians. It is through the study of party politics that some of the most fundamental processes in modern political life are to be encountered. Before going on in chapter 6 to look at parties as organisations in their own right and at their relations with the electorate, we need to get an overview of the whole system of parties as it has evolved in independent Ireland. Since one of the best ways of approaching such an overview is to look at the Irish system from a comparative perspective, this chapter begins by looking at those features of the Irish party system that outside observers might regard as unusual and then goes on to examine how these features have evolved.

THE COMPARATIVE CONTEXT

While the comparative political science literature on European party systems is enormous, with a host of studies analysing the differing origins of party systems, their patterns of change and stability and the various ways in which they may be classified and compared, this large literature also more or less neglects the case of Ireland. There are two reasons for this. First, and most simply, Ireland's status as a small and peripheral state means that it often escaped the attention of studies which have inevitably focused mainly either on the larger European states (France, Germany, Italy and the United Kingdom) or on those clusters of smaller continental countries that share common traditions and cultures (the Benelux states or the Scandinavian countries). Ireland in this sense stands alone, and has often been overlooked. Second, and more importantly, comparative political research has also tended to overlook the Irish case because it seems that the Irish party system "doesn't fit" into the more widely applicable models of party systems, in that it has long been believed that the patterns and structures of mass politics which are evident elsewhere in Europe have little relevance to the Irish case.

One of the most common ways in which to compare European party systems is to focus on the origins and genetic identity of the major parties which make up those systems, and then to group these parties into reasonably distinct sets of "party families", such as socialists, conservatives, christian democrats and liberals. Thus, for example, regardless of whether a particular socialist party in one country is more to the left than that in another, this sort of approach tends to compare such parties on the basis that, however different their current policy concerns might be, they do at least come out of the same (socialist) family.

This is of course an easy and practical way in which to compare party systems and in which to group particular countries together. By following this approach, it is possible to make a distinction between a group of countries which includes Austria, Belgium, Germany, Italy, Luxembourg, the Netherlands and Switzerland, on the one hand, and a second group which includes Denmark, Finland, Iceland, Norway, Sweden and the United Kingdom, on the other, on the basis that the centre-right of the political spectrum in the former group is dominated by a christian democratic party, whereas in the latter group the dominant centre-right party is a secular conservative one. This distinction is far from accidental, since Catholics have constituted a large proportion of the population in the first group of countries, whereas they constitute just a small minority in the latter, and, with few exceptions, christian democratic parties tended to come to the fore precisely in those countries in which there was a large Catholic population, and in which Catholic voters were mobilised in order to defend the position of the church—as regards its influence on social policy, educational policy, and so on—against the threat of growing secularism. In addition, we can also distinguish between those countries in which the left of the political spectrum was monopolised by a large social democratic party, as in the Scandinavian countries and the UK, and those where the left was divided between a social democratic party, on the one hand, and a communist party, on the other, as in France and Italy. Finally, further distinctions can be drawn between countries where there has existed a strong agrarian party (for example, Denmark, Norway and Sweden) and those in which there existed a strong liberal party (for example, Belgium, Germany and the Netherlands), as well as between those in which the traditional left is dominant (for example, the UK) as against those in which it has been challenged by the relatively recent emergence of ecology parties and new left parties (for example, Germany).

All in all, this genetic, family-oriented approach is very useful in comparing and classifying party systems. Unfortunately, however, it has never seemed very applicable to the Irish case, for it is precisely in terms of this approach that Ireland seems so exceptional.

There are a variety of factors involved here. In the first place, and most importantly, when we look at support for parties of the political centre or the right, it can be seen that the average electoral support for such parties in Ireland far exceeds that in any neighbouring European countries. During the 1980s, for example, an average of more than 80 per cent of the Irish vote in the five elections to the Dáil was won by parties of the centre-right (Fianna Fáil, Fine Gael and the Progressive Democrats), as against an average of just over 40 per cent in all the other West European countries taken together. Indeed, the only country to come close to the Irish level in this period is the United Kingdom, where the surge in support for the centrist Liberal-Social Democratic Alliance, and the repeated success of the Conservatives, raised the centre-right vote in 1983 and 1987 to a record post-war high. The next country after that was West Germany, and even here the centre-right vote in the 1980s was less than two-thirds that in Ireland (Gallagher, Laver and Mair, 1992, pp. 70-81).

Second, and related to this, Ireland also records the lowest level of electoral support for left-wing parties; in the 1980s, the Irish left (the Labour Party and the Workers' Party) polled an average of just less than 13 per cent, as against an average of almost 42 per cent in the other west European countries. In this case, the closest approximation to Ireland is the peaceful and prosperous country of Switzerland, and even there the combined vote for left-wing parties in the 1980s was exactly double that in Ireland (Gallagher, Laver and Mair, 1992, pp. 60-70). To be sure, the surge in support for Labour in the 1992 election did finally manage to lift Ireland off the bottom of this league table. Even then, however, the only country to be surpassed was in fact Switzerland, and with a total vote of 22.8 per cent (Labour, the Democratic Left and the Workers' Party combined) the Irish left remained below the average support in all other countries in Western Europe.

But this is not all, for Ireland is not only exceptional in terms of the distribution of the vote between left and centre-right, but it is also exceptional in terms of the sheer difficulty of fitting many of the Irish parties into the principal European families. In general, for example, comparative treatments would seem to suggest that Fianna Fáil is best regarded a "secular conservative" party. This means that it is a party of the centre-right which, at the same time, is not christian democratic in character, in that it did not originate as a party seeking to defend the position of the church against anti-religious forces. Even this definition results in difficulties, however. For example, other than the new conservative groupings which have emerged in the political systems of Greece and Spain, both of which have relatively recently democratised following long periods of authoritarian government, the only other major "secular conservative" parties in Europe are to be found in the United Kingdom and in the Scandinavian countries, and in practice neither variant is very similar to Fianna Fáil. The British Conservatives, as well as the Danish, Norwegian and Swedish Conservatives, owe their origins to the defence of middle and upper class privileges in the nineteenth century, and to resistance to the rising tide of liberalism and socialism, and all now define themselves in opposition to the major social democratic parties in their respective systems. None has the sort of radical, popular, anti-establishment heritage so treasured by Fianna Fáil (for a discussion of the party's origins and development, see below); none has enjoyed such close links with the organised trade union movement as has Fianna Fáil; and none could, or can, even come near Fianna Fáil in its traditional claims to represent the interests of the poor and the underprivileged. Indeed, it is only in certain very specific circumstances—as, for instance, when comparing Fianna Fáil under Seán Lemass in the early 1960s with the one-nation Conservatism of Harold Macmillan in Britain in much the same period, or when comparing the Fianna Fáil brand of nationalism with the similar patriotic appeal of the Gaullists in France, with whom Fianna Fáil has forged reasonably close links in the European Parliament—that one can identify connections between this largely idiosyncratic and very successful Irish party and some at least of its European neighbours.

Fine Gael is also relatively enigmatic. In comparative analyses it is often listed as a christian democratic party, not least because it has recently become a full member of the transnational christian democratic federation, known as the European People's Party. But there the similarities largely end, and again it is in terms of its origins that the fit is least easily made. As noted above, most European christian democratic parties emerged in countries in which Catholics constituted a large part of the population, but in which the Catholic influence on social and educational policy had been challenged by secular (for example, Belgium and

Italy) and/or Protestant (for example, the Netherlands) political forces. The point here is that while the proportion of Catholics in the population of countries such as Italy or Belgium was nominally very high, as it was in Ireland, the proportion of active or practising Catholics constituted no more than a large minority, thus leaving substantial room for the mobilisation of secular political forces, whether liberal or socialist.

This was clearly not the case in Ireland, however, where the vast majority of the population has traditionally been made up of active and practising Catholics (see chapter 2). Thus while in the rest of western Europe Catholicism was either effectively eradicated by the Reformation (in Scandinavia and the UK), or was subsequently challenged by the forces of secularism and socialism (in continental and southern Europe), political Catholicism in Ireland emerged victorious, and Catholic values were quickly and very effectively enshrined in the political system. It is for this reason that, uniquely among the Catholic countries of western Europe, christian democracy has never emerged as a distinct political movement in Ireland. Thus while it might now be possible to classify Fine Gael as christian democratic, largely if not only because of its organisational links with the other christian democratic parties in western Europe, this too stretches the argument.

Finally, and also largely as a result of the pervasiveness of Catholic values, Ireland (with Iceland) has been exceptional in the absence of a traditional "liberal" alternative. This gap in the political spectrum was partially filled in the late 1980s with the success of the Progressive Democrats, a new style of liberal party which bears many resemblances to the more recent variety of reformist liberalism which has characterised such parties as Democrats '66 in the Netherlands and (notwithstanding its name) the short-lived Social Democratic Party in the United Kingdom. Traditional liberalism, on the other hand, which owes its origins to nineteenth century secularist traditions, has always been noted by its absence from the Irish political spectrum.

In short, at least as far as the centre-right is concerned, the origins of the Irish parties bear little or no relation to those elsewhere in western Europe, and for this reason also Ireland has tended to be regarded as a unique case. It is not surprising that this should be so. The Irish parties in fact emerged from a unique experience in the period 1916-23, during which an intra-nationalist conflict and civil war centring on the country's constitutional status followed an armed independence struggle. Elsewhere in Western Europe, on the other hand, parties mainly grew out of social conflicts, and out of the struggles of classes and other social groups for political and later social rights. Indeed, if one were to search elsewhere for echoes of the Irish experience, then the closest parallel might well be found in the United States, where the modern party system also grew out of civil war and political conflict, and where the major protagonists are also often regarded as idiosyncratic and non-comparable.

In these terms, then, the Irish party system is a case apart, and as such it is also, in terms of much of the literature on comparative European politics, a case dismissed. Indeed, as John Whyte noted some time ago, "it is then perhaps a comfort to comparative political analysis that Irish party politics should be *sui generis*: the context from which they spring is *sui generis* also" (Whyte, 1974, p. 648).

IN THE BEGINNING WAS THE TREATY ...

As we have seen in chapter 1, the two major parties, Fianna Fáil and Fine Gael, originated from a split in the original Sinn Féin party, whose success in the 1918 Westminster election led to Irish independence in 1922. A crucial factor affecting the early alignment of the Irish party system was the fact that despite Sinn Féin's success, the nationalist issue remained unresolved, with partition and the oath of allegiance to the British crown as the most contentious elements in the Treaty settlement. The division within Sinn Féin on these issues and the 1922-23 civil war created a strong polarisation between pro- and anti-Treaty sides for the first decade of the new state's life.

This split in Sinn Féin was primarily political. But it was not solely political, and as the opposing forces crystallised, a marked social and economic cleavage emerged to reinforce the political opposition, with Sinn Féin (and later Fianna Fáil) tending to predominate in the economically and geographically peripheral west and south-west of the country. Already for some time before this, of course, the question of Irish independence had gone beyond the bounds of the purely political. Although many of the original problems which had contributed to sustaining the nationalist forces had been resolved—most notably the shift from tenant farming to owner occupation—this very transition had led to the emergence of new issues. In particular, there was the whole question of the emphasis to be placed on the need for economic development, industrialisation and modernisation, and the earliest policies of Sinn Féin had deliberately emphasised the constraint on development which resulted from the economic as well as the political dominance of Britain. Only through political independence, it was argued, could Ireland also achieve economic independence, in that only then would it be free to adopt the protectionist measures which were necessary to nurture the domestic economy.

During the crucial period leading up to independence, the Sinn Féin emphasis on the economic side of its policy had diminished. Subsequent to the civil war, however, this was to re-emerge as one of the major elements in the platform of the new, anti-Treaty forces. This platform, together with an emphasis on the need for more generous social provisions, had the effect of alienating Sinn Féin, and later Fianna Fáil, from the more privileged sectors of Irish society, who tended to prefer the more cautious and conservative Cumann na nGaedheal. At the same time, however, it was a programme which enhanced Sinn Féin's (and later Fianna Fáil's) appeal among the small farmers, the poor and the working class (Rumpf and Hepburn, 1977, pp. 87-107; Garvin, 1974).

The conflict between the two sides during the 1920s was therefore sharp and polarised. Indeed, not only did it involve important political and economic issues, but it also reflected a level of enmity which had found expression, just a few years earlier, in widespread armed conflict. It is worth emphasising that in almost no other country in Europe have two sides which were originally, and literally, at war with one another then gone on as fully legitimate parties to continue that contest at the electoral level within a very short space of time. It is hardly surprising, therefore, that there were many in Ireland at the time who felt that the regime itself would be unable to survive.

Survive it did, of course, and not least because of a later split in Sinn Féin, which had been the losing side in the civil war, and which initially refused to recognise the legitimacy of the new state. In 1926, led by Eamon de Valera, a minority of the party broke away to form Fianna Fáil, as we have seen in chapter 1. One year later, following the introduction of the Electoral Amendment Bill which was designed to prevent any candidate standing for election who would not declare a prior commitment to swearing the oath of allegiance, Fianna Fáil turned its back on abstentionism, and entered the Dáil.

Five years later, following its electoral victory in 1932, the new party entered government, and was to remain in office continuously until 1948. For most of the 1930s its principal opponent remained the old "pro-Treaty" wing of Sinn Féin, which, in 1933, having merged with two of the minor parties of the time, was reborn as Fine Gael. The opposition between these two parties has persisted ever since, even though, with the passing of time, and with the succession of new generations, both the original basis of their conflict and their mutual enmity have tended to wane (on the party system generally, see Carty, 1981; Gallagher, 1985; Mair, 1987; Sinnott, 1978 and 1984).

Throughout the 1920s and 1930s, as indeed has also been the case ever since then, Labour played the role of the third party in the system. Labour is in fact the oldest of the three parties, and, like its British counterpart, was formed as the political wing of the trade union movement, being formally launched in 1912 and developing into a proper political organisation in 1922. The party had "stood aside" in the crucial Westminster election of 1918 for tactical reasons. Thereafter, in the new state, it also tried to stand aside from nationalist issues, and focused principally on matters of more immediate concern to its working class constituency, made up of both urban trade unionists and farm workers. Given the importance of the intra-nationalist divide, however, it seemed inevitable that such a strategy would force Labour onto the margins of Irish politics, and this certainly proved to be the case. Initially, when Sinn Féin/Fianna Fáil refused to enter the Dáil, Labour did enjoy quite a large share of the political limelight as the principal "constitutional" opposition to Cumann na nGaedheal. Once Fianna Fáil had become legitimised, however, and particularly given that the Fianna Fáil programme also contained many of the more radical social and welfarist policies which were favoured by Labour, there seemed little potential remaining for the smaller party to play an independent role. Indeed, when Fianna Fáil first took office in 1932, it did so as a minority government with Labour support.

Labour's failure to develop into a major party along the lines of the prominent social democratic parties in the rest of western Europe has long constituted a focus of discussion among Irish political analysts, and there are several factors which can be cited to account for the party's Cinderella status (see Gallagher, 1982; Mair, 1992). Two of these factors are of particular importance. In the first place, and most obviously, the sheer salience of nationalist issues in the early years of Irish politics meant that there was simply little scope for a party which devoted itself almost exclusively to working-class socialist concerns. Indeed, the working class itself was small, since Irish society at the time had a largely rural and agricultural character (see chapter 2). Second, as Brian Farrell (1970) has argued, Labour's decision not to take part in the 1918 election played a crucial role in determining its subsequent poor fortunes, since, given the very large proportion of newly enfranchised voters, this can really be considered as the election which set the political terms of reference for the new state. Had Labour participated, argued Farrell, then it would have had the opportunity of placing socialist issues on what was essentially a wholly new political agenda; in fact, of course, Labour missed that opportunity, and thus in its own way it helped to pass the agenda over almost exclusively to nationalist concerns.

Both of these arguments therefore place a particular emphasis on the patterns which developed at the very early stages of mass politics in independent Ireland. In the beginning was the Treaty, the argument goes, and since then nothing has changed. Precisely because nationalism became the focus of the political agenda in 1918 and immediately thereafter, precisely because Sinn Féin/Fianna Fáil and Cumann na nGaedheal/Fine Gael proved to be the dominant actors on the political stage in the 1920s and 1930s, and precisely because Labour was marginalised throughout this period, we have the outcome which became so familiar throughout the 1960s, the 1970s, and even the 1980s, as may be seen from Figure 5.1: a strong Fianna Fáil, a rather less strong Fine Gael, and a Labour Party that consistently took third place. The formative years of Irish politics were therefore the crucial years, setting a pattern which has since proved almost impossible to shift. It is in this sense that people still continue to speak of the maintenance of "civil war politics" and of the uniqueness of the Irish case.

But while the particular cleavage which divided the parties in these early years may well have been unique, and while the Irish context also, as Whyte remarked, may well have been *sui generis*, the more general notion that very early patterns of politics become frozen into place is certainly not unusual. Indeed, as Lipset and Rokkan (1967) have shown, this is precisely the pattern which has tended to prevail throughout western Europe, with the cleavage structures which were dominant around the beginning of the century, when mass suffrage was first

Figure 5.1: Electoral support for Irish parties, 1922-92

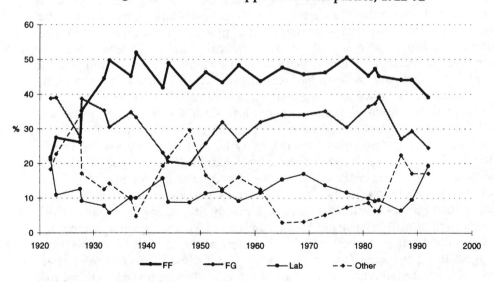

introduced, as well as the parties which mobilised on the basis of these cleavages, tending to remain frozen in place thereafter. Writing of the west European party systems of the late 1960s, they noted that these tended to reflect, "with few but significant exceptions, the cleavage structures of the 1920s", and that throughout Europe "the party alternatives, and in remarkably many cases the party organisations, are older than the majority of the national electorates" (Lipset and Rokkan, 1967, p. 50). The other European countries were, of course, unlike Ireland in that their party systems froze around cleavages which tended to reflect primarily social rather than political divisions, and involved socialist, christian, conservative and liberal parties, rather than building on the sort of nationalist parties which were frozen into place in the Irish case; nevertheless, even though the issues were different, the freezing process itself proved to be more or less the same.

That said, we should be wary of assuming any sense of inevitability or fatalism in our understanding of the factors which determined the development of the Irish party system. In Ireland, to be sure, as elsewhere in Europe, the formative years played a very important role. But this is not the only relevant factor, and it is certainly not the only factor which can be cited to explain the continued survival of the old civil war parties and the long-term marginalisation of the Labour Party.

THE DYNAMICS OF PARTY COMPETITION

In seeking to understand the evolution of the Irish party system, we need to begin with one of its most characteristic features: its domination by a single party. The dominant position of Fianna Fáil must be seen in the context of two more general issues: the mechanics of party competition and the nature of policy competition. In the light of these broader perspectives, it becomes possible to identify "watersheds", or critical turning points, in the evolution of the Irish party system.

The dominance of Fianna Fáil

The single most important element in determining the development of the Irish party system has been the persistently dominant position of Fianna Fáil. As noted above, the very early and formative years of the party system were characterised by the opposition of Sinn Féin/Fianna Fáil, on the one hand, and Cumann na nGaedheal/Fine Gael, on the other, with Labour and occasional other minor parties being marginalised by this overriding contest. After 1932, Fianna Fáil began to consolidate its own pre-eminent position, not least because its governing status and increasingly moderate approach allowed the party to extend its support far beyond the small-farmer constituency in the peripheral west, and to begin to appeal to the more "respectable" and privileged middle class (and working class) voters in the rest of the country (see Garvin, 1974), thus stealing much of the ground from under Fine Gael's feet. At the same time, support for Cumann na nGaedheal/Fine Gael itself began to slip: in 1927, when it was at its peak, the party had polled almost 39 per cent of the vote, but at the end of the 1940s, when Fianna Fáil had already been in government for 16 years, its vote had fallen to just less than 20 per cent (see appendix 2c).

Meanwhile, frustrated by the erosion of Fianna Fáil's original radical appeal, new parties had also begun to emerge on the scene in the 1940s. These included

Clann na Talmhan, a party which sought to represent the interests of the small farmers, and Clann na Poblachta, which mobilised on the basis of a strong republican and socially reformist programme. Labour also managed to reach a new peak in support by 1943, although in 1944 the party temporarily split into two. By the end of the 1940s, therefore, the party system was balanced by a relatively strong Fianna Fáil party, on the one side, and a fragmented and politically diverse collection of smaller parties, on the other. This was also a period in which there existed perhaps a greater potential for political realignment and change than had been the case for almost 20 years. In moving to the centre, Fianna Fáil had abandoned much of its original radicalism and had begun to disenchant many of its former supporters. Fine Gael, on the other hand, seemed to be heading towards the margins of Irish politics, and a new, sometimes radical, politics was also afoot. In the 1948 election, the two Labour parties, the two Clann parties, and a variety of independents—all falling more or less outside the traditional mould of Irish politics—together won a total of almost 40 per cent of the vote.

These new parties, and Labour, now had a relatively clear choice. On the one hand, they could pursue an independent line and, by mobilising an alternative politics within a system which had for some time revolved around the civil war contest, they could seek to take advantage of the problems of their established opponents, thus building the potential for a radical transformation of the party system itself. On the other hand, they could try to sink their mutual differences, and could even break bread with Fine Gael, and follow the more short-term strategy of providing an alternative government to Fianna Fáil.

In the event, it was the latter option which was favoured, and rather than turning their backs on the old civil war opposition between Fianna Fáil and Fine Gael, the various minor parties, together with some independent support, formed a loose and heterogeneous coalition with Fine Gael in an attempt to throw Fianna Fáil out of office at last. Rather than building an alternative politics, therefore, they chose instead to work towards creating an alternative government. The attempt proved successful, at least after a fashion, and the new coalition government lasted until 1951. As we have seen in chapter 1, Fianna Fáil then came back into office for three years, before being once again displaced in 1954 by a coalition of the now revived Fine Gael, the now re-united Labour Party, and the now fading Clann na Talmhan. This government also lasted for three years, with Fianna Fáil returning to office in 1957 and remaining there for a further 16 years (see appendix 3b for a list of governments).

In retrospect, this sequence of alternating governments might not seem so important—no more than a brief flurry of change in what has otherwise been a highly predictable political balance. From another perspective, however, it was a crucial moment, for it helped to clarify the character of Irish political competition in quite an unambiguous fashion. From now on, politics no longer revolved around the contest between Fianna Fáil and Fine Gael, as had been the case in the 1920s and 1930s. Indeed, in this sense "civil war" politics existed no more. Rather, and almost throughout the postwar period, politics instead revolved around the opposition between Fianna Fáil, on the one hand, and all the remaining relevant parties in the system, on the other (Mair, 1979). Thus while there have always been more than two parties contesting elections in Irish politics, the pattern of competition has often tended to reflect that of a straight two-party system, with a single party (Fianna Fáil) on one side and a varying collection of parties on the other, a pattern which persisted from 1948, when the first anti-Fianna Fáil coalition was formed, right up until 1989, when Fianna Fáil itself entered a coalition government for the first time in its history (see Farrell, 1990; Laver and Arkins, 1990).

The constraints on party competition
The most important feature of this postwar configuration involves the constraints which it imposed on party competition and party strategy, constraints which resulted from the struggle for office between Fianna Fáil, on the one side, and all of the remaining parties, on the other (see Mair, 1993). Given the size of its core electoral support and Dáil representation, Fianna Fáil was obviously the only party which was in a position to aim for a single-party majority government. As such, it was also in a position to polarise the party system into two camps—those who supported Fianna Fáil and those who did not—and to follow its own independent path, quite unconcerned with coalitions and alliances. If the party won a majority in the Dáil it would govern alone; if it failed to win enough seats to form a majority, then it would either form a minority single-party administration (as it did in 1951, 1961, March 1982 and in 1987) or it would go into opposition (as it did in 1948, 1954, 1973, 1981, and in December 1982). Indeed, in relative terms, Fianna Fáil is one of the most successful single parties in Western Europe (see Coakley, 1987, p. 159). Even in the 1980s, for example, at a time when the party was believed to be in trouble and to be losing its electoral grip, it still managed to win an average of some 45 per cent of the vote, which is approximately a quarter more than that polled by the largest party in the average Western European system. Only in Austria, West Germany and Greece did the largest party manage to win a greater share of the national vote than did Fianna Fáil, although the Social Democrats in both Spain and Sweden came very close. Moreover, because of biases in the electoral system, especially in the past, this large electoral support was also usually translated into an even larger share of Dáil seats, with the result that the party could normally hope to win a majority on its own.

Fianna Fáil's opponents, on the other hand, were much less capable of developing a wholly independent strategy. Indeed, as far as the struggle for government was concerned, their options were relatively simple, if also unappealing: both Fine Gael and Labour could plough their own independent furrows, which would mean that they would always remain in opposition; or they could form an alliance and share office together. Thus whereas Fianna Fáil's choices were those between government and opposition, the choices for Fine Gael and Labour were between *coalition* and opposition. In strategic terms, their hands were tied, and, to the extent that office mattered, neither could afford to go its own way.

In principle, of course, such a constraint may not appear particularly demanding. Throughout western Europe, coalition government is the norm rather than the exception (Gallagher, Laver and Mair, 1992, pp. 173-212), and most major parties usually find themselves obliged to share office with at least one of their potential competitors. But what is also striking about most of these other systems is that the parties involved usually have a choice of partners, in that coalition alliances are regularly reshuffled and changed, such that if Party A finds it difficult to forge an agreement with Party B, it can always turn around and try to fix up a deal with Party C instead.

In Ireland, however, such options had been foreclosed to an unusual extent—at least until the end of the 1980s. Precisely because Fianna Fáil chose to follow its own independent path, and precisely because it enjoyed a sufficient "critical mass" of support to govern alone, it was clearly out of the reckoning in any conceivable coalition. This, in turn, meant that Fine Gael had only one potential coalition partner, which was Labour, while Labour also had only one potential coalition partner, which was Fine Gael. In effect, the dominance of Fianna Fáil therefore forced these two smaller parties together, such that their choices were not simply coalition or opposition, but were rather, and more narrowly, coalition *with one another* or exclusion from government. It is in this sense that enormous constraints had been placed on the postwar patterns of party competition.

In comparative analyses, Ireland has sometimes been described as traditionally having a "two-and-a-half" party system, a system which revolved around two big parties, Fianna Fáil and Fine Gael, and one small or "half" party, Labour. In this sense it has also been seen as comparable in its structure to the traditional West German party system, which has also had two big parties, the Christian Democratic Union (CDU-CSU) and the Social Democrats (SPD), as well as one small or "half" party, the liberal Free Democratic Party (FDP). At the same time, however, the dynamics of each system were very different. In Germany, the system was such that each of the two major parties (CDU-CSU and SPD) vied with one another to win the support of the pivotal, centre-based minor party (FDP), with the latter shifting its affections from one to the other, resulting in a series of alternating governments in which it always managed to win the role of junior partner in coalition. The liberal FDP may have been only a "half" party in electoral terms, but, with the exception of the period 1966-69, it has nevertheless taken part in every government in the Federal Republic of Germany since 1961. In Ireland, on the other hand, during most of the period since the 1940s, the pattern of competition in the system did not revolve around a contest between Fianna Fáil and Fine Gael with Labour as a pivotal party in the middle; on the contrary, Labour was not only on the left of the political spectrum, and thus did not lie between Fianna Fáil and Fine Gael, but it was also persistently and inevitably aligned with Fine Gael in the enduring competition of Fianna Fáil versus the rest.

The contrast between these two patterns is crucial to an understanding of the dynamics of Irish party politics. In West Germany, *neither* of the two major parties could hope to win a majority on its own, and hence *both* needed to court the pivotal FDP. In Ireland, on the other hand, at least until very recently, Fianna Fáil was always sufficiently strong to hope to govern alone, whereas Fine Gael was always sufficiently weak to realise that it could govern only in coalition, and then only with Labour. Both West Germany and Ireland may well be characterised as two-and-a-half party systems, but their patterns of party competition were therefore fundamentally different.

In the three decades which elapsed between the end of the second anti-Fianna Fáil coalition in 1957 and Fianna Fáil's own first coalition in 1989, the only major element of change in the structural configuration of the Irish party system was the composition of the non-Fianna Fáil alternative. The coalition experience in the 1950s, in which the governments were led by a Fine Gael Taoiseach, was sufficient to pull Fine Gael back from the brink and to restore its previously faltering political fortunes. Labour also benefited from the experience, while the two Clann parties, and many of the independents, found that their support had waned. By the 1960s, therefore, the old parties were back in style, and by the end of that decade their total vote share had risen to almost 97 per cent—46 per cent for Fianna Fáil, 34 per cent for Fine Gael and 17 per cent for Labour. By then, all other options had faded.

But while the old parties had consolidated their position once again, the logic of competition remained as it had done throughout the postwar period, with Fianna Fáil on the one side and a now reduced collection of opposition parties on the other. From 1957 onwards, to be sure, Fine Gael and Labour did try to go their own separate ways, with each hoping, if only fancifully, that it might one day acquire sufficient support to challenge for government on its own. As far as the electorate was concerned, however, it seemed as if the choice remained either coalition or Fianna Fáil, and as long as Fine Gael and Labour were pursuing mutually exclusive strategies, this meant in fact that Fianna Fáil remained the only really feasible governing option. Thus even though Fianna Fáil did sometimes experience electoral losses, and even though it never did manage to poll a majority of the votes in any election in this period, it nevertheless remained in office continuously between 1957 and 1973.

It was in 1973 that the two opposition parties once more pooled their resources and decided to recognise the fact that their most feasible strategy was to combine together to establish an alternative government to Fianna Fáil. In this sense, therefore, their new strategy simply replicated that which had been pursued in the late 1940s and 1950s, when the non-Fianna Fáil parties also came together to create an alternative government. In other respects, however, there were marked differences between the two situations. In the first place, the anti-Fianna Fáil vote was now concentrated in just two parties rather than being spread over five, as had been the case in 1948, and this made the whole process of coalition negotiation that much simpler and more straightforward. Since fewer actors were involved, it was more likely that an agreement could be reached and that it would be maintained. In the second place, the new coalition was also facilitated by a change in the patterns of policy competition. It is to this issue that we now turn.

Policy competition

By the end of the 1960s and the beginning of the 1970s, both Labour and Fine Gael had moved to the left of the political spectrum and had begun to pursue what were essentially similar policy goals. The shift in Labour was most marked, even if largely rhetorical, and was symbolised most clearly in its slogan "The Seventies will be Socialist". But, perhaps surprisingly, Fine Gael had also moved to the left, abandoning many of the liberal, free-market policies which had characterised the party during the coalition period in the 1950s, and emphasising instead the need for social justice and redistribution, and for what it called "the Just Society", which was the name given to the election programme which the party first launched in 1965. Both parties therefore shared a common ground in what was a rather moderate social democratic agenda, and in a joint concern with the need for a more equitable redistribution of resources.

Fianna Fáil, on the other hand, more or less ignored such concerns, claiming that problems of poverty and injustice could best be solved simply through general economic growth. As Seán Lemass, party leader from 1959 to 1966, was wont to remark, "a rising tide lifts all boats". Such a view tended to characterise the

Fianna Fáil position throughout the postwar period, in that the party's programmes usually involved an appeal to three related elements. In the first place, as the only party capable of providing single-party administrations, Fianna Fáil persistently emphasised the need for strong and capable government, arguing that coalition alliances implied both indecisiveness and ineffectiveness. Second, as noted, the party emphasised the need for economic growth, arguing that any patterns of inequality and poverty could best be eradicated by increasing the size of the national cake. Third, and perhaps most importantly, the party stressed the need for social solidarity and the need to promote "the national interest", a plea which echoed its pre-war emphasis on territorial nationalism when it competed against Fine Gael (or, earlier, Cumann na nGaedheal), but which now, in the context of the competition between Fianna Fáil and all the other parties, became translated into an appeal for all sections of the (26-county) nation to work together in harmony. Together, these three elements combined into a more general "corporatist" ideology, which, by emphasising the importance of the national interest, deliberately set its face against any attempts to translate social conflict into politics. In other words, it was an ideology which opposed any attempt to mobilise the interests of, say, workers against employers, or of the under-privileged against the more privileged, or of the farmers against the urban dwellers, or of secular forces against the Catholic church. According to this ideology, all sections of society should, on the contrary, work together to promote the interest of the nation as a whole, of which Fianna Fáil, in turn, was the most effective guardian (see Mair, 1987, pp. 138-206).

Policy differences between the two sides were therefore quite marked, and this helped to give the 1973 coalition programme the sort of coherence which was so noticeably absent in the late 1940s and 1950s. Against traditional Fianna Fáil corporatism, Labour and the now more left-oriented Fine Gael were promoting a moderate social democratic appeal, emphasising the particular interests of the more under-privileged sections of the community rather than those of society as a whole.

Beginning with the Fine Gael-Labour coalition of 1973-77, governments alternated along the same pattern for 16 years, with Fianna Fáil returning in 1977, the coalition coming back once more in 1981, and then, following two short-lived alternating governments, coming to government once more in late 1982, before finally being displaced by a minority single-party Fianna Fáil government in 1987 (see appendix 3b). By then, however, the common political agenda which had been forged by Fine Gael and Labour had become little more than a matter of historical memory. The deep recession of the 1980s had encouraged Fine Gael's relatively well-to-do electorate to adopt a more self-interested view of politics and had undermined much of the party's commitment to redistribution. Fiscal rectitude now became the priority issue. At the same time, Labour had witnessed the gradual erosion of its electoral support during the coalition period, with its more conservative voters drifting towards Fine Gael or even Fianna Fáil, and with its more radical supporters turning towards the newly mobilised Workers' Party. Relations between the two erstwhile allies became more and more difficult, and in January 1987, following a dispute over the budget estimates, Labour withdrew from the coalition and from government. Indeed, when Fianna Fáil returned to office in 1987, the government which it replaced was a Fine Gael minority government, a caretaker administration which had remained in office for some two months following Labour's withdrawal.

In addition to the increasing divisions between Fine Gael and Labour, these last years had also witnessed a renewed and quite marked fragmentation of the party system. In the midst of the recession, the political spectrum had been widened to the right as a result of the emergence of the Progressive Democrats, a party which had initially resulted from a division within Fianna Fáil over its policies in relation to Northern Ireland, but which quickly won support from elements in both major parties on the basis of its essentially conservative economic policies and liberal stance on "moral" issues. The party made a major breakthrough in its first election in 1987, when it polled almost 12 per cent of the vote and won 14 Dáil seats. The spectrum had also been widened on the left, with the slow but steady growth of the Workers' Party, which polled almost 4 per cent of the vote in 1987 (it actually outpolled Labour in the Dublin area) and won four Dáil seats. The success of both parties also helped to drive an even greater wedge between Fine Gael and Labour, with the former moving to the right in an effort to stave off the challenge from the Progressive Democrats, and with the latter under pressure to move to the left in an effort to compete with the Workers' Party. By 1987, therefore, the anti-Fianna Fáil bloc, if such it may be called, had broken apart, and the parties, as well as perhaps the electorate, were more polarised than had been the case for decades.

Watersheds in the development of the party system
Three crucial watersheds can be identified in the overall development of the Irish party system. The *first* came in 1927, when Fianna Fáil emerged from the wilderness and decided to take its seats in the Dáil. In so doing, the party ensured that the intense conflict which had once been fought out as a civil war would now become largely a focus for electoral competition. Politics, in this sense, genuinely became war by other means, with the major dimension of competition pitting Sinn Féin/Fianna Fáil against Cumann na nGaedheal/Fine Gael, while Labour in particular struggled to promote an alternative basis for political alignment.

The *second* watershed came in 1948, when the strategies chosen by the new minor parties, and by Labour, confirmed that in future the key dimension of competition would be that of Fianna Fáil versus the rest, in which the voters would simply be asked to choose whether they wished to be governed by a single-party Fianna Fáil government or by a non-Fianna Fáil coalition, a choice which remained relevant right through to the 1970s and 1980s. The waning of the civil war opposition was also later underlined in the emergence of an increasingly relevant new policy divide, which saw Fianna Fáil insisting on its guardianship of "the national interest", as against the ever more evident social democratic appeal espoused by both Labour and Fine Gael. Nonetheless, despite the growing emphasis on this moderate social democracy, the constraints on party strategies imposed by this new pattern of competition were felt particularly hard by Labour, which found itself increasingly tied to the role of junior coalition partner in the anti-Fianna Fáil alignment, and which therefore found itself unable to mobilise an alternative political opposition. It is certainly the case that Labour had been weakened as a result of its marginalisation in 1918, and also as a result of the subsequent institutionalisation of civil war politics; but as Irish society modernised, and as the civil war opposition waned in importance, it was the strategic constraints imposed by an opposition pitting Fianna Fáil against all other parties which was to prove the most persistent bulwark against Labour's further progress.

The *third* watershed came in 1989, when this long-standing pattern of competition was broken, perhaps irrevocably, by Fianna Fáil's decision to enter a coalition with the Progressive Democrats. This last watershed was important in two ways. In the first place, precisely because Fianna Fáil now proved willing to play the coalition game, it was no longer the case that competition revolved around Fianna Fáil versus the rest. From this point on, in fact, Fianna Fáil was to become "just another party"—bigger and more successful than its opponents, to be sure, but certainly no different from them in any other important sense. This is indeed crucial, since for much of the postwar period Fianna Fáil's election propaganda was based on the fact that it was the only party which could conceivably guarantee single-party government, and hence which could ensure stability and continuity. Any alternative, it argued, would have to take the form of a coalition, and coalition government, at least according to Fianna Fáil, was, by definition, bad government. After 1989, however, it was clear that this familiar line could no longer be peddled with any degree of credibility.

Second, and perhaps more importantly, by playing the coalition game Fianna Fáil opened up the possibility that it would now remain almost permanently in office. The reason for this was simple enough: as the biggest single party, and as the party which was perhaps closest to the centre of the political spectrum, it would probably always seem easier for Fianna Fáil to find a coalition partner than would be the case for most of the other parties. Moreover, unless it was to suffer a massive and quite unprecedented erosion of support, Fianna Fáil in the future, as in 1989, would be likely to need just one other coalition partner in order to achieve a majority, whereas its smaller opponents would be required to forge deals involving three if not four parties in order to control a majority in the Dáil. Thus while Fianna Fáil's electoral position might indeed have weakened, and while it might well have abandoned its old shibboleths and become just another party, nevertheless, from a strategic point of view, it decision to become available for coalition probably placed it in a stronger position than it had been at any time in the two previous decades.

Fianna Fáil's strategic position was also enhanced by the fragmentation and polarisation of the non-Fianna Fáil side of the party system. Indeed, even if the party had retained its non-coalition policy, this process of fragmentation, as well as the numerous policy differences which divided the smaller parties from one another, would probably have been sufficient to ensure that no cohesive non-Fianna Fáil alliance could have emerged in the foreseeable future, even if, as in 1989, Fianna Fáil on its own were unable to muster a working majority. This relative advantage was to become even more apparent as the party attempted to move closer to the centre ground on issues relating to Northern Ireland and to church-state relations, in that these particular issues formerly constituted perhaps the only dimension of competition along which the various non-Fianna Fáil parties might have found common ground. That such common ground could prove relevant became all too apparent in the wake of Mary Robinson's successful election to the Presidency in 1990, and indeed it was the success of that campaign which helped to shift Fianna Fáil, judiciously, closer to a more moderate position.

Nevertheless, as the more conventional left-right political spectrum widened, and as the distances extended between the Progressive Democrats and Fine Gael, on the one hand, and Labour and the Workers' Party/Democratic Left, on the other, Fianna Fáil found itself sitting increasingly happily in the centre, ready to make deals with whatever other smaller party was willing to join it in coalition.

That said, the decision to coalesce in 1989 also carried certain risks for the party. As has been emphasised above, it was precisely Fianna Fáil's capacity to polarise party alignments into an opposition between itself, on the one hand, and all other parties on the other, which had structured and sustained the postwar party system, as well as Fianna Fáil's own position of dominance within that system. Once these constraints were loosened, however, as they were in 1989, the party system was likely to become much more volatile and unstable. The political market, in other words, was opened up, and hence those parties which had been sustained most strongly by the old alignment, especially Fianna Fáil itself, were likely to become more vulnerable.

Evidence of this new openness was clearly seen in 1992 (see Mair, 1993). Since competition was no longer structured by the opposition of Fianna Fáil against the rest, it had begun, in a sense, to cease being structured at all. Fianna Fáil clearly suffered from this change, electorally if not strategically, with its support falling to its lowest level since 1927. Fine Gael, whose role had long been reduced to that of leadership of the anti-Fianna Fáil alliance, also correspondingly suffered, falling to its lowest level of support since the nadir of 1948. Labour, on the other hand, whose fortunes had been most seriously curtailed by the traditional alignment, finally found the space in which to begin shedding its Cinderella status, and polled its highest share of the vote since 1922. Labour was later to follow the Progressive Democrats as Fianna Fáil's new junior partner in government, a move which, despite Fianna Fáil's electoral losses, did much to confirm the strategic advantage which the larger party enjoyed in the centre of the political spectrum.

In one sense, of course, it can be argued that Labour's decision to coalesce was simply a repeat of the mistakes which it had made in the late 1940s and early 1970s. Then, following earlier sporadic electoral successes, the party had gone on to join new coalition governments, only to find that its identity had become undermined and its potential for further growth had been stymied. This new situation is quite different, however. In the first place, and most obviously, Labour has entered coalition on the basis of a stronger Dáil position than ever before. Second, and more importantly, it has entered a coalition on the basis of choice rather than necessity. For the first time in its history, Labour found itself in a position (not unlike that of the small German FDP) in which it could choose between alternative governments. Throughout the postwar period, as noted above, Labour's options, however unpalatable, were relatively simple: it could either remain in opposition, or it could enter a coalition with Fine Gael. In 1992, however, the choice was widened to include the possibility of coalition with Fianna Fáil, and hence the party's bargaining position was strengthened immeasurably.

Third, and most importantly of all, Labour's decision to join Fianna Fáil rather than to try once again with Fine Gael (and the Progressive Democrats) finally confirmed the end of the old "Fianna Fáil versus the rest" party system. It was one thing for Fianna Fáil to break the mould by coalescing with the newly formed Progressive Democrats, many of whose leaders were actually former members of

Fianna Fáil (both PD ministers in the 1989 coalition government had formerly sat around the cabinet table as Fianna Fáil ministers). It was quite another thing for the party to reach across the traditional divide and form a coalition with one of "the rest". Once that had happened, everything would come up for grabs.

CONCLUSION

It is difficult to predict the future direction of the new party system that is emerging in the 1990s. The degree of stability of party systems in general depends on two related factors. The first is the stabilisation of voting patterns, which results from strong social cleavages, pinning down voters into particular alignments based on class, religion, region and other forms of collective identity. The second is the stabilisation of voting patterns, which results from a structured pattern of competition, in which voters are constrained by a limit on the range of available alternatives. In Britain, for example, the long-term stability of the party system was sustained not only by strong ties between party and class, but also by the fact that the only realistic governing alternatives were those represented by Labour, on the one hand, and the Conservatives, on the other. In Ireland, however, which was always characterised by a politics "without social bases", only the second of these factors came into play, with the overall stability being primarily ensured by the paramount need to choose between Fianna Fáil and its opponents.

This is now no longer the case. On the one hand, Fianna Fáil on its own is no longer such a credible alternative. In the future, as now, it is likely to require partners in government. At the same time, it is also no longer distinct from its traditional opponents, nor they from it. If coalition with Labour is possible, then who is to argue against the future possibility of coalition with Fine Gael? It is in this sense that all the options are now open, with both the electors and the parties being no longer constrained and hence no longer so predictable. For now, at least, the party system has become unstructured.

REFERENCES AND FURTHER READING

Carty, R. K., 1981. *Party and Parish Pump: Electoral Politics in Ireland*. Waterloo, Ontario: Wilfrid Laurier Press.

Coakley, John, 1987. "The election in context: historical and European perspectives", pp. 153-72 in Laver, Mair and Sinnott (1987).

Farrell, Brian, 1970. "Labour and the Irish political party system: a suggested approach to analysis", *Economic and Social Review* 1:4, pp. 477-502.

Farrell, Brian, 1990. "Forming the government", pp. 179-91 in Gallagher and Sinnott (1990).

Gallagher, Michael, 1982. *The Irish Labour Party in Transition, 1957-82*. Manchester: Manchester University Press.

Gallagher, Michael, 1985. *Political Parties in the Republic of Ireland*. Manchester: Manchester University Press.

Gallagher, Michael and Michael Laver (eds), 1993. *How Ireland Voted 1992*. Dublin: Folens and Limerick: PSAI Press.

Gallagher, Michael, Michael Laver and Peter Mair, 1992. *Representative Government in Western Europe*. New York: McGraw-Hill.

Gallagher, Michael and Richard Sinnott (eds), 1990. *How Ireland Voted 1989*. Galway: Centre for the Study of Irish Elections and PSAI Press.

Garvin, Tom, 1974. "Political cleavages, party politics, and urbanisation in Ireland: the case of the periphery-dominated centre", *European Journal of Political Research* 2:4, pp. 307-27.

Laver, Michael and Audrey Arkins, 1990. "Coalition and Fianna Fáil", pp. 192-207 in Gallagher and Sinnott (1990).

Laver, Michael, Peter Mair and Richard Sinnott (eds), 1987. *How Ireland Voted: The Irish General Election 1987*. Swords: Poolbeg Press.

Laver, Michael and Kenneth A. Shepsle, 1992. "Election results and coalition possibilities in Ireland", *Irish Political Studies* 7, pp. 57-72.

Lipset, S. M. and Stein Rokkan, 1967. "Cleavage structures, party systems, and voter alignments: an introduction", pp. 1-64 in S. M. Lipset and Stein Rokkan (eds), *Party Systems and Voter Alignments*. New York: The Free Press.

Mair, Peter, 1979. "The autonomy of the political: the development of the Irish party system", *Comparative Politics* 11:4, pp. 445-65.

Mair, Peter, 1986. "Locating Irish parties on a left-right scale", *Political Studies* 34:3, pp. 456-65.

Mair, Peter, 1987. *The Changing Irish Party System: Organisation, Ideology and Electoral Competition*. London: Frances Pinter.

Mair, Peter, 1990. "The Irish party system into the 1990s", pp. 208-20 in Gallagher and Sinnott (1990).

Mair, Peter, 1992. "Explaining the absence of class politics in Ireland", pp. 383-410 in J. H. Goldthorpe and C. T. Whelan (eds), *The Development of Industrial Society in Ireland*. Oxford: Oxford University Press.

Mair, Peter, 1993. "Fianna Fáil, Labour and the Irish party system", pp. 162-73 in Gallagher and Laver (1993).

Manning, Maurice, 1972. *Irish Political Parties: an Introduction*. Dublin: Gill and Macmillan.

Penniman, Howard R. (ed.), 1978. *Ireland at the Polls: the Dáil Elections of 1977*. Washington, DC: American Enterprise Institute for Public Policy Research.

Penniman, Howard R. and Brian Farrell (eds), 1987. *Ireland at the Polls, 1981, 1982, and 1987: a Study of Four General Elections*. Durham, NC: Duke University Press.

Rumpf, Erhard and A. C. Hepburn, 1977. *Nationalism and Socialism in Twentieth-Century Ireland*. Liverpool: Liverpool University Press.

Sinnott, Richard, 1978. "The electorate", pp. 35-67 in Penniman (1978).

Sinnott, Richard, 1984. "Interpretations of the Irish party system", *European Journal of Political Research* 12:3, pp. 289-307.

Whyte, John H., 1974. "Ireland: politics without social bases", pp. 619-51 in Richard Rose (ed.), *Electoral Behavior: A Comparative Handbook*. New York: The Free Press.

6 / PARTIES AND VOTERS

Michael Laver and Michael Marsh

These days we think of parties and elections as two sides of the same coin—we no longer find one without the other. Yet, although elections have been held for millennia, parties as we know them have a relatively recent pedigree, dating back only to the nineteenth century. Furthermore, Irish parties are even younger than those found in other parts of Europe, as we have seen in chapter 5, though the Labour Party claims to have been founded before the creation of the state.

The relationship between parties and elections is absolutely central to the working of parliamentary democracy, both in Ireland and elsewhere. This is because parties bring some logic and structure to the choice faced by voters on polling day. At the very least they provide voters with a choice between opposing teams of politicians, as different parties nominate different sets of candidates for the legislature and senior party politicians hold themselves out to the electorate as possible government ministers. Parties may also present voters with clear-cut policy options, allowing people to select the policies as well as the personnel of government.

Despite their central role in the democratic process, political parties in Ireland and elsewhere are typically treated as private organisations not subject to extensive public regulation. Thus, while the conduct of elections in Ireland is scrupulously regulated by laws and the constitution, the conduct of political parties, in choosing candidates or raising finance for example, is regulated only by the parties themselves.

Because choices of party leaders, policies and candidates are so fundamental to politics, we devote the first part of this chapter to the way in which Irish political parties conduct their internal affairs. We show that Irish parties are responding to changes in their environment. In particular, party leaders are tending to become more prominent, while rank-and-file members are tending to become less important, in response to a pattern of high profile and personalised campaign coverage by Dublin-based broadcast media that increasingly dominate the channels of political communication.

A parliamentary democracy such as Ireland can function effectively only if party legislators are relatively disciplined, voting for the most part according to the strategies determined by party leaders. If they do not do this—and such a situation arose in the French Fourth Republic, for example—then governments can never be sure from day to day of their legislative majority and are likely to be very unstable. Yet party legislators behave in a disciplined manner only if party membership is valuable to them, making the threat of expulsion from the party, or even of the less serious sanction of suspension from the parliamentary party, something to be taken seriously. Furthermore, the value of a party label depends very much on whether voters give their support consistently to parties rather than to individual candidates. If voters support individual candidates rather than parties, then politicians can defy the party line and generally behave as mavericks, in the knowledge that they can nonetheless hold onto their seats at the next election.

The second part of the chapter, therefore, will look at what seems to influence voters when they make their choices. We will see that there is a growing body of evidence suggesting that some at least of the traditional social bases of party support are beginning to change.

IRISH PARTY ORGANISATION

All modern political parties have a group of active supporters whose role goes well beyond the simple act of voting. These people normally join an organisation, pay a membership fee, and thereby acquire the right to participate in certain party activities. This often gives members at least the formal capacity to influence the formation of party policy, as well as the selection of party election candidates and party leaders. Participation is more significant in some parties than in others, in part because not all parties have the same rules and structures—though formal structures do not always tell us the full story.

The best way to assess the internal power structure of parties is to look at how, in practice, they make key political decisions. We therefore look below at three types of decision made by Irish political parties—candidate selection, the choice of party leader, and policy formation. First, however, we look at the general organisation of Irish parties and at how such organisations are maintained and financed. We will confine our attention to those parties currently represented in the Dáil, and in particular to the more established parties, Fianna Fáil, Fine Gael and Labour. Where the experience of any of the newer parties is significantly different, we will point this out.

Party structure

The organisational heart of most Irish parties is a central office. This provides back-up to deputies and coordinates local branches scattered all over the country. central office is staffed largely by full-time officials in larger parties but by volunteers only in smaller ones. Even Fianna Fáil, however, Ireland's largest political party, employed only ten full-time staff in late 1992, a tiny number in comparison to equivalent parties in most other European countries. This lack of resources places clear limits on the exercise of central control and in many respects Irish parties are quite decentralised, with local organisations retaining a high degree of autonomy.

The local branch (called a cumann in Fianna Fáil and a local group in the Green Party) is the basic unit of most political parties. These branches vary in size, but each party sets a formal minimum membership of around ten people (five for Labour in rural areas). A party normally has a number of branches in each Dáil constituency and these send delegates to a constituency council (variously called) which handles candidate selection and the conduct of elections. In larger parties there is also an intermediate tier at local government constituency level, which deals with local elections. Party organisation is thus constructed from the "grassroots" upwards. Despite their status as the building blocks of party organisation, the existence of particular party branches is often rather indefinite. Fianna

Fáil, for instance, estimates that it has almost 3,000 branches, although several hundred of these might not be registered in any one year. In addition, and despite the rules, some branches exist only on paper, being created to allow the supporters of certain local politicians to have more votes at constituency councils and in internal party elections. Some party leaderships have sought to contain this practice; in May 1978, Fine Gael under Garret FitzGerald introduced new procedures into its constitution to stop this tactic.

At the summit of this organisational pyramid is the national conference (called an ard-fheis in Fianna Fáil, Fine Gael and the Workers' Party, and a convention by the Greens) which in theory is the supreme policy-making body of the party. This comprises delegates from the branches, plus public representatives and party officials. It is a large and unwieldy body that meets infrequently, usually once a year. Such meetings have tended to be great social and political occasions. Whatever their limitations as policy making bodies, they function as rallies designed to reinforce the faith and commitment of the rank and file and to enable the party to demonstrate unity and enthusiasm to the outside world. Currently, such weekend conventions are giving way to more low-key one-day events, tailored much more to the demands of the broadcast media than to participation by delegates. While financial and publicity considerations provide the main explicit justification for such changes, they also reflect the declining importance of ordinary party members.

Between national conferences, the management of the party is in the hands of an executive committee. Though its name and precise composition vary from party to party, it normally comprises people elected by members, plus others representing party TDs (for more details of party organisation see Mair, 1987a and Farrell, 1992).

Figure 6.1 shows a typical party structure, in this case that of Fianna Fáil. It shows the cumann at the base, sending delegates to local and Dáil constituency organisations. Each of these units in turn sends representatives to the ard-fheis. In between meetings of the ard-fheis, the party is under the authority of the national executive, which supervises the party bureaucracy located in central office. The parliamentary party is represented strongly in the national executive; of course, parliamentarians are elected by ordinary voters (or by local councillors in the case of senators) and not by the cumainn. There are some differences of detail between this structure and those of the other Irish parties, but the essential features are the same.

Party finance

Whatever their organisational structure, all political parties need money and Irish parties are certainly no exception. Gone are the days when it was enough to have an army of dedicated volunteers willing to knock on doors, stuff envelopes and drive people to the polls on a wet and windy night, all for the love of the party. An army of volunteers is still an extremely useful asset, but a modern high-tech election campaign depends upon a coterie of specialists and a lot of expensive equipment. Computers must be bought, trained staff must be employed, offices must be rented, and phone, fax and postage bills must be covered; in addition, there are opinion polls to be commissioned, videos to be produced, posters to be printed, campaign buses and helicopters to be hired, manifestos to be published, and so on. Running a modern political party in the age of information technology is an expensive business, which costs the largest party, Fianna Fáil, about a million pounds each year. Fine Gael spent about £600,000 in 1992, Labour about £250,000 and the PDs about £200,000 (*Sunday Tribune*, 17 January 1993). Where do Irish parties get all of this money from?

Figure 6.1: Organisational structure of the Fianna Fáil party

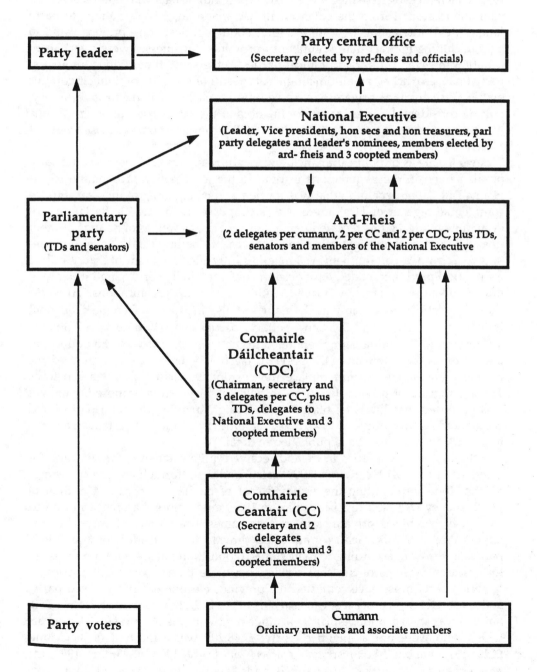

The short answer to this question is that nobody knows precisely; as both Michael Gallagher (1985, p. 130) and Peter Mair (1987a, p. 106) note, this matter is "shrouded in secrecy". This is because, while most parties get some state support, several also receive quite extensive contributions from private sources about which they are most unwilling to give any information. This was highlighted during the long-running Tribunal of Inquiry into the Beef Industry that began in 1991, which investigated allegations that certain individuals who had received favourable treatment from the government had made large contributions to party funds. Much interesting new information about political contributions came to light, including the fact that a number of prominent businesses were clearly contributing to several different political parties at the same time. Public interest in party finances reached an all-time high. As a result of the glare of publicity on this matter, it seems that private donors became much less willing to give money, putting considerable pressure on the finances of the big parties, although Fianna Fáil was reported in early 1993 to retain 300 corporate sponsors (*Irish Press*, 11 March 1993).

Several aspects of political financing were addressed in 1993, as a result of proposals agreed in the negotiations leading to the joint policy programme of the Fianna Fáil-Labour coalition that was formed at the beginning of the year. First, a confidential register of TDs' interests was proposed, requiring the declaration of even quite modest sums received personally by TDs, as well as of a range of other financial matters that might affect their capacity to be impartial public representatives. Second, a commitment was made to introduce a system of state funding for political parties, intended to undermine the potentially corrupting influence of money given in secret by private individuals and organisations. In some European countries—notably in Germany but also in Austria, Denmark, Finland, Italy, Norway, Spain and Sweden—political parties can rely on quite significant state funding. The initial sum mentioned in the Irish context was one pound per annum for every vote won in the previous election, subject to a maximum of one million pounds. This would replace the current Oireachtas grant (see below). Third, a register of private donations to political parties was proposed. Finally it was proposed that limits be placed on campaign spending by both parties and candidates. By the middle of 1993, however, only the proposal to establish a register of TDs' interests had been published in detail.

Actually, political parties in Ireland received quite extensive state funding for some time prior to 1993. Farrell (1992) calculated that, through one mechanism or another (but not counting the assumed cost of media coverage), £4 million of public money was paid to Irish parties in 1989, much more than parties received from their combined private sources. This comes in a variety of ways, but the largest slice is the Oireachtas grant, paid directly to the leaders of "qualified" parties in the Dáil, according to their status. Opposition parties, with no access to the research facilities of the civil service, get more than government parties. A qualified party must have contested the previous election as an organised party, and must have won at least seven seats. In 1992 £125,130 was paid to Fianna Fáil, but this was shared under a private arrangement with the Progressive Democrats (PDs), who were not a qualified party; £248,205 was paid to Fine Gael and £123,313 to Labour (*Administration Yearbook and Diary*, 1993, p. 456). In 1993, the two government parties, Fianna Fáil and Labour, were expected to receive

£90,000 and £39,000 respectively. Fine Gael was due to receive £256,658 and the PDs £127,512 (*Irish Times*, 9 January 1993). There is also money for administrative staff and secretaries for the Oireachtas press office, money for parties to employ a youth education officer (if they have a youth section), and allowances to TDs for travel and postage. Some of these expenses serve to defray costs that would otherwise have to be met by the parties, but TDs' allowances are much less generous than in many other countries and they do not stretch to supporting research staff for deputies of the kind that legislators in other countries enjoy. Parties have relatively few permanent employees and rely for research expertise on volunteers or, when in government, on civil servants.

In addition to this, Irish parties receive benefits in kind at election time, in the form of free airtime for "party election broadcasts". This time is made available to parties on the basis of a formula used by RTE that takes account both of a party's current Dáil representation and of the number of candidates it has nominated. This airtime is a very significant asset, though difficult to quantify; it would cost a lot if it had to be paid for. Since so many Irish homes now have access to a range of non-Irish television stations, it is difficult to know how many voters switch channels or turn the sound down when party election broadcasts fill the screen. Nonetheless, this facility does offer even small and poor parties a chance to make a case directly to the entire Irish electorate, a chance used to good effect by the Green Party, for example.

So it is certainly not true to say that Irish parties receive no state aid, though they do receive much less than those in some other European countries. The trend is for the level of state aid to increase. This may downgrade the importance of the other main sources of party finance—membership dues, fundraising activities and private contributions—although parties may simply spend ever more money as it becomes available. As we have seen, the matter of private contributions remains a controversial issue on which the main parties have traditionally been quite secretive. The other sources of finance are rather easier to assess.

Party memberships are probably declining (see below) and are therefore likely to provide a diminishing source of revenue, but the activities of members nonetheless remain very important to the finances of Irish parties. While Fianna Fáil, unusually, does not have a formal membership fee, its members assist the collection of party funds in other ways—by making a voluntary subscription, by organising a national "church gate" collection, and by participating in a members' lottery. These are very significant sources of income for the party but it is notable that returns from the church gate collection have declined sharply in recent years from a peak of almost £500,000 in 1983 to an estimated £345,000 in 1991 (Fianna Fáil, 1991). Fine Gael also has a lottery. Membership dues provide vital income for the other parties, which also organise less successful national collections. Labour has an additional source of income in trade union affiliation fees. All parties also engage in a range of ad hoc fundraising activities and functions, and the low level of state funding for parties certainly makes the need to raise cash a continuing preoccupation (for a more detailed analysis of party finance, see Mair 1987a, pp. 106-13).

Finally, it is worth noting that all parties rely heavily on their bankers at election time and are typically allowed to run quite large overdrafts in order to finance campaign expenses. This practice has become more marked as overall expenditure has increased. Currently, most Irish parties are carrying substantial debts left over from several recent elections. In early 1993 Fianna Fáil was widely reported to be £3 million in debt, having spent about £1 million in the November 1992 election. Interest payments on its bank debt are reported to have increased from £215,000 in 1991 to £500,000 in 1993 (*Irish Times*, 4 February 1993). Fine Gael were reported to owe the banks a million pounds, Labour £120,000 and the PDs £80,000 (*Sunday Tribune*, 17 January 1993). Certainly as far as Fianna Fáil was concerned, the problem of servicing bank debt had reached crisis proportions by early 1993. Drastic plans to sell the party headquarters and slash staffing levels were discussed, while interest-free loans of £1000 were sought from party members (*Irish Press*, 11 March 1993). Ultimately, the cash crises facing some of the Irish parties may provide the impetus for a shift towards much more state funding. It is possible that, for no more sinister reason than a fear of not getting its money back, a bank could seriously undermine the prospects of a particular party by taking a tough line on credit. While there is no suggestion at present that this might happen, it is at least a hypothetical prospect that sits rather uneasily with the notion of parliamentary democracy.

Party membership

This money is raised and spent by the people who make up the party: the rank and file members, party officials, deputies and, last but not least, the party leader. As we have already seen, party branches can sometimes have a shadowy existence. It is indeed only quite recently that parties have kept records of how many members they have and Fianna Fáil still does not do so. In general, most party membership figures in Ireland remain a combination of guesswork and wishful thinking. Many party members, furthermore, are merely nominal and are certainly not active. Estimates of party membership, such as they are, are reported in Table 6.1. These figures were supplied by the parties themselves, and may well involve considerable over-estimates of membership.

Table 6.1 shows the memberships of the different parties at the time of the 1992 general election, the votes won by different parties and the ratio between these figures. Fianna Fáil claims roughly one member for every nine voters. It is striking that in all other major parties the ratio is much lower, with Labour having only

Table 6.1: Party members and voters, 1992

	Members 1992	Voters 1992	Number of voters per member
Fianna Fáil	75,000	674,650	9
Fine Gael	25.000	422,106	17
Labour	10,000	333,013	33
PDs	7,000	80,787	12
Greens	1,200	24,110	20

Note: The total excludes votes cast for "other" parties and candidates. Information on membership of Democratic Left and of the Workers' Party in the Republic was not available.
Source: Marsh, Wilford, Arthur and Fitzgerald (1993).

one member for every 33 voters. Around two-thirds of all those belonging to an Irish political party seem to belong to Fianna Fáil; if this is the case, it gives the party a real organisational advantage at election time.

Overall, however, relatively few people belong to political parties in Ireland. The figures above suggest that something like 120,000 people are party members, less than six per cent of the electorate and well below the European average of 13 per cent (Gallagher, Laver and Mair, 1992, Table 5.1). This reflects the fact that parties are more narrowly political in Ireland than in some other parts of Europe. Many European social democratic and christian democratic parties have sought to provide organisations that cater for the whole of a member's social life from the cradle to the grave. Fianna Fáil, which has seen itself as a national movement, comes closest to this model and perhaps for this reason has always promoted a wider concept of party membership. The smaller more radical parties, such as the Workers' Party or Sinn Féin, tend to place very heavy demands upon members and demand a very high level of year-round commitment. The other Irish parties, however, are essentially electoral organisations.

Party membership also appears to be in decline in Ireland. Fine Gael leader John Bruton freely admitted (*Irish Times*, 22 January 1991) that his party's membership level was a long way down from that attained in the early 1980s, while Fianna Fáil also seems sure that its membership is not what it used to be. Activists seem to be less active, judging by the results of recent national collections, and even a recent party report admitted that membership was "static" while the age profile of members showed that the party was getting collectively older (Fianna Fáil, 1991). The few thousand members picked up by new parties such as the PDs, Greens, Workers' Party and Democratic Left are not enough to offset the membership losses suffered by the traditional parties.

Party candidates and officials

In general the nomination of candidates for elections is a highly decentralised process in Ireland, allowing considerable participation by rank and file members. In recent years, however, there are signs that the party leadership would like to exert much more control over this.

Candidate selection varies little between the different parties. Typically it is carried out by members delegated by the various local party branches in the area in which the election is to take place. For Dáil elections, each branch in a Dáil constituency sends delegates to a constituency convention which decides both how many candidates to select and who these people are to be. Direct membership participation in this process can quite extensive, on one estimate ranging from about ten per cent (in the PDs) to over 40 per cent (in Fine Gael) though indirect participation in the process is even higher (Gallagher, 1988, p. 126). In the case of the Green Party and Democratic Left, candidate selection is handled directly by the membership as a whole, and not via a delegate convention.

The criteria for candidate selection in Ireland seem to be essentially pragmatic. What is most valuable to an aspiring candidate is a track record in winning votes or, if he or she has not stood for election before, being well enough known in the area to stand a good chance of doing so. Neither the political views of the aspiring candidate nor his or her potential as a legislator seem to carry much weight. When several candidates are selected by the same party, there seems to be little concern to achieve any social balance (by age, gender or social class for example), though in rural areas candidates will almost always come from different parts of the constituency, particularly where this significantly crosses a county boundary.

The nomination of candidates by local branches is subject to some control by central party organisations. Typically, the centre has considerable formal powers. These allow the national executive or party leadership to veto a particular candidate, to nominate additional candidates, and to decide how many candidates should stand in any particular area—in fact, to take all key decisions on candidate selection. In practice, it is quite common for the central party to determine how many candidates there should be in each constituency, but other powers have been exercised only rarely. Local members have become accustomed to choosing candidates and it is local activists, of course, who must do the voluntary work that helps to get these nominees elected. They also argue that the local party, because of its knowledge of the constituency, has the necessary expertise to identify the candidates best equipped to win. Attempts by central party organisations to "parachute" a prominent outsider into a local constituency have usually been deeply resented at local level. In the same way, vetoing a candidate can be risky if local activists rally around the excluded person, who then stands as an independent. Smaller parties such as Labour have been vulnerable to such threats in the past; in the larger ones, the party label has proved more effective, giving the party leadership stronger de facto control over party affairs.

This reluctance to intervene has been less evident over the last few elections, although use of a party leader's veto remains rare. Local parties are often effectively under the control of local deputies, whose personal supporters may occupy all key posts. This has sometimes meant that candidate selection has favoured the interests of particular local incumbents, at the expense of the party in general. In Fine Gael in particular, many deputies have been suspected of engineering the selection of a weak running mate, or no running mate at all. Opportunities to win an extra seat were not taken because the incumbent feared the risk to his or her own seat. The Fine Gael leadership intervened often in the 1980s to alleviate this danger, adding candidates to the list of those nominated (see O'Byrnes, 1986). The Fianna Fáil national executive has done the same, and is likely to intervene more in future, especially in marginal constituencies. Concern about the quality of deputies as legislators has also justified greater involvement, often informal, by the party leadership.

In addition to candidates, members elect a number of other party officials. Branch members elect branch officials, as well as nominating delegates to constituency conventions and national conferences. A party's national executive committee also contains a number of people directly elected by the annual conference. Although this committee is formally the decision making body within the party between meetings of the annual conference, in most parties it defers in practice to the party leader.

Party leaders
It is arguable that the choice of party leader is the most important decision facing any party. Elections are as much about who governs as about what leaders do when they govern, so that the party leader is a key figurehead of any party's campaign. In Fianna Fáil and Fine Gael, furthermore, the party leader is a potential Taoiseach, so these parties, when they choose a leader, make a decision of major national significance.

While rank-and-file members participate quite fully in the selection of local candidates, they have no direct say in the choice of a national party leader. In Fianna Fáil, Fine Gael, the PDs and Democratic Left, selection of the parliamentary leader (effectively *the* leader, even when there is some other formal post such as party President) is made solely by parliamentarians. Fianna Fáil, the PDs and Democratic Left restrict the vote to members of the Dáil; Fine Gael allows senators and members of the European Parliament a vote as well. The Labour Party used to operate the system currently employed by Fianna Fáil but, under new rules adopted in 1989, the election of a Labour leader (who must be a member of the parliamentary party) involves party members as a whole. It is certain that this change will alter the character of the election, given the need for candidates to campaign much more publicly than has been common in the past.

Even where they have no formal role, however, rank-and-file members of any party have some indirect influence on who becomes leader. In the election of a new Fianna Fáil leader in 1992, for example, most deputies consulted their constituency members before the vote took place, and several local parties held meetings, following which clear messages were sent to their local deputies. The voice of the ordinary party member was particularly evident in 1983, when the then Fianna Fáil leader, Charles Haughey, in "the night of the long phone calls", used his popularity amongst the party rank and file to improve his standing with deputies on the eve of a challenge to his position.

When the decision on the party leadership is confined to parliamentarians, a single question seems to be uppermost in everyone's minds—who is most likely to boost party support in the next election? Most new leaders have been selected after a very muted campaign, and certainly not one that has put issues to the fore. As with candidate selection, it is the perception of a person's vote-winning ability that is decisive. However, when the electorate is extended to all party members, who may have little to gain directly from election victories and who may be more concerned that certain core values of the party be maintained, then the situation may be rather different. Hence issues and policies will probably have a higher profile in future leadership elections within the Labour Party.

The formation of party policy

While the ordinary member continues to have a real say in candidate selection, the member's voice may be little more than an echo of the party leadership when it comes to deciding the policies on which these candidates campaign. The formation of party policy in Ireland, as in most other democracies, presents a series of fascinating contrasts between theory and reality. In theory, as we have seen, the official policy of each of the main Irish parties is made at an annual conference involving a large number of party representatives, both local and national, as well as activists and ordinary members. In practice, this body is too large, too diffuse, and meets too rarely to make effective strategic decisions about party policy. A partial exception is the Labour national conference, which has in the past laid down the law on matters such as coalition—for example, binding the party leadership not to go into coalition without coming back to a special delegate conference for permission to do this. Although the national conference was downgraded in Labour's new (1991) constitution, a special delegate conference was nonetheless required before Labour could enter coalition with Fianna Fáil in 1993 (Farrell, 1993). The Workers' Party has also made momentous decisions about its future policies and organisations at national conferences, and it was as a consequence of a vote at a special delegate conference that the party split in 1992, with six of the seven deputies leaving the party to found what became the Democratic Left.

For the most part, however, national conferences that fill large halls are seen as far too cumbersome to generate effective party policy documents. This task normally falls to the party's national executive. Even here, however, the purview of the official decision-making body is limited, especially when the party concerned is in government. When senior party politicians make up the cabinet and only one party is in power, the effective policy making body of the party is the cabinet—it is as simple as that. A national executive might make some decision that conflicted with a cabinet decision, but it would have very little real control over the individuals concerned, and its decisions would have relatively little effect. In the popular mind, party policy would certainly be cabinet policy, not some theoretical policy propounded by the national executive. The policy of a government party, in effect, is the policy promoted by the cabinet minister with jurisdiction over the area concerned. A wise Irish voter wanting to find out about Fianna Fáil policy on third level education, therefore, will look not at the party's official election manifesto, but at the policies that the Fianna Fáil Minister for Education promotes while in office. The role of the relevant minister in setting policy can be seen quite clearly by tracing the effects of a series of cabinet changes over the 1992-93 period. In a number of key policy areas, perhaps the most dramatic of which was the availability of condoms, new ministers introduced quite new policies.

Even when a party is in opposition, its parliamentary party designates a set of senior politicians to "shadow" cabinet ministers in the Dáil and to act as party spokespersons on the policy areas concerned. They make the party's Dáil statements on these policies, attack the government ministers concerned, and are the people to whom the media turn for "official" party reaction. Members of this "shadow cabinet" develop policy expertise in the area for which they are responsible, and are in effect the main engines of policy development for the party, whatever the party rulebook might say.

Irish parties: the balance sheet

Irish parties, with their strange names and roots in a civil war, are often seen to be outside the European mainstream, but in many respects they are not so different from their European counterparts. Some of the trends that we have identified in Ireland can be found elsewhere. Falling membership, centrally directed campaigns and financial difficulties characterise parties in many countries. In many ways, indeed, the structure of Irish parties is essentially quite modern. In much of Europe, so-called "mass" parties replaced more informal earlier structures that existed simply to support parliamentary groups. Mass parties grew out of social movements, and were concerned with far more than simply elections. Over the last few decades, however, it has become clear in Europe that the era of the mass party is over. All parties, whatever their origins, are coming to resemble one another in their central concern with fighting and winning legislative elections. This concern is very apparent in Irish parties, and goes some way to explain the increasing role of the party elite. The major role played by the parliamentary leadership in Ireland is also typical. Attempts to construct parties in which deputies are under the firm control of the party organisation have, for the most part, been unsuccessful. As far as both the selection of national leaders and the choice of de facto policies are concerned, party TDs and in particular the most senior party politicians are the key decision makers.

In an attempt to buck this trend, the Green Party in Ireland, like its counter-parts elsewhere, has tried to construct a more democratic organisation. There is no party leader, merely a "coordinator" elected by the Coordinating Committee. Local groups elect "facilitators". Delegates to higher bodies should normally serve for a short, limited term to ensure rotation of office, and all members may attend any party meeting as observers. Decisions, say the party's rules, should be reached by consensus where possible. Efforts are made to consult widely within the party before policy decisions are made. Yet, before the party can really claim to be different, these procedures will have to be tested when it has a significant parliamentary presence, something which is currently no more than an aspiration.

All this is not to say that modern Irish parties are just like those nineteenth century elitist organisations that the mass parties replaced. Ordinary members do play a role, and this is not confined to funding the organisation which they sup-port. In particular, they exercise considerable influence on the choice of candi-dates who will bear the party label at election time. Furthermore, as we argued in the introduction, the power of the party leadership is made possible only by the fact that voters tend to give their support to national party labels rather than to individual local candidates. To a large extent, therefore, the internal affairs of Irish parties are determined by the voting behaviour of the Irish electorate—the matter to which we now turn.

PATTERNS OF VOTING BEHAVIOUR IN IRELAND

When political scientists study patterns in the votes cast for different political parties, they usually have in mind some kind of "model" that sets out to explain why people vote at all. Two different models of voting behaviour have become current in recent times. One of these assumes that voting is a form of self-expression; the other assumes that people vote in order to have an effect on how society is run. We briefly describe these models before discussing how much each of them can add to our understanding of voting behaviour in Ireland, and we go on to look at the importance of political issues, social background and personality factors as determinants of voting choice.

Two models of voting behaviour

The "party identification" model is based on the idea that voting is an act of self-expression. Every individual in society is "socialised" into a set of beliefs and atti-tudes by a complex process involving parents, teachers, church, friends, peers and the mass media. As a result of this process of socialisation, people may come to "identify" with a particular political party. Thus US voters may come to see themselves as being either "Democrats" or "Republicans", while Irish voters, ac-cording to this account, might come to identify themselves closely with Fianna Fáil, Fine Gael or Labour, for example. Such attachments change only very slowly, and go much deeper than a vote cast at any particular election. Thus a Republican identifier in the US may "defect" and may vote for the Democrats at a given election—under the influence of some particular candidate, issue, or scandal—but will continue to identify with the Republicans and see a vote for the Democrats as a deviation from this. In the most boring election imaginable, with no hot issues, scandals or colourful candidates, every voter would vote according to his or her party identification.

While the "party identification" model sees voting largely as an expression of identity, the "rational choice" model is based on the idea that casting a vote is a purposeful act designed to achieve something. Every individual in society has a set of desires. Some of these may be very basic human needs—the desire for food, warmth and shelter, for example. Other desires are products of the socialisation process—the desire for a united Ireland, for example, or the desire for nuclear disarmament. The rational choice model assumes that people vote in such a way as to bring their desires closer to fulfilment. A person thus votes for the party that seems most likely to guarantee food, warmth and shelter, or to bring about a united Ireland or nuclear disarmament, if these are the desires that he or she wants to satisfy. According to this approach, voters have no psychological loyalty to any given party, but rather pick the party that seems most likely to deliver what they want at each election. They may of course vote over and over again for the same party, but they do this because the same party is always their best choice, not because they are particularly loyal to it.

Most popular accounts of party choice in Ireland set great store by traditional party loyalties, and thus fit better with the party identification model. The origins of the two main Irish parties are typically traced to the civil war, and party loyalties are said to have been handed down within families from that point onwards. It is assumed that most families can be classified quite easily as "Fianna Fáil families" or "Fine Gael families", for instance, and that Irish people socialised into voting a particular way stay loyal, more or less regardless of the current policies of "their" party (for an engaging and lucid presentation of this view see Waters, 1991). Yet there is also some recognition that the importance of such traditional loyalties is probably less now than it may have been in years gone by. Dick Walsh, recalling a 1960s television programme which showed party activists seated on a hillside pointing out the party affiliations of the different households scattered around the valley, suggested that the exercise would be impossible in 1992: "[they] could safely base their judgements on tradition and the assumption that families voted en bloc; nowadays they couldn't even be sure that everyone went to mass" (*Irish Times*, 18 January 1992).

Notwithstanding traditional loyalties, it is common to assume that the hopes and fears of the electorate constrain Irish parties in the choice of policies that they can offer. It would be seen by most people as electoral suicide for a party to promote abortion on demand, for example, or to suggest that Northern Ireland security forces be allowed to patrol on both sides of the border. Thus most commentators do feel that Irish parties cannot trade on the loyalty of their supporters to promote just any old policy on anything—in other words they feel that, at least in part, Irish voters do choose whom to support on the basis of party policy positions.

Unfortunately, we have little evidence to examine the merits of these two approaches in the Irish case. Survey evidence from other countries, however, and evidence relating to the stability of voting patterns in Ireland and elsewhere over

very long periods and across generations (see chapter 5) suggests that the party
identification approach explains a great deal about how Irish voters make up their
minds about which party to support. Survey evidence also shows, however, that
this is not the full story; a rational choice element has always been present, and it
may, indeed, have been getting stronger in recent years.

Issues
Despite the apparent closeness of the two main parties on key dimensions of policy, discussion of issues does play a major role in election campaigns in Ireland,
as it does elsewhere. According to the opinion polls, by far the most important issue in recent elections has been unemployment. Asked during the 1992 election
what were "the main issues the parties should be addressing in this election campaign", fully 86 percent of those surveyed cited unemployment (Marsh and
Sinnott, 1993). Both taxation and the health service were also highly rated in recent campaigns, with interest rates being an additional preoccupation in 1992
(Laver, Marsh and Sinnott, 1987; Marsh and Sinnott, 1990; Marsh and Sinnott,
1993; Sinnott, 1994: Table 6.7). In these campaigns, "social" issues such as abortion, divorce and contraception, as well as the Northern Ireland problem, rated
very low on the priorities of most voters. The low rating of the abortion issue was
particularly striking in 1992, since controversial referendums on the issue were
held at the same time as the election. Despite this, only four percent of voters
rated abortion as one of the main issues in the election (Marsh and Sinnott, 1993).
Above all, therefore, Irish voters seem to be concerned at election time with economic policy.

On the face of it, however, few Irish people seem to vote on the basis of the
policies that parties put forward—even their economic policies. Asked during the
1992 campaign about the most important factor in making up their minds how to
vote, only 20 per cent of respondents cited "the policies of the parties" (Marsh
and Sinnott, 1993). This may be because Irish voters feel that the economic policies of the main parties are so similar that there is nothing much to choose between them.

In such circumstances voters, many of whom clearly do regard economic policy as very important, may choose between parties on the basis of their perceived
competence to run the economy, rather than their stated policies. A way for voters to make this decision is to reward incumbent governments that have presided
over an economy that has done well, and punish incumbents that have presided
over an economy that has done badly. One implication of this is that, if politicians
believe that voters think this way, then they will attempt to manipulate the
economy so that it appears to be performing well in the run-up to an election—
and this is certainly a popular perception among political commentators about
what governments do, in Ireland as well as elsewhere in Europe. This creates a
sequence of economic boom and bust known as the "political business cycle".

The effect of economic performance on political popularity in Ireland has been
explored by Borooah and Borooah (1990). They analysed the impact of key economic indicators on the opinion poll lead of successive Irish governments over
the opposition during the period 1974-87. They found that the popularity of government parties could indeed be well explained by the economic performance
with which they were associated. In particular, government popularity went
down when unemployment went up, and vice versa. Other economic indicators

with a significant impact on the popularity of government parties were real wage rates, the exchange rate, the number of new dwellings constructed and, to a lesser extent, real interest rates. This relationship was particularly strong for manual workers—the economic indicators explained over 80 per cent of the variation in the government parties' lead among this group. Borooah and Borooah (1990, p. 70) also found that, while governments typically suffered from "popularity deficits" for most of their time in office, they "managed to stage recoveries when they most mattered namely at election times". This implies some attempt on the part of governments to manage the economy for electoral gain but Irish governments have not been able to manipulate the economy well enough to be able to hold on to power. There has, indeed, been a change in the party composition of the government after every Irish election since 1969.

To sum up, government popularity in Ireland responds strongly to economic indicators in general and to the level of unemployment in particular. At the same time, opinion polls suggest that economic issues in general, and most especially unemployment, are the most highly rated by the electorate. Taken together, these findings strongly suggest that many (though not necessarily most) Irish voters make explicit choices based on their views about economic policy and performance when they vote, rather than simply affirming a traditional partisan loyalty.

A changing pattern of voting behaviour?

In the absence of evidence to the contrary, we would be rash to turn our backs on the widely-held view that support for the traditional "civil war" parties is to some extent based upon enduring party loyalties. Looking at things in these terms, however, baseline support for the traditional parties does seem to be declining as folk memories of the bitterness of the civil war fade. The combined vote share of Fianna Fáil and Fine Gael has declined from about 85 percent in the two 1982 elections to about 64 percent in 1992, for example. Polls carried out for the European Commission suggest that the number of Irish people saying they "feel close" to a particular party has declined markedly since these polls began in the early 1970s (Schmitt, 1989), and it is reasonable to see in these results a decline in the appeal of the traditional parties.

Some argue that the electorate is becoming more volatile, and general fluctuations in levels of party support were greater in recent elections than they had been since the 1940s. Almost 40 percent of voters for the main parties in 1989—Fianna Fáil, Fine Gael, Labour, the PDs, Democratic Left and the Greens—indicated an intention to vote differently in 1992. The comparable intended shift between 1987 and 1989 was 28 percent (see Sinnott, 1994: Table 6.1). The surge in Labour support at the 1992 election saw the party's vote share jump from 9.5 percent in 1989 to over 19 percent in 1992. Perhaps most significantly of all, the shift of voters from parties of the right to parties of the left in 1992 was unprecedented in Ireland, and very unusual in a more general European context (Mair, 1993, pp. 163-5). Moreover, new parties have emerged in Ireland, something that would be impossible if inherited and unchanging party loyalties determined the votes of everyone in the land. The past few elections have seen the emergence of several new parties—the PDs, the Workers' Party, the Greens and Democratic Left—and this might lead us to wonder whether the traditional pattern of Irish party loyalties is breaking down.

Figure 6.2: Electoral support for "traditional" and "new" parties, by various social groups, December 1992

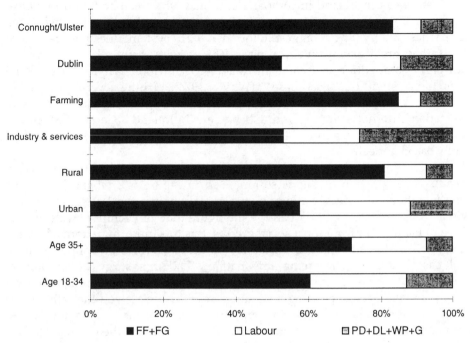

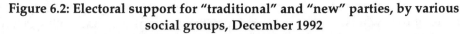

We can find some evidence that this might be the case when we compare the patterns of party support for new and "traditional" parties, and for Labour, between rural and urban, between farming and non-farming and between young and old voters. Figure 6.2 uses results from an *Irish Times*/MRBI poll taken in December 1992—support figures for each party were very close to the final election results.

The figure shows a very clear tendency for support for the new parties and Labour to be concentrated among younger and more urban voters, and to be much lower among farmers and more rural voters. Support for the "civil war" parties is at its highest among older and rural voters, and among small farmers. The number of people living in urban areas and the number working in the non-farming sector is increasing. The number living in rural areas and working in farming is decreasing. This is one major possible explanation for the trend away from the traditional parties and towards the others, highlighted in the size of the combined vote losses of Fianna Fáil and Fine Gael in 1992. Labour's dramatic gains in this election were made for the most part in urban areas (especially Dublin). As a result, the urban-rural contrast in Irish voting patterns became much more marked. Since social mobility in Ireland continues to reduce the size of the more elderly, the rural and the farming sections of the electorate, the demographic profile of support for the traditional parties bodes ill for their future development.

This chart makes it clear that there is some social patterning in the party preferences of Irish voters, but the relationship between social class and voting behaviour is very weak in Ireland in comparison to that which can be found in almost every other European country. In particular, the contest between the two "civil war" parties, still by far the biggest in the Irish party system, does not seem to be based to any great extent on social class. This is why many who have written about party competition in Ireland have agreed with John Whyte in describing this as "politics without social bases" (Whyte, 1974). Writing several years later, R. K. Carty re-emphasised this line of argument with the bold claim that "social characteristics do not structure voting behaviour in Ireland" (Carty, 1981, p. 24). In this sense the largest parties fit the label of "catch-all" parties, because of their broadly based appeal.

These assertions are based on the sort of survey evidence that is reproduced in appendix 2e. A portion of this is summarised in Figure 6.3, which depicts the voting intentions of each social grade immediately before the 1992 election. It is obvious from the bottom, black band in the figure that very similar levels of support go to Fianna Fáil from most social groups. It is this uniform pattern of Fianna Fáil support that has been cited since 1969 as evidence for the "politics without social bases" thesis. Reinforcing this pattern, Labour's surge of support in November 1992 was if anything more pronounced among non-manual than among manual workers, creating a situation in which it received the same levels of support among each. Considering support for each of the three main parties, there are no major differences in the voting behaviour of middle class and working class voters in Ireland (though Fine Gael tends to have been more attractive to the middle class and Labour to the working class in the past). In contrast to the pattern to be found in many other western European countries, knowing whether a voter has a manual or a non-manual occupation does not help us much in predicting how he or she is likely to vote (see Franklin, Mackie and Valen, 1992, p. 387).

Figure 6.3: Support for parties by social grade, December 1992

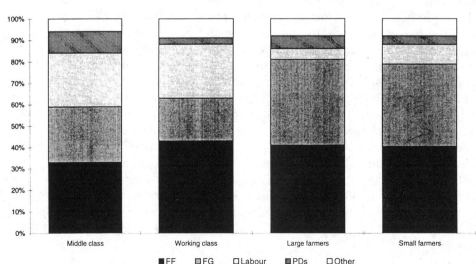

Nonetheless, Figure 6.3 does show some quite interesting patterns. As we have already noted, farmers are very much more likely to vote for either Fianna Fáil or Fine Gael than they are to vote for any of the other parties, and the table shows that the traditional distinction between the voting behaviour of large and small farmers may be beginning to disappear. Thus the increasing volatility of the Irish electorate has certainly not been brought about by the farming sector—farmers were much less likely than others to vote for Labour, or for one of the new parties. In addition to this, there are at least some patterns in the voting behaviour of the non-farming sector. In particular, the Progressive Democrats were much more likely to receive support from middle class than from working class voters. Despite the catch-all basis of Fianna Fáil support, furthermore, the party did receive somewhat more support from the working class than from the middle class. The social bases of Irish voting behaviour may be weak—but they are noticeable nonetheless. We do get some clues about which party a voter is likely to support if we know his or her position in the occupational structure.

Voting behaviour and personalities

While it may be necessary to examine the finer details of opinion polls to see the influence of social class on electoral behaviour, the importance of personalities is more obvious. Election campaigns tend to be dominated by party leaders. For the big parties, each leader is in effect its nominee for Taoiseach. This leads to an understandable focus on personalities that extends to the leaders of the smaller parties. There has been adverse reaction to this tendency, with commentators complaining that Irish elections are assuming a "presidential" character, rather like the "beauty contests" for the presidency of the United States. Certainly, media coverage does focus on party leaders, and most recent elections have culminated in a "great debate" between the leaders of Fianna Fáil and Fine Gael. But the parties have been as much to blame. Election posters frequently feature little more than the party leader's face, while slogans such as "Dessie can do it" and songs such as "Arise and follow Charlie" have all personalised election campaigns.

There is certainly a strong perception in many quarters that a popular leader is worth votes to a party. Fine Gael strategy in the early 1980s focused in particular on Garret FitzGerald. The party's opinion research showed that he was more widely liked and trusted than Fianna Fáil's leader, Charles Haughey, and Fine Gael strategists thought that emphasising the contrast between the two would work to their advantage. Fianna Fáil also built election campaigns around Charles Haughey, seen by party strategists as someone who could motivate rank-and-file members and attract long-term supporters. Des O'Malley featured prominently in PD campaigns, particularly in 1987, when he was seen by party strategists as their greatest electoral asset. Labour's successful election campaign in 1992 was built very much upon the personal popularity of its leader, Dick Spring, whose opinion poll ratings at the time were far above those of the other party leaders. For the same reasons, an unpopular leader is typically held to damage a party's election prospects, as Charles Haughey found to his cost in early 1992, when forced out of the Fianna Fáil leadership in favour of Albert Reynolds by a party scared of the negative effects of the "Haughey factor" in the upcoming election.

Notwithstanding these perceptions, there is no clear evidence that leaders have a decisive effect on voting behaviour. Studies have shown the popularity of British leaders to have some effect on that of their parties, but such links have generally not appeared to be very strong (see, for instance, Mishler, Hoskins and Fitzgerald, 1989). Even a big popularity gap between rival leaders may be worth no more than one or two per cent of the vote. Yet, when asked during the 1989 election campaign, between 14 and 20 per cent of Irish voters claimed that the choice of Taoiseach is the most important element in their electoral calculation (Marsh and Sinnott, 1990; unfortunately this question was not asked in 1992). In addition, even when surveys show a high degree of consistency between respondents' voting intentions and their perceptions of who would make the best Taoiseach (Marsh and Sinnott, 1990), we cannot tell from such results which of these two things, party choice and leader perception, follows from the other.

Our focus, like that of election campaigns, has so far been on national leaders, but it must be remembered that, when the electors finally go to the polls, the votes cast are given to individual local candidates. Moreover, even though the emphasis in national election campaigns is on parties, much of the activity at local level revolves around those candidates. Activity within any given constituency is certainly aimed at increasing party votes, but most candidates are also concerned to maximise their individual performances. Because the Irish electoral system forces voters to indicate a preference for an individual candidate, many candidates are effectively in competition with others of their own party, as well as with candidates from other parties. Indeed, quite a high proportion of the turnover of TDs from one election to another (over a third in 1992) happens because a TD from one party is beaten for the seat by a rival from the same party, rather than by an opponent from another party; there is rarely such a thing as a "safe seat" in Ireland.

Once more, evidence about the effect of individual candidates on voting behaviour is difficult to assess. Certainly, when voters are asked in opinion polls about the extent to which their voting decision is affected by parties, issues, leaders and candidates, they are more likely to claim that they make up their mind on the basis of the local candidates on offer than to mention any other factor. When asked during the 1992 election campaign, around 37 per cent of voters said that picking a candidate to represent the needs of the constituency is the most important thing for them when they vote, a figure very close to that found in previous elections (Marsh and Sinnott, 1993, p. 98). Such responses should not be taken at face value, however. Electoral casualty lists often testify to the vulnerability of a TD who goes it alone and dispenses with the protection of a party label. Some survive, but most perish, particularly those who jump ship from one of the major parties.

More detailed examination of STV election results provides quite convincing evidence that the party affiliation of candidates guides the choices of most voters. About 80 per cent of voters give their second preference vote to a candidate of the same party as their first preference candidate, where this is possible (Gallagher, 1978). When a Fianna Fáil candidate is eliminated from a count, for example, most of his or her votes will go to another Fianna Fáil candidate. It seems likely, therefore, that when people say that candidates are the most important thing when they are voting, what they mean is that, for a given choice of party, they decide which of that party's candidates to vote for according to their personal record or potential.

Even so, just as voting patterns imply that most people vote for party first and candidate second, they also reveal that some do not. Some candidates are able to attract at least some votes across party lines, and incumbents in particular can expect to attract personal support to add to that which they attract by virtue of their party label. In 1989, a special "panel" survey—one that interviewed people at the start of the election campaign and re-interviewed them after election day—found that one third of those who changed their minds about which party to vote for during the course of the campaign did so out of a desire to support a particular candidate (Marsh and Sinnott, 1990, Table 5.17).

CONCLUSION

Elections in Ireland, as in all parliamentary democracies, are largely about parties. Parties nominate most of the candidates who stand in elections, and candidates with well known party labels attract the overwhelming majority of the votes. Parties dominate the campaign with their manifestos and press conferences, and the leaders of the parties provide the focus of most media attention. Yet parties on the whole get a bad press in Ireland. Nineteenth century commentators often saw them as private bodies which interfered with the public democratic process, and there are echoes of these complaints today. Despite these reservations, it can be seen that parties organise and simplify much of the electoral process. Without them, voters would have very little information about the candidates on offer, and would have even less information about the link between their vote and the formation of a government. We might feel that parties could do their job much better if they had more resources, perhaps from public funds, but this might also change the balance between the centre and the grass roots of the party, and downgrade the importance of membership still further.

Irish parties do not have large memberships, but they do have enough members to give the larger parties a presence in most parts of the country, something which provides a personal link between the representatives in the Dáil and the ordinary citizen. Party membership allows a relatively large number of people to get more involved in politics, and to participate more fully than those who simply fill in a ballot paper, but it is deputies, party spokespersons and party leaders who do most to set the policy direction of the party. Ordinary members exercise some influence, particularly on their party's recruitment process, and they often seek rather more. On occasion this creates a tension between leadership and the rank and file which is particularly marked in parties, such as Labour, that emphasise their "democratic" character.

For voters, a party label provides a simple cue, enabling people to make sense of what is sometimes a quite complex choice at election time. Although votes can only be cast for individuals, most electors seem to behave as if they are voting for parties. In the last analysis political scientists still remain unsure as to why voters select one party rather than another. Much of the evidence is consistent both with the argument that party choices are based on habits learned early in life, and with the view that electors assess parties by what they say and what they do, particularly in relation to the economy; not until there is evidence from specially designed election studies can this confusion be resolved.

Even so, there are limits to the reach of parties. Some independent candidates do get elected at a typical Irish election, and voters still decide which of their chosen party's candidates they would most like to send to Dáil Éireann. Local party politicians can build a reputation and organisation that is essentially personal; this can transcend their party label, allow them some independence and offer us a glimpse of what politics might be like without party organisation.

Ultimately, however, parliamentary democracy in Ireland works as it does because people vote for parties rather than individuals at election time, and do so in a way that is predictable, at least in some measure. This makes the social patterns in party choice a fundamental basis of Irish party politics. It also suggests that if such social bases are changing, we can expect change in the Irish party system. The rise of new parties and the modest decline of the old ones suggest that this process is already under way, but we may expect the old parties to make every effort to adapt to the changing circumstances and to maintain their central place in Irish politics.

REFERENCES AND FURTHER READING

Borooah, Vani K. and Vidya Borooah, 1990. "Economic performance and political popularity in the Republic of Ireland", *Public Choice* 67:1, pp. 65-79.

Bowler, Shaun and David M. Farrell, 1990. "Irish voter rationality: the 1987 Irish general election revisited", *Economic and Social Review* 21:3, pp. 251-68.

Carty, R. K., 1981. *Party and Parish Pump: Electoral Politics in Ireland*. Ontario: Wilfrid Laurier Press.

Farrell, David M., 1992. "Ireland", pp. 389-457 in R. S. Katz and Peter Mair (eds) *Party Organisations in Western Democracies, 1960-1990: a Data Handbook*. London: Sage.

Farrell, Brian, 1993. "The formation of the partnershp government," pp. 146-61 in Gallagher and Laver (1993).

Fianna Fáil, 1991. *Commission on the Aims and Structures of Fianna Fáil: Interim Report*. Dublin: Fianna Fáil.

Franklin, Mark, Tom Mackie, Henry Valen et al., 1992. *Electoral Change: Responses to Evolving Social and Attitudinal Structures in Western Democracies*. Cambridge: Cambridge University Press.

Gallagher, Michael, 1978. "Party solidarity, exclusivity and inter-party relationships in Ireland, 1922-1977: the evidence of transfers", *Economic and Social Review* 10:1, pp. 1-22.

Gallagher, Michael, 1985. *Political Parties in the Republic of Ireland*. Manchester: Manchester University Press.

Gallagher, Michael, 1988. "Ireland: the increasing role of the centre", pp. 119-44 in Michael Gallagher and Michael Marsh (eds), *Candidate Selection in Comparative Perspective: the Secret Garden of Politics*. London: Sage.

Gallagher, Michael, Michael Laver and Peter Mair, 1992. *Representative Government in Western Europe*. New York: McGraw-Hill.

Gallagher, Michael and Michael Laver (eds), 1993. *How Ireland Voted 1992*. Dublin: Folens; Limerick: PSAI Press.

Gallagher, Michael and Richard Sinnott (eds), 1990. *How Ireland Voted 1989*. Galway: Centre for the Study of Irish Elections and PSAI Press.

Laver, Michael, Peter Mair and Richard Sinnott (eds), 1987. *How Ireland Voted: the General Election of 1987*. Swords: Poolbeg Press.

Laver, Michael, Michael Marsh and Richard Sinnott, 1987. "Patterns of party support", pp. 99-140 in Laver, Mair and Sinnott (1987).

Mair, Peter, 1987a. *The Changing Irish Party System: Organisation, Ideology and Electoral Competition*. London: Frances Pinter.

Mair, Peter, 1987b. "Ireland 1948-1981: issues, parties, strategies", pp. 134-59 in Ian Budge, David Robertson and Derek Hearl (eds), *Ideology, Strategy and Party Change*. Cambridge: Cambridge University Press.

Mair, Peter. 1993. "Fianna Fáil, Labour and the Irish party system", pp. 162-73 in Gallagher and Laver (1993).

Marsh, Michael and Richard Sinnott, 1990. "How the voters decided", pp. 94-130 in Gallagher and Sinnott (1990).

Marsh, Michael and Richard Sinnott, 1993. "The voters: stability and change", pp. 93-114 in Gallagher and Laver (1993).

Marsh, Michael and Rick Wilford, 1990. "Irish political data, 1989", *Irish Political Studies* 5, pp. 129-60.

Marsh, Michael, Rick Wilford, Paul Arthur and Rona Fitzgerald, 1993. "Irish political data, 1992", *Irish Political Studies* 8, pp. 169-214.

Mishler, W., M. Hoskins and R. Fitzgerald, 1989. "Parties in the balance: a time series analysis of long-term trends in Labour and Conservative support", *British Journal of Political Science* 19:2, pp. 211-36.

O'Byrnes, Stephen, 1986. *Hiding behind a Face: Fine Gael under FitzGerald*. Dublin: Gill and Macmillan.

Schmitt, Hermann, 1989. "On party attachment in western Europe and the utility of Eurobarometer data", *West European Politics* 12:2, pp. 122-39.

Sinnott, Richard, 1994, forthcoming. *Irish Voters Decide*. Manchester: Manchester University Press.

Waters, John, 1991. *Jiving at the Crossroads*. Belfast: Blackstaff Press.

Whyte, John H., 1974. "Ireland: politics without social bases", pp. 619-51 in Richard Rose (ed.), *Electoral Behavior: a Comparative Handbook*. New York: Free Press.

7 / PARLIAMENT

Michael Gallagher

As we saw in chapter 3, the constitution provides for a parliamentary system of government. Ireland's parliament consists of two houses: the lower and directly elected Dáil, currently consisting of 166 members elected from 41 constituencies, and the upper house, the indirectly elected Seanad, which has 60 members. The power of the Seanad is very limited, and we shall concentrate on the Dáil in this chapter.

In classical liberal democratic theory, parliament plays a key role in the democratic process. The people elect a parliament, to which the government is accountable. This, in fact, is what enables democratic states to claim that they are democratic. Set against this theory, many people have found practice rather disappointing right across western Europe. Parliaments may still be elected by the people, and may even elect governments, but it seems that once a government gets into office it can go its own way largely unchecked by parliament. And, even in the context of these generally low expectations of how much control a parliament can really exercise over a government in any country, it has frequently been argued that the Dáil stands out for its exceptional weakness. Twenty years ago, Ward (1974, p. 241) described the Dáil as "supine", and Dinan (1986, p. 71) sums up an academic consensus with his judgement that it is "a woefully inadequate institution". From the practitioners' side of the fence, former Labour TD and minister Barry Desmond once described Dáil Éireann as "a sleepy middle class, quasi-professional, male dominated, conservatively deliberative, poorly attended debating assembly" (Desmond, 1975, p. 6). In this chapter we shall look at what parliament is supposed to do and ask how well it does it.

The constitution assigns two main functions to the Houses of the Oireachtas. These are the appointment of the Taoiseach and the government (Articles 13 and 28) and law making, or more broadly policy making (Articles 15 to 27). The constitution also declares (Article 28.4.1) that "The Government shall be responsible to Dáil Éireann". This gives us three dimensions on which to assess the performance of the Dáil: the appointment of governments, policy making, and scrutiny of government behaviour.

APPOINTMENT AND DISMISSAL OF GOVERNMENTS

The formal position, as laid out in Article 13.1 of the constitution, is that the Dáil nominates the Taoiseach and approves the composition of the government, whereupon the President appoints them. The Dáil can also dismiss a Taoiseach and a government, by passing a vote of no confidence (Article 28.10). However, at least up to the 1980s, the Dáil's real power in this area has usually been fairly nominal, almost to the same degree as the President's.

The reason, of course, is that the decision on who is to be Taoiseach and who is to form the government has usually been made not by the Dáil but by the voters at general elections. The vote of the Dáil after the election merely puts the seal on what the voters have decided. For example, at the 1977 election Fianna Fáil won a majority of the votes and 84 of the 148 seats, and when the new Dáil met, the Fianna Fáil leader, Jack Lynch, was duly elected as Taoiseach on the bloc vote of the Fianna Fáil TDs. When this happens, Ireland displays many of the features of the archetypal "Westminster" or majoritarian model that generally characterises countries such as Britain, Canada and New Zealand. In the purest form of this model, each general election produces a clear "winner", in that one party wins an overall majority of seats, and this party then forms a stable government until the next general election, without having to fear much interference from parliament (see Lijphart, 1984, ch. 1). The voters, rather than parliament, choose the government. If no one party has won an overall majority, a "bare majority" coalition—that is, a government that does not contain any parties over and above those that are strictly necessary for ensuring that the government has a majority—is the most acceptable alternative. In contrast, a "consensus" model is more accurate for many west European countries that use PR electoral systems, in which elections do not throw up a clear winner (Lijphart, 1984, ch. 2). In these countries, weeks can elapse after an election before a government emerges, a process that entails lengthy negotiation and bargaining between prospective coalition partners (see Gallagher, Laver and Mair, 1992, ch. 7). The task of putting together a government that will be supported by the legislature is by no means a formality, and the result is often an "oversized" coalition government that contains "surplus" parties that are invited into the government so as to make it more broadly based and representative of the whole electorate.

Government formation in Ireland is becoming a more complicated process, but this does not mean that Ireland is moving towards the consensus model. It is clear that the basic instincts of the main political parties remain essentially majoritarian. One explanation for Ireland's general adherence to the Westminster model is the strong British influence on Irish political culture (see chapter 2), which has led to a view of elections as decisive battlegrounds whose victors can expect largely untrammelled power until the next election. Another is that the nature of the party system has led to a persistent "Fianna Fáil versus the rest" cleavage (see chapter 5), and often either Fianna Fáil, or a coalition of other parties, has won a majority or near-majority of seats. However, since 1977 the picture has changed. None of the six subsequent elections produced a clear "winner", and on each occasion government formation was not straightforward.

In some ways, the picture of Ireland as a classic example of the Westminster model in this regard has always been rather deceptive. Only 10 of the 25 governments elected following general elections from 1922 to 1992 inclusive have actually held a majority of Dáil seats (two others held exactly half the seats). One reason why governments have nonetheless been fairly stable is that the Dáil, unlike most European parliaments, always contains a few, or sometimes many, independent TDs, who through benign abstention or occasional support may enable a minority administration to remain in office. For this reason, up to the late 1970s it was understandable that observers attached little importance to the Dáil's formal powers in the area of appointing a government.

However, since the end of the second world war there have been eight occasions when a general election did not produce a clear outcome. The first was in 1948, when Dáil strength was spread among six parties and a number of independents. A government emerged after intensive negotiations among the leaders of all parties except Fianna Fáil, at which they agreed to form Ireland's first coalition government. Much the same happened in 1954, except that there were fewer parties in the coalition (see appendix 3c). However, in these two cases all the serious negotiating took place before the Dáil convened. By the time it did meet, the deal had been struck, so once again the Dáil was just formally ratifying a decision that had been taken elsewhere.

In the 1980s, though, the Dáil's role was harder to ignore. After the 1981 election, uncertainty as to who would form the next government persisted right up to the point when the vote was taken in the Dáil. Even though Fine Gael and Labour had agreed to try to form a coalition administration, these two parties had only 80 of the 166 seats and thus needed the backing of independent TDs to secure a Dáil majority. After the February 1982 election, it was Fianna Fáil that needed support from the Workers' Party and independent TDs to enable it to form a minority government. The aftermath of the November 1982 election was more like the scenario of 1948 and 1954, in that although the election did not produce a decisive verdict, a coalition deal was made after the election between parties that had a Dáil majority, so the Dáil's approval of this government was just a formality. In 1987, though, the Dáil reclaimed centre stage, as it seemed for a while that no potential government could secure its approval. When the Dáil met it was known that 82 of the 166 TDs would be voting for Charles Haughey as Taoiseach and 82 would be opposing him, with independent Tony Gregory uncommitted. The suspense continued until Gregory declared that he would abstain on the crucial vote, thus enabling Haughey to be elected Taoiseach on the casting vote of the Ceann Comhairle (Speaker). In 1989, for the first time ever, the Dáil was unable to elect a Taoiseach at its first post-election meeting. It took a further two weeks and two meetings of the Dáil before Fianna Fáil and the PDs agreed to form a government that controlled exactly half of the Dáil seats. This was the first occasion on which Fianna Fáil, hitherto a staunch defender of the principle that a party should be either in government on its own or in full-blooded opposition, agreed to share power with another party (Farrell, 1990; Laver and Arkins, 1990). Government formation after the 1992 election was an even more protracted process—again, the new Dáil was unable to elect a Taoiseach at its first meeting, and the Fianna Fáil-Labour government was not installed until eight weeks after the election (Collins, 1993, pp. 193-209; Farrell, 1993).

When we look at the Dáil's role in dismissing governments, the same picture emerges: a superficial compliance with the purest version of the Westminster model concealing a more complex reality. The Westminster model does not anticipate a parliament throwing a government out of office—on the contrary, the parliament's support is generally taken for granted by government. Sure enough, the Dáil has dismissed a government on only two occasions. The first was in November 1982, when the minority Fianna Fáil government was beaten by 82 votes to 80 on a confidence motion, precipitating the resignation of the government and a general election. Even this could be explained away as an aberration caused by the recent death of one Fianna Fáil TD and the absence through illness of another. The second was in November 1992, when the PDs left the government and joined the opposition benches, whereupon a motion of no confidence in the Fianna Fáil minority government was passed by 88 votes to 77 (Girvin, 1993, p. 12; Mitchell, 1993).

However, there have been seven other occasions when a government has gone to the country rather than continue in a situation where defeat on a confidence motion seemed only a matter of time. This happened in August 1927, 1938 and 1944, when the minority governments of the day were in a weak position and preferred to call a general election at a time of their own choosing rather than wait for the Dáil to pull the plug. Prior to calling the 1951 election, the first Inter-Party government had been losing support from some of its own backbenchers in the wake of the traumatic "Mother and Child" affair. Six years later the same fate befell the second Inter-Party government, and this factor was coupled with a weakening of its Dáil position due to by-election defeats. In January 1982 the minority coalition government was defeated in a vote on its budget, an item so basic to any government's programme that failure to get it through the Dáil is regarded as tantamount to losing a vote of confidence, and it resigned at once. In January 1987 Labour pulled out of the coalition government, leaving Fine Gael with only 68 seats and facing certain defeat had the Dáil met again. In other words, one reason why governments have so rarely been dismissed by the Dáil is that when they have seen defeat staring them in the face, they have usually jumped off the cliff rather than waiting to be pushed.

The Westminster model in its purest form, then, no longer adequately captures the reality of the Dáil's role in appointing and dismissing governments. However, it remains true that Irish governments do not routinely fear dismissal by the Dáil; governments are not regularly made or broken on the floor of the house. In this, of course, the Dáil is in line with virtually every other parliament in Western Europe—Finland and Italy are the only real exceptions. The idea of parliaments constantly making and unmaking governments is neither realistic nor especially attractive. The classic example of a parliament wielding this power occurred in the dying days of the French Fourth Republic, where the last six governments lasted for an average of only 23 days each. Few would recommend "strengthening" the Dáil so that this pattern could be replicated. If parliament has a role, it must lie in one of the areas to which we now turn.

MAKING POLICY

The constitution, by assigning law-making powers exclusively to the Oireachtas (Article 15.2.1), reflects one of the central tenets of classical liberal democratic theory: the legislature (parliament) makes laws and the executive (government) carries them out. This might lead us to expect, if we leave aside for the moment the role that the European Community now possesses in this area (see chapter 12), that the government is merely the striking arm of parliament, carrying out parliament's will whether it likes it or not. However, only the very naive really expect to find this kind of relationship between government and parliament in any parliamentary democracy, and it is more common to find the view expressed that parliament, in Ireland even more than in many countries, has come to be a mere "glorified rubber stamp" (Dinan, 1986, p. 76) for whatever proposals government puts before it.

In the area of policy making, as in appointing governments, we can distinguish between the Westminster and consensus models. In the Westminster model, parliament is not seen as a real maker of laws. Rather, parliament provides a forum where the issues raised by a government proposal can be fully aired. The government is obliged to justify its measure and the opposition gets the chance to make the case against it (and, generally, to keep the government on its toes), but ultimately the government sees its plans approved by parliament pretty much as a matter of course. There is no feeling that the views of the opposition need to be taken into account or that the agreement of the opposition is required for the passage of legislation—after all, the opposition is the opposition because it "lost" the last election and the government won it. To bring the opposition into the policy-making process could thus be seen as undemocratic, since it would reduce the significance of the choice made by the voters at elections. In the consensus model, in contrast, government is obliged to take seriously the feelings of parliament, including the feelings of the opposition. While in the last resort it is the government that governs, governments prefer not to railroad their legislation through against strong resistance; they try to find a consensus within parliament for their proposals and are willing to take on board constructive suggestions from the opposition.

Ireland's law-making procedure is closely based, in the letter and in the spirit, on that of Westminster. Bills can be introduced in either house—in the past, almost all government bills were introduced in the Dáil, but in recent years the number introduced in the Seanad has grown. The formal progress of a bill is the same through each house, but since in the event of a disagreement between Dáil and Seanad it is the former that prevails (see p. 144 below), we shall concentrate here on the Dáil. A five-stage process is provided for bills, though most bills can bypass the first stage (see Figure 7.1). The second stage is the general debate on the principle of the bill. The third (committee stage) involves a detailed examination of each section of the bill. The fourth and fifth stages consist of tidying up the decisions made at the committee stage and formally passing the bill. After this, bills go to the other house and then to the President, who signs them into law or, very rarely, refers them to the Supreme Court for a verdict on their constitutionality (see pp. 52-3 above). With the fourth and fifth stages being largely formal, only the second and third stages offer the house any real opportunity to affect the content of a bill.

The second stage debates are, at least in theory, the big events in the life of the Dáil, as it is here that the broad lines of bills are argued out. However, in practice debates have a very ritualistic quality about them. All too often they are highly predictable affairs. The relevant minister opens the event by outlining the rationale for the measure to be introduced, after which a succession of opposition deputies use the occasion to pour cold water on the bill under discussion and also, very often, to criticise the general ineptitude of the government and its mismanagement of the country's affairs. There is little incentive for the opposition to offer constructive alternative proposals since the likelihood of any government deputy crossing the floor to vote for them is practically zero.

Figure 7.1: The stages of a bill initiated in Dáil Éireann

Stage	Matters decided
First stage	Formal introduction of bill, securing agreement that the bill proceed to second stage. Virtually all bills (government bills, and private members' bills introduced by a "group" of at least seven deputies), can be presented to the house without needing this formal agreement, and enter the process at the second stage.
Second stage	Debate on the broad principle of the bill. The details of the bill are not discussed at this stage, and the substance of the bill cannot be amended. The vote taken after the second stage debate (assuming there is one – a significant number of bills are passed by agreement of the house, without the need for a vote) determines whether the bill is allowed to proceed to almost certain acceptance or is rejected.
Third stage	Committee stage. The bill is examined in detail by a committee (in the past, almost invariably, the "committee" consisted of the whole Dáil; from 1993, specialist 30-member committees undertake this task). The bill is discussed section by section. Amendments may be proposed, provided they do not conflict with the principle of the bill, since this was approved by the house at the second stage.
Fourth stage	Report stage. Usually a formal tidying up of amendments made at third stage. New amendments may be proposed provided that they do not conflict with amendments rejected at the third stage.
Fifth stage	The final and formal passing of the bill. Speeches at this stage tend to be shorter and more ritualistic versions of those on the second stage. The bill now goes to the Seanad for discussion.
Final stages	When it returns from the Seanad the Dáil discusses the changes, if any, proposed by the Seanad. If it accepts them, the bill is sent to the President, for signing into law or, in the President's discretion, for referral to the Supreme Court for a verdict on its constitutionality. If the Dáil does not accept the Seanad's suggested amendments, it sends the bill back to the Seanad for reconsideration. The Seanad may fall into line with the wishes of the Dáil or it may reaffirm its amendments, in which case it can delay but not veto the passage of the bill.

Note: Bills can also be initiated in the Seanad. In this case they then go to the Dáil after being passed, but, in the event of the Dáil deciding to make amendments, they are treated as if they had been initiated in the Dáil (Article 20.2.2 of the constitution).

TDs are not supposed to read speeches from a prepared text, but they may use "notes", which are sometimes very extensive. There is no time limit on speeches, and some stretch to astonishing lengths in order to pad out the available time. When the Dáil debated parliamentary reform early in 1983, former government chief whip Bertie Ahern admitted that he had had to persuade government TDs to come into the Dáil chamber and "keep talking for 45 minutes" on more or less any subject that could be deemed relevant to the bill, while Fine Gael's Bernard Durkan said that "the first thing I tried to learn when I was elected here was how to speak for half an hour on a subject that could be dealt with in ten minutes" (*Dáil Debates* 339: 658, 27 January 1983 and 339: 1136-7, 3 February 1983). Much of the time in Dáil debates is taken by "having people waffle on", as Ahern put it. The Dáil usually meets for three or four days a week (Tuesday, Wednesday, Thursday and sometimes Friday) for around 30 weeks of the year, and tends to meet less frequently than the average parliament in Europe. In 1991 it sat for 99 days and in 1992 for 92 days; this is less than the 224 days that parliament met in Greece, 170 in the United Kingdom and 149 in France, though more than the 70 in Belgium or 66 in West Germany (the figures are the average for these countries

Table 7.1: Sittings and business of Dáil Éireann in the 1930s, 1960s and 1980s

	1934-38 (average per annum)	1964-68 (average per annum)	1984-88 (average per annum)
Sitting days	72	78	92
Sitting hours	478	568	765
Bills considered by Dáil	66	52	63
Bills promulgated as laws	49	32	32
Bills carried over to following year	14	15	27

Source: For the 1930s, *Sittings of Dáil Éireann; Public Bills in the Dáil; Private Bills in the Dáil*. All published annually by the Stationery Office, Dublin. For the 1960s, *Returns relating to Sittings and Business of the 17th Dáil* (Dublin: Stationery Office, 1967) and *Returns relating to Sittings and Business of the 18th Dáil* (Dublin: Stationery Office, 1971). For the 1980s, *Returns relating to Sittings and Business of the 24th Dáil* (Dublin: Stationery Office, 1990) and *Returns relating to Sittings and Business of the 25th Dáil* (Dublin: Stationery Office, 1991).

over a five-year period in the early 1980s—see IPU, 1986, pp. 276-309). The average figure for the 10 EC parliaments for which information is available was 117 days. Table 7.1 shows that the Dáil met more frequently in the late 1980s (the latest period for which full figures are available) than either 20 or 50 years earlier, but actually passed fewer bills than in the 1930s.

Not surprisingly, second stage speeches, at least once the minister and the main opposition spokesperson have had their say, are not made to a packed and expectant Dáil chamber. It is not uncommon to find only two TDs in the chamber for such speeches: an opposition backbencher ploughing through a mini-thesis on the multiple shortcomings of the measure under discussion, and a bored-looking cabinet or junior minister who has long since ceased to pretend to listen to what is being said. If the opposition is feeling recalcitrant, one of its TDs will demand a quorum (20 TDs), without which the Dáil technically cannot conduct its business. This means that government backbenchers have to stream out of their offices and into the Dáil chamber to make up the numbers for a while, but they soon drift back again and hope that the opposition tires of the tactic. Attendance is particularly low when the government of the day commands a large majority (as the outcome of votes in the Dáil becomes a foregone conclusion) and on Fridays.

While some profess indignation at the low level of attendance in the Dáil chamber, it is hard to criticise those TDs and ministers who conclude that they have more useful ways of spending their time. Dáil debates are often dialogues of the deaf, set pieces with a strong element of theatre in which TDs speak for the record or in order to get publicity at local level—as in the House of Commons, "debate" is a rather flattering term for "a series of largely unconnected speeches often delivered to a near empty House" (Borthwick, 1988, p. 72). The word wrongly implies that each speaker is responding to what has been said previously, or that at the end the minister deals systematically with criticisms made from the opposition benches. The heavy emphasis laid on debates demonstrates again the Dáil's derivation from Westminster and the traditional British view of parliament as a symbol of democracy rather than as an effective working body, though we should remember that attendance in the chamber tends to be low in nearly all parliaments these days (especially on Friday afternoons). Arter (1990, p. 124) notes that the sparse attendance at plenary debates in the Swedish

Riksdag has given rise to comment there; only a handful of members of the Norwegian Storting attend debates except when votes are taken (Laegreid and Olsen, 1986, p. 195); while a Danish joke has it that a deputy wanting to keep something secret should announce it from the rostrum of the Folketing, as then it is certain that nobody will hear it.

The only chance of a government bill being defeated at the second stage arises not from the possibility of some of the government's backbenchers being convinced by the brilliance of the arguments from the opposition but from dissent within its ranks, or if it does not control a majority of TDs in the first place. Such defeats are very rare, but they are not unheard of. In January 1982, as we have already mentioned, the minority coalition government's budget was defeated. In April 1983, the government's proposed wording of the anti-abortion amendment to the constitution was defeated due to defections among conservative government backbenchers. The 1987-89 minority Fianna Fáil administration was defeated six times in the Dáil, though none of these defeats concerned legislation. More significantly, this government did not bring before the house a bill to approve the redrawing of constituency boundaries in a way that would have made life more difficult for the smaller parties at the next election, because of a well-founded fear that any such bill would be defeated there.

The assumption made so far is that all bills are government bills, and in practice it has been the case that only government bills can expect to pass into law. Indeed, the constitution states (Article 17.2) that no motion or resolution shall be passed, or law enacted, that involves spending public money unless the Dáil receives a written message, signed by the Taoiseach, recommending the measure on behalf of the government. This is a stipulation in many countries, clearly motivated by the fear that were it not in force, parliament might vote for the spending of money but against government efforts to raise it. Moreover, when the 1987-89 Fianna Fáil government sustained Dáil defeats on motions apparently "directing" it to take certain steps, it ignored the motions, dismissing them as being merely declaratory. The standing orders of the Dáil contain provision for "private members' bills", which are usually introduced by an opposition deputy. From 1937 to 1988 only six such bills were passed, all in the 1950s (Morgan, 1990, pp. 103, 231), although the device has recently been shown to be still of some relevance due to the passage of two private members' bills introduced by Fine Gael frontbencher Alan Shatter: one on marital breakdown in 1989 and one on adoption in 1991. Even unsuccessful private members' bills may have an impact, since the government sometimes secures the withdrawal or defeat of the bill by promising to take some action itself.[1]

The opposition, then, is unlikely to secure the defeat of a government bill or the passage of a bill of its own. If the Dáil is to make any impression on legislation, this must come at the third, "committee", stage of a bill's progress, where the opposition can hope to have some influence on the final shape of the bill. All bills are discussed by specialist 30-member committees, on which the parties are represented in proportion to their Dáil strengths. Although discussion on the broad principle of the bill is ruled out, this having been settled at the second

---

1. Private members' bills should be distinguished from private bills, which differ from public bills in that they apply only to certain bodies or localities (an example is The Limerick Markets Act, 1992). Private bills, of which there are only a handful per decade, must be introduced in the Seanad and have a distinctive method of enactment (for details see Morgan, 1990, pp. 103-4).

stage, TDs can raise points about specific sections: they can point out anomalies, inconsistencies, loopholes, imprecise phraseology, and so on. If the points raised are consistent with the basic intention of the bill, the minister might well accept them and modify the bill accordingly. If the minister does not want to accept opposition amendments, then they will fail.

The fact that the plenary discussion of the principles of a bill in the Dáil precedes the committee stage is more significant than is often realised. In many countries, a bill is examined in detail by a small committee of parliament *before* it goes to the whole house; in the Westminster model, the sequence is usually the other way around and "the committee is bound by the principle of the bill to which the House has agreed" (Laundy, 1989, p. 73). Shaw finds that this is a very important factor in deciding the significance of parliamentary committees in policy making: "if a committee can consider a bill before it is taken up on the floor, the chances of the committee influencing or determining the outcome tend to be greater than when the lines of battle have been predetermined in plenary meetings" (Shaw, 1979, p. 417). Small committees of deputies who have acquired some expertise in a particular area are more likely to reach a consensus if the issues at stake have not been heavily politicised by partisan debates on the floor of the house, and the chances of the government's proposals getting through unaltered are correspondingly lower. For this reason, governments in Westminster model countries prefer to leave the committee stage until after the plenary discussion, so that any changes made by the committee are likely to be minor.

It is clear, then, that the Dáil cannot be seen as an active participant in the process of making laws, let alone broader policy. Governments are usually more concerned to bring the major interest groups round to their way of thinking (see chapter 10) than to placate the Dáil, whose backing they tend to take for granted. The Dáil is often seen as legitimising legislation rather than really making it, and the value of its existence is questioned. However, there are two points that need to be made before the Dáil's role in the legislative area is dismissed as of little value. First, even if its only function *was* to legitimise legislation, this could still be seen as important. Norton (1990c, p. 147) points out that parliaments play an important symbolic role, and that for many people the fact that all legislation has to be passed by a parliament consisting of the elected representatives of the people is more important in making them feel that they are ruled democratically than the question of how much real power that parliament wields.

Second, it would be wrong to infer from the rarity of government defeats that Ireland suffers from "cabinet dictatorship" or an "elected dictatorship" between elections (Morgan, 1990, p. 82). The Dáil will do what the government wants provided, and only provided, the government has the backing of a majority of TDs. In situations of minority government, the government will be able to get its legislation through only if it takes care not to introduce any proposals that would induce the opposition to combine against it. For example, the fact that the minority Fianna Fáil government of 1987-89 suffered no defeats on any of its legislative proposals is testimony to its sensitivity to its minority position, not to its control of the Dáil (Girvin, 1990, p. 7). Moreover, even when the government parties have a Dáil majority, it is easy to overlook the fact that the government has to pay a price to retain the backing of its TDs. Ministers have to show their backbenchers some respect in order to keep them trooping loyally through the government lobbies. When the party is in power, weekly meetings of its parliamentary party (attended by TDs, senators and MEPs) hear from ministers about their plans and expect this to be a genuine process of consultation. If a TD raises a doubt or a question, it is politically difficult for the minister to brush this aside as dismissively as an opposition TD might be dealt with in the Dáil chamber—ministers, after all, want to be personally popular with their own TDs, for a variety of obvious reasons. A sensible minister will "wear a velvet glove, albeit having a mailed fist within it", when dealing with government backbenchers (Rose, 1986, p. 14). The power of the parliamentary party should not be overstated—evidently, the initiative in making policy lies with the government, not with backbenchers. But, equally, it would be wrong to imagine that the government has a completely free hand from its own party; if a proposed policy or piece of legislation arouses broad antagonism from government TDs at a parliamentary party meeting, it is unlikely to be pressed further, as occurred early in 1991 when government proposals to make contraceptives available to 16- and 17-year-olds ran into Fianna Fáil backbench resistance. An awareness of what the parliamentary party will and will not stand for is bound to be a factor in determining what policies the government tries to introduce.

With this qualification, then, it is the government and not the Oireachtas that has the initiative in the shaping of laws and policies. Once again, the Irish pattern is not especially exceptional, even if the Oireachtas is less active in this area than are most parliaments. Of course, in presidential systems of government such as the USA, parliament can be quite strong, because the survival of a government is not at stake: if a presidentially-backed bill is defeated in Congress, the administration does not fall. But things are very different in the parliamentary systems of government by which Western European countries are governed. When a government is answerable to and can be dismissed by parliament, measures proposed by the government are very unlikely to be rejected by parliament. When bills go to a specialist committee before they reach the floor of the house, parliament can exercise significant influence over their final shape, but where the Westminster model prevails it would be unrealistic to expect a policy-making role for parliament. All that we might hope for is that the Dáil keeps a vigilant eye on what government is up to, the topic that we now examine.

SCRUTINISING THE BEHAVIOUR OF GOVERNMENT

As we have just said, the initiative in making policy lies with government rather than with parliament. However, this does not freeze parliament out of the political process entirely. Even if it does pass virtually all the government's proposals, it still has a choice as to how to follow this up. Does it merely sit back supinely and allow the government to act as it wishes? Or does it keep the government under careful scrutiny, checking on whether it has behaved as it said it would and on whether public money has been spent as the government promised, keeping the government on its toes and exposing its mistakes? How effective is the Dáil in making the government answerable and accountable? The Dáil has three main methods of trying to compel the government to justify its behaviour: debates, parliamentary questions and committees.

Debates

As well as the debates on bills, which we have already discussed, the Dáil may debate other motions. Two that are relevant to the scrutiny function of the Dáil are, first, motions of confidence in the government and, second, formal motions on topics such as the adjournment of the house. From time to time an opposition party is prone to table a motion of no confidence in the government, to which the government almost invariably responds by tabling a motion of confidence in itself. The resultant debate, naturally, ranges over the entire gamut of the government's activity, with opposition TDs using the occasion to obtain publicity for their criticisms of the government rather than really expecting to oust the government—as we have already mentioned, only twice (in 1982 and 1992) has a government actually lost such a motion. The adjournment debate held at the end of some sessions (a debate ostensibly on a topic such as "That Dáil Éireann do adjourn for the summer recess") is similar in content, as various ministers defend the government's record while opposition TDs disparage it.

Parliamentary questions

On each Tuesday, Wednesday and Thursday when the Dáil sits, one hour and a quarter is set aside for parliamentary questions (PQs). Ministers face questions, on successive sitting days, in rotation. Questions must be put down three working days before they are due to be answered, to give the minister and departmental civil servants time to discover the information sought. Questions may seek very detailed information; they may relate to an individual constituent or to the constituency of the TD asking the question, or they may ask about a topic of national significance or a matter of government policy. Some questions seek a written answer, which the TD receives within three working days, but others are put down for oral answer, which means that the TD must wait until the relevant minister's day for answering questions comes around but does have the advantage that the TD can respond to the minister's reply by asking a "supplementary" question. A TD dissatisfied with the minister's reply can raise and elaborate upon his or her grievance during the "adjournment debate" that occupies the last 50 minutes of each day's sitting, and the minister is obliged to reply more fully. This, though, receives little media coverage because of its late hour, except in the relevant provincial newspapers. Deputies may ask any number of questions for written answer, but no TD can put down more than two on any one day that seek an oral answer; the order in which the latter questions appear on the order paper (which determines which ones will be reached, since time constraints mean that on average only about 20 questions are answered orally each day) is settled by lottery. This has led to the practice known in Britain as "syndication" (Irwin, Kennon, Natzler and Rogers, 1993, pp. 50-2), whereby a number of Fine Gael TDs put down identical or near-identical questions in order to boost the chances of the question being drawn in a high position in the lottery.

The number of questions has risen greatly over the years (see Table 7.2). Over the 50-year period covered in Table 7.2, the number of questions for oral answer doubled while the number of written questions rose fifty-fold. This matches experience in the United Kingdom, where the number of questions doubled from the late 1940s to the late 1960s and had doubled again by the late 1980s (Irwin, Kennon, Natzler and Rogers, 1993, p. 27). The number of questions to the Minister for Social Welfare rose from an average of 152 a year in the mid-1960s to 2,285 a year in the mid-1980s, when this department, together with Environment and Education, accounted for about half of the questions asked. The exponential rise in the number of written questions (in part a sign of the increased volume of constituency work) is a fairly recent phenomenon; as late as 1978 there were more questions for oral than for written answer. During the 1970s, in fact, the number of questions put down for oral answer (most of which were not answered orally due to time constraints) reached a peak of 6,056 in 1971, over 12 times as many as the number of questions put down for written answer (Smyth, 1979, p. 51). Only during the 1980s did the number of oral questions fall to roughly manageable proportions (as TDs realised that there was little point in putting down for oral answer questions that, due to limitations on time, would almost certainly receive a written answer in any case) and the number of written questions escalate enormously.

Table 7.2: Parliamentary questions in the 1930s, 1960s and 1980s

	1934-38 (average per annum)	1964-68 (average per annum)	1984-88 (average per annum)
Questions for oral answer	984	4,043	2,011
Questions for written answer	179	249	8,740
Private notice questions	1	3	39
Total questions	1,164	4,295	10,791

Notes: All figures are averages, so, due to rounding, columns do not necessarily add to the total figures. Private notice questions are questions of which the minister receives no prior notification: Dáil Standing Order 31 provides that questions "relating to matters of urgent public importance" may be "asked on private notice", subject to the permission of the Ceann Comhairle.
Source: For the 1930s, *Questions in the Dáil*, published annually by the Stationery Office, Dublin. For the 1960s, *Returns relating to Sittings and Business of the 17th Dáil* (Dublin: Stationery Office, 1967) and *Returns relating to Sittings and Business of the 18th Dáil* (Dublin: Stationery Office, 1971). For the 1980s, *Returns relating to Sittings and Business of the 24th Dáil* (Dublin: Stationery Office, 1990) and *Returns relating to Sittings and Business of the 25th Dáil* (Dublin: Stationery Office, 1991).

The rise in the number of questions receiving written answers has continued in the period since 1988: in 1991 11,200 were asked, together with 2,100 that received oral answers, while in 1992 the respective figures were 11,000 and 1,900 (the practice of syndication, described above, slightly inflates these figures). As in Britain, oral questions tend to be policy-related while questions for written answer are more often concerned with local matters or individuals. Some analyses have criticised the volume of questions, arguing that those relating to individuals are not the sort of questions TDs should be asking and constitute "wasteful duplication" of the work of the Ombudsman (Anon, 1983; Anon, 1986). Certainly, the prominent recurrence of the same few names among those asking questions about individual constituents does suggest that many TDs find other less public ways of obtaining similar information. The only attempt to cost parliamentary questions was made in 1982, when it was calculated that the average cost of dealing with a question was about £40. When a similar question was asked ten years later, the Minister for Finance indicated that the equivalent cost in 1992, based on the 1982 figure, would be around £64 (*Dáil Debates* 415: 1831-2, 13 February 1992). The fact that most questions are tabled by opposition TDs affirms the political motive of putting down a question—government deputies ask very few questions, even of a local nature.

In many ways the odds at question time are stacked in the ministers' favour. After all, they have had at least three days to think of a reply and, besides, there is nothing to prevent them from giving an evasive reply. In addition, they need not answer supplementary questions at all, if necessary using the formula that "that is a separate question", if by chance the supplementary asked is one that they did not anticipate and hence did not have their officials prepare an answer to. At question time, the minister has civil servants sitting across the aisle waiting to pass to him or her the relevant information or documents, while the TD asking the question does not have access to this kind of back-up.

However, there is a limit, in practical political terms, to the extent to which a minister can evade a question without giving the impression that he or she has something to hide. The stature of a minister who seems unable to give convincing answers to questions will drop, among both government deputies and journalists. Question time is the liveliest part of the Dáil schedule, so it gets good media coverage. If a minister performs ineptly at question time, this is likely to receive coverage on television news, and journalists' assessments of the minister are less likely to be favourable. Consequently, parliamentary questions can be quite effective in probing some alleged ministerial misdemeanour. However, they are not designed to enable the monitoring of government policies on a continuous basis—if this is to be done, the most appropriate mechanism is a system of committees.

Oireachtas committees

Committees are a feature of almost all modern parliaments, but their significance varies greatly. Where government is not directly accountable to parliament, parliament may work mainly through committees: examples include the US Congress and the European Parliament. In parliamentary systems, committees tend to be more powerful in countries closer to the consensus model than where the Westminster model applies. In the traditional Westminster model, which Ireland took over in 1922, committees have no great significance.

When a fully-fledged committee system is up and running, parliament has a number of committees, each consisting of around 10 to 30 deputies depending on the size of the parliament, with a specific function. Some committees monitor the performance of government in specific policy areas, such as agriculture or education. Others might be assigned to review policy in some area, such as taxation or pensions, and to examine or suggest legislation. If committees are to be strong and effective, they will have the power to insist that ministers and civil servants appear before them to explain their decisions, and they will also need the resources to hire outside experts and research staff in order to examine topics systematically. If they are to work properly they need to operate to some extent on non- or cross-party lines, as otherwise they will just replicate the division on the floor of parliament. Sometimes "small group psychology" creates an identification with the committee that rivals, though rarely displaces, identification with party. Ministers and civil servants know that they might one day have to give detailed justifications of the decisions they make and so, it is hoped, they take more care to make the right ones.

Because the idea of a strong committee system was not part of the Westminster system in 1922, it did not form part of the original procedures of the Oireachtas either. Until the 1980s, committees were few in number, and even some of those that did exist were mere "housekeeping" committees, looking after the internal affairs of Leinster House. Most of the non-housekeeping committees are "joint" committees—that is, they contain members from both Dáil and Seanad. The most important committee up to the 1980s was the Public Accounts Committee, which has the function of considering the accounts of government departments in the light of the annual reports of the Comptroller and Auditor General, who checks that public money has been spent in the way that the Oireachtas decided it should be. However, a study of the operation of this committee from 1961 to 1980 spoke of the unconscientious attitude of its members, superficial and unplanned questioning, and haphazard treatment of officials (O'Halpin, 1985, especially pp. 507-8). Two other committees set up in the 1970s were more successful. In 1973 the Committee on the Secondary Legislation of the European Communities was established to monitor developments within the EC affecting Ireland, and its reports were often of high quality, although the Oireachtas generally showed little interest in them (see pp. 242-3 below). The Committee on State-Sponsored Bodies was created in 1978 and soon established a reputation for thorough investigation of this sector of the economy, where information had previously been hard to come by (Chubb, 1992, pp. 202-3).

Discontent grew on all sides of the house during the 1970s with the seeming irrelevance of the Dáil. In 1975 Labour backbencher Barry Desmond published a "Plea for Reform" of the Dáil, and five years later Fine Gael published proposals to strengthen the Dáil's committee system (Desmond, 1975; Fine Gael, 1980). The Fine Gael-Labour coalition government that came into office in December 1982 instigated a Dáil debate on Oireachtas reform in early 1983, an event that put on the record a widespread feeling among deputies that procedures needed a major overhaul. Later that year an expanded committee system was duly established.

Altogether, 17 committees were set up during the lifetime of the 24th Dáil, eight of them entirely new. Each had a brief that crossed departmental boundaries: for example, there were committees on Women's Rights; Marriage Breakdown; Public Expenditure; Small Businesses; Crime, Lawlessness and Vandalism; Cooperation with Developing Countries; and so on. The decision not to have departmentally-related committees was not fully explained—the reason may have been a fear, expressed by John Bruton (the minister responsible for introducing the reforms), that such committees would end up arguing for more resources for "their" departments. An Agriculture committee, for example, would probably consist mainly of farmers, and they would call for more money for agriculture (Dáil Debates 339: 1266-7, 8 February 1983). While this is indeed a danger, and occurs in some parliaments, it is hard to see how committees can effectively monitor the work of departments if they are not given a brief requiring them to do that. In the great majority of parliaments, parliamentary committees do correspond to ministerial departments, and the scrutiny function is performed more effectively as a result (IPU, 1986, pp. 630-49; Olson and Mezey, 1991, p. 15).

This bold experiment in Oireachtas reform drew mixed reviews. One problem that soon became apparent was that in relation to the size of the pool from which committee members could be drawn, there were simply too many commit-tees. Only the 166 TDs and 60 senators could become members, and from this num-ber the 30 cabinet and junior ministers had to be deducted. At the peak of the committee system, there were 256 committee places to be filled (175 by TDs and 81 by senators), so many Oireachtas members found themselves overstretched by multiple commitments, and some committee meetings had to be embarrassingly postponed because they were inquorate (the quorum in a 30-member committee, for instance, would be 11). The research, staffing and accommodation demands made by the expanded Dáil committee system imposed a great strain on Leinster House resources (Arkins, 1988, p. 94). In addition, the spread of committees was criticised. O'Halpin (1986, pp. 3-4) described the committees as "a haphazard collection"—some major areas of government activity, such as economic affairs, employment, foreign policy, agriculture, Northern Ireland and education escaped scrutiny (due mainly to the decision that committees should not "shadow" gov-ernment departments), while some of the committees had "vague or ill-considered" remits. Arkins (1988, p. 94) speaks of "an uncoordinated mish-mash of committees", which resulted partly from the way in which some committees were set up as parts of deals between government and opposition.

Despite these reservations, most assessments of the expanded system saw clear benefits. Zimmerman (1988, p. 286) concluded that it improved executive account-ability by compelling policy makers to justify the decisions they had made; the committees were "successful to an extent in obtaining information needed to make useful recommendations for improving the system of control". Arkins (1988, p. 97) describes the achievements of the committee experiment as "considerable". The coalition government took up some of the suggestions made by committees, and after 1987 some of the decisions made by the new Fianna Fáil ministers were influenced by ideas highlighted by the committees with which they had been involved while in opposition. Specialist committee work improved the expertise of backbenchers generally. The expanded committee system also provided the Oireachtas with "well researched ammunition with which to pester the execu-tive".

Oireachtas committees have no permanent existence—each is constituted afresh at the start of each parliament. Consequently, after 1987 the number of committees reconstituted was a clear verdict on the 1983 experiment, as far fewer were brought into existence. As of mid-1992 there were only 13 committees, and six of these were "housekeeping" committees, concerned with the running of Lein-ster House. The other seven committees were Commercial State-Sponsored Bod-ies, Crime, Employment, Irish Language, Public Accounts, Secondary Legislation of the European Communities, and Women's Rights.

The Fianna Fáil-Labour coalition's "Programme for Government" in 1993 revi-ved the idea of a much more extensive committee system. Five of the non-housekeeping committees were reconstituted (the exceptions being those on Crime and Employment), and these were joined by five new committees (see Table 7.3): Foreign Affairs (with sub-committees dealing with the Secondary Legislation of the EC and Cooperation with Developing Countries), Enterprise and Economic Strategy (covering the departments of Agriculture; Enterprise and Employment; Marine; Tourism and Trade; Transport, Energy and Communications), Finance and General Affairs (covering the departments of Taoiseach; Environment; Finance),

Legislation and Security (covering the departments of Defence; Equality and Law Reform; Justice), and Social Affairs (covering the departments of Arts, Culture and the Gaeltacht; Education; Health; Social Welfare). The last four of these consider the committee stages of bills emanating from the specified departments, and also discuss the financial estimates of their departments. It remains to be seen how much further the committees go in attempting to scrutinise the affairs of the departments within their ambit. This initiative undoubtedly constitutes a significant step towards the "comprehensive" committee system that observers of the Oireachtas have long advocated. Early assessments indicated some teething troubles, including dissatisfaction at the committees' lack of power to compel ministers and civil servants to appear before them, and low attendance at some meetings, caused partly by the fact that most TDs (other than ministers) belong to more than one committee.

Table 7.3: Oireachtas committees in 1993

Committee (type)	TDs	Senators	Total
Commercial State-sponsored Bodies (Joint)	7	4	11
Enterprise and Economic Strategy (Dáil)	30	-	30
Finance and General Affairs (Dáil)	30	-	30
Foreign Affairs (Joint)	25	5	30
Irish Language (Joint)	7	4	11
Legislation and Security (Dáil)	30	-	30
Public Accounts (Dáil)	12	-	12
Social Affairs (Dáil)	30	-	30
Women's Rights (Joint)	11	6	17
Housekeeping committees			
Consolidation Bills (Joint)	3	3	6
Procedure and Privileges (Dáil)	18	-	18
Procedure and Privileges (Seanad)	-	12	12
Selection (Dáil)	13	-	13
Selection (Seanad)	-	11	11
Services (Joint)	9	9	18
Standing Orders (Joint)	3	3	6
Total	228	57	285

Source: Information supplied by the Houses of the Oireachtas.

Certainly, past experience has disappointed those who have held unrealistic expectations about the possibility of an expanded committee system radically transforming relations between government and parliament to the latter's advantage. It has made it clear that there are a number of fundamental reasons why, despite the extensive reforms introduced in the 27th Dáil, hopes should not be pitched too high.

First, most governments have not been keen to see an effective system emerge. Government ministers, like everyone else, would prefer not to have to work under close scrutiny. Opposition frontbenchers would like to see the government on the rack, but they look forward to being in government themselves one day and thus have some reluctance to see too many checks on ministers. Fianna Fáil in particular has never been keen on the idea, and its agreement to strengthen the committee system in 1993 represented something of a volte face. In 1983 its then leader Charles Haughey made clear his reservations, saying that "the running of the country ... is a matter for clear hard decisions by the Government", not for committees, and that discussion of those decisions should take place in the Dáil chamber (*Dáil Debates* 343: 2380, 21 June 1983).

Second, for much the same reasons, the civil service is not enthusiastic about a system of committees that can summon officials and demand to know why particular decisions were made. Senior civil servants are said to have "resented being quizzed" by the Public Expenditure Committee, one of the most active of the committees of the 1982-87 Dáil (Arkins, 1988, p. 96). There are problems in reconciling such a system with the traditional "corporation sole" concept, under which the minister is deemed ultimately responsible for all decisions made within his or her department. Civil servants can be reprimanded only if they act outside their powers or outside the minister's policies. If some misdemeanour is committed as a result of a civil servant carrying out a routine function in line with departmental policy, the minister rather than the civil servant is to blame. Consequently, when the committee system was expanded in the mid-1980s, the Department of the Public Service issued guidelines for civil servants (see Zimmerman, 1988, pp. 276-8). These guidelines stressed that civil servants appearing before Oireachtas committees did so on behalf of their minister and should clear with the minister in advance what they intended to say. They were not to tell a committee at what level a decision was made, nor were they to reveal information about the advice given by civil servants to the minister. This protected civil servants who had given poor advice to their minister, preserving the position that only the minister could be held accountable. Equally, it prevented civil servants who had cautioned against a policy that turned out to be a blunder from telling the committee, "I told him it was foolish, but he did it anyway".

Third, there are questions as to how far a strong committee system can be reconciled with a parliamentary system of government—especially when the Westminster model operates. When government TDs must be loyal to the government in the Dáil chamber, they may not be likely to criticise it within a committee, so cross-party agreement might be difficult to preserve unless committees refrain from too direct an assault on government. Comparisons with the strong committee system in the US Congress or the European Parliament are misleading since government survival is not at stake there. In most parliamentary systems, certainly, committees are usually more significant than Oireachtas committees have traditionally been, but they do not come anywhere near to displacing government from its dominant position in the political process. Moreover, members of the American Congress and the European Parliament do not usually aspire to places in government, unlike backbenchers in parliamentary systems. In Ireland, 30 out of 80-100 government deputies will be in cabinet or junior ministerial posts—almost all Fianna Fáil TDs, and many of those from other parties, can nurture quite realistic hopes of one day savouring the delights of office, provided they keep their noses clean. A backbencher who wants promotion might well decide that going along with the party line is a safer option than becoming a trenchant inquisitor of his or her own party in government and, like the opposition frontbenchers, may not want to weaken the powers of the offices to which he or she aspires.

Fourth, TDs are not well equipped to enquire closely into the actions of government. As we have seen, the 1983 reforms strained resources greatly. TDs and senators have very limited facilities for research. The Oireachtas library, for example, contained about 52,000 titles in the mid-1980s, compared with 430,000 titles in the library of Finland's Eduskunta or 160,000 in the Danish Folketing, not to mention even larger holdings in the parliaments of bigger countries (IPU, 1986, pp. 728-53). Indeed, even TDs' basic facilities are modest—it was only in 1982 that each TD finally got his or her own secretary. Before then, many TDs had answered all their letters personally in longhand. TDs' salaries (around IR£30,000 a year) do not allow them to employ personal staffs beyond, in some cases, a constituency secretary. Moreover, TDs have heavy demands on their time from other sources, especially constituency work (see chapter 8). In the past, many TDs probably had more interest in their constituents' problems than in the potential rewards of committee work. That has changed since the late 1970s, but even those TDs who would like to devote themselves to parliamentary duties are reluctant to spend too much time on committee work. TDs fear that devoting their energies to Oireachtas committee work for four years and neglecting their clinics would be a recipe for electoral suicide. It may be, though, that the provision of more expert assistance and research advice for the committees would enable TDs to contribute effectively to committee work without placing their seats in jeopardy.

Overall, the Dáil's mechanisms for scrutinising the government are not as effective as they might be. However, the Dáil, while playing, as we have seen, little part in influencing policy, compares quite well with many parliaments when it comes to keeping an eye on government, despite the glib but frequently heard generalisations to the effect that it is among the feeblest parliaments in Europe. For example, the Swedish Riksdag is weak in this area, having only one committee trying to supervise the work of government departments (Arter, 1990, p. 136). Similarly, the French National Assembly is very ineffectual as a watchdog over government: "the procedures for controlling executive power, for scrutinising or debating or questioning executive acts, are completely inadequate", and the only real checks on the executive are fear of violence in the streets or of losing the next election (Frears, 1990, p. 50).

SEANAD ÉIREANN

Our discussion so far has concentrated mainly on the Dáil but, as we mentioned at the start of the chapter, the Oireachtas also has an upper house, Seanad Éireann. The lifespan of each Seanad matches that of the Dáil, except that Seanad elections take place a couple of months after the corresponding Dáil election. The Seanad has 60 members: 43 are elected from five "panels", six are elected by university graduates and the other 11 are appointed by the Taoiseach. The five panels are Agriculture, Culture and Education, Industry and Commerce, Labour, and Public Administration, and those nominated for a panel are required to have "knowledge and practical experience" of its subject (Article 18.7.1 of the constitution). This might give the impression that the Seanad is a vocational body containing representatives of the main interest groups. However, even if this is what some expected in 1937 when the format of the new upper house was first outlined, the reality is otherwise because of the composition of the electorate (which is defined by law and not by the constitution). The electors for the 43 panel seats are members of city and county councils, the Dáil and the outgoing Seanad—those qualified under more than one heading receive only one vote. At the January 1993 Seanad election, the electorate for the panel seats comprised 965 people, of whom 786 were affiliated to one of the three main parties (Coakley, 1993, p. 140). Not surprisingly, since the great bulk of the voters are practising party politicians, so are the people they elect, and, by and large, the senators elected from the panels are similar in background to TDs—indeed, they are often former or aspiring TDs, or both.

The six university senators are returned from two panels. Graduates of the National University of Ireland return three senators, with the other three elected by TCD graduates. The principle of special graduate representation has been criticised as elitist, and the details of representation give more weight to Trinity graduates than to the more numerous NUI graduates, not to mention graduates of other third-level institutions who are excluded from the election. However, it has been pointed out that very few of the university senators are members of a political party (Coakley, 1993, p. 142), and defenders of the university seats maintain that these six senators are often an innovative and independent force in an Oireachtas otherwise firmly controlled by the parties. The 11 senators appointed by the Taoiseach are usually chosen so as to ensure that the government has a secure majority in the Seanad, and to give a boost to politicians who have a chance of winning an extra seat for the party at the next Dáil elections.

The Seanad is by far the weaker of the two houses. A few of the powers of the Houses of the Oireachtas, it is true, are shared equally among both chambers; thus, the declaration of an emergency (see pp. 55-6 above), the impeachment of a President or the removal of a judge need acquiescence from both Dáil and Seanad. In the area of legislation, the Dáil is unequivocally the superior chamber. Bills come before the Seanad, but at most it can merely delay them for 90 days. If it rejects a non-money bill, reaches no decision or suggests amendments that are unacceptable to the Dáil, the Dáil can simply overrule it (Article 23.1 of the constitution). In the case of a money bill, the Seanad is given only three weeks in which to make its "recommendations", which again the Dáil may overrule (Article 21). If it rejects a bill (other than a bill to amend the constitution) and the Dáil overrules it, it may invoke the "Article 27 procedure", under which a majority of senators and a third of the members of the Dáil may petition the President not to sign the bill but instead to submit it to a referendum. No such petition has ever been presented—indeed, the Seanad has not rejected a government bill since July 1964. Not surprisingly, the Seanad is often dismissed as a mere "talking shop", and some (including the Progressive Democrats) have called for its abolition, pointing to the abolition of comparable chambers in Denmark (in 1953), New Zealand (1950) and Sweden (1970). The Seanad meets less frequently than the Dáil—for only 68 days in both 1991 and 1992—and senators are paid less than TDs (IR£18,000 a year).

Defenders of the Seanad argue that despite its lack of power, it plays a useful role in the legislative process, as debates on bills are usually conducted in a more reflective and constructive, non-party spirit than in the Dáil. Moreover, in recent years the Seanad has been more keen than the Dáil to discuss the reports issued by Oireachtas committees and, besides, contentious issues that TDs are reluctant to grapple with are sometimes raised in the Seanad, often by university senators. In addition, the task of setting up an effective Oireachtas committee system would be even more difficult without the 60 senators—though with only 19 senators sitting on non-housekeeping committees in 1993, this resource was being under-utilised. In any case, the Seanad is useful to the political parties, and since any proposal to abolish it would have to come from them, it is likely to remain in existence, whether or not its currently insignificant place in the political system is enhanced.

WEAKNESS OF PARLIAMENT

From what we have said so far, it is clear that in relations between government and parliament, the government is generally the dominant partner—although in times of minority government, a situation quite common during the 1980s, the position is not quite so clear cut. There are many reasons for governmental dominance, some applicable to most parliaments—hence the frequent references to a "decline of parliaments" during the twentieth century—and some specific to the Oireachtas.

For one thing, the role of the state, and hence of government, has grown considerably during the twentieth century. Government business has become much more complex, and it is more difficult for all but those directly and continuously involved to monitor its work. The level of specialisation and expertise required is such that everyone else, including the backbench member of parliament, is effectively an amateur in the policy-making process.

Second, the development of the mass media has provided an alternative and often more effective means of making governments accountable. Ministers cannot so easily wriggle out of awkward situations when being grilled by an interviewer on the television as they can in parliament.

Third, parliaments tend to be conservative institutions, slow to adapt to changes in the outside world. The Dáil has tended to look only as far as another notoriously conservative parliament, the House of Commons, when considering reforms. Thus an expanded committee system was introduced in 1983 only after Westminster had adopted one in 1979, and broadcasting of Dáil proceedings on radio (in 1986) and on television (in 1991) began several years after the Commons had taken these steps. The Dáil has been slow to demand that its members declare their interests in a register maintained for that purpose, as is done in most European parliaments. The Fianna Fáil-Labour programme for government in January 1993 promised that such a register would soon be introduced, though it was evident that not all Fianna Fáil or Fine Gael backbenchers viewed the prospect with enthusiasm.

Fourth, new patterns of decision making virtually bypass parliament. In many European countries, including Ireland, the major interest groups, especially the employers' and farmers' organisations and the trade unions, play a central role in economic policy making (see chapter 10). When the government agrees a package with these interests (such as the 1987 Programme for National Recovery or the 1991 Programme for Economic and Social Progress), parliament can do little except chew over a fait accompli. The Dáil's weakness also reinforces the tendency of these groups to concentrate their lobbying efforts on government ministers and senior civil servants, where the real power lies, leaving ordinary TDs with few interests to represent other than those of their constituents. In addition, a growing number of policies are made at EC level, again undermining the traditional notion of domestic parliaments as law-making bodies (see chapter 12). Moreover, the courts, utilising their role as interpreters of the constitution, have become increasingly active in effectively changing the law in a number of respects (see chapter 3).

Fifth, as we have already observed, TDs have other demands on their time, especially constituency work (see chapter 8). Even the most nationally-oriented deputies cannot spend all their political lives on parliamentary work, because they are expected to service the needs of their constituents and fear losing their seats if they neglect this work. Interestingly, although in Ireland the impact of the pressures of constituency work on parliament is often seen in a negative light, as a "problem" that should be fixed, in other countries it is viewed positively. Citizens who need advice or assistance could use some alternative extra-parliamentary channel, so the fact that they often contact their local MP or deputy is seen in both Britain and France as beneficial to the political system and testimony to the relevance of parliament (Norton, 1990b, pp. 24-5; Frears, 1990, p. 50). In contrast, the very low level of contact between individuals and deputies on constituency matters in the Netherlands is held to produce "mutual isolation" and to contribute to the low esteem in which Dutch people hold their parliament (Gladdish, 1990, pp. 115-16).

Finally, and most importantly, deputies behave not as individuals but as members of a party. When it comes to the crunch, deputies in most parliaments follow the party line; when political life is dominated by political parties, as is the case throughout Europe, deputies' orientation to party is stronger than their orientation to parliament. As we saw earlier, this is not necessarily a bad thing—to govern effectively, governments need to be able to rely on their own backbenchers to support them through thick and thin. Deputies stay in line because they know that rebellion will probably harm their own chances of promotion within the party, because they are reluctant to appear to be siding with the opposition, and because government legislation is likely to be broadly acceptable to them since they have their say on it at meetings of the parliamentary party. Having said this, the solidarity of party voting in the Dáil is extraordinarily high, to the extent that a government TD voting against any government bill, apart from those very rare cases where a free vote is allowed, is likely to be expelled from the parliamentary party. Indeed, in July 1993 the Fianna Fáil parliamentary party adopted a rule under which voting against the whip, or even abstaining, on any issue would henceforth mean automatic expulsion from the parliamentary party. In most European parliaments a rather higher degree of independence is usually allowed, although persistent mavericks will eventually have to pay the price. One reason for the difference may be that Irish governments have often had very small Dáil majorities, or no majorities at all, so that any crack in solid party voting could lead to a government defeat. In addition, governments have clung to an especially rigid version of the Westminster model, whereby a government that cannot get its legislation through resigns. British governments used to operate under this convention until it was effectively rewritten when the Callaghan minority government in the 1970s soldiered on despite losing votes on some major bills. However, the Dáil, in this as in other aspects, remains "more British than the British themselves", and governments in effect attach an implicit confidence motion to most of their bills. The threat of a general election therefore hangs in the air when a government bill seems in danger of defeat, a powerful incentive for government backbenchers not to rock the boat. As Laundy (1989, p. 86) puts it, it may be a "misconception" that a government must resign if it sustains a defeat, but "since it helps to keep their followers in line, governments have little interest in discrediting this myth".

CONCLUSION

The relationship between government and parliament is often seen in adversarial terms, and the question is asked: which controls which? Since the Dáil patently does not control the government, it easy to conclude that the government controls the Dáil and that the Dáil is therefore an irrelevant rubber stamp.

This chapter has shown that such a conclusion would be an oversimplification. The relationship between government and parliament in nearly every country is less stark and more symbiotic than the adversarial perspective would suggest, with a degree of give and take between the two. It is true that the Dáil hardly ever throws a government out, or even rejects one of its proposals, but this is partly because the government takes care not to propose anything that the Dáil might not accept. It is true that government backbenchers almost invariably file faithfully through the "Tá" (Yes) lobbies when votes are taken on government bills, but this is partly because the government clears its plans with these backbenchers in advance at meetings of the parliamentary party. It is true that the initiative in policy making lies with the government rather than with the Dáil, but that is the case in most European parliaments, though the Dáil would certainly be more effective if bills were examined by an Oireachtas committee before being discussed by the full Dáil. By means of parliamentary questions and a potentially powerful system of committees, the Dáil can exercise a degree of scrutiny over government that compares favourably with the position in some other countries.

However, there is no doubt that parliament could be more effective in carrying out this role of keeping an eye on the behaviour of government than it has been in the past. The most obvious reform has always been the establishment of an expanded committee system, with committees directly paralleling government departments, and the 1993 scheme represents a major move in that direction. This is likely to be as far as the Oireachtas can go in extending its influence. In a political system where the Westminster model is widely accepted as setting the correct groundrules for the relationship between government and parliament, and where TDs or senators defying the party whip do so at their peril, the Oireachtas has little chance of ever becoming a major player in the policy-making process.

REFERENCES AND FURTHER READING

Anon, 1983. "Dáil questions on social welfare", *Relate: Information Bulletin of the National Social Service Board,* December, pp. 2-5.

Anon, 1986. "No answers for Dáil questions", *Consumer Choice,* October, pp. 294-6.

Arkins, Audrey, 1988. "The committees of the 24th Oireachtas", *Irish Political Studies* 3, pp. 91-7.

Arkins, Audrey, 1990. "Legislative and executive relations in the Republic of Ireland", pp. 90-102 in Norton (1990a).

Arter, David, 1990. "The Swedish Riksdag: the case of a strong policy-influencing assembly", pp. 120-42 in Norton (1990a).

Borthwick, Robert, 1988. "The floor of the house", pp. 53-75 in Ryle and Richards (1988).

Chubb, Basil, 1992. *The Government and Politics of Ireland,* 3rd ed. Harlow: Longman.

Coakley, John, 1993. "The Senate election", pp. 135-45 in Gallagher and Laver (1993).

Collins, Stephen, 1993. *Spring and the Labour Story.* Dublin: The O'Brien Press.

Desmond, Barry, 1975. *The Houses of the Oireachtas: a Plea for Reform.* Dublin: the author.

Dinan, Des, 1986. "Constitution and parliament", pp. 71-86 in Brian Girvin and Roland Sturm (eds), *Politics and Society in Contemporary Ireland.* Aldershot: Gower.

Farrell, Brian, 1990. "Forming the government", pp. 179-91 in Gallagher and Sinnott (1990).

Farrell, Brian, 1993. "The formation of the partnership government", pp. 146-61 in Gallagher and Laver (1993).

Fine Gael, 1980. *Reform of the Dáil.* Dublin: Fine Gael.

Frears, John, 1990. "The French parliament: loyal workhorse, poor watchdog", pp. 32-51 in Norton (1990a).

Gallagher, Michael and Michael Laver (eds), 1993. *How Ireland Voted 1992.* Dublin: Folens and Limerick: PSAI Press.

Gallagher, Michael, Michael Laver and Peter Mair, 1992. *Representative Government in Western Europe.* New York and London: McGraw-Hill.

Gallagher, Michael and Richard Sinnott (eds), 1990. *How Ireland Voted 1989.* Galway: Centre for the Study of Irish Elections and PSAI Press.

Girvin, Brian, 1990. "The campaign", pp. 5-22 in Gallagher and Sinnott (1990).

Girvin, Brian, 1993. "The road to the election", pp. 1-20 in Gallagher and Laver (1993).

Gladdish, Ken, 1990. "Parliamentary activism and legitimacy in the Netherlands", pp. 103-19 in Norton (1990a).

Inter-Parliamentary Union, 1986. *Parliaments of the World: a Comparative Reference Compendium,* 2nd ed. Aldershot: Gower.

Irwin, Helen, Andrew Kennon, David Natzler and Robert Rogers, 1993. "Evolving rules", pp. 23-72 in Mark Franklin and Philip Norton (eds), *Parliamentary Questions.* Oxford: Clarendon Press.

Laegreid, Per and Johan P. Olsen, 1986. "The Storting: a last stronghold of the political amateur", pp. 176-222 in Suleiman (1986).

Laundy, Philip, 1989. *Parliaments in the Modern World.* Aldershot: Dartmouth.

Laver, Michael and Audrey Arkins, 1990. "Coalition and Fianna Fáil", pp. 192-207 in Gallagher and Sinnott (1990).

Lijphart, Arend, 1984. *Democracies: Patterns of Majoritarian and Consensus Government in Twenty-one Countries.* New Haven and London: Yale University Press.

Mitchell, Paul, 1993. "The 1992 general election in the Republic of Ireland", *Irish Political Studies* 8, pp. 111-17.

Morgan, David Gwynn, 1990. *Constitutional Law of Ireland,* 2nd ed. Blackrock: Round Hall Press.

Norton, Philip (ed.), 1990a. *Parliaments in Western Europe.* London: Frank Cass.

Norton, Philip, 1990b. "Parliament in the United Kingdom: balancing effectiveness and consent?", pp. 10-31 in Norton (1990a).

Norton, Philip, 1990c. "Conclusion: legislatures in perspective", pp. 143-52 in Norton (1990a).

O'Halpin, Eunan, 1985. "The Dáil Committee of Public Accounts, 1961-1980", *Administration* 32:4, pp. 483-511.

O'Halpin, Eunan, 1986. "Oireachtas committees: experience and prospects", *Seirbhís Phoiblí* 7:2, pp. 3-9.

Olson, David M. and Michael L. Mezey, 1991. "Parliaments and public policy", pp. 1-24 in David M. Olson and Michael L. Mezey (eds), *Legislatures in the Policy Process: the Dilemmas of Economic Policy*. Cambridge: Cambridge University Press.

Rose, Richard, 1986. "British MPs: more bark than bite", pp. 8-40 in Suleiman (1986).

Ryle, Michael and Peter G. Richards (eds), 1988. *The Commons under Scrutiny*. London: Routledge.

Shaw, Malcolm, 1979. "Conclusion", pp. 361-434 in John D. Lees and Malcolm Shaw (eds), *Committees in Legislatures: a Comparative Analysis*. Oxford: Martin Robertson.

Smyth, J. McGowan, 1979. *The Houses of the Oireachtas*, 4th ed. Dublin: Institute of Public Administration.

Suleiman, Ezra N. (ed.), 1986. *Parliaments and Parliamentarians in Democratic Politics*. New York: Holmes and Meier.

Ward, Alan J., 1974. "Parliamentary procedures and the machinery of government in Ireland", *Irish University Review* 4:2, pp. 222-43.

Zimmerman, Joseph F., 1988. "An innovation: backbench committees", *Administration* 36:3, pp. 265-89.

8 / DÁIL DEPUTIES AND THEIR CONSTITUENCY WORK

Michael Gallagher and Lee Komito

In chapter 7 we looked at the parliamentary roles of Dáil deputies. In this chapter we concentrate on a different aspect of the work of TDs, looking at the business on which they spend a lot of their time, namely constituency work. We begin by looking at the backgrounds of TDs, since this reflects the expectations people have of their deputies, and then go on to describe their constituency work. We discuss its causes, examining several explanations that have been put forward, and then consider the consequences it has for the political system.

BACKGROUNDS OF DÁIL DEPUTIES

To become a member of parliament, local roots are very important in Ireland, as in almost all countries. Virtually all TDs live in their constituencies—outside Dublin, in particular, there are very few exceptions, most of whom are ministers. Most TDs were born, raised and educated in their constituencies, and have always lived there. Similarly, most TDs have a background as county or city councillors—again, something that is by no means unusual in a cross-national context. At the time of the 1992 election, 103 (62 per cent) were members of a local authority. Of the TDs elected in 1992, 73 per cent were on a local authority before entering the Dáil, and 90 per cent had been on a local authority at some stage (for analysis of the 27th Dáil, see Gallagher, 1993, pp. 71-5). Moreover, most TDs are members of local voluntary associations, and many have extensive kinship networks throughout the constituency. It is very hard for outsiders, or even for native sons or daughters with no established local base, to break through—they are unlikely to be picked as candidates, never mind get elected. A short cut to acquiring a local political base is to have a political pedigree. In the 1992 Dáil, a remarkable 39 of the 166 TDs (23 per cent) were related to one or more present or past TDs who had preceded them into the Dáil—perhaps a uniquely high level for any modern parliament. Only 20 of the TDs elected were women (see chapter 11 for fuller discussion of this).

As for TDs' occupations, one trend in recent years has been the increase in full-time deputies, who now make up a strong majority of the Dáil. Looking at the jobs deputies did before entering the Dáil, 47 per cent were professionals of one sort or another (teachers being the most numerous), with 21 per cent having a "commercial" background (mainly small businessmen, publicans and so on), 17 per cent being employees and 12 per cent farmers. The strength of "commercial" TDs makes the Dáil unusual in a comparative context, but this proportion has been declining in recent years, as has the number of farmers, while the number of professionals has been increasing. Some jobs are well suited to the insecurity of political tenure that characterises Irish political life. For example, teachers can take unpaid leave of absence and know that their jobs are waiting for them if they ever lose their Dáil seat. In other cases, political office complements the politician's previous occupation. "Commercial" occupations often provide the opportunity to make local contacts, as they may put the holder (a publican or an auctioneer, for example) in touch with people and enable the holder, being self-employed, to take time off at will for political purposes. By the same token, political office has been known to provide additional business for solicitors, publicans, auctioneers, insurance brokers, or other occupations in which clients can be attracted by publicity or the aura of power.

So the average TD, if there is such a person, is male; he lives, was born and has many contacts in his constituency, and belongs to the local council. The fact that this is typically the profile of those elected by the people tells us something about what Irish people expect from their deputies, and helps to explain the heavy load of constituency work that falls upon the shoulders of TDs.

BROKERAGE AND WHAT IT ENTAILS

In all parliaments, members have both a national parliamentary role and a local constituency role. In the former they are expected to play a part in legislative business and in scrutinising the way in which the government is running the country (see chapter 7). In their local role they keep in touch with the people who elected them, looking after the interests both of their constituencies generally and of individual constituents. Observers have often remarked on what they see as the over-concentration by Dáil deputies on constituency business at the expense of parliamentary work.

The most appropriate word to describe what TDs do in their role as constituency representatives is "brokerage", which should be distinguished from the related concept of clientelism. A broker deals in access to those who control resources rather than directly in the resources themselves; there might be situations in which a person wants something but is unable or unwilling to obtain it from the person who has it, in which case the services of a broker may be useful. Once the service has been provided, the brokerage relationship ends. The main difference between brokerage and clientelism is that clientelism implies a more intense, more permanent relationship. It involves "clients", people who are in some way tied in to the person who does things for them, whereas "brokerage" implies a relationship that is not institutionalised. Thus to say that Irish politics are characterised by clientelism would suggest that TDs have clienteles, sizeable bodies of people who are linked directly to them and who are in some way in their debt. To say that Irish politics are characterised by brokerage would imply that there are many people who do not have any dealings with TDs, and that even the people who do use TDs as brokers are not under any direct obligation to them as a result. Although the term "clientelism" has caught on in some circles as a way of describing constituency work, most reliable research suggests that brokerage rather than clientelism is what happens in Ireland.

This does not mean that there is no clientelism at all in Irish politics—the term is applicable to various aspects of internal party activities. The relations between party activists and politicians, as well as between politicians at different levels of the political system (councillor, TD, minister), do involve long-term, diffuse, personal commitments. It is at times of electoral competition (for party selection or public votes), as well as internal competition for party office, that such loyalties become evident.

Brokerage in Irish politics can take many forms. As carried on by TDs, it can involve, for instance, advising constituents about the benefits for which they are eligible; advising them how to get one of these benefits (a grant, allowance or pension); taking up with the civil service an apparently harsh decision or a case of delay; or helping, or seeming to help, someone to obtain a local authority house or even a job. It can also involve activity on behalf of a community, town, or residents' association, for example to persuade central or local government to improve water or sewerage services or street lighting, or to attract industry to the constituency. Some brokerage activities allegedly involve pulling strings, as in the apocryphal threat to have a garda transferred or demoted unless a pending drink-driving case is stopped, or in smoothing the path for dubious planning applications, so in some people's eyes brokerage has unsavoury connotations because it is regarded as using undue influence to give certain people unfair advantages.

Unquestionably, TDs do a lot of brokerage work—indeed, they spend most of their time doing it. There are quite a few pieces of evidence over the years, and they all point in the same direction. Dick Roche (who later became a TD himself) found from interviewing 115 TDs in 1981 that the average TD reported handling about 140 representations a week—though admittedly some of these were insignificant, such as a request for a form (Roche, 1982). Moreover, whichever way their work was measured it was clear that the volume of constituency work had gone up greatly since earlier surveys in the 1960s—the large increase in parliamentary questions in recent years (see Table 7.2 in the previous chapter) can be taken as a rough indicator of this. The main subject matter of representations was delay, usually concerned with the Department of Social Welfare or local authority housing. Kelly (1987, p. 139) reports a rather lower figure for the Labour TD Michael D. Higgins's load in 1982, about 3,000 cases in the year or 60 a week, and this may be a more reliable figure since it is based on a count of actual cases as opposed to TDs' reports of what they do. Whatever the precise figure, it is clear that a lot of time and work is involved: in holding several "clinics" each week in the constituency where constituents come to present their problem to the TD, and in exchanging letters or phone calls with constituents and with officials to follow up these cases. Since there is a TD for every 20,000 people, Kelly's figures imply that each TD, assuming Higgins was typical, has about 30 casework contacts a week per 10,000 constituents.

Does all this activity serve any useful purpose—do people benefit from asking TDs for assistance? Early studies came to very different conclusions. Sacks, who conducted research in County Donegal, concluded that politicians could actually achieve very little. They nonetheless manage to create and retain clienteles by dispensing what he calls "imaginary patronage"—that is, they convince people that they have achieved something for them even though in reality they haven't (Sacks, 1976, pp. 7-8). Nearly all the constituency work TDs do is carried out, he implies, solely to create the impression that the TD is making an effort. Certainly, some of it might be of this nature: many requests concern cases where the constituent will get the benefit anyway without anyone's help (such as an old age pension) or won't get it as he or she is simply not eligible. Similarly, from the civil service side of the fence, Dooney and O'Toole (1992, p. 190) write that "officials are not impressed by representations" from politicians and that the "elaborate" representations procedure "very rarely has the effect of having administrative decisions reversed". The implication is that TDs are largely going through the motions in order to impress their constituents with their industry rather than genuinely expecting to have any impact on decisions already reached by the civil service. However, it might seem implausible that most or all TDs' work falls into this category; it is doubtful whether TDs can build up, and preserve for many years, a reputation as hard-working and effective constituency politicians simply by dispensing imaginary patronage, unless their constituents are exceptionally gullible.

Bax, whose research was in County Cork, came to the opposite conclusion, namely that TDs have considerable power, deriving in some cases from their influence over the appointment of senior county council officials; they could install an associate in a position of power and use him or her thereafter. He gives an example (Bax, 1976, p. 49) of a TD who helped the county engineer get his job; the engineer then steered contracts to a businessman who was a friend of the TD, and the businessman gave jobs to people recommended by the TD. Another example (p. 64) concerned a TD bribing some councillors and council officials to get them to accept a tender from a businessman friend of his.

There is, it is true, evidence to support the claim that there are at least some strings to be pulled. The prominent civil servant Peter Berry mentions in his memoirs a case in 1962 concerning the appointment of an immigration officer at Cork Airport (*Magill*, June 1980, p. 46). The selection board put forward four names in ranked order, but the relevant minister, Charles Haughey, appointed the fourth, explaining that he had received representations on his behalf from Jack Lynch, a Cork TD and also a minister. Berry records other cases of ministers' use of patronage. In addition, some cases became public in the 1980s. In 1983, the Labour Court ruled that Seán Doherty, the former Minister for Justice, had used influence with the Minister for Public Works to get a constituent a job as a lock keeper in 1982, even though an interview board had ranked this person only fourth. Doherty responded that the Labour Court "should keep its snout out of my affairs" (*Irish Times*, 14 May 1983). In November 1984, it was alleged that the Minister for Defence, Patrick Cooney, had appointed to a clerical post in the army someone not recommended by the interview board but who had close family links with Alan Dukes, the Minister for Finance. Denying that anything improper had occurred, the minister counter-charged that he had discovered four occasions when Paddy Power, one of the TDs making the allegations, had appointed people ranked lower than first by the respective interview boards while he had been Minister for Defence in 1982 (*Dáil Debates* 354: 255-68, 20 November 1984). Analyses of the distribution of funds from the national lottery in 1988 and thereafter showed that significantly more money went to constituencies with ministers than those without ministers.

Even so, politicians' scope for pulling strings is less than it once was. The principle of appointment on merit rather than through string-pulling was established early on, with the creation of the Civil Service Commission and the Local Appointments Commission. Over the years, the writs of these bodies have been progressively extended. Rate collectors were one of the last sizeable job categories excluded from their scope, and with their inclusion there are now very few types of civil service job where a politician's support can help an applicant. However, the army, the police and the boards of semi-state companies are exempted from the scope of these Commissions.

In discussing string-pulling, we must also bear in mind that in Ireland, as in every other country, it is not unknown for businesses or others to donate money to individual politicians or to political parties in the hope or expectation of receiving a reward from the investment. The long-running Beef Tribunal that held public hearings from 1991 to 1993 under Mr Justice Hamilton heard many allegations concerning financial donations and favouritism shown by government ministers to certain companies. At local level, scope for enrichment exists because rezoning of land may result in a substantial financial gain for the landowner. Politicians have some power to permit exemptions from general planning rules, and there have been persistent suggestions that politicians sometimes benefit, directly or indirectly, from favourable planning decisions (Komito, 1983; see also a series of articles in *Irish Times*, 12-16 July 1993). The absence of laws compelling disclosure of political donations in Ireland, on the part of either the donors or the political parties, provides plenty of scope for rumour and suspicion to flourish.

Although cases such as those mentioned above make news when they emerge and show that politicians can pull some strings, recent research suggests that most of the brokerage work conducted by ordinary backbench TDs is more mundane and less questionable ethically. It also suggests that the analyses of both Sacks and Bax are oversimplifications. Even if TDs and ministers can do some string-pulling, this is nowhere near as central to their work as Bax suggests. But it would also be wrong to conclude that there is hardly any point in seeking the help of a TD as there is little he or she can do, as Sacks implies. A consensus has emerged that TDs can be helpful, but not by getting people things to which they are not entitled. Instead, the value of contacting a TD lies in the fact that this can enable people to find out about the existence of benefits, grants or rights that they would otherwise have been unaware of, and/or to discover how to obtain these entitlements.

This was the conclusion of research conducted in Dublin in the late 1970s and early 1980s. It found that politicians' "claim to power or influence rested on their ability to monopolise and then market their specialist knowledge of state resources and their access to bureaucrats who allocated such resources" (Komito, 1984, p. 174). Politicians could tell people what they were eligible for and how to secure it; this involved little work for the politician but saved constituents, many of whom are "bureaucratically illiterate", a lot of work (pp. 182-3). Working-class people, it found, made much more use of TDs' services than did middle-class people. In addition, a TD's intervention sometimes forced a case to be reviewed, a decision to be speeded up or a service to be provided (p. 183). Indeed, there is now a special exclusive "hotline" in the Department of Social Welfare to enable TDs to enquire about individual cases (statement by Minister for Social Welfare— *Dáil Debates* 421: 778-9, 23 June 1992).

Kelly found much the same from her analysis of Michael D. Higgins's caseload. Despite the picture presented by Dooney and O'Toole (1992, pp. 188-91), according to which representations from politicians rarely have any effect, Kelly (1987, p. 145) found that in many instances the TD was able to secure a benefit for people after they had initially been turned down by the civil service, and he also got cases speeded up. He achieved this not by pulling strings but because of his expertise: his knowledge of how best to present the case and of what sort of supporting documentation was needed. Some people had been corresponding with the wrong department, while others had omitted steps like quoting their social welfare number or obtaining a doctor's certificate to back up their case. Similarly, the ability of the Ombudsman to have officials reverse decisions rests not on any "pull" or power to force a body to accept his recommendation, but on his right to obtain access to all the documents connected with a case and the expertise of the Ombudsman's staff in assessing cases (*Annual Report of the Ombudsman*, 1993, pp. 1, 156).

So the research of Komito and Kelly suggests that neither Bax nor Sacks got it quite right: they find no evidence of TDs interfering on a major scale with the equitable operation of the political or administrative system, but, equally, it is not true that TDs cannot achieve anything. The picture to which their research points is that most brokerage work involves rather routine activity, attending many clinics and local meetings, writing letters, helping people to sort out their social welfare problems and so on, rather than anything more corrupt or devious. The TD's role, in fact, resembles that of a lawyer, who operates not by bribing the judge but by ensuring that the case is presented better than the ordinary citizen would be able to present it. In many ways, politicians' brokerage activities are similar to the activities of a range of professional mediators (such as priests, advice centre personnel and trade union officials); the difference derives from their special access to the state bureaucracy and their specific motives in carrying out brokerage functions.

CAUSES OF BROKERAGE

Before examining explanations for the high brokerage load on TDs, we should note that constituency work is not, as some people seem to imagine, a peculiarly Irish phenomenon. In fact, "grievance chasing" is part of the role of the parliamentarian virtually everywhere: "members of every type of legislature say that they are subjected to an incessant flow of such [particularised] demands, and they indicate that coping with them requires a substantial portion of their time and resources" (Mezey, 1979, p. 159). For example, in France the role of the *député* is seen by voters as "interceding with central government on behalf of individuals or councils, rather than as a legislator or watchdog over executive power or debater of the great issues of the day", and so deputies spend most of their time on constituency work (Frears, 1990, p. 46). Even members of the British House of Commons, sometimes seen as relatively nationally oriented, are on the receiving end of a sizeable volume of constituency demands; just as in Ireland, the leisurely pace of the past has been replaced by a pattern of frenetic activity. In the late 1980s, MPs were estimated to devote about three hours a day to dealing with constituency correspondence and to spend virtually every weekend in their constituencies (Norton and Wood, 1990, p. 198). Another study of MPs described them as "self-generating workaholics" who actively seek constituency work because they find it more satisfying than the pointlessness of life on the backbenches: "Members of Parliament are preoccupied with endless meetings, ceaseless letters, difficult constituency problems ... There is the sense of an 'endless treadmill' of late nights and early mornings, perhaps allowing little time for reflection" (Radice,

Vallance and Willis, 1990, p. 154). This is particularly the case in constituencies in the Scottish and Welsh peripheries, where voters expect their MPs "to display a commitment to constituency service, perhaps above all other responsibilities", and the role of "local promoter" is all-important for an MP (Cody, 1992, pp. 351-2). More broadly, relationships (which may or may not be of the patron-client form) based on personal linkages tend to exist in all types of society—modern or traditional, western or eastern, developed or pre-modern (Eisenstadt and Roniger, 1984). Given this pattern, it might be surprising if Irish voters did *not* make heavy brokerage demands on their TDs.

Even so, the perception of Irish politics as "clientelist" and somehow anomalous seems to be so widespread that it is worth trying to explain the high volume of casework descending on TDs, as well as why such a high level of casework is seen as both clientelist and reprehensible. Four factors in particular are frequently mentioned: political cultural attitudes to the state, the small scale of society, the electoral system and the nature of the Irish administrative system.

A historically developed suspicion of the state

In all peasant societies, the capital city and the machinery of central government tend to be looked on with some suspicion. In Irish history, this factor was reinforced by the non-indigenous nature of the ruling elite. In the words of Chubb (1992, p. 210), brokerage is

> deeply rooted in Irish experience. For generations, Irish people saw that to get the benefits that public authorities bestow, the help of a man with connections and influence was necessary. All that democracy has meant is that such a person has been laid on officially, as it were, and is now no longer a master but a servant.

The argument is that the political culture of the nineteenth century and before, when central government was for obvious reasons perceived as alien, remote and best approached via an intermediary, has carried on into the post-independence state. Former Taoiseach Garret FitzGerald comments that Dublin "is still widely perceived in rural Ireland as if it were even today a centre of alien colonial rule" (FitzGerald, 1991, p. 364). Given that so many other aspects of pre-independence political culture have a bearing on contemporary politics (see chapter 2), this is perfectly plausible, and it is hard to avoid some cultural explanation when seeking reasons as to why people in some countries (such as Ireland and France) approach deputies on matters that people in other countries (such as those in Scandinavia) would take elsewhere. Surveys testify to people's belief that a TD is the best person to approach if one wants to be sure of getting one's entitlements (Farrell, 1985, p. 243; Komito, 1992).

This cultural explanation would become dubious, however, if linked too closely with the notion of a "dying peasant culture" or with a suggestion that people's tendency to approach their TDs springs from an atavistic misconception of the way in which the civil service works and of how to interact with it. After all, the volume of brokerage is clearly increasing rather than decreasing as urbanisation and the decline of agriculture proceed. Political culture and the legacy of the past are part of the explanation, but we need to look also for causes in present-day Ireland: "rather than an outmoded style of behaviour, brokerage is an effective solution to a particular set of problems" (Komito, 1984, p. 191). This also means that there is no reason to expect brokerage work to go away as "modernisation" continues.

Small size of society

In all societies, informal networks of trust exist within and alongside formal structures. While such networks exist in large industrial societies (Komito, 1992, p. 143), they may be particularly significant in small societies where, even if it would be an exaggeration to say that "everybody knows everybody else", it is at least true that many people have some kind of direct or indirect access to decision makers that bypasses the formal structure. The Republic of Ireland is clearly, in relative terms, a small society, with only three and a half million people, and a survey conducted in the early 1970s found that respondents were inclined to think of many others besides politicians as potential brokers. Altogether, of the 70 per cent of respondents who answered a question as to whom they would consult if they had a problem with the authorities, 54 per cent opted for a politician, 4 per cent for a state official and 42 per cent for some other specific individual, such as a solicitor, a priest or a business person (for details see Komito, 1992).

The small scale of Irish society also has an impact on people's perceptions of their deputies' role. At the 1992 election, for example, there was one deputy for every 15,404 electors and for every 10,391 valid votes. Very few other countries have as high a ratio of deputies to voters. With such a small number of voters to represent, it is hardly surprising that deputies find themselves asked to play the role of "mediator-advocate vis-à-vis the local and national administrative bureaucracies", as Farrell (1985, p. 242) puts it. A reinforcing factor in Ireland is the high degree of centralisation of decision making, nearly all of which takes place in Dublin. Local government is weak, with very few powers. The upshot is that national parliamentary representatives get requests for help on what in many other countries would be purely local matters.

The STV electoral system

This is sometimes suggested as a cause of brokerage since, as we saw in chapter 4, STV puts candidates of one party in competition with each other and thereby forces them to establish an edge over their so-called running mates. Moreover, given that the Oireachtas is not very strong, backbench deputies cannot easily establish a reputation as outstanding parliamentarians and fight internal party battles on this terrain. So, once the demand for brokerage activity arises, TDs have to respond to it, even though many of them wish there was less of it.

The electoral system powerfully reinforces the tendency of TDs to immerse themselves in constituency work, but it does not really explain where the work comes from in the first place. If 60 cases come in every week, TDs must deal with them, but STV itself does not explain why they come in. Even allowing for the fact that TDs eagerly advertise their availability and actively seek problems to solve, and maybe thereby generate more constituency work than would arise otherwise, this still leaves a lot that arises from other causes.

The nature of the administrative system and the lack of alternative mechanisms

The argument here is essentially that some citizens need brokers to obtain their entitlements. This is the conclusion of Roche and implicitly of others, such as Komito, Kelly and Zimmerman. As Roche (1982, p. 103) puts it: "Irish complaint behaviour is a manifestation of a breakdown at the interface level between Ireland's public institutions and the Irish public". In other words, some people turn to TDs to help them due to the frustration that results from their own direct dealings with the state apparatus.

This arises because of the nature of the machinery with which citizens come into contact. All bureaucracies tend to develop certain characteristics, such as inflexibility, obsession with precedent, secretiveness, rigid adherence to the rules and perhaps impatience with people who do not fully understand the rules. In Ireland, there is also very little occupational mobility between the public service and the wider economy, or even between the different public service departments. Thus the "culture" that develops within a department is not tempered by the introduction of new personnel at middle or upper levels. Zimmerman (1978, p. 33) gives an example of people having difficulty in coping with the bureaucracy: he quotes from a newspaper letter written by a man complaining about the treatment of people trying to discover where they stood in the queue for Dublin Corporation houses. The letter reported that one person was reduced to tears by the curt and cold manner of the official on the other side of the hatch. Others, too, speak of a bureaucratic tendency to send out standard replies that do not address a specific query, not to explain fully what someone is entitled to or why some application has been turned down, or of delay in dealing with cases and even of files getting lost.

The problem was exacerbated in the 1960s and 1970s by the rapid growth in state intervention: the number of services being provided increased rapidly, as did the number of people looking for these services. The resultant long queues demonstrated the inability of the state to respond to this increased demand. The difficulties in getting a phone installed, and the lengths to which people were willing to go in order to hasten the process, illustrated the problem. Long delays in processing a social welfare claim, for instance, were the result of increases in the number of people applying for assistance and of an increasingly complex application procedure to decide eligibility. Structural improvements (such as computerisation) have reduced processing delays; the result may not suit the applicant, but at least the answer is known more quickly. For example, the number of complaints made to the Ombudsman about Telecom Éireann dropped by two-thirds from 1987 to 1992 following the introduction of itemised billing (*Annual Report of the Ombudsman*, 1993, p. 5), suggesting that when people know how a decision has been reached, they are less likely to complain about it. Similarly, the need for assistance, simply to find out where in the queue an application sits, is somewhat less. This has, to some degree, lessened the scope for brokerage interventions by politicians—their ability to get fast answers or move cases to the front of the queue is now a less valuable commodity.

Unfortunately, the increase in efficiency has not been matched in most areas by any marked increase in transparency: the rules for determining eligibility remain complex, and thus the need for the assistance of someone who understands the system remains. Furthermore, there has been no great increase in the amount of trust extended to civil servants and their activities, and thus the need for someone who can be trusted to act on one's behalf remains.

All of this leaves many people wanting assistance from someone willing to help them. When this happens, contacting a TD often seems the most suitable mechanism by which a grievance might be redressed. The civil service has an appeal procedure, but those whose problems spring from "bureaucratic illiteracy" are unlikely to be able to make much use of this. A report in the early 1980s concluded that the composition, procedure and location of appeal hearings led to claimants identifying the appeal system (with some justification) as a mere extension of the bureaucracy that had made the initial adverse decision rather than as an independent structure: "many claimants do not have a great deal of faith in the appeal system before the hearing but most have even less once the hearing is over" (Coolock Community Law Centre, 1980, p. 35; see also Hogan and Morgan, 1991, pp. 245-6). A more promising step is to seek assistance from a Citizens Information Centre (CIC). There are 80 such centres around the country; they operate under the auspices of the state-funded National Social Services Board (NSSB) but are run by volunteers (over 1,150 of them in 1991). They not only give information on social welfare entitlements but, where appropriate, also take up cases with the relevant office or department. In 1991 they dealt with 119,261 queries, compared with 39,000 in 1979 (National Social Services Board, 1992, p. 25). This is clear evidence of public demand for assistance in dealing with the state bureaucracy. However, the restricted opening hours of CICs, and perhaps the limited ability of their volunteers to persuade public officials to reverse a decision, mean that these centres clearly do not meet the full demand.

One valuable channel for obtaining rectification of grievances, as opposed to merely providing information, is the office of the Ombudsman, which was established in January 1984 (see Hogan and Morgan, 1991, pp. 279-317, for the powers and operation of the office). The Ombudsman has the role of investigating complaints from members of the public who feel that they have been treated unfairly by public bodies. He has the power to demand any information, document or file from a body complained against and can require any official of that body to attend before him to give information about a complaint (*Annual Report of the Ombudsman*, 1993, p. 155). The office received about 3,000 complaints in each of the years 1988-92, compared with the approximately 5,000 received in 1985, 1986 and 1987 (*Annual Report of the Ombudsman*, 1993, p. 5). It is clear that the Ombudsman's office has been able to assist a significant proportion of those whose cases fall within its jurisdiction: of the cases dealt with in 1992, 16 per cent were resolved in favour of the complainant and assistance was provided in a further 34 per cent of cases (*Annual Report of the Ombudsman*, 1993, p. 7). Moreover, details of some of the cases outlined in the annual reports of the office show how difficult it has sometimes been even for the Ombudsman, endowed as he is with statutory powers to demand all the files relating to a case, to persuade the bureaucrats concerned that they should review a decision, highlighting the difficulties ordinary citizens can encounter.

However, if Higgins's 1982 caseload described above is typical, TDs collectively receive approximately half a million cases a year, and clearly most of these do not come to the Ombudsman. One reason, no doubt, is that TDs seem more available and accessible than the Ombudsman, despite the latter's willingness to be of assistance. It may be significant that high-profile visits by members of the Ombudsman's staff to various parts of the country tend to result in an increase in complaints from just those areas (*Annual Report of the Ombudsman*, 1993, p. 5), implying that some cases go to politicians simply because politicians seem more accessible than any other channel of complaint. Another reason why most people do not go to the Ombudsman is that many cases coming to TDs result from a lack of information as to how best to utilise the administrative system (or just disgruntlement with a decision) and do not involve possible maladministration—as John Whyte (1966, p. 16) puts it, they are problems on "a humbler scale" than would warrant the attention of the Ombudsman. In the words of the NSSB, "the problem for most people in writing to the various Departments seems to be (i) not knowing exactly which section to address their letter to and (ii) the standard letter of reply may not deal satisfactorily with their enquiry" (National Social Services Board, 1992, p. 7).

So, almost by default, people wanting assistance turn to public representatives, who cannot afford to be abrupt or offhand—TDs' jobs, unlike those of civil servants, may depend on how helpful and approachable they are. Moreover, through experience TDs can probably steer them in the right direction: as one TD put it, "there is hardly a Deputy in this House who is not at least as conversant with the supplementary welfare allowance scheme as are the community welfare officers" (Proinsias De Rossa, *Dáil Debates* 428: 834, 25 March 1993).

To suggest that the nature of the Irish administrative system is part of the explanation for the high volume of brokerage demands made to TDs might seem to imply that civil servants are the villains of the piece. However, it would be unfair to put all the blame on them. Often they do not have enough training to be as helpful to the public as they would like to be and, as in most bureaucracies, the most junior people are placed across the desk from the public—promotion means getting away from the public. Moreover, offices and working conditions are sometimes not ideal, and the long queues for services may be the result of political inactivity rather than administrative inattention.

But civil servants are not entirely blameless either, since they, or the civil service collectively, could behave in such a way that people would not need to use brokers in their dealings with them. As has been argued before (Komito, 1984, pp. 188-9), the tacit cooperation of bureaucrats is needed for the brokerage system to operate—a system that suits both politicians and civil servants, especially at the local level. For one thing, it protects the bureaucrats to some extent, since politicians form a barrier between them and the public. Without politicians acting as brokers, many more people would be tackling them directly; as it is, politicians form an unofficial complaints tribunal. In this capacity politicians also provide an unpaid monitoring service; they can assess whether people really have been dealt with harshly, or have lost out on the benefit of the doubt. If a TD or councillor then makes a firm complaint about a particular case, the civil servant or local official can be fairly sure that it is a valid complaint, since the politician does not want to jeopardise his or her ongoing relationship with the official on behalf of an undeserving constituent. So politicians in effect do some preliminary screening of cases and then present the strongest among them in a manner tailored to the expectations of the civil service, which helps the officials. In return, civil servants may well give special priority to representations from TDs and respond more sympathetically than to letters of complaint or injury from ordinary members of the public (cf. the special TDs' "hotline" mentioned on p. 154 above). In addition, officials consider politicians to be more "trustworthy". Politicians have a stake in maintaining good relations with officials, so officials can rectify errors without any adverse comment. Members of the public, having no stake in the status quo, cannot be similarly trusted; officials are less likely to admit errors, which means that they are also less likely to rectify such errors.

Higgins (1982, p. 124) makes much the same point when discussing brokerage on local authorities. He suggests that on county councils there is an implicit bargain between councillors and officials. The latter do not publicly disparage councillors' brokerage activities—that is, they do nothing to dispel the notion, fostered by politicians, that a public representative has got someone something by pulling strings. Nor do they improve their responsiveness to members of the public, something that could make brokers unnecessary. In return, he says, councillors do not insist on as much accountability from officials as they could, something that would make life uncomfortable for officials.

CONSEQUENCES OF BROKERAGE

Some of the consequences of brokerage are highly tangible, while others are less so. Brokerage work affects the operation of the political and administrative systems, and some suggest that it plays a part in shaping political culture. We shall look at its impact on the Dáil, the government and the civil service, ask whether it produces clientelist politics, and consider its effects on people's attitudes towards politics and the state.

Impact on the Dáil and the government
This is the most obvious and tangible consequence. If TDs have to deal with 60 cases a week, then this reduces the time available for parliamentary work. This is part of the reason why TDs in the past showed little interest in Dáil reform— rightly or wrongly, they believed, and many still do, that to devote time to Dáil work at the expense of brokerage work in the constituency could be electorally suicidal. However, as we saw in chapter 7, there are obviously many other reasons why the Dáil is weak, and it is open to question how much stronger it would be if TDs had less constituency work. Moreover, there is no reason why, with an adequate provision of support staff, politicians should not be able both to provide a brokerage service for constituents and to be active parliamentarians.

It is also sometimes suggested that even ministers are overburdened with constituency work and are unable to devote enough time to government business. However, in recent years ministers have used civil servants to do most of their constituency work for them. A series of parliamentary questions tabled in March 1993 by Eamon Gilmore TD asked about the size of each minister's private office and constituency office. It turned up the information that the 15 cabinet ministers collectively had 127 civil servants in their private offices and 81 in their constituency offices, while the figures for the 15 ministers of state were 81 and 60 respectively (*Dáil Debates* 427: 1804-96, 11 March 1993 and 428: 519-20, 24 March 1993). The distinction between the "private office" and the "constituency office" may be more apparent than real; indeed, one minister acknowledged that "staff are not formally divided between constituency and other duties. The situation varies from day to day in each office and staff carry out appropriate duties as the need arises" (Joe Walsh, Minister for Agriculture, *Dáil Debates* 427: 1854, 11 March 1993). Given that each cabinet and junior minister has, therefore, an average of 11 civil servants, paid for by the taxpayers, to assist in his or her constituency and political work, it is hard to believe that brokerage can be a major burden on the shoulders of ministers.

Impact on the work of the civil service

We noted earlier that TDs may do some preliminary screening of cases before deciding which ones to take up with officials. However, even if a TD can see that a constituent's chances are negligible, he or she may not want to say this to the constituent. It is less risky electorally to forward the case to the civil service, perhaps putting down a parliamentary question, though of course without using up credit with contacts in the civil service by claiming that it is a deserving case. When this happens on a large scale, there is an obvious cost to the civil service in terms of time and money. Each question has to be followed up fully and all the details have to be investigated, even if the answer turns out to be something straightforward such as the person simply not being eligible. If, as sometimes happens, the person has not even applied for the grant they are complaining about not having received, or there is some confusion over their social welfare number, the search is much longer. The cost is virtually impossible to quantify. Examining these representations also costs civil servants time that could be spent dealing with other things, so, ironically, some TDs, by clogging up the works with pointless representations, may exacerbate the delays they complain about (Dooney and O'Toole, 1992, p. 190).

Relationship with clientelist politics

As we noted earlier, some people use the term "clientelist politics" to describe politics in Ireland; journalists and politicians alike are prone to speak of "our clientelist system". The picture painted by Bax and Sacks is one of politicians doing favours (real according to Bax, imaginary according to Sacks) for people and in return being rewarded by a vote at the next election. The suggestion is that politicians gradually build up a sizeable and fairly stable "clientele" of people who are under some obligation to them; the politicians are able to "call in the debts" at election time. Most voters, it is implied, are part of some politician's clientele.

However, words like "clientele" are not very apposite to describe those who give a first preference vote to a particular Dáil candidate. TDs simply do not possess "clienteles". Many, perhaps most, people have never contacted a politician at all. In the early 1970s, only 17 per cent of those questioned in a Dublin survey had ever contacted a politician for any reason (Komito, 1989, p. 185). There is no more recent evidence on contacts between voters and TDs, but a 1991 poll found that only 24 per cent of respondents said they had contacted a city or county councillor since the 1985 local elections. Contact had been higher among rural than urban dwellers and among working-class people than middle-class respondents (Irish Marketing Surveys, 1991, Table 12/1). Moreover, even those who are helped by a politician cannot be taken for granted. For one thing, many of them "do the rounds" of the clinics, hoping to improve their chances by getting several TDs to chase up their case. For another, even if a TD does do something for a constituent, the secrecy of the ballot means that he or she has no way of knowing whether the favour is returned at the ballot box. Many of the key characteristics of clientelism, such as the solidarity binding "clients" and "patrons", are simply not present in Irish electoral politics (Farrell, 1985, p. 241).

Thus, an earlier study concluded that "politicians believed that they were inevitably dependent on the votes of anonymous constituents with whom they could have no direct links" (Komito, 1984, p. 181). Far from resting comfortably atop pyramids of loyal supporters, they come across as "professional paranoids", permanently insecure, always busy at brokerage work but never sure that any of it will pay electoral dividends. They promote a high community profile, advertise clinics, turn up at residents' association meetings and so on, not to build up a clientele but simply to earn a reputation as hard-working people. They hope that even people who never actually need a broker are impressed and will conclude that the TD will be there if they ever need him or her. Brokerage and clientelism, then, are very different things, and much as TDs might wish that they could build up solid clienteles by their constituency work, its rewards are much less certain than this.

The term "clientelism" may be used by some commentators partly because of its pejorative and nefarious connotations; it has overtones of manipulation and string-pulling, of a mode of behaviour that some feel Ireland should be moving away from, in contrast to the more neutral "brokerage". Eisenstadt and Roniger (1984, p. 18) observe that the tendency develops in many societies to perceive less formalised relations of this kind as "slightly subversive to the institutionalised order, to fully institutionalised relationships or to membership of collectivities". As we shall now see, brokerage in Ireland has been criticised on precisely these grounds.

Individualisation of social conflict

Higgins (1982, p. 133) suggests that brokerage "disorganises the poor"; it encourages them to seek an individual solution to a problem such as poverty rather than to see the problem as fundamental to society and take part in collective action to try to redress it. It encourages vertical links, from the TD to the constituent, rather than horizontal ones between people in the same position, such as the poor or the unemployed. Brokerage encourages competition rather than co-operation between people in similar vulnerable positions. It reinforces and perpetuates individualism—social conflict is individualised. Thus, he concludes (p. 135), it is "exploitative in source and intent". Its origins lie in the dependency of the poor, "the structural fact of poverty", and in the uneven distribution of resources such as wealth, knowledge and access, and it perpetuates this dependency by heading off any demand for more fundamental changes. Hazelkorn, in whose view at least some of TDs' constituency work should be described as clientelism rather than as brokerage, also argues that it redirects incipient class conflict into channels that emphasise the role of individuals rather than of classes: "the effect has been to retard the political development and consciousness of the economically dominated classes" (Hazelkorn, 1986, p. 339).

It may well be that politicians' brokerage work reduces the level of alienation among those who seek their assistance, and thereby acts as a force for the stability of a social structure marked by clear inequalities rather than for change. However, it would be a mistake to attribute too much explanatory power to brokerage. It is probably more realistic to see the availability of public representatives as a response to a demand rather than as a cause of it—as a manifestation of a tendency to seek an individual solution rather than as a cause of this. TDs' willingness to help individual constituents cannot really be held responsible for the absence of socialism in Ireland. There are other societies in which it could be argued that class conflict is minimised and wealth is unevenly distributed (such as the United States of America); yet few have seen such societies as characterised by clientelism. At best, a number of different causes seem capable of producing the same effect; at worst, one is labelling a symptom as a cause. Besides, as we have seen, people in most countries expect their public representatives to take up the cudgels on their behalf when they have a problem, so the fact that TDs do a lot of brokerage work cannot of itself count for much in explaining the distinctive features of Irish politics.

Impact on people's perception of the state

There is general agreement that brokerage affects perceptions of the state, but some disagreement about exactly how it does this. Once more, Bax and Sacks, operating at different ends of the country, come to opposite conclusions.

Bax (1976, pp. 51-2) suggests that brokerage, at least in societies at certain stages of development, has an integrative effect; it brings citizens and the central state machinery closer together. Brokers can serve the function of humanising the state in the eyes of people who would otherwise see it as remote and would feel alienated from it. Brokers transmit values in each direction—they keep the people and the state apparatus in contact with each other, strengthening links between them.

Sacks (1976, pp. 221-5), in contrast, feels that brokerage is primarily negative in its effects. Far from bringing people into contact with the state, it actually keeps them at arm's length from it. TDs and their machines are in effect intermediaries between citizens and the state. They propagate the notion that a citizen has a better chance of getting something from the state if he or she approaches it via a TD, and this perpetuates citizens' negative and suspicious views of the state. This reinforces personalism and localism, the tendency to trust only those with whom one has some personal or local connection, which Sacks sees as being important elements in Irish political culture. He also argues that the state is one of the major factors with the potential to bring about change and modernisation, but the potential impact of the state is much reduced by brokerage, since TDs and their machines refract the outputs of the state to serve their own ends.

There is some truth in both of these views, but neither gives the whole picture. Bax is right to emphasise the linkage role performed by brokerage. The points picked up by TDs in their clinics give valuable feedback on the impact of government policies, especially in areas such as social welfare and health, and can be fed into the policy-making process. However, as Bax acknowledges, there is also an element of manipulation involved. Sacks, in contrast, makes the mistake of assuming that people's use of brokers is irrational and that for the most part they could do just as well on their own (Sacks, 1976, p. 216). It may be true that brokerage does reinforce the suspicion that some people have of the state apparatus, as some politicians seek to convey the impression that they can pull strings on a constituent's behalf. But it is an exaggeration to suggest that brokerage actually causes this suspicion or is the only factor keeping it alive.

More realistically, brokerage can be seen as a factor working to sustain the status quo. To quote from earlier research, "it does not alter the circumstances which originally fostered it, and may only provide superficial relief while actually creating a greater need for fundamental, but postponed, changes" (Komito, 1984, p. 191). It perpetuates itself because, like charity, it helps people without removing their vulnerability. Specifically, it helps people to obtain their entitlements but removes the urgency to create a situation in which people do not have to rely on brokers at all, for example by making the administrative machinery more responsive and accountable to ordinary people. In this way, it might be advantageous in the short term but disadvantageous in the long term. It deals with the symptoms but does nothing about the causes. Its most positive consequence has been the extension of trust, meaning that citizens are more likely to feel themselves to be members of or even to some degree participants in the political system, rather than to be alienated, and perhaps victimised, subjects of the system. This has contributed to the overall stability of the political system. Given the lack of trust extended to the colonial state, the creation of this "community of trust" was no small feat, and may have been crucial to the development of participative democracy. It may be argued that it has also helped to perpetuate inequality. Of course, it is not the case that if all TDs suddenly stopped doing any constituency work, the result would be radical reform that would produce a civil service that satisfied everyone all the time, let alone a social revolution. However, the need for a more citizen-friendly administration might well become more apparent, and to that extent brokerage can be seen as a palliative, postponing the day when major surgery will have to take place.

There is some reason to believe that, in the 1990s, the system of trust may be beginning to break down. There has been an increase in grass-roots organisations that are very disenchanted with both politicians and civil servants and, finding the formal structures of the state unsatisfactory, are instead turning towards informal or ad hoc self-help groups. Brokerage politics are essentially a stop-gap, and when the gap to be bridged between government and some of the governed becomes too great, their inadequacy as a long-term solution is made manifest.

CONCLUSION

Dáil deputies are predominantly local people, whose route to the Dáil typically takes them through a local council. Their constituents expect them to be active constituency representatives, taking up their personal or communal problems or grievances with the relevant government department. This can be explained by the nature of Irish political culture and by the highly centralised, perhaps over-bureaucratic nature of the decision-making process in Ireland. The volume of constituency work takes time that TDs could, at least in theory, devote to their parliamentary responsibilities, and also has an impact on the functioning of the civil service. Among observers of Irish politics, constituency work tends to be regarded as a negative phenomenon. It is often branded "clientelism", a term with a multitude of unfavourable connotations (largely due to the private and individual, rather than public and collective, nature of politician-voter interactions). Yet, it is clear that Irish politics are not clientelistic in the conventional sense of the term. Indeed, a heavy constituency workload is the norm for parliamentarians around the world—what happens in Ireland may differ in degree, but not in kind, from the general pattern. Although the high volume of casework does have some political consequences, we should not make the mistake of attributing every supposed defect in the Irish body politic to brokerage.

REFERENCES AND FURTHER READING

Annual Report of the Ombudsman 1992, 1993. Dublin: Stationery Office.

Bax, Mart, 1976. *Harpstrings and Confessions: Machine-style Politics in the Irish Republic*. Assen: Van Gorcum.

Chubb, Basil, 1992. *The Government and Politics of Ireland*, 3rd ed. Harlow: Longman.

Cody, Howard, 1992. "MPs and the peripheral predicament in Canada and Britain", *Political Studies* 40:2, pp. 346-55.

Coolock Community Law Centre, 1980. *Social Welfare Appeals*. Dublin: Coolock Community Law Centre, Special Report 2.

Dooney, Seán and John O'Toole, 1992. *Irish Government Today*. Dublin: Gill and Macmillan.

Eisenstadt, S. N. and L. Roniger, 1984. *Patrons, Clients and Friends: Interpersonal Relations and the Structure of Trust in Society*. Cambridge: Cambridge University Press.

Farrell, Brian, 1985. "Ireland: from friends and neighbours to clients and partisans: some dimensions of parliamentary representation under PR-STV", pp. 237-64 in Vernon Bogdanor (ed.), *Representatives of the People? Parliaments and Constituents in Western Democracies*. Aldershot: Gower.

FitzGerald, Garret, 1991. *All in a Life: an Autobiography*. Dublin: Gill and Macmillan.

Frears, John, 1990. "The French parliament: loyal workhorse, poor watchdog", pp. 32-51 in Philip Norton (ed.), *Parliaments in Western Europe*. London: Frank Cass.

Gallagher, Michael, 1993. "The election of the 27th Dáil", pp. 57-78 in Michael Gallagher and Michael Laver (eds), *How Ireland Voted 1992*. Dublin: Folens and Limerick: PSAI Press.

Hazelkorn, Ellen, 1986. "Class, clientelism and the political process in the Republic of Ireland", pp. 326-43 in Patrick Clancy, Sheelagh Drudy, Kathleen Lynch and Liam O'Dowd (eds), *Ireland: a Sociological Profile*. Dublin: Institute of Public Administration.

Higgins, Michael D., 1982. "The limits of clientelism: towards an assessment of Irish politics", pp. 114-41 in Christopher Clapham (ed.), *Private Patronage and Public Power*. London: Frances Pinter.

Hogan, Gerard and David Gwynn Morgan, 1991. *Administrative Law in Ireland*, 2nd ed. London: Sweet and Maxwell.

Irish Marketing Surveys, 1991. *Irish Independent/IMS poll, 30 May–7 June*. Dublin: Irish Marketing Surveys.

Kelly, Valerie, 1987. "Focus on clients: a reappraisal of the effectiveness of TDs' interventions", *Administration* 35:2, pp. 130-51.

Komito, Lee, 1983. "Development plan rezonings: the political pressures", pp. 293-301 in John Blackwell and Frank J. Convery (eds), *Promise and Performance: Irish Environmental Policies Analysed*. Dublin: Resource and Environmental Policy Centre, University College Dublin.

Komito, Lee, 1984. "Irish clientelism: a reappraisal", *Economic and Social Review* 15:3, pp. 173-94.

Komito, Lee, 1989. "Voters, politicians and clientelism: a Dublin survey", *Administration* 37:2, pp. 171-96.

Komito, Lee, 1992. "Brokerage or friendship? Politics and networks in Ireland", *Economic and Social Review* 23:2, pp. 129-45.

Mezey, Michael L., 1979. *Comparative Legislatures*. Durham, NC: Duke University Press.

National Social Services Board, 1992. *Annual Report 1991*. Dublin: National Social Services Board.

Norton, Philip and David Wood, 1990. "Constituency service by Members of Parliament: does it contribute to a personal vote?", *Parliamentary Affairs* 43:2, pp. 196-208.

Radice, Lisanne, Elizabeth Vallance and Virginia Willis, 1990. *Member of Parliament: the Job of a Backbencher*, 2nd ed. Basingstoke: Macmillan.

Roche, Richard, 1982. "The high cost of complaining Irish style: a preliminary examination of the Irish pattern of complaint behaviour and of its associated costs", *IBAR—Journal of Irish Business and Administrative Research* 4:2, pp. 98-108.

Sacks, Paul M., 1976. *The Donegal Mafia: an Irish Political Machine*. New Haven and London: Yale University Press.

Whyte, John, 1966. *Dáil Deputies: Their Work, its Difficulties, Possible Remedies*. Dublin: Tuairim pamphlet 15.

Zimmerman, Joseph F., 1978. "Role perceptions of dual office holders in Ireland", *Administration* 26:1, pp. 25-48.

9 / THE GOVERNMENT

Brian Farrell

Most modern representative democracies have adopted cabinet systems of government, which come in a variety of forms. In some countries, cabinets are composed almost exclusively of single-party majorities; in others, many or most cabinets are coalitions. Some countries expect relatively straightforward outcomes of general elections to create a stable government; others provide elaborate and time-consuming procedures for government formation. Some demand that only parliamentarians can become ministers and set little store by expertise; in others specialists are preferred and ministers are not allowed to take seats in the assembly. In many the prime minister plays an influential, even dominant, role; in others the prime minister has very limited authority.

In chapter 7 we looked at the appointment of governments and their relationship with the Dáil. This chapter examines some main themes in the operation of the Irish cabinet system, including the composition of the government, the way the government works, the role of the Taoiseach, and the performance of Taoisigh in office, and outlines a possible approach to evaluating and comparing these Irish leaders.

FACTORS SHAPING THE IRISH SYSTEM

Ireland can be clearly located within the classical Westminster model of cabinet government (Farrell, 1988a; Weller, 1985). At the outset, the first Dáil embodied the essential features of the Westminster model in its constitution. A popularly-elected chamber, the Dáil, chose its majority party leader as prime minister; in turn, he picked parliamentary party colleagues as ministers. Even more important than these fundamental institutional arrangements, three core conventions of the Westminster model were absorbed into the Irish system: the doctrine of collective responsibility (requiring, at a minimum, that all ministers acquiesce in governmental decisions), the principle that individual ministers are answerable to parliament for the functioning of their departments, and a commitment to cabinet confidentiality that has built into a formidable tradition of executive secrecy.

If the Westminster model was a formative influence in the creation of the Irish cabinet system, two other factors have powerfully shaped its operation. The first is that these inherited arrangements and conventions have been rooted within a written, and increasingly rigid, constitutional framework. From the sketch outlined in the Dáil constitution of 1919, through the flexible provisions of the Irish Free State constitution, to the articles of the 1937 constitution, the formal size, structure and responsibility of government have been codified. Occasional innovations deviating from the Westminster model have been short-lived (such as the "extern" ministers introduced in the Irish Free State constitution), although undoubtedly the very existence of a written constitution and of judicial review represents a significant departure from the uncodified and flexible Westminster system. The second factor is the accumulated experience—political, procedural and personal—built up in more than 70 years of Irish government. If the modern Irish cabinet system remains close to its Westminster origins, it is considerably removed from the contemporary British cabinet system (for which, see Burch, 1988).

THE COMPOSITION OF THE GOVERNMENT

The basic powers, structure and size of the Irish government are outlined in Article 28 of the constitution. This provides that the government shall consist of not less than seven and not more than 15 members. All are required to be parliamentarians; specifically, the Taoiseach, Tánaiste and Minister for Finance must be Dáil deputies. Two other ministers may be chosen from the Seanad, although this option has rarely been exercised. All ministers are nominated by the Taoiseach, approved by the Dáil and appointed by the President. The Taoiseach "may at any time, for reasons which to him seem sufficient" request ministerial resignations (Article 28.9.4). The Taoiseach is not required to identify the reasons, and ministers who refuse to resign may be, and have been, dismissed. Thus in the "arms crisis" of 1970 the appointments of the Ministers for Finance and for Agriculture and Fisheries (Charles J. Haughey and Neil Blaney) were terminated when they refused to resign; during the presidential election campaign of 1990 the Minister for Defence (Brian Lenihan) was dismissed after controversial allegations regarding much earlier attempts to influence President Hillery; and in 1991 the Ministers for Finance and for the Environment (Albert Reynolds and Pádraig Flynn) were dismissed following their stated intention to support a motion of no confidence in Mr Haughey's leadership of Fianna Fáil. On the resignation of the Taoiseach, all other ministers are deemed to have resigned.

The executive power of the state is exercised by, or on the authority of, the government. The constitution requires it to "meet and act as a collective authority" and holds it collectively responsible for the departments of state administered by ministers. The same article (28.4) describes the government as "responsible to Dáil Éireann" and requires that it present annual estimates of income and expenditure to the Dáil for consideration. Article 28.10 requires the Taoiseach to resign "upon his ceasing to retain the support of a majority in Dáil Éireann", unless the President grants a general election and the Taoiseach secures a majority in the new Dáil. Article 13 gives the President absolute discretion to refuse a general election to a Taoiseach who has ceased to retain majority support in the Dáil, as discussed at p. 53 above.

This constitutional outline gives an incomplete, and in many ways misleading, account of Irish government (Farrell, 1988b). It ignores the reality that political parties—either singly or in coalition—form governments and can usually command disciplined Dáil support. As already indicated in chapter 7, this political reality (reinforced by the Standing Orders of the Dáil and by the virtual monopoly of the executive in regard to authorising public expenditure enshrined in Article 17.2 of the constitution) tends to make it difficult to exercise any effective parliamentary control over government. The cabinet, in large measure, is a small

closed group of senior deputies, bound by shared interest, experience and responsibility, and able to use its control of the executive organs of the state to push
through its own policies.

Size

In terms of size the Irish system is comparable to other European cabinets. A combination of low turnover rates, excessive ministerial longevity and a reluctance to
fill the constitutional maxima meant that in the early decades of the state very
few politicians gained ministerial experience. Although the pace of recruitment
and replacement has accelerated in more recent decades, the total number of Irish
ministers remains very small.

In the first quarter century of the state's existence, from 1922 to the general
election of 1948, only 30 different individuals were appointed as ministers. Over
the next decade, to the retirement of de Valera as Taoiseach in 1959, a further 25
were recruited. In the following 20 years under Lemass, Lynch and Cosgrave as
successive Taoisigh, 36 new ministers were appointed. The emergence of Haughey
and FitzGerald, and a flurry of three general elections in the early 1980s, led to a
relatively rapid turnover: 28 new ministers, including three women, were nominated, between Haughey's first government in 1979 and the end of FitzGerald's
second coalition in 1987 (these figures correct the tabular statement of ministerial
appointments 1922-82 in Farrell, 1987a; see also Coakley and Farrell, 1989, and
appendix 3c).

More recently, the pace has again slowed down: in 1987 Haughey appointed
only four new ministers and subsequently named a fifth to succeed Ray Mac-
Sharry on his appointment as EC commissioner; only one new minister was
appointed in the formation of the 1989 Fianna Fáil-Progressive Democratic
coalition (both PD ministers in this cabinet had been originally appointed by
Lynch in 1970 in the major reshuffle caused by the arms crisis). In 1991 Haughey
filled one cabinet vacancy by re-promoting a colleague dropped in 1989 and subsequently named two new ministers to replace dismissed colleagues. In 1992, Albert
Reynolds departed from this pattern and appointed five first-time ministers to
his first cabinet; in forming the 1993 cabinet four of these were retained and Séamus Brennan (originally appointed in 1989) dropped to make space for Labour.
Spring ignored previous governmental experience; apart from himself and Ruairí
Quinn (who had served for three years in FitzGerald's second government), the
four other Labour nominees were new ministers and included Niamh Bhreathnach, appointed minister just a month after entering the Dáil. Overall, then, in
the period 1922-93 only 136 ministers served in Irish cabinets.

Ministerial selection

The selection of ministers is a prerogative of the Taoiseach. Constitutionally,
the choice is limited to members of the Oireachtas, in practice to TDs (only three
senators have served as ministers, all briefly: Joseph Connolly, 1932-36; Seán
Moylan, 1957; James Dooge, 1981-82). Politically, the selection is always made
from the winning side. The Taoiseach in a single-party government is less limited than a coalition leader, who must negotiate the number and allocation of
departments with another party leader but has virtually no influence on that
leader's ministerial selections. Since the minority party is typically over-

represented in relation to its Dáil strength, a coalition Taoiseach is that much more constrained.

No Taoiseach has ever detailed the criteria for ministerial selection. Parliamentary seniority and long continuance in office were a marked feature of the Irish system (see Chubb 1974, pp. 82ff and Farrell 1987a, pp. 142ff), and on average ministers can expect to have to serve for about seven to nine years as a TD before entering the cabinet. However, there were always notable, though not necessarily successful, exceptions: Noel Browne (1948), Kevin Boland (1957), Martin O'Donoghue (1977) and Alan Dukes (1981) were all made ministers on their first day in the Dáil, and Niamh Bhreathnach (1993) in effect comes into this category as well (she entered parliament when the 27th Dáil first met on 14 December 1992, and became a minister when the Fianna Fáil-Labour government was eventually formed on 12 January 1993).

More recent party leaders have been prepared to ignore seniority claims (Farrell, 1993b). They have shown no compunction about ignoring any previous front-bench role as party spokesperson. Certainly, when a party moves from opposition to government, there is no automatic right of succession from the position of spokesperson to that of minister with responsibility for the same subject. Smaller parties invariably find the seniority of their nominees more relevant than previous shadow positions. This indifference to previous party responsibility for specific policy areas mirrors a more general cavalier attitude towards ministerial selection. Few clear professional criteria appear to be employed. Seniority, measured in terms of parliamentary service, has certainly not been a dominant consideration in recent Irish ministerial selection.

Haughey's first cabinet (in 1979) dropped four members of the Lynch government and appointed two deputies who had been elected only two years previously (Albert Reynolds and Michael Woods). FitzGerald's initial choice (1981) was even more adventurous. He ignored the seniority claims of three former ministers, allotted Agriculture to a newly elected deputy (Alan Dukes), gave Foreign Affairs to Senator James Dooge, and chose three other ministers who had served only a single term in the Dáil (John Boland, Jim Mitchell and Paddy O'Toole). In 1992, Albert Reynolds made an almost clean sweep, dropping eight members of the outgoing Haughey cabinet and moving three others to different departments. This adventurous selection, though, included only one relatively inexperienced deputy (Brian Cowen, who was first returned in a by-election in 1984). In 1993, Spring, as noted above, was also ruthless in his choices.

There is a notable discrepancy in regard to promotions from the rank of junior minister to the cabinet. In the case of Fine Gael-led coalitions (in part arising from their 16-year period in opposition prior to 1973) few former juniors have been appointed. However, successive Fianna Fáil Taoisigh have been more prepared to recruit from these ranks, rather than directly from the backbenches. Evidently they believe that some ministerial apprenticeship is desirable.

It is more difficult to assess the extent to which competence and ability has been a major criterion in selection. The first generation of the Irish political elite were "politicians by accident", divided by a largely symbolic constitutional issue. The ties of loyalty that created the original revolutionary generation became partisan bonds separating them into two opposing groups in a bitter civil war. Capacity was only one critical criterion for either recruitment or promotion;

political reputation or influence, loyalty and proximity to the leader became primary functional prerequisites. The highly competitive character of the electoral system and its consequent fuelling of intraparty rivalry has meant that there has been far less stress on professional and technical competence than on political skills and "reliability" in recruiting the senior elite. An examination of cabinet-making by Haughey, FitzGerald, and Reynolds shows how far the traditional emphasis on loyalty to the leader has remained a dominant condition of ministerial selection (Farrell, 1987a and 1987b).

At the very least it is evident that Taoisigh have preferred to surround themselves with colleagues of like mind. Some, like Cosgrave in 1973, deliberately sought to include a range of party views in the cabinet. Others, like Haughey (who was elected party leader by only 44 to 38 votes over George Colley in 1979), were virtually forced to reappoint disaffected colleagues; Colley was made Tánaiste and given a veto on ministerial appointments to both Justice and Defence. Both FitzGerald and Reynolds have argued that their choices were based on merit and capacity, and the former justified breaching conventions in appointing Dooge and Dukes on these grounds (see FitzGerald, 1991, p. 363). Even so, it is difficult to avoid the conclusion that, like Haughey in his later cabinets, a prime consideration was to reward, and make use of, their own supporters within their parties. The exigencies of coalition—curtailing some of the Taoiseach's freedom of choice—may have given added impetus to an inherent tendency to favour their own faction, although in 1993 Spring's nominations show a party leader eager to bring potential left-wing critics inside the governmental tent.

The secretariat

In terms of the secretariat, there is an even smaller pool of experience. Until 1979 the Secretary of the Department of the Taoiseach also served as Secretary to the Government. In that year, following the abolition of the Department of Economic Planning and Development, these two main functions were separated and allotted to two separate secretaries. But only a very small number of senior civil servants have been appointed to these sensitive posts: in all there have been only seven cabinet secretaries in the period 1922-93. Since 1979, the separate post of Secretary to the Department of the Taoiseach has had three incumbents. Staffing levels in the Department are remarkably low by any standards; the cabinet secretariat is particularly small. It is augmented by a handful of personal advisors to the Taoiseach.

This small group caters for the Taoiseach both as head of government and as a minister. It is responsible for preparing the agenda of cabinet meetings, circulating memoranda among ministers, recording decisions and generally assisting the Taoiseach in fulfilling his functions. These include, for instance, keeping the President informed, coordinating government business in the houses of the Oireachtas, preparing replies to parliamentary questions and, increasingly, preparing for major EC meetings and Anglo-Irish summits. The Department of the Taoiseach has also sometimes acquired responsibility for a range of other governmental activities, including the Central Statistics Office and, until the creation of the Department of Arts, Culture and the Gaeltacht in 1993, various cultural institutions.

The secretariat's main purpose is to service the government as a corporate entity. In particular, it maintains a constant check to ensure that all documentation submitted to government conforms to the detailed requirements of the *Government Procedure Instructions* (Farrell, 1988a, 1993a). First drawn up in the early 1920s, these specify the format for memoranda and lay down certain general principles: that policy proposals should be submitted in advance to the cabinet in writing, that where the interests of other departments are involved there should be prior consultations and, in particular, that the provisional sanction of the Minister for Finance should be sought in advance. There are specific instructions to cover the procedures relating to legislation. There are procedures designed to reconcile, or at least qualify, differences of opinion between departments prior to submission. The Secretary to the Government, who regularly attends at cabinet, draws up the decisions of the government (the only—and generally extremely uninformative—minutes of government meetings), transmits relevant parts to other departments for action and, from time to time, monitors their implementation.

The Department and advisors also assist the Taoiseach in preparing for government business; this includes supplying summaries and observations on submissions by other ministers. The increasing scale and complexity of issues considered by government and, in particular, the "internationalisation" of much public policy has encouraged Taoisigh to supplement the expertise available to them by appointing special advisors. Sometimes these are assigned to specific policy areas but they tend to become part of an internal *cabinet* (a small team of advisors) that a Taoiseach consults on a variety of issues. Also operating in the Taoiseach's Department is the Government Information Service under the Government Press Secretary, invariably a political appointee close to the Taoiseach (see Farrell, 1993a).

THE WORK OF THE GOVERNMENT

Formerly the cabinet met twice weekly during parliamentary sessions. The present practice is to have weekly meetings (on Tuesdays during Dáil sessions, Wednesdays at other times) except during holiday periods—Christmas, Easter and the month of August. When necessary, however, the cabinet can be, and is, convened rapidly. On occasions, when ministers may not be readily available, urgent matters of a non-controversial nature are decided by way of "incorporeal meeting", i.e. ministers are contacted by telephone (see Dooney and O'Toole, 1992, p. 7). Attendance is limited to ministers, the Attorney General, the Secretary to the Government and the Minister of State at the Department of the Taoiseach (who acts as chief whip and coordinates the legislative programmes). Generally, discussion at cabinet is limited to the Taoiseach and a group of the most senior and influential ministers who sit around and across the centre of a cigar-shaped table at Government Buildings in Upper Merrion Street. Other ministers contribute on matters relating to their own departments, sometimes in terms of regional and personal interests and occasionally on broader contentious topics. But a chronically overloaded agenda does not encourage unnecessary or long-winded interventions.

Despite elaborately-framed procedures, the cabinet remains an arena in which the complex, controversial and perennially unresolvable compete for attention and time against the immediate, commonplace and critical. The agenda may include anything from 10 to 30 separate items; invariably there are also non-agenda items requiring discussion. Topics may include technical implications of a new EC directive, the appointment of a Supreme Court judge, a major legislative proposal, the dismissal of a junior civil servant, a ministerial order affecting excise rates, the latest industrial relations problem, difficulties within the parliamentary party or parties, or precise decisions curtailing expenditure on services.

Structure and relative underdevelopment

The structure of government in Ireland has barely changed in 70 years. In particular, there has been no development of a cabinet committee system, nor any extension of the powers of junior ministers, either of which might be expected to reduce the burden of cabinet decision-making. Junior ministers were initially termed "Parliamentary Secretary" and limited to seven; in 1978 the title "Minister of State" was substituted and the number increased to 10, and a further five posts were later created. Ministers of State are attached to a particular government department and are dependent on their ministers in submitting matters for cabinet consideration. There have been occasional efforts to identify the functions and specify the responsibilities of individual Ministers of State but, to date, it appears that no Taoiseach has been able to offer such junior ministers access to the cabinet without the prior approval of the relevant minister. They do not normally attend cabinet meetings and cannot have the same involvement in the framing of public policy as a minister.

Similarly, cabinet committees—with the rarest of exceptions—have not flourished. In Britain and elsewhere, the cabinet has reduced its work load by transferring to these committees of ministers (both standing and ad hoc committees) discussions of, and indeed decisions on, particular issues and policy areas (see Hennessy, 1986). In Ireland, the original cloak of secrecy over the existence, number, membership, functions and procedures of such committees, so effectively breached in Britain in recent decades, has been rigorously maintained. They are not an acceptable subject for parliamentary questions, and ministers are not very forthcoming. It appears, however, that there is not a great deal to hide. There are few, if any, "standing" committees. From an early stage, the use of committees appears in cabinet proceedings, frequently in an effort to resolve disputes between ministers and/or departments. Although there are some indications that committees are more common in coalition than in single-party governments, the record shows that—irrespective of the government—such committees met infrequently (and sometimes not at all), were not normally serviced by the secretariat and rarely appear to have reported back to cabinet. One result is that far more cabinet papers (about 800) are handled each year by the Irish cabinet than by its British counterpart, which makes more extensive use of cabinet committees and handles only about 60 to 70 cabinet papers a year (Farrell, 1987b, p. 149).

A major attempt at structural reform that might affect the operation of government in the future was introduced by the Fianna Fáil-Labour "Partnership Government" in 1993. The Labour Party, sensitive to the difficulties it had encountered in the past in securing adequate and speedy implementation of government policy, proposed the appointment of "programme managers" in each department (Farrell, 1993b). Akin to ministerial advisors, they are responsible for "monitoring, organising and getting the programme up and running in each Department and [are] to meet at regular intervals to ensure that that is happening" (Albert Reynolds, *Dáil Debates* 427: 128-9, 2 March 1993). It is indicative of a difference of approach and governmental experience between the two parties that all but one of the Fianna Fáil ministers appointed serving civil servants; none of the Labour appointments has been a civil servant. The provision for joint meetings of the managers might suggest a significant departure in a system that resists any regular meetings of departmental secretaries. But the role of the programme managers is only evolving and it is difficult to see them, either collectively or individually, diverting existing modes of government business significantly.

Collective responsibility

Within this busy world of the cabinet, the doctrine of collective responsibility laid down in the constitution is upheld in procedure and practice. Admittedly, there have been some significant breaches. In 1979, following discussion with the Taoiseach, the Minister for Agriculture, James Gibbons, who publicly opposed a government Family Planning Bill (and abstained in the Dáil vote on it), was not required to resign; in 1974 the Taoiseach, Liam Cosgrave, and the Minister for Education, Richard Burke, both voted against another contraception bill introduced in government time by their colleague the Minister for Justice. But these are exceptions to a general rule that normally denies ministers the right to record private dissent, let alone public opposition, to cabinet decisions. Typically the net of collective action is spread even wider.

The *Government Procedure Instructions* (1983 edition, paragraph 19), elaborates:

> The doctrine of collective responsibility requires that each Minister should inform his colleagues in Government of proposals he or a Minister of State at his Department intends to announce, and, if necessary, seek their agreement. This applies, in particular, to proposals for legislation which can be initiated only after formal approval by Government.

The rationale offered for collective responsibility is that it permits ministers full and frank argument in reaching decisions in private while maintaining a united front once decisions are formulated. It is a cornerstone of the system. This emphasis on collective responsibility permeates the operation of the whole governmental system and contributes to its outstanding characteristic: the remarkable concentration on the cabinet itself as a clearing house for all government business decisions and the established and accepted emphasis on government continuity.

The joint principles of collective responsibility and cabinet continuity are reinforced by a firmly entrenched commitment to a high level of executive secrecy. All governmental systems, even the relatively "open" Scandinavian systems, recognise the advantages of maintaining a level of confidentiality regarding top government decision-making. In the Irish case the established attachment to virtually absolute cabinet confidentiality was upheld by the Supreme Court in 1992. Chief Justice Finlay, leading for the majority of the court (in a case regarding the admissibility of evidence regarding cabinet discussions before the Tribunal of Inquiry into the Beef Industry) stated:

> confidentiality is a constitutional right which, in my view, goes to the fundamental machinery of government and is, therefore, not capable of being waived by any individual member of the government, nor ... by a decision of any succeeding government (see Farrell, 1993a; Hogan, 1993).

Role of the minister

This concentration on the cabinet severely restricts the freedom of ministers. It is more than a formal constitutional convention. With the rarest of exceptions, ministers seek cabinet approval before initiating or implementing policy changes. Approval is not a matter of the government automatically rubber-stamping proposals from ministers; it is clear (despite such rare exceptions as Donogh O'Malley's unapproved announcement of the "free education" scheme) that the cabinet acts as a genuine and comprehensive constraint on policy initiation by individual ministers. In particular, there are stringent controls exercised by the Department of Finance which circumscribe ministerial action; even quite small items of new expenditure are frequently referred back to the whole cabinet. It follows that policy initiatives must be carefully processed through the detailed mechanisms of the cabinet system and are unlikely to be implemented unless the approval of other ministers and departments is secured.

Typically, a minister, as well as being a member of the government, is the head of a department; to date only one "Minister without Portfolio", i.e. without formal responsibility for a department, has been appointed (in 1939). According to the Ministers and Secretaries Act, the minister is a "corporation sole"—responsible for everything done by the department. In practice even this internal administrative function is subjected to cabinet scrutiny. Clearly some ministers are more assertive than others but, in general, they take care to keep their colleagues in government informed in advance. Apart from any other consideration, this sharing of information and responsibility helps ministers to cope with party and constituency pressures. (For further discussion see "Ministerial autonomy and collective responsibility" in Farrell, 1994.)

Ministers must also cope with the civil service machine. Personnel changes are not easily accomplished and the system tends to guard incumbents and established hierarchies against ministerial interference. Departments usually have their own agenda, and ministers who try to move too far or too fast may soon discover the peril of not waiting for, or ignoring, the advice of their civil servants. In their role as "accounting officers" for their departments, departmental secretaries may, if necessary, invoke the considerable weight of the Department of Finance to restrain a minister who is seen to be promoting unacceptable projects.

On the other hand, few politicians become ministers without some degree of ambition, shrewdness, energy and capacity. They are not ciphers to be manipulated nor subservient lackeys. Inevitably, tensions, disagreements and conflicts will arise within a cabinet system. There will be forceful expressions of strongly held views and interests. To guide disparate ministers towards a collective decision, without alienating those who express contrary views, and to maintain the cabinet in being, requires considerable political skill. Here the role of Taoiseach is critical.

ROLE OF THE TAOISEACH

The Taoiseach plays a pivotal and multi-functional role in the political system. In a classic description, the longest serving Secretary to the Government, Maurice Moynihan (1969, p. 19), identified the Taoiseach as "the captain of the team":

> In this capacity, he is the central coordinating figure, who takes an interest in the work of all departments, the figure to whom Ministers naturally turn for advice and guidance when faced with problems involving large questions of policy or otherwise of special difficulty and whose leadership is essential to the successful working of the Government as a collective authority, collectively responsible to Dáil Éireann, but acting through members each of whom is charged with specific Departmental tasks. He may often have to inform himself in considerable detail of particular matters with which other members of the Government are primarily concerned. He may have to make public statements on such matters, as well as on general matters of broad policy, internal and external. He answers Dáil Questions where the attitude of the Government towards important matters of policy is involved. He may occasionally sponsor Bills which represent important new developments of policy, even when the legislation, when enacted, will be of particular concern to the Minister in charge of some other Department of State. His Department is the sole channel of communication between Departments generally and the President's secretariat, except in minor and routine matters. Through his Parliamentary Secretary, whose Office is also included in the Department of the Taoiseach, he secures the coordination, in a comprehensive parliamentary programme, of the proposals of the various Ministers for legislative and other measures in the Houses of the Oireachtas.

The Taoiseach is also a major figure in partisan politics. With the exception of John A. Costello, all Taoisigh have been party leaders. In relation to government, three particular functions require comment. The Taoiseach is chairman of the cabinet, manager of ministers, and increasingly seen as chief executive of the state. As Ireland has moved from an unexamined assumption of single-party majoritarian government as the norm to a recognised acceptance of coalition, each of these functions has been affected.

Chairman of the cabinet

Procedure, practice and power make the Taoiseach master of the cabinet. The Taoiseach determines the order in which items on the cabinet agenda are taken, the time given to consideration of each item, who is to speak, and when a decision should be reached—or postponed. It is evident that circumstance and personality influence the skill and the will with which this chairmanship is effected. But in practice, ministers do not challenge the Taoiseach's control of the agenda.

Again, the Taoiseach is extremely influential in determining the outcome of cabinet discussions. Votes are taken only infrequently, usually on less important issues, and not recorded. Nor is there a quorum for cabinet meetings. Typically decisions are consensual in character and dissent is not minuted. A minister whose proposals are being resisted will usually require the Taoiseach's support to be successful. On highly contentious issues, matters may be referred to a committee of ministers. If resolution is not possible and the Taoiseach expresses no strong view the matter may be deferred indefinitely. There are no vetoes as such. However, in practice, specific opposition by the Taoiseach acts as a veto.

These powers are likely to be maximised in single-party governments, unless factionalism creates problems. In coalition cabinets, the Taoiseach's chairmanship is likely to be more muted. Care must be taken to avoid divided decisions where the cabinet splits along party lines. Control of the agenda will usually be shared with another party leader serving in cabinet. Equally it is important that the junior party's ministers acknowledge and respect the Taoiseach's overall responsibility and authority. An instructive example of what happens when these conventions are not observed is provided in the transition from Haughey to Reynolds during the Fianna Fáil-PD coalition in 1992 (Farrell 1993b; Girvin, 1993, pp. 8-12).

Manager of ministers

A significant part of the Taoiseach's power arises from the fact that he or she nominates ministers and allocates their portfolios, and may rearrange this deployment of ministers at will. Although, as a matter of courtesy, the Taoiseach informs the Dáil of these appointments, there is no question of seeking parliamentary approval either for the initial appointments to particular departments on the formation of government or for subsequent shuffles. It is evident that senior politicians can and do hold out for more prestigious appointments, although there is no formal hierarchy of ministers. It is also clear that they may be refused by a strong-minded Taoiseach; in 1982 George Colley declined to join the government when refused appointment as Tánaiste, and in 1987 Haughey resisted Albert Reynolds's demands to have Energy added to his portfolio of Industry and Commerce.

In the past, ministerial changes were infrequent in Irish politics. There was caution in making initial appointments and reshuffles were very rare. Even with a change of Taoiseach, ministers were rarely dropped, though, as we have seen, this pattern has changed recently. Midterm reshuffles have also been rare. They are often difficult to manage and may not always achieve their intended objective. In the major reshuffle of September 1939, de Valera managed to place Lemass in a strategic position (although he never explicitly acknowledged this intention; see Farrell, 1983, pp. 53-6). FitzGerald's effort to shuffle the Fine Gael ministers in 1986 without introducing any new blood was a failure (FitzGerald, 1991, pp. 621-5; Hussey, 1990, pp. 196-202).

Similarly, no Taoiseach has shown the taste for ministerial butchery said to be a prerequisite for British prime ministers. The smaller scale of the Irish system is partly responsible; choices are reduced by the size of parliamentary parties. In the past, also, some backbenchers neither aspired to nor competed for office. The increased professionalisation of TDs has largely eliminated that problem and, as competition has increased, this has enhanced the choices available to a Taoiseach, confirming and extending his or her role as manager of ministers.

On the other hand, the increased frequency of coalition government imposes constraints on the Taoiseach's choices in managing ministers. Portfolios have to be negotiated with another party leader; selection of nominees is ceded to the other party. Sometimes this creates political difficulties for the major party: conspicuously in 1948 Clann na Poblachta refused to serve in a government headed by the Fine Gael leader Richard Mulcahy and in 1993 Reynolds was forced to demote a Fianna Fáil minister to make space for a Labour nominee. The Taoiseach in a coalition may be forced to concede extra influence to the junior party, such as the replacement of the Fine Gael-appointed Peter Sutherland as Attorney General by the Spring nominee, John Rogers, in 1984 (it might be noted that the selection of the Attorney General is specifically reserved to the Taoiseach in Article 30.2 of the constitution). The Taoiseach has no real political function if difficulties arise within other parties in coalition, even if these directly affect cabinet personnel; in 1951 it was Clann na Poblachta party leader Seán MacBride, not Taoiseach Costello, who sought the resignation of Noel Browne that effectively brought down the government; in 1983, following the resignation of Frank Cluskey, Labour leader Spring selected Quinn as replacement without any discussion with the Taoiseach; and FitzGerald's botched reshuffle in 1986 was affected by the refusal of Labour minister Barry Desmond to relinquish his Health portfolio.

Chief executive

The Taoiseach has always been recognised as the chief executive in the Irish cabinet system. In Ireland, as elsewhere in Europe (especially in other EC member states), the "challenge of internationalism" has forced some political and administrative adjustments enhancing that role (OECD, 1990).

Changes in the management structure and staffing of the Taoiseach's Department over the last 20 years have been largely overshadowed by political events and the personalities involved. Lynch, recognising the need for reform, recruited an independent economic advisor, Dr Martin O'Donoghue, in the early 1970s and in 1977, after his election to the Dáil, nominated him as minister to the newly created Department of Economic Planning and Development.

Two years later, on his accession, Haughey abolished this Department and absorbed its officials into his own department. Many saw this as merely a political manoeuvre to demote an unwanted minister. However, as we have already noted, Haughey also separated the functions of Secretary of the Department of the Taoiseach and Secretary to the Government, an indication that he was seeking to strengthen the Taoiseach's office to cope with its additional responsibilities by developing an administrative remit within his own office. Haughey's successor, FitzGerald, inherited this framework but made little attempt to use it fully. He preferred to rely on a personal advisor on economic affairs (see Honohan, 1988) and secured comprehensive written reports from Foreign Affairs to keep abreast of EC, Northern Ireland and international affairs generally. It was evident that FitzGerald recognised the need to strengthen the capacity of his office to deal with EC coordination. However, little was achieved. The Taoiseach trusted his Foreign Ministers and played an active role himself when required.

Haughey saw the solution in the internal development of the Taoiseach's Department. On resuming office in 1987 he appointed a minister of state at the Department of the Taoiseach with special responsibility for the coordination of government policy and EC matters. The minister appointed, Máire Geoghegan-Quinn, was reappointed in 1989 and played an important part in preparing for and carrying through Ireland's EC presidency in 1990 (see pp. 241-2 below). Haughey further enhanced the influence of the Secretary of the Taoiseach's

Department. This is most graphically illustrated by the fact that the last Secretary of the Department of the Taoiseach in large measure negotiated, and oversaw through monthly meetings, the implementation of two successive national understandings on pay, taxation and public policy agreed between the government and the major "social partners", i.e. trade union and business representatives. He also sat on a number of major state boards, including the recently developed Financial Services Centre, and effectively acted as chief of staff for the Taoiseach while Haughey held that office. His successor as Secretary, while less prominent as a public personality, has continued to play this executive role over a wide range of activities on behalf of the Taoiseach.

Coalition also affects this executive function of the Taoiseach. In a power-sharing situation it becomes more difficult—and dangerous—for the Taoiseach to act without consulting the leader of another party in government. Indeed, it is a marked feature of the partnership government formed in 1993 that an attempt has been made to institutionalise this changed relationship. This has been done by enhancing the role of the Labour leader in his function as Tánaiste (Farrell, 1993b). Although constitutionally it is clear that the Tánaiste is a *deputising* prime minister who functions in the absence of the Taoiseach, the attempt is being made to convert Spring into a *deputy* prime minister. A separate Office of the Tánaiste has been established, with its own secretariat and with a Labour-nominated minister of state in charge. Its central function is to brief and advise the Tánaiste generally on all government policy matters, and it is now established practice that all government papers are sent to the office, which also exercises a role in monitoring the implementation of the Programme for Government.

These innovations, and the general shift from single-party to coalition government as the norm, mark some important restraints on the power and influence of Taoiseach. But the broad thrust of developments over recent decades has considerably enhanced the executive office of the Taoiseach, increased the capacity to probe policy proposals and to monitor the implementation of decisions, and further entrenched the Taoiseach's influential—even conclusive—chairmanship of the cabinet. The question remains: has there been a decisive, systemic change in the role of the modern Taoiseach compared with that of earlier office-holders?

CHAIRMAN OR CHIEF?

To date only nine men have held office as head of government since the foundation of the Irish state. It is difficult to build any general theory on such a small selection of cases (O'Leary, 1991), but worth attempting a broad sketch based on more than a profile of personality types. The Taoiseach is at once an individual and an institution; whatever about personal life experiences and circumstances, any individual's performance will be modified, shaped and affected by the established pattern of the office.

What is required is some broad typology to encompass all these factors within recognisable terms; what is suggested is a broad judgment of the overall performance and behaviour of each Taoiseach as "chief" or "chairman". "Chiefs" are distinguished by a tendency to accumulate political resources, concentrate decision making or control of decision making in their own hands, and—above all—

make use of their strategic position to mobilise the machinery of government for action. "Chairmen" are prepared to allow others to share resources, responsibilities and publicity, reluctant to move beyond established procedures and slower to act. These two types should not be seen as separate and distinct categories; each remains confined within the particular disciplines of the cabinet system.

In essence, then, these ideal types are poles that mark the continuum of political leadership within cabinet systems. Specific incumbents may aspire to operate closer to one end of the spectrum; particular circumstances may drive them to the other. The "chief" may be consumed by the desire to be first but is nevertheless forced to act in concert with colleagues; the "chairman" accepts the limitations of collective responsibility, but may well convert them—by necessity or by design—into a power base for highly effective leadership. The same Taoiseach may at different times, or even with regard to different issues or personalities during the same period, alternate between the two. A brief sketch of the nine office-holders illustrates something of the complexities involved in attempting to analyse the role of Taoiseach (for short biographies of each, see appendix 4).

W. T. Cosgrave (1922-32)

Cosgrave became leader by accident, following the sudden deaths of Griffith and Collins. A participant in the Easter Rising in 1916, he won a seat for Sinn Féin in the Kilkenny by-election in 1917 and became Minister for Local Government in the first Dáil. In the early months of 1922, he chaired meetings of the Provisional Government in the absence of Collins.

He did not aspire to be a charismatic leader; he had inherited a team and stressed cabinet rather than personal leadership, consulting other colleagues in allocating departments to ministers. At the same time, Cosgrave was prepared to demote ministers to junior rank (Edmund Duggan in 1922, Séamus Bourke in 1927) and successfully steered his government through a series of cabinet crises involving the loss of ministers (both Richard Mulcahy and Joseph McGrath left during the "Army Mutiny" in 1924; Eoin MacNeill resigned over the Boundary Commission report in 1925; in 1927 J. J. Walsh resigned without notice and Kevin O'Higgins was assassinated). Against this turbulent background, to maintain power for ten years was a major political achievement; little wonder that contemporary colleagues insisted that Cosgrave's informal title, "the Boss", expressed the reality of cabinet relationships.

Cosgrave took over an Ireland in transition to independence during a civil war. His first government produced a wide range of legislation covering courts, police and public administration which has continued to provide the basic institutional framework of the Irish state. It was a remarkable record of reconstruction, achieved at a time when the very legitimacy of the state was being challenged and a large section of organised public opinion led by de Valera's Sinn Féin was refusing even to recognise, let alone participate in, the Dáil. An American contemporary observer recorded:

> Acts were passed dealing with the organisation of local government, the land problem, pensions, beet-sugar subsidies, police, the civil service, the courts, currency, electricity supply, fisheries, housing, intoxicating liquors, railways, roads, tariffs and unemployment. In the field of external affairs the Irish government successfully pressed its claims for a greater degree of independence than was formally described in the constitutional law of the British Empire (Moss, 1933, p. 24).

But Cosgrave was a conservative in social and economic affairs and the concentration on the political aspects of independence did little to reduce inequalities in an underdeveloped society. On the other hand, he did facilitate the entry of Fianna Fáil into full parliamentary politics and, only ten years after the civil war, accepted the results of the 1932 general election and handed the established apparatus of the new state to his political opponent, Eamon de Valera.

Eamon de Valera (1932-48, 1951-54, 1957-59)
In all, de Valera completed almost a quarter century of executive leadership as President of Dáil Éireann (1919-22), President of the Executive Council and Taoiseach. His longevity in office makes any brief balanced judgment difficult. Known as "the Chief", his actual performance was more cautious and less assertive than the title suggests. Frequently accused by opponents of running a one-man band and of exercising an almost hypnotic dominance over his ministers, the record shows that he was the leader of a team that included strong-minded and assertive ministers.

That team came to power (as a minority government) in 1932; four of the original nine ministers chosen by de Valera were still in cabinet when he ceased to be Taoiseach on becoming President in 1959. They were undoubtedly committed to their leader but were also ready, in the privacy of the cabinet room, to argue and disagree about the direction and pace of public policy. Cabinet meetings were frequent and exhaustingly long; ministers were free to thrash out decisions. In measure, this may have been a technique of leadership by attrition; in measure it reflected de Valera's determination to bring colleagues towards consensus and never again to preside over a cabinet split such as that which led to civil war in 1922.

In 1932 the government had an articulated programme. There was no debate on the main thrust of its constitutional aim: to dismantle as much as possible the unacceptable parts of the Treaty settlement. For this de Valera (who acted as Minister for External Affairs as well as head of government between 1932 and 1948) was virtually exclusively in charge. Typically, de Valera drafted Bunreacht na hÉireann with his chosen civil servants rather than through the cabinet (Keogh, 1988; Fanning 1988). Similarly, ministerial colleagues did not dispute his handling of neutrality during the second world war. However there was considerable divergence within the de Valera governments on particular aspects of economic and social policy. Lemass pressed a radical, strongly interventionist policy of protectionism through the 1930s; he was opposed by the more orthodox Minister for Finance, Seán MacEntee. The long-stated Fianna Fáil policy of maintaining maximum numbers on the land, enshrined in the constitution, conflicted with efforts to promote greater agricultural productivity. Far from being the driver of an acquiescent team of ministerial work-horses, de Valera was often referee in vigorous and competitive fights between ministers and departments concerned, as in all governments, to secure maximum resources for their own schemes and policies.

He avoided political showdowns in cabinet; no minister ever resigned; none was seen to be sacked. De Valera's management of his team was subtle, even oblique, but achieved its purpose. Thus in 1939 when he installed Lemass as Minister for Supplies, with extraordinarily wide-ranging powers, de Valera also shifted MacEntee from Finance; however, this patent demotion was obscured by changing all ministers' portfolios, with the exception of that of James Ryan. De Valera was prepared to tolerate, and able to manage, a considerable degree of friction within cabinet. In time, this consumed an increasing amount of his time and energy; he tended to become the adjudicator rather than the initiator of policy.

Yet his input into economic and social policy for many years could be obscured by his rhetoric. The much quoted radio address of 1943 on "the Ireland we have dreamed of", with its ideal of a frugal, rural idyll, scarcely represented the real thrust of Fianna Fáil policy under de Valera. Through the 1930s a small set of mainly urban-based ministers shaped the priorities and allocated the resources of government; Lemass was preeminent and it was with Lemass, in a tiny cabinet committee in the early 1940s, that de Valera attempted the task of post-war planning (Farrell, 1983a, 1983b).

After 16 continuous years in power, defeat in 1948 marked an understandable decline in de Valera's capacity. He was to lead two further administrations, in 1951 and 1957, but a combination of age, almost total blindness and innate conservatism made for a passive mode. De Valera was slow to promote younger men or to entertain new ideas. Cabinets remained essentially consensual, with de Valera refereeing struggles between ministers, but decision-making was painfully slow-moving, at the pace of the last minister to be convinced. To the end, he remained "the Chief", but now a chief content to be rather than to lead.

John A. Costello (1948-51, 1954-57)

Costello was a reluctant Taoiseach, heading Ireland's first coalition government with severely curtailed powers. A busy, successful senior counsel, he served as Attorney General from 1926 to 1932 and, from his election to the Dáil in 1933, as a Fine Gael frontbencher. He presided over the most disparate administration ever formed in the Irish system; five parties ranging from a conservative Fine Gael, through Clann na Talmhan and two Labour parties to Clann na Poblachta. The only Taoiseach who was not party leader, he was chosen because the Fine Gael leader, Richard Mulcahy, was unacceptable to others in the coalition. In addition, he was asked to become Taoiseach only after all the ministerial portfolios had been distributed among the parties and, therefore, lacked the customary power to "hire and fire".

Given the strong ideological and personal diversities in a government formed without any agreed programme (except the desire to oust Fianna Fáil after an uninterrupted 16 years in office) and without any experience of coalition, this Inter-Party administration strained some of the inherited conventions of a cabinet system designed for single-party government. The exclusion of the cabinet secretary from government meetings did not help. There were inevitably disagreements. It says much for Costello's skill as a chairman that there was only one resignation, at the very end of his first term. While most attention has concentrated on the two controversial issues of Noel Browne's "Mother and Child" Scheme and the decision to repeal the External Relations Act, the first Inter-Party government achieved some noticeable success in revitalising land policy, developing agriculture, and introducing the Industrial Development Authority and Córas Tracht-tála. It also helped to heal the rift in the Labour Party.

Defeated in 1951, Costello formed the second Inter-Party government three years later. With a more confined party grouping and considerably enhanced prestige it was easier for him to exert influence as Taoiseach. There was none of the earlier lack of cabinet discipline. He insisted that the secretary attend cabinet and take minutes. Costello was conscious that some ministers had lost the freshness of their first term and was ready to prod individual ministers to act or to intervene in support of particular policies. But perhaps Costello's enduring contribution to the development of the Taoiseach's office was that, having advocated coalition as early as 1946, he was able to break the established mould and actually head two coalition governments. In later years, as an elder statesman, he encouraged Fine Gael to adopt the "Just Society" social democratic programme that subsequently paved the way for the National Coalition of 1973.

Seán Lemass (1959-66)

Inheriting, as uncontested successor to party founder Eamon de Valera, an overall majority government, an inert economy and a conservative society, Lemass was a consciously modernising Taoiseach. He attempted to galvanise the economy by an emphasis on expanding industrial growth, exports and overseas investment; promoted free trade with Britain and Europe; set out to convert the large state-sponsored segment (much of it his own creation as long-serving Minister for Industry and Commerce) into developmental corporations; hinted at the need to modify the policy of neutrality; and participated in cross-border talks with the prime minister of Northern Ireland. Critics have argued that his claim that "rising tides lift all boats" was belied by continuing and perhaps increasing relative social deprivation.

In two elections (1961 and 1965) as party leader he failed to secure Fianna Fáil's traditional target of an overall majority. In cabinet, his leadership was assertive, brisk and businesslike; he commented that "de Valera's cabinets began on time, mine ended on time" and made a virtue of rapid decision making. He responded to the challenge of resignation by a senior minister (Paddy Smith) in 1964 by appointing a young, urban-based minister (Charles J. Haughey) to the key department of Agriculture. In 1966, without any pressure from colleagues, party or public, he chose to retire. Lemass exhibited a wide range of behaviour associated with the "chief". He was assertive in advancing policies in the cabinet and in public, prepared to use ministers to float ideas, to circumvent normal procedures on occasion and to chair cabinets with decisive consequences.

Jack Lynch (1966-73, 1977-79)

Following an internal contest that revealed a degree not merely of rivalry but of factionalism within the Fianna Fáil party, Lynch began by continuing policies already in place, established a considerable reputation as a vote winner (especially in southern regions) and secured an overall majority of seats in the 1969 general election. Almost immediately the outbreak of a new—and still continuing—phase of violence within Northern Ireland provoked an atmosphere of instability. May 1970 was the occasion for the "arms crisis" in which, as we have mentioned, Lynch forced the resignation of a Minister for Justice, sacked the Ministers for Finance and for Agriculture, and accepted a fourth ministerial resignation; he successfully reshuffled the cabinet and survived a vote of no confidence.

In the 1973 election, despite a marginal increase in first preference votes for Fianna Fáil, he lost six seats and went into opposition.

Over the next four years, Lynch reorganised the party and framed an attractive, expansionist package of policies (including the abolition of domestic rates and of car tax, and a programme of "full" employment). This secured an overall majority of votes and a 20-seat majority in the 1977 general election. A combination of factors (including internal party dissatisfaction with his moderate policy on Northern Ireland, factionalism, the continuing economic pressures generated by the oil crisis, the failure to control public finances, and declining electoral performance, as manifested in European Parliament, local and by-elections) precipitated a slightly premature resignation in December 1979.

Originally viewed, erroneously, as a "caretaker Taoiseach", Lynch was slow to exert his authority until the cabinet crisis of 1970. Subsequently more evidently in charge, he was prepared to allow ministers latitude in pursuing policies. In his last period in office, there appeared to be a drift in economic management which, combined with Ireland's rapidly growing population and the factors mentioned above, greatly reduced his authority. Lynch, a reluctant candidate, began as a classic "chairman" (in May 1970 he acknowledged that many of his cabinet colleagues had entered the Dáil and/or cabinet at the same time as he had). Forced to act as chief during the arms crisis of 1970, he also showed that a Taoiseach who is not prepared to resign cannot easily be forced to stand down. In his last period in office, he again preferred the chairman role.

Liam Cosgrave (1973-77)

Son of the first Irish prime minister (W. T. Cosgrave, 1922-32), he had survived considerable internal party dissatisfaction immediately before becoming head of the National Coalition of Fine Gael and Labour in 1973. Committed to an agreed 14-point programme of a broadly social democratic nature, this administration was confronted by the impact of the oil crisis on a small, open, trading economy, the pressure of population growth and the need to attempt some resolution of the Northern Ireland problem. The latter led to the creation of a short-lived "power-sharing executive" of unionist and nationalist politicians in Belfast, the former issues proved intractable, and there was a serious rise in overseas borrowing and a general malaise in the public finances.

Cosgrave, a committed party man, was a remarkably successful coalition leader who secured the admiration and loyalty of Labour ministers. This helped him to survive two political crises (when he voted against his own Fine Gael minister's bill permitting limited access to contraceptives in 1974, and when he refused to dismiss, or accept the resignation of, a minister whose public insult provoked the resignation of President Ó Dálaigh in 1976). A redrawing of electoral constituencies, designed to assist the coalition, magnified the effects of a disastrous defeat in 1977 (see p. 79 above); Cosgrave promptly resigned as Fine Gael leader. The circumstances of coalition inevitably drive a Taoiseach towards the "chairman" pole. In selecting his nominees for office, maintaining harmony between the coalition partners, and managing cabinet, Cosgrave proved a skilful chairman. Yet he exhibited a more vigorous leadership in promoting Northern Ireland policy and showed determination in resisting pressure on contentious issues.

Charles J. Haughey (1979-81, 1982, 1987-92)

Elected to leadership by backbenchers against a candidate favoured by the cabinet and party hierarchy, Haughey faced internal opponents and a parliamentary opposition that was deeply suspicious and bitterly hostile. Recognising the need to tackle the problems of public finance and economic management, his plans to secure a personal mandate in an early election were foiled in part by the H-Block controversy in Northern Ireland, and he was defeated in 1981. The sudden collapse of the first FitzGerald coalition on its budget proposals gave rise to a brief and accident-prone Haughey government in 1982, severely restricted by its minority status, dependence on left-wing parliamentary support and continuing internal challenges to his leadership. Two of his ministers (Desmond O'Malley and Martin O'Donoghue) resigned when pressed to support his party leadership and he lost parliamentary support. Following his defeat in November 1982 there was another challenge to his leadership (occasioned by revelations that journalists' phones had been tapped for party political purposes) and in 1985 a number of dissident Fianna Fáil members left and established the Progressive Democrats.

In some ways this strengthened Haughey's position within Fianna Fáil, and, although the party's vote dropped slightly at the 1987 general election, he was able to form his third, minority, administration. With internal opposition neutralised, Haughey tackled the problems of the public finances with energy and skill, and engineered a broad agreement with the social partners that stabilised pay rates, reduced inflation and made inroads into the public service that some described as Thatcherite. The process was greatly assisted by an unforced commitment from Fine Gael leader Alan Dukes not to oppose corrective, if unpopular, measures required to restore economic confidence.

Nevertheless, after a series of government defeats on relatively minor issues, Haughey called for a majority mandate in a new general election in 1989 (Girvin, 1990). In the event, he again failed to secure a majority and, after a complex series of manoeuvres, persuaded Fianna Fáil to relinquish its traditionally hostile rejection of all forms of coalition (Farrell, 1990). He then formed a coalition administration with the PDs, two of whose members (both former Fianna Fáil ministers) received cabinet posts. He held centre stage and received much favourable publicity during Ireland's presidency of the EC in 1990, and he concluded another "Programme for Economic and Social Progress" with the social partners.

Dissatisfaction and dissent continued. Despite apparent public satisfaction with the coalition's performance, many in Fianna Fáil resented what was seen as the undue influence of the PDs, as exemplified in the forced dismissal of Brian Lenihan during the 1990 presidential election campaign and the withdrawal of Haughey's nomination of Dr Jim McDaid to government a year later when the PDs made it clear that they would not support McDaid's nomination in the Dáil vote. Haughey resisted a further challenge to his leadership of the party in November 1991 (he won a motion of confidence among his TDs by 55 votes to 22) and dismissed two senior ministers, as already indicated. However, a combination of factors (including declining popularity in the polls, concern about a series of allegations regarding political intervention in business decisions, and, finally, Senator Seán Doherty's charge that the Taoiseach had been aware of improper telephone tapping in 1982) eventually forced him to resign before he was willing to go.

More than with most previous incumbents, Haughey's career reveals the importance of distinguishing between style and performance at different stages. Initially, his instinct to tackle economic problems was frustrated by the need to cope with internal dissension. Similarly, attempts to assert leadership in the short-lived 1982 government foundered on the need to retain support within both party and parliament. By 1987, he was uncontested leader, master of a cabinet of his own creation and able to show the leadership energy and flair that had distinguished his earlier ministerial career in a variety of departments. His handling of the delicate task of steering Fianna Fáil into coalition and subsequent leadership in coalition revealed the range of his political talents. But in the end he could not resist the demands of senior party colleagues for his removal as an electoral liability. Although he was frequently noted for his "presidential" style, and as a vigorous promoter of favoured policies, Haughey's instinct to be "chief" was curtailed by factionalism within his party, failure to secure a parliamentary majority, and economic circumstance. Cautious in initiating, or even taking an unambiguous stand on, contentious social issues, he showed great skill in imposing himself on the Fianna Fáil party. Over time he developed the office of Taoiseach (increasing its staff and functions), silenced or removed internal critics, and played a "chief"-like role at Anglo-Irish and European summits. The limits on his desire to be "chief" enforced by the need to act as "chairman" were illustrated in his painstaking negotiation of the coalition agreement with the Progressive Democrats in 1989. Haughey is likely to be seen as a leader whose frustrated instinct to be "chief" enabled him to act as a remarkably effective "chairman" who tried to hold on to office too long.

Garret FitzGerald (1981-82, 1982-87)

Succeeding to the leadership of Fine Gael in 1977, FitzGerald set about reforming the structures of the party, expanding its support and personnel, developing policies that combined orthodox economic management with a progressive and liberal approach to social issues, and pressing for a resolution of the Northern Ireland crisis. This restored the party's vote in 1981; careful vote management greatly increased its number of seats and enabled it to form a minority coalition government with Labour. This government immediately faced a crisis in the public finances necessitating unpopular measures; a second stringent budget in January 1982 was its downfall.

The November 1982 general election revealed a national consensus regarding national economic management and an uneasy political response to a proposed constitutional referendum on abortion. Fine Gael achieved its best ever performance in both votes and seats (see appendix 2b) and formed a much more tightly negotiated coalition with Labour. FitzGerald promoted the New Ireland Forum (whose proceedings took place in 1983-84) and concluded the 1985 Anglo-Irish Agreement that currently affects the administration of Northern Ireland. He was less successful in promoting liberal issues (including a restricted divorce jurisdiction) within the Republic and, in part because of internal cabinet disagreements, there was a continuing crisis in the public finances. Labour refused to support a stringent budget in 1987 and following its withdrawal and a slump in support for Fine Gael in the subsequent election FitzGerald resigned as party leader.

FitzGerald was adventurous in pressing pluralist policies but was not an effective manager of economic policies. His discursive style of chairing cabinet may have defused but did not resolve internal disagreements. His own determination to advance Northern Ireland policies led him to operate as a chief rather than a chairman in this area (FitzGerald, 1991, p. 425) but seems to have reduced the time, energy and skill required to deal with other issues. His academic background and the circumstances of coalition inevitably pushed FitzGerald towards the "chairman" end of the spectrum (although ironically colleagues and observers rated him poorly in terms of chairing skills at meetings, especially of his cabinet). On the other hand, he showed determined leadership in promoting a social democratic image for his party, placing contentious social issues on the national agenda and achieving a significant institutional breakthrough on the intractable problem of Northern Ireland.

Albert Reynolds (1992-)

It is early to attempt any evaluation of Reynolds. His initial appointments represented an adventurous extension of a tendency among more recent Taoisigh to put their mark on the cabinet at the outset. His (much criticised) handling of the Maastricht referendum in June 1992 exhibited a canny capacity to calculate a range of diverse and divisive pressures and produce an effective result. He has managed to distance himself from the more conservative and cautious stance of his predecessor on contentious social issues without provoking, to date, any conservative backlash. On the other hand, the (far from complete) evidence available suggests that he either misjudged, or was indifferent to, his PD colleagues in government. A series of incidents culminating in his evidence before the Beef Tribunal precipitated a vote of no confidence (see Farrell, 1993b; Girvin, 1993, pp. 8-12). Reynolds failed to lead Fianna Fáil to the stated goal of an overall majority, but, following negotiation of Ireland's demands on the EC structural and cohesion funds at Edinburgh in December 1992, he did successfully conclude a new coalition with Labour. In the process, he may have broken finally the Fianna Fáil taboo against coalition government and secured for his party an indefinite period in office—perhaps with shifting political partners.

CONCLUSION

The performance of recent Taoisigh suggests that there has been a significant change of balance within the Irish system. In the early stages, many factors combined to limit the exercise of executive leadership: the constitution and the legal system, the processes of cabinet government and civil service procedures, the familiar and ambiguous public attitudes to authority, the pressures of party colleagues and supporters, and the patterns and practices established by predecessors. More recent developments have sharpened the focus on the leader: electioneering methods and coverage identify the party leader as symbol of the party; increasing use of summits in Anglo-Irish and EC negotiations elevate the Taoiseach's role as the authoritative voice of government and national leader; as the growing professionalisation of politics appears to sharpen inter-ministerial rivalries and disagreement the Taoiseach is invoked as the final court of appeal; and there has been an increase in the influence of the Taoiseach's department within the civil service, and especially in its capacity to colour media coverage.

These developments, elevating the role of Taoiseach as "chief", should not be allowed to diminish the central importance of having a "chairman" in charge. In particular, the negotiation, formation and management of coalitions as against single-party governments are more likely to be achieved by a patient "chairman" than an assertive "chief". Yet, in all types of government, the ultimate authority of the Taoiseach cannot be lightly challenged and, at critical junctures, it is the solitary exercise of leadership by the "captain of the ship" that is required. That is more than a metaphor for a public relations emphasis on presentation; it is the reality of how the system operates. But, overall, the Irish system of government is essentially collective in character. Ministers do matter, even if the Taoiseach matters most. The cabinet remains the arena in which ultimate, and collective, decision making takes place. The substance of those decisions may well be determined less by the personalities of politicians than by the processes of policy development discussed in the next chapter.

REFERENCES AND FURTHER READING

Blondel, Jean and Ferdinand Müller-Rommel (eds), 1988. *Cabinets in Western Europe*. London: Macmillan.

Burch, Martin, 1988. "The United Kingdom", pp. 16-32 in Blondel and Müller-Rommel (1988).

Chubb, Basil, 1974. *Cabinet Government in Ireland*. Dublin: Institute of Public Administration.

Coakley, John and Brian Farrell, 1989. "Selection of cabinet ministers in Ireland, 1922-1982", pp. 199-218 in Mattei Dogan (ed.), *Pathways to Power: Selecting Rulers in Pluralist Democracies*. Boulder, San Francisco and London: Westview Press.

Collins, Stephen, 1992. *The Haughey File*. Dublin: The O'Brien Press.

Dooney, Seán and John O'Toole, 1992. *Irish Government Today*. Dublin: Gill and Macmillan.

Dwyer, T. Ryle, 1987. *Charlie: the Political Biography of Charles J. Haughey*. Dublin: Gill and Macmillan.

Fanning, Ronan, 1988. "Mr de Valera drafts a constitution" pp. 33-45 in Brian Farrell (ed.), *De Valera's Constitution and Ours*. Dublin: Gill and Macmillan.

Farrell, Brian, 1971. *Chairman or Chief? The Role of Taoiseach in Irish Government*. Dublin: Gill and Macmillan.

Farrell, Brian, 1983a. *Seán Lemass*. Dublin: Gill and Macmillan.

Farrell, Brian, 1983b. "De Valera: unique dictator or charismatic chairman?", pp. 35-46 in J. P. O'Carroll and John A. Murphy (eds), *De Valera and his Times*. Cork: Cork University Press.

Farrell, Brian, 1987a. "Government formation and ministerial selection", pp. 131-55 in Howard R. Penniman and Brian Farrell (eds), *Ireland at the Polls 1981, 1982 and 1987: a Study of Four General Elections*. Durham, NC: Duke University Press.

Farrell, Brian, 1987b. "Aftermath and government formation", pp. 141-52 in Michael Laver, Peter Mair, and Richard Sinnott (eds), *How Ireland Voted: the Irish General Election 1987*. Swords: Poolbeg Press.

Farrell, Brian, 1988a. "Ireland. The cabinet system: more British than the British themselves", pp. 33-46 in Blondel and Müller-Rommel (1988).

Farrell, Brian, 1988b. "The constitution and the institutions of government: constitutional theory and political politics", pp. 162-72 in Litton (1988).

Farrell, Brian, 1990. "Forming the government", pp. 179-91 in Gallagher and Sinnott (1990).

Farrell, Brian, 1993a. " 'Cagey and secretive': collective responsibility, executive confidentiality and the public interest", pp. 82-103 in Ronald J. Hill and Michael Marsh (eds), *Modern Irish Democracy: Essays in Honour of Basil Chubb*. Dublin: Irish Academic Press.

Farrell, Brian, 1993b. "The formation of the partnership government", pp. 146-61 in Gallagher and Laver (1993).

Farrell, Brian, 1994. "Odd man out? The role of ministers in the Irish political system", in Michael Laver and Kenneth A. Shepsle (eds), *Cabinet Ministers and Parliamentary Government*. Cambridge: Cambridge University Press, forthcoming.

FitzGerald, Garret, 1991. *All in a Life: an Autobiography*. Dublin: Gill and Macmillan.

Gallagher, Michael and Richard Sinnott (eds), 1990. *How Ireland Voted 1989*. Galway: Centre for the Study of Irish Elections and PSAI Press.

Gallagher, Michael and Michael Laver (eds), 1993. *How Ireland Voted 1992*. Dublin: Folens and Limerick: PSAI Press.

Girvin, Brian, 1990. "The campaign", pp. 5-22 in Gallagher and Sinnott (1990).

Girvin, Brian, 1993. "The road to the election", pp. 1-20 in Gallagher and Laver (1993).

Hennessy, Peter, 1986. *Cabinet*. Oxford: Basil Blackwell.

Hogan, Gerard, 1993. "The cabinet confidentiality case of 1992", *Irish Political Studies* 8, pp. 131-7.

Honohan, Patrick, 1988. "The role of the adviser and the evolution of the public service", pp. 7-44 in Miriam Hederman (ed.), *The Clash of Ideas: Essays in Honour of Patrick Lynch*. Dublin: Gill and Macmillan.

Hussey, Gemma, 1990. *At the Cutting Edge: Cabinet Diaries 1982-1987*. Dublin: Gill and Macmillan.

Keogh, Dermot, 1988. "The constitutional revolution: an analysis of the making of the Constitution", pp. 4-84 in Litton (1988).

Litton, Frank (ed.), 1988. *The Constitution of Ireland 1937-1987*. Dublin: Institute of Public Administration.

Moss, Warner, 1933. *Political Parties in the Irish Free State*. New York: Columbia University Press.

Moynihan, Maurice, 1969. *The Functions of the Department of the Taoiseach*. Dublin: Institute of Public Administration.

OECD, 1990. *Aspects of Managing the Centre of Government*. Paris: Organisation for Economic Cooperation and Development, OECD Occasional Paper.

O'Byrnes, Stephen, 1986. *Hiding behind a Face: Fine Gael under FitzGerald*. Dublin: Gill and Macmillan.

O'Leary, Brendan, 1991. "An Taoiseach: the Irish prime minister", *West European Politics* 14:2, pp. 133-62.

Weller, Patrick, 1985. *First Among Equals: Prime Ministers in Westminster Systems*. Sydney, London and Boston: George Allen and Unwin.

10 / POLICY MAKING

Eunan O'Halpin

National policy making is a complex business. Governments perpetually experience difficulties in making decisions, in sticking to them, in carrying them out, and in achieving the results desired. In Ireland there is an apparently widespread assumption that the national policy process developed since independence is inadequate for the demands placed upon it (Barrington, 1980, pp. 221-3; Lee, 1989, pp. 633-6; Garvin, 1991, pp. 43-5). In the mid-1930s, and almost continuously since the seminal Devlin report of 1969 on public service organisation, an assortment of nostrums have been proposed to improve matters, ranging from the reorganisation of central administration to changes in the voting system to a reform of local government. While there is broad agreement on the inadequate performance of the existing system, however, there is no consensus on how to improve it.

In considering the Irish policy system, this chapter explores a number of broad themes. These include the role of the civil service, of interest groups, and of politicians, political parties and the communications media in the process by which policy is formed, operated, reviewed and adapted.

SOME VIEWS OF THE POLICY PROCESS

There is a large body of literature on policy making, and any number of models are available (see the useful discussions in Burch and Wood, 1989, pp. 22-49, and Self, 1985, pp. 79-138). Three have emerged as the most widely discussed, each of them useful in analysing policy making in Ireland, though each appears individually inadequate as a comprehensive explanation of the policy process. The *bureaucratic* model suggests that only government officials have the knowledge, expertise and position to lead politicians through the policy maze to the decision the bureaucrats think best. The *corporatist* model suggests that voters, parties and perhaps even governments are irrelevant to policy making, which is the monopoly of major interest groups representing the various components in society. These negotiate with each other and with the state to minimise social disruption and to produce an agreed outcome. The *pluralist* model attributes preponderant power in policy making in particular areas at particular times to individual interest groups, who may be in competition with other interest groups which they aim to exclude from the policy process. Unlike the corporatist model, it does not imply that a small number of groups control the whole process; instead, it allows an important role for the government in mediating between these groups and in intervening to protect the general public interest.

In Ireland, as elsewhere, there is no consensus either on the precise definition of terms such as "corporatism" and "pluralism" or on their application to the national policy process. Thus the growth since the early 1960s of institutions and

processes through which government can negotiate with various economic interest groups to produce agreement on key issues such as pay increases, industrial
peace, and aspirational agendas for economic and social development, a phenomenon described as "tripartism", has been the subject of considerable debate. One
author argues that this institutionalisation of consensus seeking represents the
incorporation of organised economic interests into policy making and is thus
plainly corporatist; another maintains that, the government aside, the participants in these processes have never shown either the capacity or the will to
move beyond the defence of their individual sectional interests, and have
avoided the "too close involvement in responsibility for public policy" which
thoroughgoing corporatism would imply (Lalor, 1982, pp. 74-97; Hardiman and
Lalor, 1984, p. 84).

Whichever model or combination of models we opt for, it is clear that other
actors, too, play a part in the process. The constitution might seem to imply that
the individual voter has the final say. In recent years an increasing number of
the decisions that matter have come to be taken at European Community level
(see chapter 12). And, given the scope of High Court and Supreme Court decisions
in recent decades, the judiciary can also be seen as playing a role in policy making
(see chapter 3).

However, the three models we have outlined call our attention to the fact
that three sets of actors are preeminent in the policy-making process: the government, the civil service and interest groups. We shall examine closely the role
of each of them in this chapter, before going on to look more briefly at some less
significant actors: voters, parties and the media.

THE ROLE OF THE GOVERNMENT AND THE CIVIL SERVICE

Although the constitution implies that the government merely carries out the
policies decided by the Oireachtas, the reality is very different, as we saw in
chapter 7. The government's monopoly on legislative initiative, and virtual
immunity from informed review or criticism, has fostered a distinctive style of
rule in Ireland. Executive government is strong, though not necessarily very effective. Furthermore, whatever the manifesto pledges of the party or parties from
which it is formed, in the Irish system the government is largely reactive. Most
of its energies go into the management of existing national business, of which
there is enough to occupy all but the most energetic and innovative of ministers.
In most areas decisions tend to follow from what has gone before, and there is an
inbuilt propensity to add to activities rather than to substitute a new for an existing one.

Formal responsibility for policy lies with the government, and responsibility
for handling policy in particular areas lies with the relevant minister. In a formal sense, ministers lay down policy and their officials simply implement their
decisions. In practice, the process is more complex.

Ministers are birds of passage, their tenure dependent on the Taoiseach and
the electorate. The average life of a Dáil is only about three years, and during
that time many ministers can expect to be involved in at least one reshuffle of
portfolios. A minister's policy timescale is, inevitably, relatively short. He or
she will probably be in another post or out of office before the outcome of a policy

decision can be appraised. Moreover, as Séamus Ó Buachalla has illustrated in his study of education policy since independence, the calibre and commitment of ministers varies considerably (Ó Buachalla, 1988, pp. 250-90). A minister may be well informed and decisive about his or her portfolio and carry sufficient weight in cabinet to get government support and money—the late Donogh O'Malley, who in "a short period" in the 1960s "transformed" the system of secondary education, is an example of what civil servants would term a "good minister" (Ó Buachalla, 1988, p. 285; McNamara, 1990, p. 79). Additionally, the minister may have brought in a trusted "special advisor" from outside the department for help in getting to grips with his or her brief (O'Halpin, 1991, pp. 289-90; FitzGerald, 1991, p. 310). On the other hand, given the lack of systematic criteria in selecting ministers (see p. 170 above), a minister may have been given a department for purely political reasons and have little interest in the department's policy area. One former official, who served no fewer than 10 ministers during his 20 years as secretary of the old Department of Posts and Telegraphs, politically a very junior ministry, described them as "for the most part, modest men who came ... without much in the way of ideas but who recognised that the best way to get results was to allow an old and well-tried machine to function efficiently". What all had in common was an inability "to fight their corner in the Cabinet Room or with the Minister for Finance who controlled the supply of money" (Ó Broin, 1985, pp. 162-3).

Even a "good minister" may be more inclined to use his or her term of office in a particular department to embark on new policies than systematically to study how existing ones are performing. Moreover, there are many other demands on a minister's time (Murray, 1990, pp. 130-1). Gemma Hussey, who served in the FitzGerald government from 1982 to 1987, recorded the "considerable shock" of her British opposite number on hearing "the extent of my involvement with my constituency and with the party nationally, in addition to Cabinet responsibilities" (Hussey, 1990, p. 172). Finally, the modern state is highly interventionist, and thus is being drawn into ever more complex and detailed decisions which depend enormously on expert advice. Where does this leave civil servants, the primary source of information, analysis and advice to ministers on policy, and the instrument through which action is taken once policy has been settled by ministers?

At first glance, it suggests that as permanent officials they cannot but have great influence on policy. They are in a position to press the merits of one course of action against another on ministers, to control the flow of information upon which a ministerial decision will be based, and even to delay or impede the execution of a policy with which they do not agree. But in legal terms civil servants have no independent role in policy making: under the law each minister is a "corporation sole", the effect of which is that civil servants can act only in the name of the minister (O'Halpin, 1991, pp. 295-6; Garvin, 1991, p. 51). It is, consequently, difficult to be precise about their actual role. However, even if officials all loyally serve the minister of the day, their individual and collective views and beliefs plainly affect the formulation, adoption and implementation of policy. What evidence is there of their influence on what the state does?

Public perceptions give us few clues. There is no equivalent in the Irish popular imagination to Sir Humphrey, the devious Oxford-educated mandarin of the BBC's *Yes, Minister* and *Yes, Prime Minister* series. Nor, it would appear, do the

Irish see their officials as autocratic technocrats on the French or German models, or as the budget-maximising busybodies of national government so loathed by the American right. The popular image of the Irish civil servant is rather of a lowly clerk, a cheap-suited, Fáinne-wearing bumbler, or a cold-eyed spinster with a rosary, a sharp tongue and a well-worn pair of knitting needles. This contrast may reflect differing expectations of public bureaucracy: in twentieth century Britain, the higher civil service has routinely been accused both by the left and by the right of promoting and pursuing a middle of the road approach whatever the wishes of the government of the day; in France and Germany national bureaucracy claims much of the credit for the phenomenal success of postwar economic reconstruction and development; in the United States the federal government has always been mistrusted because it embodies national intervention against state and local particularism. In Ireland, most public and political commentary on the civil service focuses on its alleged inflexibility in the delivery of services to individuals or communities, not on any supposed thwarting of the national will or on an excessive propensity to tax and to spend. In other words, the popular assumption appears to be not that the civil service is disloyal, manipulative, self serving or hidebound in its higher reaches, but instead bureaucratic, overstaffed and inefficient at lower levels in producing the benefits supposed to flow from policy. Does research bear this out?

The bureaucrat as bogeyman

Contrary to popular belief, the Irish civil service is not all that large. Government departments now employ about 28,000 people, which is about half the number employed in the health services, to carry out an enormous miscellany of functions ranging from tax collection to animal disease eradication, and from economic policy formulation to the protection of national treasures. The vast majority of these civil servants are engaged on clerical, manual or industrial work, from the keeping of records to the restoration of old buildings, and have no individual influence on policy. Generally speaking, indeed, the greater the numbers employed in a particular department, the less influential that department is in policy terms: until January 1984, when the state companies An Post and An Bord Telecom were set up, about half of all civil servants were employed in the old Department of Posts and Telegraphs on work ranging from the collection and delivery of post to the development and operation of telecommunications networks. The two biggest departments in the civil service today are the Revenue Commissioners and Social Welfare. This is not because either is especially powerful or prestigious, but because each needs a large number of clerical staff for the millions of individual cases dealt with each year by the taxation and social welfare systems.

In terms of influence on policy, therefore, we have to concentrate on the higher ranks of the civil service, the 2,000 or so officials who hold posts for which the minimum entry requirement for those not already in the civil service is an honours university degree or a professional qualification. Most such civil servants are recruited either at school-leaver or at graduate level, and are permanent employees of the state. Governments may come and go, but the officials will remain until retirement or death intervenes. There are benefits and drawbacks in these arrangements. In terms of policy formulation, it means that in any one area officials collectively can bring vast experience to bear on an issue; it may also mean, however, that they become so closely associated with a policy line and so fixed in their ways that they find it difficult to accept the need for innovation. One former Taoiseach has observed that "some resistance to change is ... to be expected from the civil service, each department of which tends to have its own attachment to policies developed in the past" (FitzGerald, 1991, p. 301). This phenomenon is not unique to Ireland. It sometimes takes a severe shock, or a very determined minister, to get the permanent officials moving in the direction that the government desires.

Whatever the position in other countries, however, what Irish evidence there is suggests that most ministers have been happy enough with both the quality and the honesty of the officials who served them (O'Halpin, 1991, p. 292), although one commentator maintains that the "tradition of mutual trust between politicians and civil servants which had been built up since the 1930s has been damaged in recent decades" (Garvin, 1991, p. 45). Generalisations about relations between ministers and officials must, however, be qualified by the reflection that in Ireland, unlike other democracies, there is no tradition of memoir writing among former ministers. Since the foundation of the state only a handful have published accounts of their time in office, and very few have left collections of papers available for research. We might, therefore, assume what other evidence suggests, that the general silence of ex-ministers about the quality of advice and the loyalty of their officials implies satisfaction (Andrews, 1982, pp. 120-1). Of the few who have written about their experience in office, the acerbic former Minister for Health Noel Browne speaks highly of the civil service (Browne, 1986, pp. 121-2).

On the other hand, Gemma Hussey, while generally appreciative of her officials, had some complaints about a lack of support from the Department of Education during crucial negotiations on teachers' pay in 1985, a point indirectly supported by her Taoiseach (Hussey, 1990, p. 181; FitzGerald, 1991, p. 624). Garret FitzGerald himself deplored the attitude of Department of Finance officials, admittedly supported by their minister Richie Ryan, to the plans of the 1973-77 Cosgrave coalition government in which he was Minister for Foreign Affairs: Finance's "opposition to our proposal to replace estate duties with an annual wealth tax went well beyond the normal pattern of civil service resistance to change". This, however, was "an untypical response, demonstrating the distance civil servants *can* go in challenging Government policy rather than the distance they normally *do* go in warning Governments of the consequences of their actions" (FitzGerald, 1991, pp. 298-300). Despite this reassurance, FitzGerald does instance other episodes of what he saw as official incompetence or obstruction (FitzGerald, 1991, pp. 393-4, 403, 446-7). Overall, his memoirs give the impression that he found parts of the civil service, particularly the Department of Finance, politically neutral but somewhat hidebound and slow to respond to clear directions from government. It is impossible to say whether this indicates a deeper malaise in the civil service, or whether it largely reflects a natural tension within the cabinet and within the bureaucracy between those who have to manage the economy and levy taxes, and those who want to spend public money (Doyle, 1987, pp. 73-4).

If the general probity of officials is not in much doubt, there nevertheless has been considerable criticism of the influence of senior civil servants on policy. For decades this focused on their concern with the minutiae of day-to-day administration at the expense of strategic thinking about long-term issues, and on their cast of mind (Public Services Organisation Review Group, 1969). The late Todd Andrews, one of the giants of state service from the 1930s to the 1960s, applauded the loyalty and ability of senior civil servants but deplored their innate caution and conservatism, describing them as adept at thinking of excellent reasons for not doing anything new and dismissive of outside advice and technical expertise (Andrews, 1982, pp. 119-21, 298-9). These observations are broadly supported by the comments of the secretary of one department, who retired in 1989: "The whole ethos of the civil service, if we go back twenty-five or thirty years, was against initiative. You did not stick your neck out. There used to be a premium on caution coupled with a fear of making a mistake." He went on, however, to stress that things had changed: "The modern generation, even of civil servants, are more enterprising, they are prepared to take chances" (McNamara, 1990, p. 78).

Whether or not it is true that senior civil servants are now more inclined to innovate, the government's stated concerns about the performance of the civil service shifted considerably in the 1980s. The 1985 White Paper *Serving the Country Better* said nothing of substance about the civil service's policy formulation role, concentrating instead on the need to improve service to the community by strengthening management and structures (see the discussion in Stapleton, 1991, pp. 328-32). This concern with results is largely attributable to the experience of the 1970s and early 1980s. The problem in those years was not a paucity but a surfeit of expensive policy innovations, the indiscriminate acceptance of which plunged the state into acute financial crisis (Doyle, 1987, pp. 72-4; Honohan, 1988, p. 20; Lee, 1989, pp. 624-5).

Where does this leave the civil service? Is it a bastion of conservatism or a hotbed of new ideas? The answer nowadays is, probably, a bit of both—as has been the case since 1922. In the area of health policy, for example, recent research has shown that, at crucial times in the history of the state, civil servants have provided many of the ideas and much of the impetus for radical reform and development (Barrington, 1987, pp. 155-61). On the other hand, Lee has pointed to the penny-pinching, fatalistic attitude of the Department of Finance during the 1920s, 1930s and 1940s as a key factor in Ireland's uninspired economic and social performance since independence, although this argument owes something to Keynesian hindsight and is not one that all historians would accept unreservedly (Lee, 1989, pp. 563-77; Fanning, 1978, pp. 632-4). Furthermore, while a case can certainly be made that Finance was overpowerful in the first decades of the state's existence, when the country's economic performance was weak, this can hardly be the explanation for the policy disasters of the 1970s and early 1980s, when traditional Finance caution was swept aside by a succession of spendthrift governments, prompting the secretary of that department to the caustic observation that the "consistent view taken over thirty-five years by politicians, administrators and the so-called commercial state sector has been that it was the function of the Department of Finance to raise money and theirs to spend it" (Doyle, 1987, p. 74).

The relative influence of the civil service across the policy spectrum seems to depend on the political climate, the interests and inclinations of individual ministers, and the perceived nature of public feeling on particular issues. If a new law is necessary to initiate or continue a policy, civil servants are entirely at the whim of their political masters: departments are full of proposals for new legislation which may take a long time to reach the cabinet table. For instance, legislation to establish the National Archives was held up for years by the collapse of the first FitzGerald coalition in 1982. It is a fair guess that successive Ministers for the Environment saw little point in having a battle in cabinet and in the Dáil for legislation to control stray dogs, until in the mid-1980s there were a number of widely publicised dog attacks on children, which both highlighted the unsatisfactory state of the law and created a climate of public outrage that facilitated the smooth passage in 1986 of a strong measure that might otherwise have drawn criticism from dog owners.

On the other hand, civil servants sometimes have enormous discretion in carrying out existing policy, and over time they may in practice reorient it by the way in which they administer it. An example is immigration control. Since independence this has been almost completely untouched by public scrutiny or discussion, or even overt ministerial direction. In that time it has been enormously successful in its broad objective: preventing foreigners from settling in Ireland lest they take Irish people's jobs or become a burden on the state. In administering it, however, the Department of Justice has also brought into play factors not mentioned in the relevant legislation, arguing that to admit certain categories of foreigner would excite religious or racial passions. In 1953 the department proudly informed the government that, despite the massive postwar refugee crises as millions of people were displaced from eastern and central Europe, fewer than 3,000 aliens had rights of permanent residence in Ireland. Furthermore, in the aftermath of the Holocaust, Irish policy remained markedly hostile towards Jews: "the question of the admission of aliens of Jewish blood presents a special problem and the alien laws have been administered less liberally in their case" due to "a fairly strong anti-Semitic feeling throughout the country" because "Jews have remained a separate community within the community ... have not permitted themselves to be assimilated, and ... for their numbers ... appear to have disproportionate wealth and influence" (Department of Justice, 1953). Was this bureaucratic xenophobia, or did the officials simply gauge the public mood correctly? The moral, political and even economic implications of immigration policy have never been seriously examined in the Dáil, although the subsidiary issue of the treatment of would-be asylum seekers has received some media attention in recent years.

Special advisors, programme managers and policy making

All governments have on occasion sought advice and guidance on policy issues from outside the civil service, sometimes through the importation of politically congenial counsellors, sometimes through informal dialogue with trusted friends. For example, the distinguished Dublin solicitor Alexis FitzGerald exercised considerable unofficial influence on economic policy during the two Costello governments of 1948-51 and 1954-57; ironically, the reputation he then earned as an *eminence grise* stood against him when he was formally appointed "special advisor" to the first FitzGerald government in 1981-82, and he was "depressed and frustrated" by his lack of practical influence (Williams, 1987, pp. 32-4). The last 20 years have seen considerable developments in the appointment and use of special advisors by ministers. Some have been civil servants seconded from normal departmental duties; others have been imported into the civil service to bring what one termed "political sensitivity" to the consideration of policy issues

(Honohan, 1988, p. 26). While it is now established practice for ministers to appoint such advisors, their functions vary considerably. Some ministers have used advisors to provide independent advice on policy questions for which they are directly responsible, some to guide them on broader issues facing the government collectively, and others for straightforward party political advice and to manage constituency affairs (Honohan, 1988, pp. 28-9; O'Halpin, 1991, pp. 289-90). With the arguable exception of Martin Mansergh as advisor to the Taoiseach on Northern Ireland affairs, Fianna Fáil seems to have been less inclined to use such appointees in a substantive policy role than have other parties when in government. This probably reflects Fianna Fáil's vast experience of working with the civil service, and some corresponding unease amongst other parties that the bureaucracy may have become conditioned to think along Fianna Fáil lines through long exposure to Fianna Fáil governments (Garvin, 1981, pp. 204-5).

Such considerations probably played their part in the innovations insisted on by the Labour Party as part of its December 1992 coalition deal with Fianna Fáil. Under this each minister can now appoint both a "special advisor" and a "programme manager". To the familiar ambiguity about the roles of special advisors, as usual a mixture of civil servants and imported talent, is now added the mystery of what programme managers are intended to do. Are they there simply to facilitate the flow of business within and across departments, or are they an echo of the old Soviet concept of party commissars, attached to state organisations to ensure that the party's priorities remain paramount? Judging by appointments thus far, most Fianna Fáil ministers appear to regard the job of programme manager as administrative, and have appointed civil servants to the positions. Judging by *their* selections, Labour ministers, whose idea it was, seem to want programme managers to serve as an interface between the party, its coalition partner, and the bureaucracy. It may be some years before the value of these innovations can fairly be assessed, either in terms of policy co-ordination or of producing results.

INTEREST GROUPS

Interest groups can be defined as organisations or movements, permanent or transient, which seek to influence government on behalf of their members or in furtherance of a policy decision or outcome favoured by their members. For example, the Law Society sets out to defend the interests of solicitors, while An Taisce presses continuously for state action to protect and to restore Ireland's physical heritage. Interest groups clearly play an important role in policy formulation and operation. For the purposes of this chapter, they can be divided into two broad categories: those with a *sectional* base, such as trade unions, farmers' associations or professional bodies, and those that are *cause centred*, such as Greenpeace or SPUC (for an outline of various definitions of interest groups see Jordan and Richardson, 1987, pp. 19-40). Interest groups are frequently in competition for favourable decisions from government: in questions of safety regulations for industrial workers, for example, trade unions and employers' organisations are likely to have different opinions on what is adequate and on what measures industry can afford to adopt. Similarly, there are interest groups that support and others that oppose, say, the further rezoning of land around Dublin to allow the construction of more private housing.

Sectional groups

The relationship of individual groups with the government will vary over time for political and other reasons. In Ireland there is a long-standing tradition of tripartite consultation in aspects of policy involving government and what are currently termed "the social partners", that is representatives of various economic interests. In its present form this dates back to the early 1960s, and it is part and parcel of a style of governance aimed at keeping everyone moderately content, perpetually seeking a national economic and social coalition (Hardiman, 1988). In those respects it resembles the consensual approach of mainland European social democracies, though without achieving the same economic success. It contrasts sharply with the dismissive approach to organised labour adopted by the Thatcher governments in Britain from 1979 to 1990. Some commentators see it as an essentially corporatist approach, others as a more opportunistic means by which government can suppress incipient tensions between labour and capital, town and country, rich and poor, and producers and consumers, others again simply as a way of assuring wage stability and industrial peace (Morrissey, 1986, pp. 91-4). Although common in varying degrees to all parties when in government, it seems to suit Fianna Fáil's Peronist instincts best.

In addition to this process of national consensus building, individual sectional groups have constant dealings with the relevant government departments. For example, relations between the farmers' organisations and the Department of Agriculture, while sometimes stormy, are always extremely close. Farmers' associations represent stakeholders in that policy area, and they also possess much relevant information. Consequently, in the words of a former secretary of that department, they play "a very important role in the evolution of agricultural policy" (McNamara, 1990, p. 81). Each side needs the other. As in other countries, scrutiny suggests that so close a relationship sometimes leads to the exclusion from influence of competing groups, or even to the neglect of the collective good: for example, much evidence has emerged in recent years, during the Beef Tribunal proceedings and elsewhere, to suggest that public health considerations in agricultural production have never been taken very seriously in Ireland, because the department is producer- rather than consumer-oriented.

Cause centred groups

Cause centred groups have become significant and conspicuous factors in national politics in the last two decades. Whether ad hoc groups formed to press for a single measure, such as the legalisation of divorce, or associations with a permanent mission such as the Simon Community or Greenpeace, their visible activities and influence have increased considerably. This is most notable in relation to social, moral and environmental issues, where the main political parties have difficulty in reconciling conflicting pressures for conservation and development, for the defence of traditional morality and recognition of changed social realities, or for the defence of the interests of the majority and of minorities. There is a tendency in the national media to romanticise some groups, to contrast their sincerity and sense of concern about poverty, marital breakdown, pollution or inner city blight with the cynicism and opportunism of party politicians. But politicians are at least elected by and answerable to the general public. Cause centred groups are not. Furthermore, however noble their cause, such groups may have their own interests to pursue as well: for example, the aid agencies and charities engaged in lobbying for more government aid to the third world themselves frequently seek grants, favourable tax status and other special benefits from the state.

We should note, furthermore, that not all such groups promote desirable, environmentally friendly, liberal causes: as many have been formed to oppose the provision of halting sites and homes for travellers as to fight against rapacious developers, polluting industries or gaming machines. In national affairs, cause group tactics have been used most effectively in recent years by those fighting to reimpose a decidedly Catholic version of public morality. In this they were notably successful in the 1980s, much to the angst of better known groups urging the opposite view. The anti-abortion group the Society for the Protection of the Unborn Child (SPUC) appeared out of the blue in 1981 and, despite the obvious discomfort of all the major political parties, eventually induced the government to call a referendum to consider an amendment to the constitution that would guarantee the rights of the unborn child. In 1986 the government proposed a further amendment to allow divorce (see chapters 2 and 3), only to see this rejected by the people after a campaign in which the forces of moral conservatism showed themselves to be far better skilled in modern pressure group techniques than those who sought to modernise Irish society.

Interest group politics

Individual interest groups pursue their aims through a combination of public and private pressure on government, politicians and other interest groups, and by using the mass media. They form tactical coalitions to achieve particular ends; they compete for government attention, sympathy and favours; and they frequently argue their case in terms of the general good. On one public issue, such as continued state funding for denominational education, the main churches speak with one voice; on another, such as marital breakdown, they take opposite sides. Beyond the most generalised appeals for concessions towards Irish agriculture, "the farmers" turn out to be a heterogeneous assortment of conflicting interests. The same applies to "business"—an umbrella term that includes both bankers and the self-styled entrepreneurs who loathe them quite as much as they do officialdom (McCann, 1993, pp. 47-50). An interest group may be no more than an alliance of people or institutions having collective interests to further with government. To take a contemporary example, consider the beef processing industry. Beef processors collectively have lobbied and pressurised government to improve the environment for their activities by grants, tax breaks, export assistance, foreign trade negotiations and so on. Yet, except in pursuing these collective interests, they compete ferociously amongst themselves for stock, for markets, for plant, and for favours from government. Thus, while they could scarcely be described as a happy family, they will unite against the outside world.

Depending on issues and circumstances, interest groups pursue their aims and exercise their influence on policy through public or private channels, directly or indirectly. The major formal economic interest groups have representation on the boards of state companies and agencies, on ad hoc and permanent advisory and review bodies, and at European Community level. They have the resources to carry out their own research and analysis of what interests them, they are accustomed to making their case in public, they have ready access to the bureaucracy in Dublin and in Brussels, and they lobby continuously (O'Carroll, 1987, p. 105; McCann, 1993, pp. 39-47). At national level, the relevant professions are heavily represented on bodies that exercise considerable statutory power, such as the Medical Registration Council, the Dental Board, the Law Society and the Opticians Board. This amounts to self-regulation by the professions, and has recently come under scrutiny by the courts and by government, as a divergence between the public interest and professional self-interest has become steadily more apparent. Regulations have been used not simply to maintain the highest standards of practice but also to protect the vested interests of those already in practice and to restrain innovation, competition and price cutting. Thus the Law Society has been forced by the courts to change its admission and examination procedures for aspiring solicitors, and the Medical Registration Council has been successfully sued by non-Irish doctors claiming unfair treatment. The Bar Council has also been subjected to public and government criticism for its rules regarding the employment of barristers, and in recent years it has made significant changes to these in response.

The difficulties experienced by the 1973-77 Cosgrave coalition with its wealth tax illustrates how effectively interest groups can extract concessions from an ill-prepared and divided government. The wealth tax was part of the price exacted by the Labour party for participation in government with Fine Gael. It was a capital tax, i.e. a tax on assets, intended to increase the burden of taxation on the well off, as part of a broader initiative in tax reform. It had not been carefully thought out beforehand, and so was open to much legitimate technical criticism, and in isolation it was singularly unattractive to most Fine Gael members of the cabinet (Sandford and Morrissey, 1985, pp. 13, 154). They accepted it only with great reluctance as an unavoidable element of the coalition's agreed programme. There was also opposition within the bureaucracy, with the Department of Finance arguing vigorously for an alternative approach (FitzGerald, 1991, pp. 298-9). This lack of unity of purpose weakened the government's position, "since Fine Gael were trying to implement a fundamental decision *they* had not made" (Morrissey, 1990, p. 31). Devising the tax was a complex matter, and neither ministers nor officials could be certain in advance of its precise impact in every case. This uncertainty opened the door for interest groups both to scaremonger and to seek concessions for their members from a government that did not have an adequate grasp of its own proposals: "Both the agriculture and the business lobbies appealed directly to the government and were very influential", with agriculture being especially successful. The result was that the government, unnerved by this wave of pressure, precipitately made concessions: the yield of the proposed tax "would have been at least four times" that of the measure ultimately enacted, which was an "ineffective tax with minimal support" (Morrissey, 1990, pp. 33-4). Tax reform has remained an area of Irish public policy in which organised sectional groups, particularly the farmers, continue to reign supreme.

Has the power of interest groups grown?
There is no doubt that economic and social interest groups have become conspicuous, formal parts of the fabric of Irish and European Community government in

the last three decades (Girvin, 1989, pp. 210-11). In the words of one former official, there has been a "proliferation of organisations desiring to participate in
the policy process". This "makes extra demands on the civil service which in the
past could formulate policies in an atmosphere of quiet contemplation" (O'Connor, 1991, p. 365). This phenomenon certainly reflects an increase in influence for
some groups; for others, however, it may simply be that they now have to operate in a more open environment, and to compete with other interests, for example
groups defending the interests of consumers of professional services, which used
not to exist. This in turn may serve to reduce the power of some long-established
groups: the fact that lawyers and doctors now have to fight their corner publicly,
and to change what they cannot justify, surely indicates that they are relatively
less influential than previously. The same applies to the churches: as Irish society has developed and secularised since the 1960s, so the Catholic church has
had to address the government far more publicly than in the days when a private word, or even a minister's fear of upsetting the bishops, was enough to suppress developments of which the hierarchy might not approve (Whyte, 1980).
First in health, then in social policy and in education, the Catholic church has
seen its preeminent influence slowly wane. Furthermore, unlike trade unions and
business associations, which are admitted as of right to the discussion of policy
in Brussels, churches have no formal input at all into the policy system at European level.

Do interest groups strengthen or weaken Irish democracy?
Depending on one's point of view, a compelling case can be made for or against the
present involvement of interest groups in the policy system. On the "for" side, it
is argued that such groups help to bridge the gap between government and citizen; that they can represent the interests of their members far more powerfully
and coherently than these members acting individually could; and, to the extent
that they are in competition with one another, that no interest group has a
monopoly of influence with the government.

On the "against" side, it can be argued that interest groups, whether sectional
or cause groups, are disproportionately powerful—one secretary of the Department of Finance complained of the disastrous consequences for the national finances of decades of "plain bullying" by sectional groups (Doyle, 1987, p. 72). On that
analysis, the country is in danger of becoming ungovernable, as the collective
interest is completely lost sight of in the pursuit of deals with the most powerful
interest groups. Take the issue of tax reform: no one in public life has demurred
from the argument of the authoritative Commission on Taxation, and of many
other respected commentators, that the existing system of direct taxation is "unfair, muddled and complicated", a mess of allowances, exemptions and high nominal rates that disproportionately benefits the better off and the self-employed
(Commission on Taxation, 1982, p. 29). Yet the pressures generated by the sectional groups threatened with more taxation has rendered radical reform impossible: instead of redistributing the burden of taxation more equitably by broaden-
ing the tax base, government has tried to keep everyone happy by slowly reducing the marginal rate of income tax. Efforts to broaden the tax base have been
frustrated by interest group pressure: the failed wealth tax was followed by the
fiasco of the farm tax, introduced in 1984 to replace agricultural rates, emascu-
lated by farmer pressure and unceremoniously scrapped by the new Fianna Fáil

government in 1987 "just when the tax began to yield significant revenues" (O'Connor, 1993, p. 21). In addition to their considerable power in public policy, it can also be argued that interest groups are sometimes highly unrepresentative; that they suppress or manipulate grassroots opinion, and may sacrifice their members' real interests for the chance to influence the formulation of policy, becoming a partner instead of an adversary of the government; that the process of national negotiation of which sectional groups are part frequently prevents the adoption of rational long-term policies lest these mortally offend some key group; that interest group politics effectively excludes the weakest and poorest in Irish society; and that interest groups undermine the relationship between voters and politicians on which Irish democracy rests.

Whichever side of the argument one comes down on, it is clear that interest groups play an important role in Irish life. Whether negotiating with the government and each other on national economic and social development, or protesting in the streets against the country's laws on abortion, sectional groups and cause groups are likely to remain a permanent part of the Irish policy system. The conclusions of a recent study seem apposite:

> our message is that the system can work—can be worked—better or worse. Some pressures will be undesirable—but that judgement will depend on political goals sought. Sometimes groups will frustrate government, but at other times they will stimulate or carry out government policy. Whether governments utilise the capacity of groups skilfully or turn the opportunities into opposition is the test of successful governance (Jordan and Richardson, 1987, pp. 290-1).

VOTERS, PARTIES AND THE MEDIA

In theory, general elections give voters a chance to express their policy preferences. In practice, though, elections appear to play little part in terms of selecting policies, although they are very important in terms of deciding who gets to make the choices. While the last two decades have seen a marked increase in the turnover of governments, differences in the policies on offer do not seem to have been the determining factor in electoral outcomes. Nevertheless, the political parties put some effort into policy formulation, at least for manifesto purposes. But party manifestos are catchall documents: it is difficult to argue a definite link between, say, Fianna Fáil's 1987 election commitment to appoint a junior minister for horticulture and the party's overall performance. In addition, the nature of the Irish party and voting systems militates against clearcut policy choices by the voters. Furthermore, the electorate seems conditioned to accept manifesto commitments largely in the spur of the moment spirit in which they are usually made. There is little sign either that the national electorate exacts revenge on a party that forgets its policy promises or rewards one that honours them in government. The 1987-89 Fianna Fáil government's experience illustrates the point: when the party emerged as the qualified victor of the 1987 election, Mr Haughey visited the Department of Finance for a briefing on the poor state of the national finances and then promptly recanted on manifesto promises. That government subsequently won high approval ratings in opinion polls for its prudent financial and economic management and its negotiation of the Programme for National Recovery, even though this did not translate into electoral success in 1989. In summary, political parties are at most an intermittent source of policy ideas, and general elections seldom serve as plebiscites on competing sets of policies, or even necessarily on policy performance.

Discussion of policy making would be incomplete without reference to the national news media. The national press, radio and television are very important in forming public perceptions on policy issues because they are the principal means by which the public obtains news and analysis of national and international affairs. News and analysis are not neutral, value free commodities. The personal or political beliefs of journalists, editors and producers obviously have an impact on their treatment of public issues no matter how dispassionate and impartial they attempt to be. While the Irish media seem reasonably free of major political censorship—with the obvious exception of the legal ban on broadcast interviews with members of Sinn Féin and of various republican and loyalist paramilitary groups—relations between the government and the state-owned radio and television stations have always been somewhat delicate (Andrews, 1982, pp. 271, 285-7). The broadcast media and the national press are, nowadays, also routinely attacked by conservative cause groups as hotbeds of social and moral liberalism.

One of the most striking developments in the media in recent decades has been the political dealignment of the national press. The *Irish Press* and the *Irish Independent* historically have had very close links with Fianna Fáil and Fine Gael respectively, while the *Irish Times* for many years catered primarily for ex-unionists. The position has changed enormously since the 1950s, and none of these papers could now be described as partisan. This stands in honourable contrast to Britain, where the majority of the tabloid and middlebrow press not only supports the Conservative Party but runs propaganda campaigns against the other parties. There, at election time the national press is used not to inform the public but blatantly to put across a party political line. Finally, we may note that the media themselves constitute an interest group. For example, they speak with one voice against the present libel laws, because these inhibit their activities. Furthermore, some observers felt that RTE's Radio One, in order to protect its position, campaigned shamelessly on air against the government's plans to end the state's monopoly on broadcasting in 1989.

POLICY OUT-TURN

Some policies appear broadly successful, others not. The determining factor is not always the degree of deliberation, consultation and expert assessment that goes into a decision, nor the resources committed to carrying it through. For example, the introduction of an amnesty for tax avoiders in 1988 produced receipts many times greater than the Department of Finance had expected. On the other hand, the state's programme of bovine TB eradication initiated in 1954 has failed completely in its declared aim, despite exhaustive discussion, consultation, and analysis: over one billion pounds have been spent without any appreciable change in the reported incidence of the disease (O'Connor, 1986). In this Augean stable the thrust of policy for successive governments transparently became to placate the main interest groups involved—the farmers and the vets—rather than to take definitive action to dispose of the disease problem once and for all.

To take two more examples of success and failure: under de Valera Ireland was able to maintain its long-declared policy of neutrality during the second world war despite its almost total neglect, for short-term financial reasons, of the military and economic preparations that its defence experts advised would be necessary. Army numbers were actually reduced in the winter of 1939-40 to save money, a unique exhibition of *sang froid* in the midst of a major European war (Chief of Staff, 1936; Duggan, 1990, pp. 180-1). On the other hand, no government since independence has enjoyed much success with Irish language policy despite considerable expenditure and strict state control of the education system.

There appears to be an almost endemic reluctance in Irish government to treat the review of policy as an integral part of the policy process. In an area such as economic policy, performance is measurable against targets using published data, and so outside commentators can provide informed analysis on it. In most policy areas, however, few other than those directly involved will have the insight, the expertise and the information to offer an authoritative assessment of performance. Within government the pressure is always to move things along, to avoid trouble, to dampen public dissatisfaction, and usually to keep the main interest groups involved happy. It is easy to see why: ignoring these precepts carries major risks. The Minister for the Marine ultimately lost his cabinet seat because of the 1988-90 rod licence dispute, a furore that arose from his department's proposals for an apparently rational solution to the chronic problems of inland fisheries development. The provision of health services provides a further illustration of the unwelcome consequences of systematic policy review. Health administration has been the subject of uncommonly rigorous analysis in the past 15 years as costs have escalated. Yet successive governments have found it intensely difficult to act on any part of that analysis, not due to doubts about its validity but because of the short-term political implications of upsetting the main interest groups. It might make financial, managerial and clinical sense to shut Roscommon hospital in line with established policy on the provision of sophisticated medical services in regional centres; Roscommon town voters thought differently in the last two general elections, returning an independent "hospital" candidate pledged to fight any downgrading. In 1989 he was able to secure significant concessions from the Fianna Fáil-Progressive Democrats coalition in return for his support, though his bargaining power was dramatically reduced following the 1992 election.

CONCLUSION

Policy making in Ireland is characterised by the complexity of the process. The Oireachtas is conspicuously weak. Sectional groups have a strong and formalised influence in economic bargaining, in regulatory bodies and in the state apparatus generally. Cause groups have become more noticeable and more vigorous in the last two decades, sometimes in alliance with established sectional groups, sometimes in opposition to them. It was largely through their efforts that three constitutional referendums were held in the 1980s: on abortion, on divorce and on the Single European Act (see table on referendums in appendix 2h). The civil service operates as an influence for continuity rather than for radical change, and for the most part governments are concerned to manage as best they can rather than to innovate in national affairs. There seems to be a low level of linkage between policy issues and electoral performance, and a consistent reluctance to spell out publicly the probable long-term consequences of policy decisions.

A number of models of policy were briefly outlined at the start of this chapter. All are useful in illustrating different sources of pressure, ideas and power in the system; none is individually adequate to explain the intricacies of the Irish policy making system. Thus it can be argued that the Incorporated Law Society's relationship with government, where it enjoys "the right to regulate its members' affairs in exchange for accepting some responsibility", fits Peter Self's definition of "corporate pluralism" (Self, 1985, p. 87). Equally, however, recent years have seen successful legal challenges to the manner in which it and analogous bodies have exercised such public power. In the same way, the almost incestuous relationships between the farmers' associations and the Department of Agriculture have come under pressure from other interest and cause groups precisely because they are so close. If there is a propensity for corporatist style arrangements between government and dominant interest groups in some parts of the Irish system, there appear to be countervailing pressures from those marginalised in or altogether excluded by these relationships. Depending on the sector, the issue, the circumstances and the time, policy making in Ireland can fairly be described as pluralist, as corporatist, or as a combination of the two.

However the system is characterised, the Irish experience in policy making suggests that there is no magic mix of elements that will automatically produce an optimum outcome. Expert knowledge, political commitment, interest group support, adequate structures, public understanding, money, a benign international environment, attainable objectives and sheer good luck may all be needed. In Ireland, so far as can be judged, governments have seldom hit on the appropriate combination in any policy area.

REFERENCES AND FURTHER READING

Andrews, C. S., 1982. *Man of no Property: an Autobiography*, volume 2. Dublin: The Mercier Press.

Barrington, Ruth, 1987. *Health, Medicine and Politics in Ireland 1900-1970*. Dublin: Institute of Public Administration.

Barrington, T. J., 1980. *The Irish Administrative System*. Dublin: Institute of Public Administration.

Browne, Noel, 1986. *Against the Tide*. Dublin: Gill and Macmillan.

Burch, Martin and Bruce Wood, 1989. *Public Policy in Britain*. Oxford: Martin Robertson.

Chief of Staff, 1936. Memorandum for Minister for Defence, 22 September 1936, University College Dublin archives, MacEntee papers, P67/191(3).

Commission on Taxation, 1982. *First Report of the Commission on Taxation: Direct Taxation*. Dublin: Stationery Office.

Department of Justice, 1953. Memorandum for Government, 28 February 1953, National Archives, Department of the Taoiseach, S.11007B/2.

Doyle, Maurice, 1987. "Comment", pp. 71-6 in Seán Cromien and Aidan Pender (eds), *Managing Public Money*. Dublin: Institute of Public Administration.

Duggan, J. P., 1990. *A History of the Irish Army*. Dublin: Gill and Macmillan.

Fanning, Ronan, 1978. *The Irish Department of Finance 1922-58*. Dublin: Institute of Public Administration.

FitzGerald, Garret, 1991. *All in a Life: an Autobiography*. Dublin: Gill and Macmillan.

Garvin, Tom, 1981. *The Evolution of Irish Nationalist Politics*. Dublin: Gill and Macmillan.

Garvin, Tom, 1991. "Democracy in Ireland: collective somnambulance and public policy", *Administration* 39:1, pp. 42-54.

Girvin, Brian, 1989. *Between Two Worlds: Politics and Economy in Independent Ireland*. Dublin: Gill and Macmillan.

Hardiman, Niamh and Stephen Lalor, 1984. "Corporatism in Ireland: an exchange of views", *Administration* 32:1, pp. 76-88.

Hardiman, Niamh, 1988. *Pay, Politics and Economic Performance in Ireland, 1970-1987*. Oxford: Oxford University Press.

Honohan, Patrick, 1988. "The role of the adviser and the evolution of the public service", pp. 7-44 in Miriam Hederman (ed.), *The Clash of Ideas: Essays in Honour of Patrick Lynch*. Dublin: Gill and Macmillan.

Hussey, Gemma, 1990. *At the Cutting Edge: Cabinet Diaries, 1982-1987*. Dublin: Gill and Macmillan.

Jordan, A. G. and J. J. Richardson, 1987. *Government and Pressure Groups in Britain*. Oxford: Clarendon Press.

Lalor, Stephen, 1982. "Corporatism in Ireland", *Administration* 30:4, pp. 74-97.

Lee, J. J., 1989. *Ireland 1912-1985: Politics and Society*. Cambridge: Cambridge University Press.

McCann, Dermot, 1993. "Business power and collective action: the state and the Confederation of Irish Industry 1970-1990", *Irish Political Studies* 8, pp. 37-53.

McNamara, Tony, 1990. "Interview: a conversation with Donal Creedon, secretary, Department of Agriculture and Food (1988-89)", *Administration* 38:1, pp. 70-86.

Morrissey, Martin, 1986. "The politics of economic management in Ireland, 1958-1970", *Irish Political Studies* 1, pp. 79-95.

Morrissey, Oliver, 1990. "Scanning the alternatives before taxing with consensus: lessons for policy making from the Irish wealth tax", *Administration* 38:1, pp. 21-40.

Murray, C. H., 1990. *The Civil Service Observed*. Dublin: Institute of Public Administration.

Ó Broin, León, 1985. *Just like Yesterday: an Autobiography*. Dublin: Gill and Macmillan.

Ó Buachalla, Séamus, 1988. *Educational Policy in Twentieth Century Ireland*. Dublin: Wolfhound.

O'Carroll, J. P., 1987. "Ireland: political dominance of business", pp. 84-113 in M. P. C. M. van Schendelen and R. J. Jackson (eds), *The Politicisation of Business in Western Europe*. London: Croom Helm.

O'Connor, Robert, 1986. *A Study of the Bovine Tuberculosis Eradication Scheme*. Dublin: Economic and Social Research Institute.

O'Connor, Tom, 1991. "A civil service career—some reflections", *Administration* 38:3, pp. 365-72.

O'Connor, Tom, 1993. "The farm tax—a political casualty", *Seirbhís Phoiblí* 14:1, pp. 21-31.

O'Halpin, Eunan, 1991. "The civil service and the political system", *Administration* 38:3, pp. 283-302.

Public Services Organisation Review Group, 1969. *Report*. Dublin: Stationery Office.

Sandford, Cedric and Oliver Morrissey, 1985. *The Irish Wealth Tax: a Case Study in Economics and Politics*. Dublin: Economic and Social Research Institute, ESRI paper 123.

Self, Peter, 1985. *Political Theories of Modern Government, its Role and Reform*. London: George Allen and Unwin.

Stapleton, John, 1991. "Civil service reform, 1969-87", *Administration* 38:3, pp. 303-35.

Whyte, J. H., 1980. *Church and State in Modern Ireland 1923-1979*. Dublin: Gill and Macmillan.

Williams, T. Desmond, 1987. "Alexis FitzGerald", pp. 32-4 in Patrick Lynch and James Meenan (eds), *Essays in Memory of Alexis FitzGerald*. Dublin: The Incorporated Law Society.

11 / WOMEN IN IRISH POLITICS

Yvonne Galligan

This chapter examines the representation of women in Irish politics. It shows how few women there are in political life in Ireland, analyses the causes of women's low level of participation in politics and considers the consequences of women's under-representation in terms of policy outputs. The chapter concludes by suggesting that the relationship between women and the political process appears to be changing. This gives rise to pressure for adaptation of the political system on two fronts: representation and policy-making. The extent to which it can change depends on a number of conditions being fulfilled. If this does not happen, the under-representation of women in the legislature and in decision-making centres of the political parties will cause the continuation into the twenty-first century of the "democratic deficit" that has existed since the founding of the state.

WOMEN IN POLITICAL INSTITUTIONS

In November 1990, the Irish electorate chose Mary Robinson as the country's first woman President, making Ireland only the second country in Europe (after Iceland) to have an elected woman head of state. To an outside observer, this could give the impression that women are strongly represented in Irish political life. Yet such is not the case. Women have always been under-represented in Ireland's political institutions, as we shall see when we look at their record in government, parliament, local government and the political parties.

Government

With the exception of the appointment of Countess Markievicz as Minister for Labour in the government elected by the first Dáil in 1919 (a largely symbolic appointment in the circumstances of the time), no woman held a cabinet post until December 1979 when Máire Geoghegan-Quinn was promoted from a junior ministry to become Minister for the Gaeltacht in Charles Haughey's first Fianna Fáil administration. Of the 136 people who have held full ministerial positions from independence to date, only five (4 per cent) have been women. In the seven administrations formed between 1979 and 1993, 11 women politicians have held full ministerial positions or junior ministries. Before 1993, there was never more than one woman in the cabinet at any time. With the installation of the Fianna Fáil-Labour coalition government in January 1993, the number of women holding cabinet posts increased to two, and three of the 15 junior ministerial positions were allocated to women. Thus, at government level, the overall representation of women in ministerial positions increased modestly from one out of 25 (4 per cent) in December 1979 to five out of 30 (17 per cent) in January 1993.

Parliament

During the half century from the beginning of the state in 1922, the average Dáil contained only four women (3 per cent of all TDs). Over the 26 elections held between 1922 and 1992, only 53 individual women were elected to the Dáil. The figures for women TDs and candidates in 1977, low as they were, represented record levels at the time (see Table 11.1 and Appendix 2d), highlighting women's near invisibility in parliamentary politics up to that point. In recent years there has been some increase: on average, 12 women were elected to each Dáil from 1977 to 1992. Nine of these were elected for the first time in the November 1992 general election, the largest number of new women TDs ever returned to parliament at one time. With a total of 20 women (12 per cent) in the Dáil since 1992, Ireland is now in sixth place in terms of gender balance in parliaments of the EC member states and not far off the EC average of 13 per cent. Gardiner (1992, p. 22) observed that, while women's electoral opportunities increased in the early 1980s, this was offset by the focus of politics and party manifestos shifting away from gender to economic concerns, with parties less inclined to select women candidates. From 1977, when politicians and political parties "discovered" both the women's vote and the appeal of women candidates to the electorate, the number of women being selected as party candidates has risen, but it has yet to reach 20 per cent of all candidates (see Table 11.1). The success of the election and presidency of Mary Robinson has been an important factor in political parties turning their attention once again to running women candidates in a general election (Brown and Galligan, 1993).

Table 11.1: Women candidates and TDs at elections, 1977-92

Election	---- Candidates ----			----- Deputies -----		
	Total	Women	%	Total	Women	%
1977	376	25	6.6	148	6	4.1
1981	404	41	10.1	166	11	6.6
1982 (Feb)	366	35	9.6	166	8	4.8
1982 (Nov)	365	31	8.5	166	14	8.4
1987	466	65	13.9	166	14	8.4
1989	371	52	14.0	166	13	7.8
1992	482	89	18.5	166	20	12.0

Source: Calculated from Nealon's *Guides*, various editions 1977-87; Walker (1992, pp. 228-76); Department of the Environment (1993).
Note: The figures for candidates refer to the number of candidacies; candidates running in more than one constituency are counted as many times as they stood. This particularly affects the figure for the 1987 general election, when an independent candidate, Barbara Hyland, ran in 13 constituencies.

The pattern of women's representation in the Seanad, the upper house, is not very different. Over the 40-year period from 1937 to 1977, there were only 19 female senators in total in the second chamber. There was a perceptible increase in the number of women senators from 1977 onwards, when Jack Lynch, as Taoiseach, included three women among his 11 appointees. For the following decade, membership of the Seanad was utilised by women politicians, in the same way as by many of their male colleagues, as a base from which to develop a Dáil career. Although less powerful political institutions usually contain proportionally more women members than more important ones (such as the lower house of parliament), women have not been represented in significantly higher numbers in the Seanad than in the Dáil. One criticism made of the Taoiseach, Albert Reynolds, and Tánaiste, Dick Spring, in 1993 was their failure to increase the overall balance in gender representation in the Seanad through the Taoiseach's nominees, only one of whom was a woman.

Women's representation on parliamentary committees varies markedly (see Table 11.2). Overall, women, who make up 12 per cent of the membership of the Houses of the Oireachtas, comprise 14 per cent of the total membership of these committees. There is little difference in the participation levels of women and men in the committee work of the Oireachtas—80 per cent of women TDs and 79 per cent of male TDs are involved in committees. The pattern is similar for senators—62 per cent of women and 67 per cent of men from the upper house are members of at least one committee. What is striking, however, is the pattern of male and female representation on the various committees. Women parliamentarians are in a majority on the Committee on Women's Rights and are represented in significant numbers on the new Select Committee on Social Affairs. In contrast, they are noticeably absent from the committees dealing with the ordering of parliamentary business (Consolidation Bills, Standing Orders and Procedure and Privileges) and have little or no representation on the committees concerned with monitoring the expenditure of public money and economic policy (Public Accounts, Commercial State-sponsored Bodies, Enterprise and Economic Strategy). As parliamentarians generally volunteer for positions on various committees, this suggests that women TDs and senators have, as a group, specific policy interests that are different from those of male TDs.

Table 11.2: Women on parliamentary committees in 27th Dáil, 1993

Committee	Type	Size	Number of women	% women
Commercial State-sponsored Bodies	Joint	11	0	0.0
Consolidation Bills	Joint	6	0	0.0
Irish Language	Joint	11	2	18.2
Foreign Affairs	Joint	30	2	6.7
Services	Joint	18	2	11.1
Standing Orders	Joint	6	0	0.0
Women's Rights	Joint	17	10	58.8
Enterprise and Economic Strategy	Dáil	30	1	3.3
Finance and General Affairs	Dáil	30	2	6.7
Legislation and Security	Dáil	30	3	10.0
Procedure and Privileges	Dáil	18	3	16.7
Public Accounts	Dáil	12	0	0.0
Selection	Dáil	13	3	23.1
Social Affairs	Dáil	30	10	33.3
Procedure and Privileges	Seanad	12	1	8.3
Selection	Seanad	11	1	9.1
Total		285	40	14.0

Source: Information made available by the Clerk of Dáil Éireann, 1993.

Local government

The pattern of women's representation in local government has been similar to that in the national parliament. Studies of a range of European countries in the 1980s show that women have generally fared slightly better in terms of their representation at local level than in national assemblies. Norris (1987, p. 116), for instance, has calculated that the average proportion of women in local government bodies in 24 western democracies in the mid-1980s was 15 per cent while their average representation in the lower houses of parliament was 13 per cent. Randall (1987, pp. 105-6) also notes a greater presence of women in local politics than at national level. However, it is important to remember that the differences are not always significant in individual countries. There is no significant difference in Ireland. In 1934, 13 women councillors were elected to local authorities (Manning, 1987, p. 158). By 1967, this had increased to 26, representing 3 per cent of the total number of councillors, the same level as the representation of women in the Dáil (Randall and Smyth, 1987, p. 206). The number of women in local government continued to increase gradually, and, following the 1985 local elections, the percentage of local authority seats filled by women (just over 8 per cent) was again very similar to the representation of women in the Dáil (see Table 11.3). In the aftermath of the Robinson presidential victory, expectations were high in 1991 that women would finally break into local government in significant numbers. Yet the local elections of that year saw only a modest increase in women's representation. If this gentle rate of growth were to continue, it would take 13 more elections, and be well into the second half of the twenty-first century, before women have the same share of local government seats as men.

Table 11.3: Women's representation in local government, 1967-91

Year of election	Total candidates	Women candidates	Number of seats	Number of women elected	% seats held by women
1967	n.a.	63	795	26	3.3
1974	1811	86	795	42	5.3
1979	1812	n.a.	806	55	6.8
1985	1915	229	883	71	8.0
1991	1974	285	883	103	11.7

Source: Randall and Smyth (1987, p. 206); Donnelly (1992, p. 23); Department of the Environment official returns.
Note: The figures relate to County Councils and County Borough Councils. Urban District Councils and Town Commissions are not included.

Political parties

Women, then, are largely absent from the electoral arenas, and much the same is true of their position in the political parties, which is particularly important given that the parties dominate the candidate selection process (see chapter 6 above). Although the level of women's participation in party politics has increased over the last two decades, this growing activism within the formal party political structures has not been fully reflected in the numbers of women holding positions on the national executives of the major parties (see Table 11.4). The pattern is such that it is unlikely that women will ever be represented in significant numbers at senior party decision-making levels unless there is a strong commitment to balancing the gender representation at the top. The form that this commitment to providing for gender equality takes and the extent to which it is acted upon varies from party to party (Brown and Galligan, 1993, pp. 186-7).

Table 11.4: Women's representation on national executives of the main political parties, 1983-93

	Fianna Fáil %	Fine Gael %	Labour %	Progressive Democrats %
1983	16.6	23.5	8.3	-
1985	11.1	12.5	13.8	-
1987	16.6	21.6	16.2	n.a
1989	21.0	n.a	15.4	37.5
1991	7.9	27.0	17.0	27.5
1993	12.6	23.7	21.0	28.0

Source: For 1983-89, Farrell (1992, p. 444); 1991 and 1993 data supplied by the political parties.

We can see a similar pattern in party office-holding at constituency level, particularly in Fianna Fáil and the Labour Party (Table 11.5). In the case of Fine Gael, there are significantly fewer women on the national executive than at officer level in the constituencies. Table 11.5 shows that the position of constituency secretary is the one most associated with women's office-holding at this level in the hierarchy of the parties. The role of constituency chairperson is male-dominated.

Table 11.5: Women's constituency office-holding by party, 1993

	Fianna Fáil %	Fine Gael %	Labour %	Progressive Democrats %
Constituency chair	2.2	24.4	8.3	11.4
Constituency secretary	19.6	63.4	41.6	61.1
Constituency treasurer	16.3	45.1	13.8	20.3
Average women's office holding at constituency level	12.7	44.3	21.2	30.9

Source: Information supplied by the political parties.
Note: While the Green Party does not adopt this form of organisation, 40 per cent of its constituency co-ordinators are women.

While the reasons for this dichotomy in position holding are complex and deserving of further study, the general consensus among party spokespersons questioned on this matter is that the position of constituency secretary entails a range of demands and skills that are more available among women than men—secretarial and administrative skills, flexibility in terms of time, attention to detail and a willingness to provide continuity over the long term. The position of constituency secretary is seen as being a key one in the smooth running of the constituency, as it entails supporting the elected representatives, liaising with the central party organisation, and keeping in touch with party members in the constituency. The position of constituency chairperson, on the other hand, is one with a significantly greater political content. It is also one that requires a knowledge of the rules and procedures of meetings, generally seen as being a skill more associated with the life experiences of men. So, we can tentatively conclude, in the absence of hard data, that the patterns of constituency office-holding reflect the gender-related patterns of power in society, where women are more likely to be found in supportive roles and men dominate the overt decision-making positions. This idea will be explored more fully in the next section.

WOMEN IN SOCIETY

The dearth of women in positions of power in parties and political life is, of course, only part of the wider pattern of women's relative absence from decision-making centres generally. This section provides a brief summary of the levels of women's representation on state boards and in the civil service, the judiciary, trade unions and other economic interest groups, and the extent of women's participation in the paid workforce.

In a survey of the numbers of women serving on state boards in 1970, the Commission on the Status of Women noted that there was only one woman among the board members of the 10 leading state-sponsored bodies. This figure had increased to 12 per cent by 1985 (Randall and Smyth, 1987, p. 194). Three years later, 298 out of 2,336 members (13 per cent) of the boards of 50 state-sponsored bodies were women (*Development of Equal Opportunities*, 1988, p. 61). In 1993 the Fianna Fáil-Labour government declared its intention to increase the gender representation on state boards to 40 per cent by 1997. The 1992 government equality report shows that there is still some considerable way to go before this target is reached. Nevertheless, some improvements can be detected, with 315 women serving on state boards out of a total of 2,073 members (15 per cent). Of these, 206 (65 per cent) were government appointees (*Development of Equal Opportunities*, 1992, pp. 77-8). The report notes that "the percentage of Boards without female membership has fallen from 40 per cent in 1987 to 30 per cent in 1992" (*Development of Equal Opportunities*, 1992, p. 4). This modest increase has been accompanied by an effort on the part of the boards of state bodies to include women among their members. Thus, the record of these organisations in including women among their appointees has begun to improve. As the equality report states:

> what is obvious is that women are being appointed, at last, to key boards such as the
> Industrial Development Authority, Nitrigin Éireann Teoranta, the Central Bank, the
> Agricultural Credit Corporation and the Industrial Credit Corporation. These boards
> have a strategic role in public policy making and have a significant impact on the devel
> opment of the economy yet, formerly, they were dominated by men (*Development of Equal
> Opportunities*, 1992, p. 4).

The poor record of women's representation in the senior levels of the civil service was highlighted with the publication of research that found that there were no women among the senior positions of secretary and deputy secretary, that only two per cent of the assistant secretaries and three per cent of the principal officers were female, and that the majority of women employed in the civil service filled the lower clerical and typing grades (Eager, 1991, p. 19). This study reflected the conclusion of the Joint Committee on Women's Rights (JCWR) report on equal opportunity in the civil service, which found that, despite the existence of an equal opportunity policy since 1986,

> [while] women make up 63 per cent of the total general service grades in the Civil Service, they are concentrated in the Clerical Officer and Clerical Assistant grades, with declining representation in the ascending grades to a total absence of women in the two top echelons. This preponderance of women in two of the lowest grades helps to retain and reinforce the idea of male superiority (JCWR, 1991, pp. xii-xiv).

This pattern is repeated in the judicial arena—until Ms Justice Denham was appointed in December 1992, there had never been a woman on the Supreme Court. Table 11.6 shows the relative levels of gender representation among the judiciary. Indeed, the number of women working as justices at the level of the district court has actually decreased since 1985, even though about half of all solicitors and one quarter of barristers are women (Connelly and Hilliard, 1993, p. 232).

Table 11.6: Women in the judiciary, 1993

Court	Total number of Justices	Number of women	%
Supreme Court	5	1	20.0
High Court	16	1	6.2
Circuit Court	17	0	0.0
District Courts	46	4	8.7
Total	84	6	7.1

Source: Connelly and Hilliard (1993, p. 216).

The numbers of women in decision-making positions in the organisations of the "social partners"—the trade union, employer and agricultural interests influential in shaping government economic policy—are also low. Women have consistently formed over a third of trade union membership since the 1980s. In 1991 the total female membership of the 73 trade unions affiliated to the Irish Congress of Trade Unions (ICTU) was 37 per cent. However, women held only 27 per cent of the places on the executive committees of the 20 unions that represented 97 per cent of the female membership (ICTU, 1992a, pp. 2, 7). Between 1982 and 1991, three women filled reserved seats on ICTU's executive. According to the ICTU women's committee, there should be 10 women on the executive to effect a gender balance in representation on that body (ICTU, 1992a, p. 15). However, in 1993, only five (18 per cent) of the 28 executive council members were women, with four of these holding reserved positions. None of the senior official positions in the Confederation of Irish Industry, the Federation of Irish Employers or the Irish Farmers' Association in the last decade has been held by a woman.

It has been noted in other countries that the level of women's participation in employment has had an effect on the levels of participation of women in other areas of public life. From 1926 to date, women have made up 30 per cent of the total workforce in Ireland (Blackwell, 1990, p. 3; ICTU, 1992b, p. 1). However, this apparently static figure hides significant changes in the composition of the female labour force. In 1926, over three-quarters of women in employment were single. Between 1926 and 1986, the number of married women engaged in employment increased five-fold (Kennedy, 1989, p. 47). In the decade 1981-91, the proportion of married women in the labour force rose from 17 per cent to 25 per cent, and married women accounted for 40 per cent of the female labour force from 1987 to 1992 (ICTU, 1992b, pp. 1-2). Women's labour force participation rate in 1989 in Ireland was, at 37 per cent, the second lowest in the OECD; only Spain, with 33 per cent, had a lower percentage of women participating in the workforce. The average rate of female labour force participation among all countries in the OECD was 60 per cent (OECD, 1991, p. 256). Despite the dramatic rise in the numbers of married women engaging in economic activity in Ireland in the last decade, they are concentrated in lower-paid and part-time jobs and are not represented in management positions in any degree proportionate to their numbers in the workforce.

WOMEN IN POLITICS: WHY SO FEW?

The previous pages have examined the extent of the under-representation of women in politics and in decision-making centres. We must now look at the reasons for this under-representation. In doing so, we will discuss some of the factors that have acted as barriers to women's participation in public life, beginning with attitudes towards women's role in society and ending with a focus on obstacles inherent in the Irish political system that have developed from social expectations and practices.

The main factor inhibiting women's participation is generally recognised as being the degree to which a society holds negative attitudes towards the involvement of women in politics. In a study of obstacles to women's political participation in Ireland, Randall and Smyth (1987, p. 200) noted that:

> Irish women have until the very recent past been subject to a particularly intense, if complex, process of socialisation, through the agency of family, school and the Church, into an acceptance of an extremely traditional division of labour between the sexes and its implications for women's political role.

For these authors, the socialisation process, which transmits traditional assumptions about women's role in society (a feature, to varying degrees, of all societies in the liberal democratic world), has been reinforced in Ireland through the Roman Catholic church, which continues to prioritise a home and family-based role for women. This, argues Inglehart (1981), leads to women in predominantly Roman Catholic countries having less interest than men in politics, and so being less inclined to participate in the political process and its institutions.

This view is modified by later surveys measuring changes in men's and women's attitudes towards gender roles over a period of time. These studies pinpoint the existence of two contradictory sets of attitudes regarding women and politics held by the Irish public (Wilcox, 1991a, 1991b; JCWR, 1988). On the one hand, there is evidence that suggests increasingly favourable attitudes towards women and men having equal status in society. This is accompanied by a growing acceptance of women having a role in public life, with the finding that "attitudes in the population are ... supportive of equality in the public sphere, i.e. in business and political life and in the workplace" (JCWR, 1988, p. 95). However, there are indications that attitudes in Ireland towards women's participation in public life are less egalitarian than those in other EC countries (Wilcox, 1991a, p. 131). In addition, Irish men and women appear least willing to favour equality in gender roles within the context of home and family, in contrast to French and Italian women, who are among the most supportive of equality in a family context, and to both men and women in Denmark and the Netherlands, where a consistent level of egalitarianism on all types of gender roles is recorded (Wilcox, 1991a, pp. 130-1, 144). In a further study of the attitudes of European women and of feminism, Wilcox (1991b, p. 529) concluded that

> Irish women are among the most supportive of general gender equality, of equality in politics and increased numbers of women in the legislatures and of the goal of radically transforming society. After controls for demographic variables, they are more likely than others to find women's issues salient. Yet they are the least likely to favour equality in the family and among the least likely to trust women in non-traditional professions.

Thus, two views of women's role in society, which are difficult to reconcile with each other, coexist in Ireland. On the one hand, participation of women in public activity, be it employment, politics or other public functions, is viewed with greater equanimity now than it was 15 years ago. Yet there is a high degree of social pressure on women to have children, and, with no social supports, women are expected to combine their "traditional" home responsibilities with their activities in the public sphere (JCWR, 1988, pp. 81, 93-4). The expectation held by a majority of the population is, therefore, that women wishing to become involved in activities outside the home will combine both public and domestic responsibilities, leading them to assume the responsibility of a "dual burden" that men do not need to assume to the same extent.

Although Ireland still has the highest family size in the EC, women TDs have significantly smaller families than their male counterparts. This suggests that for women with political ambitions the practicality of pursuing this time-consuming career in tandem with child-rearing is an issue of greater significance than it is for their male colleagues. The issue of family size is related to the access of women to family support systems which male politicians can in general avail of more readily than women. While family demands may not deter politically ambitious women, they nonetheless appear to constitute a factor that women seeking political opportunities have to consider to a greater degree than men do.

However, the socially determined constraints on women wishing to engage in a political career are not as all-encompassing in the 1990s as they were 20 or more years ago. The greater acceptance of a broader role for women, the availability of contraception enabling women to limit family size, the higher level of education now enjoyed by women and the more extensive occupational opportunities available to women should suggest that women and men will have similar access to political careers. Nonetheless, certain obstacles remain more salient for women than for men.

If, as research has repeatedly shown, both education and occupation are relevant factors in the development of a political career for both women and men, then one must ask in what way they are significant. This can be answered in one word: networks. Given the significance of localism in Irish politics, the building of a personal support base or "bailiwick" in a constituency is a matter of considerable importance for both aspiring candidates and incumbents (Randall and Smyth, 1987, pp. 204-5). One of the most effective methods of doing this is through local government service. However, as we have seen, there are relatively few women in local government. One way of overcoming this disadvantage is through the development of local networks based on occupation. However, while professions such as teaching, law and business may appear to offer opportunities for building local support bases, it seems that the utility of these occupations lies in the economic independence and relative flexibility of time they offer rather than being the foundation for personal bailiwick-building.

Local voluntary activity presents another method of building a public profile, yet an impressionistic view would lead one to conclude that this route to a political career is under-utilised by women. If this is the case, then one must ask: do women who are involved in local voluntary community activity choose not to engage in the political party process or do they not see their participation in local issues as being of a political nature? Whatever the reason, and we must await further study of this aspect of women's participation in politics, it appears that women with political ambitions try to follow the common routes of entry into political life. However, the influence of localism is one that many aspiring women politicians find difficult to counteract if they have not had the opportunity to break into a brokerage network through local authority service. Significantly, women political hopefuls are increasingly looking to party elites for "sponsorship" at the candidate selection stage in order to compensate for a lower degree of access to local networks.

The low number of women in local government is significant, given the importance of a local authority background in getting elected to the Dáil. At the 1992 election, 17 (85 per cent) of the women elected to the Dáil had a record of local government service before entering the Dáil. This was rather higher than the figure for men (105, or 72 per cent). But with only a little over 11 per cent of local councillors being women even after the 1991 local elections, the pool of experienced women among the local authority members from whom the parties draw the majority of their candidates is very small.

Finally, while family connections have been important in determining routes to political power in Ireland, this has traditionally been a more significant factor for women than for men. From 1927 to 1973, the majority of women TDs elected were related through family or marriage to former TDs. During the 1980s, while the significance of the family connection declined, it still remained twice as important on average for women as for men. However, there are indications from the 1992 election that the significance of family is declining for women and remaining stable for men. Comparing the 1989 and 1992 elections, we find that in 1989, six (46 per cent) women TDs were related in varying ways to former members of the Dáil, while the corresponding figure in 1992 was seven (35 per cent). In other words, while in 1989 just over half of the women TDs had no connections with earlier TDs, in 1992 almost two thirds had no such family political history. The proportions of men with family connections to politics did not change as dramatically as that of women over the same period: in both elections, just over three-quarters of male TDs (76 per cent in 1989 and 78 per cent in 1992) were unrelated to a previous incumbent.

However, the above explanations, which focus on social and socio-political factors, do not fully account for the small number of women in politics. We must also look at the barriers embedded in the political system itself, and particularly at the selection process of the political parties.

During the 1980s, the record of the parties in selecting women candidates improved. Since 1977, the party executives have played an increasing role in promoting women candidates, removing some of the almost complete discretion previously held by local party units over the candidate selection process (see p. 112 above). Recent research confirms the critical role of party officials when it comes to the participation and selection of women candidates and their perceived opportunity for success (Fawcett, 1992). However, this involvement of the parties' central authorities in candidate selection, while being important for individual women, has not significantly redressed the gender imbalance in candidate tickets (Gallagher, 1988; Galligan, 1993a). As long as significantly fewer women than men are selected to contest elections, the opportunities for women to secure a place in the political process will continue to be limited. As Darcy (1988, p. 74) notes:

> Growth in the short term depends on increasing the proportions of women among new candidates (something that has been slightly declining over this decade), creating more opportunities for new people and increasing the re-election chances of women incumbents.

Surveys asking whether voters would have more confidence in a man or a woman as a parliamentarian were conducted across the EC in 1975, 1977, 1983 and 1987. The results do not suggest any innate hostility among Irish people towards the idea of women TDs: for the most part, Irish respondents (both men and women) are more likely to express a preference for a woman parliamentarian, and Irish women are less likely to express a preference for a man, than their counterparts in the EC as a whole (see Table 11.7). However, this willingness in principle to express more confidence in a woman may not always carry through to behaviour in the polling booth, as there are some indications of at least a modest

Table 11.7: Confidence in men and women as parliamentarians, 1975-87

		% saying more confidence in a man				% saying more confidence in a woman			
		1975	1977	1983	1987	1975	1977	1983	1987
Ireland	Men	42	63	38	33	10	7	4	4
	Women	33	45	20	17	24	27	14	21
EC	Men	42	47	34	27	6	6	4	3
	Women	33	33	27	19	11	16	9	11

Source: Commission of the EC (1983, p. 126); Commission of the EC (1987, p. 62).

voter and system bias against women candidates. A study of a number of general elections between 1948 and 1982 found that non-incumbent women candidates of Fianna Fáil, Fine Gael and Labour received on average 595 fewer votes than men candidates with the same credentials (Marsh, 1987, p. 70).

DOES THE UNDER-REPRESENTATION OF WOMEN MATTER?

Women and public policy

There is no doubt that for much of the state's history, women have received discriminatory treatment in law and public policy. Public policy was constructed within a constitutional context that, in Article 41.2 of the 1937 constitution, prescribed a homemaking role for women:

> 1° In particular, the State recognises that by her life within the home, woman gives to the State a support without which the common good cannot be achieved.
> 2° The State shall, therefore, endeavour to ensure that mothers shall not be obliged by economic necessity to engage in labour to the neglect of their duties in the home.

From this clear statement of the role of women, shaped by the values of conservative Catholic social thinking and accepted by the majority of men and women alike, public policies were enacted that reinforced the socially inferior position of women and their dependency on men as providers. As Scannell (1988, p. 127) notes in summing up the relationship between women, the law and the constitution:

> For almost thirty years after the constitution was adopted, the position of women in Irish society hardly changed at all. The common law relegation of women to domesticity and powerlessness continued. Laws based on the premise that women's rights were inferior to those of men survived in, and indeed even appeared on, the statute books.

Scannell outlines a long list of examples of discrimination against women in law and public policy from the 1930s to the 1960s; these included a ban on the employment of married women in the civil and public service, and unfavourable treatment as compared with men in employment, unemployment allowances, the tax code, family law, health and social policies relating to fertility, family property, legal aid and social security matters. While he was Attorney General, Declan Costello (1975, p. 68) described the status of married women before the 1970s as one involving "gross discrimination".

From 1957, some of the more obvious manifestations of gender inequality in law began to be redressed. The Married Women's Status Act of 1957 was the first attempt to accord some measure of equal treatment to female spouses in the context of family policy. It gave married women the right to sue and be sued, to enter into contracts and to hold property in their own name—rights already enjoyed by unmarried women and by all men, irrespective of their marital status. In 1957 also, the ban on the employment of married women teachers, which had existed since 1932, was removed by a ministerial order, although the prohibition on the employment of married women remained in operation in the civil service until 1973. The Guardianship of Infants Act, which was passed in 1964 and came into force in 1967, gave mothers an equal say in all decisions relating to the upbringing of their children—prior to this, fathers had had sole rights in child-rearing matters. The 1965 Succession Act gave a widow a legal entitlement to a share in her husband's estate on his death, ending the state of affairs in which a wife could be completely disinherited by a husband in his will.

However, major discriminatory measures remained in operation. During the 1970s, pressure for changes in legislation and other aspects of public policy began to emerge from three main sources: the judiciary, the feminist movement and the European Community. According to Scannell (1988, pp. 129-30), these agencies were more important catalysts in the initiation of change in the status of women than either politicians or parliament, suggesting that the political system was forced to respond to external pressures but was not prepared to initiate change. While EC directives and judicial decisions acted as important catalysts for specific legislative changes, the re-emergence of the women's movement in the early 1970s prompted a public discussion of gender-based discrimination in law and public policy.

Evidence suggests that women's lobby groups have had a more immediate influence on specific aspects of law than have the efforts of women TDs. In 1972, the Commission on the Status of Women, established by the government two years earlier, recommended that action be taken to remove discrimination in the areas of the home, employment, social welfare, taxation, family law, jury service, public life and education. This report provided the government with a blueprint for legislative reform, particularly in the areas of employment and social welfare policies, much of which was implemented in the course of the 1970s.

With the dissolution of the Commission on the Status of Women upon the presentation of its report, the task of lobbying for legislative change was taken up by a range of women's interest groups that had grown out of the women's movement. For example, the Council for the Status of Women, a non-partisan interest group formed in 1972 from a core of traditional women's organisations, is now regularly consulted by government and makes frequent submissions on a variety of issues directly affecting the position of women in society (Fitzsimons, 1991). The family law reform group AIM (Action, Information, Motivation), established in 1972 as an offshoot of the women's movement, was instrumental in lobbying for changes in legislation relating to the family, which materialised during the 1970s and early 1980s. The Rape Crisis Centres succeeded in having the legislation dealing with sexual violence against women radically amended in 1990. The status of children born outside marriage was finally regulated with the abolition of the concept of illegitimacy and the enactment of provisions giving equal rights, as far as possible, to all children in the Status of Children Act (1987), after a decade of lobbying by Cherish and other single-parent support groups. These are some instances of the work of feminist issue groups in securing legislative reform that reflected the needs and demands of women.

If lobbying efforts were not sufficient to secure change, then there was always the national and European judicial process. The McGee (1973), de Búrca (1976) and Airey (1979) cases, which respectively established the right of married couples to import contraceptives for their own use, the right of women to serve on juries and the right of women to free legal aid, are seen as important cases leading to legislative reform of benefit to women. The principle of equality for women in social welfare entitlements was conceded by the government in 1990 following a judgment from the European Court of Justice in a case brought by two women,

Cotter and McDermott, against the state. More recently, a confluence of three sets of judicial findings on aspects of abortion—from the European Community's Court of Justice in 1991, the European Court of Human Rights in 1992 and the Supreme Court in the "X" case of 1992—led to constitutional referendums in November 1992 that indicated clear majorities against an absolute ban on abortion and in favour of liberalising the ban on the right to travel and on information about abortion (Kelly, 1993, pp. 205-7).

Despite these advances in women's rights, there remain many important issues relating to women's lives that legislators have shown a reluctance to tackle. These range from the relatively non-contentious area of providing in law for equal rights and status between women and men to legislating on very emotive and politically difficult issues such as abortion, family violence, sexual harassment in the workplace and pornography.

Little, too, has been done to change the concept of women's status of dependency on men through marriage. This notion of female dependency continues to underpin many aspects of public policy, particularly in the area of social security, with changes being brought about only in a piecemeal fashion arising from the requirement to implement EC directives. In general, improvements in the situation of women in society have been in the context of the family and relationships within it, rather than in the context of women as independent adults. The reluctance of legislators to address the issue of women as independent rather than dependent adults with the same rights as men is clearly shown in the fact that no legislation exists recognising and establishing women's rights of access to social and recreational institutions (such as golf and tennis clubs), to credit facilities and to services that are available to men. Despite pressure from the combined forces of women's groups, the Joint Committee on Women's Rights, and the Employment Equality Agency seeking the enactment of legislation recognising the status of women as equal to men outside the context of the family, there is as yet no provision to this effect. However, the programme for government agreed between Fianna Fáil and Labour in 1993 suggests that these issues will be tackled as part of a broad agenda of social reforms.

Women, political attitudes and representation

The differential treatment of women and men demonstrated above raises the question of whether public policy would have been different had there been more women in politics, and whether a greater number of women in future could make a difference. In his comparative study of Eurobarometer surveys on gender, Wilcox concluded that "it is possible that Irish women believe that there are important differences between men and women, and that these differences necessitate representation of women in the legislature" (Wilcox, 1991a, p. 131). We can approach this by examining the extent of male-female differences in political attitudes and priorities. Although, as we have seen, there appears to be a discernible gender difference in attitudes towards female and male legislators, this does not carry through to stated voting intentions for political parties. The broad overall pattern is in line with studies of voter preference in Europe which report no gender gap in voter behaviour (Wilcox, 1991b, p. 537).

On most issues, no marked differences in attitudes between women and men have surfaced. For instance, in the 1992 general election there were at most minor differences in political priorities. There was little discernible difference in attitudes on employment policies, but women's second concern was the health service, which ranked only fourth among men (84 per cent of women described it as "very important" as against 76 per cent of men). Both men (81 per cent) and women (82 per cent) attached considerable importance to having trust in those holding ministerial office (Marsh, Wilford, Arthur and Fitzgerald, 1993, p. 201). At the 1990 presidential election, when for the first time there was a woman candidate, there was little evidence of a gender gap in voting. The last pre-election poll found that women supported both Mary Robinson (41 per cent) and Brian Lenihan (40 per cent) in almost equal measure, and men also divided fairly evenly (39 per cent opted for Lenihan and 37 per cent for Robinson).

Surveys of social attitudes and voting intentions towards two major conflictual issues that have confronted Irish society during the past decade, namely abortion and divorce, have also revealed a dual perception. On the one hand, the third report of the Joint Committee on Women's Rights found no significant differences in the attitudes of men and women concerning the conditions under which abortion and divorce might be permitted. However, this finding was based on a survey conducted after these issues had been decided by two referendums, in 1983 and 1986 respectively, and a different pattern emerged from polls taken during the campaigns. Women were significantly more supportive than men of a "Yes" vote in the closing stages of the 1983 campaign on the "pro-life" amendment, with 75 per cent stating an intention to vote in favour as against 62 per cent of men (Girvin, 1986, p. 79). Moreover, polls taken during the debate on divorce indicate that there was a distinct gender gap in voting intentions towards the end of the campaign, with women once again adopting a more conservative position than men. Women's support for removing the constitutional ban on divorce dropped by 27 per cent between April and June 1986, in comparison with an 8 per cent decline in men's support for divorce, and the last pre-referendum poll found that while 49 per cent of men favoured legalisation of divorce, only 31 per cent of women did (MRBI, 1986, Table 1).

Polls taken prior to the June 1992 referendum on the Maastricht treaty and the November 1992 referendums on abortion, travel and information confirm the general proposition that women are inclined to choose a more conservative political option than men. These were very complex political issues, with the EC referendum on the Maastricht treaty inevitably involving discussion of the protocol relating to abortion in Ireland (Holmes, 1993, p. 106). Abortion was the most important issue for women prior to the Maastricht referendum (26 per cent of them identified it as one of "the major issues involved"), followed by the right to travel (22 per cent) and the closer union of EC countries (22 per cent). For men, the most important issue on the eve of the referendum was the financial aid it would bring to the country (28 per cent), with the possibility of the introduction of abortion ranking third (21 per cent). While of itself the prioritising of issues is neither conservative nor progressive, it is certainly true that men were more likely to support the Maastricht treaty than women were (55 per cent as against 44 per cent; see Marsh, Wilford, Arthur and Fitzgerald, 1993, pp. 193-4). There was more uncertainty among women on how to vote, given the widespread media coverage of the potential problems of the abortion protocol. Women's lack of enthusiasm for Maastricht, then, cannot be put down simply to the holding of conservative political views.

Opinions on abortion were more clear-cut when the abortion-related referendums took place in November 1992. Girvin (1993, pp. 120-1) notes that "a number of opinion polls highlighted the diversity of opinion on the issue ... Opinion polls taken at the end of September found that significant majorities favoured the right to travel (65 per cent) and information (76 per cent)". This masks the fact that there was some degree of difference in the opinions of men and women, with men being slightly more in favour of the right to travel than women (68 per cent as against 62 per cent). There was no real difference in opinions on the right to information question. On the substantive issue of abortion, 46 per cent of women who were polled clearly opposed the addition of a limited abortion clause into the constitution as against 38 per cent of men (Marsh, Wilford, Arthur and Fitzgerald, 1993, p. 199). However, when asked a general question on the availability of abortion, women indicated a greater preference for the two most conservative options presented than did men (47 per cent as against 35 per cent—see Marsh, Wilford, Arthur and Fitzgerald, 1993, p. 197). Thus we are led to conclude that when a question exploring general attitudes to abortion is asked, women will adopt a less liberal position than men. This appears to be carried through to voting behaviour, as a post-election survey found that women were more likely to have voted "No" for conservative reasons while men were more likely to have voted "No" for liberal reasons (Kennelly and Ward, 1993, pp. 129-30).

To date, it is arguable whether the increased participation of women in parliament has led to significant differences in legislation. One of the reasons advanced for the ineffectiveness of women TDs in representing women's rights is their scarcity in the parliamentary arena. Evidence from countries in which the numbers of women parliamentarians have increased to significant proportions suggests that women legislators can effect change in the direction of women's rights only when they begin to constitute a substantial minority, perhaps about a third, of parliamentary representatives (Dahlerup, 1988; Sinkkonen and Haavio-Mannila, 1981). Thus, applying this argument to Ireland, we could say that without a substantial increase in the number of women elected to the Dáil, women's issues will continue to be ignored by legislators. This line of thinking has been advanced by observers of Scandinavian and north European politics. However, its relevance to Irish political circumstances remains unproven.

There are two factors that might militate against the fulfilment of this thesis in an Irish context. The first relates to the consciousness of parliamentarians, particularly women TDs, of gender differences on policy issues. The "large minority" thesis appears to work in Scandinavian countries partly because there is a generally high level of social and political awareness of gender issues. This perspective was highlighted during the late 1970s and through the 1980s by the activities of a strong women's movement in the case of Denmark and Norway and by the pursuit of an egalitarian social policy by successive Swedish governments. Legislators' awareness of the gender dimension was given a further impetus with the election of parliamentarians sympathetic to feminist demands. In Ireland, legislators have not been particularly conscious of feminist issues, the women's movement was a weak and short-lived phenomenon, and few feminists have been elected to the Dáil. To date, then, there has been little expression of a feminist voice in the Oireachtas apart from some notable individuals, both men and women. The advent of a larger number of women parliamentarians, then, may not in itself change policy priorities unless their political agenda is one of gender equality. A second reason is the dominance of party discipline, which regulates the policy positions of all deputies, both women and men. The conflict between reconciling party policy and personal beliefs was illustrated by the resignation of Nuala Fennell from the position of Fine Gael spokesperson on Women's Affairs during the Maastricht referendum campaign in 1992 in order to represent a more strongly feminist view on women's issues. However, it is significant that during the political debate on the right to travel and information on abortion services in February and March 1992, some of the women TDs in the 26th Dáil formulated a position representing a broadly "feminist" stance that crossed party boundaries, which they presented to the Taoiseach as women legislators rather than as party politicians.

The institutionalisation of women's interests
Gradually, as issues of women's rights and status in society became part of the political agenda, political structures evolved that institutionalised the expression of these demands. First, the Women's Representative Committee was established by the Fine Gael-Labour coalition government in 1974 to oversee the implementation of the recommendations of the Commission on the Status of Women. It was replaced in 1978 by two organisations, the Employment Equality Agency (a statutory body) and the Council for the Status of Women. The establishment of the junior ministry for Women's Affairs and Family Law Reform in 1982 and of the Joint Oireachtas Committee on Women's Rights in 1983 brought a woman-centred focus on policy and legislation into the mainstream of the political system. More recently, the report of the Second Commission on the Status of Women, suggesting extensive public policy reforms, has been accepted in a positive way by the government (Galligan, 1993b). A renewed political commitment to the principle of equality was indicated in 1993 with the appointment of a Minister for Equality and Law Reform.

If successive governments have shown some desire to incorporate women's demands into the governmental and legislative process, the political parties have not shown the same degree of enlightenment. For example, parties have been slow to adopt measures that would facilitate the selection of women in significantly greater numbers (Galligan, 1993a). In policy terms, however, parties are recognising the fact of women's less favoured position in policy and practice and are slowly adopting a more gender-sensitive approach. The Equal Status Bill drafted by the Labour Party in 1989 and defeated in the Dáil by the government parties in 1992, and the call by Fine Gael in 1991 for a constitutional amendment guaranteeing equal rights for women, are two cases in point.

Nonetheless, the more enduring structural adaptations which have incorporated the "women's agenda" have involved a minimal disruption, or none at all, to the political system, and so far have had limited results. They have been more successful as internal sensitising agencies in shaping the attitudes of legislators towards the status of women than as policy output agencies. Only time will tell whether the work of the Department for Equality and Law Reform will provide the country with a substantial body of equality legislation.

CONCLUSION

The relationship between women and politics in Ireland seems to be in a transitional phase. There appears to be a desire among the female electorate in particular to see a greater number of women representatives in parliament. Yet women are still under-represented among election candidates. Women considering a career in public life do so in a social environment that expects them also to fulfil traditional home-based duties. The number of women candidates has increased since 1977, but still comprises less than 20 per cent of all candidates in national elections. This is due to a combination of social and structural factors that inhibit women's political activity and to a resistance within the parties to giving serious consideration to providing gender balance on candidate tickets. While the success of Mary Robinson may encourage more women to present themselves for selection as candidates, the prognosis for a greater level of active participation by women in political life remains poor unless parties adopt strong affirmative action strategies similar to those successfully employed in some other European parties, such as the German Social Democrats, the Norwegian Labour, Liberal and Centre parties, and the Austrian and German Greens.

In policy terms, some progress has been made. A range of issues raised by women since the 1970s, particularly those relating to women's rights within the family and in employment, have been incorporated into the political process and legitimated over the last two decades. Nonetheless, a political resolution of conflicts based on sexuality and recognition of the equal status of women as independent adults has proved more difficult to arrive at. There is a skeletal institutional framework now in existence focusing on women's status and legislative rights that did not exist 20 years ago, but its powers have, until recently, been mainly persuasive rather than legislative. Women's interest groups have been incorporated into policy networks in specific areas, with varying degrees of success. All political parties now profess to be gender-sensitive and are indicating signs of a commitment to women-centred issues and a gender-based perspective on certain areas of social policy. Progress, in fact, has been piecemeal rather than substantive. The political dialogue of the 1990s, with the emphasis now being placed on participatory democracy, provides women with a climate that appears more receptive to the articulation of a women's view of the political world. Parties are using this dialogue to varying degrees, and in the process are slowly incorporating women and women's perspectives. However, in terms of the political representation of women, Ireland still has a long way to go before women are elected to the Dáil in the same proportions as men. There is a considerable amount of work for politicians concerned with legislating for equality between women and men. Progress is required on both fronts in order that the voice and needs of one half of the population are adequately catered for in the political system.

REFERENCES AND FURTHER READING

Blackwell, John, 1990. *Women in the Labour Force (Supplement)*. Dublin: Employment Equality Agency.

Brown, Alice and Yvonne Galligan, 1993. "Changing the political agenda for women in the Republic of Ireland and in Scotland", *West European Politics* 16:2, pp. 165-89.

Commission of the EC, 1983. *European Women and Men in 1983*. Brussels: Commission of the European Communities.

Commission of the EC, 1987. *Men and Women of Europe in 1987*. Brussels: Commission of the European Communities.

Connelly, Alpha (ed.), 1993. *Gender and the Law in Ireland*. Dublin: Oak Tree Press.

Connelly, Alpha and Betty Hilliard, 1993. "The legal system", pp. 212-38 in Connelly (1993).

Costello, Declan, 1975. "Legal status of women in Ireland", *Administration* 23:1, pp. 68-70.

Dahlerup, Drude, 1988. "From a small to a large minority: women in Scandinavian politics", *Scandinavian Political Studies* 11:4, pp. 275-98.

Darcy, R., 1988. "The election of women to Dáil Éireann: a formal analysis", *Irish Political Studies* 3, pp. 63-76.

Department of the Environment, 1993. *General Election 1992: Election Results and Transfer of Votes*. Dublin: Stationery Office.

The Development of Equal Opportunities, March 1987–September 1988: Coordinated Report, 1988. Pl. 6056. Dublin: Stationery Office.

The Development of Equal Opportunities: Second Coordinated Report, October 1988–February 1992, 1992. Pl. 8850. Dublin: Stationery Office.

Donnelly, Seán, 1992. *Poll Position: an Analysis of the 1991 Local Elections*. Dublin: Seán Donnelly.

Eager, Clare, 1991. "Splitting images—women and the Irish civil service", *Seirbhís Phoiblí* 12:1, pp. 15-23.

Farrell, David M., 1992. "Ireland", pp. 389-457 in Richard S. Katz and Peter Mair (eds), *Party Organizations: a Data Handbook on Party Organizations in Western Democracies, 1960-90*. London: Sage.

Fawcett, Liz, 1992. "The recruitment of women to local politics in Ireland: a case study", *Irish Political Studies* 7, pp. 41-55.

Fitzsimons, Yvonne, 1991. "Women's interest representation in the Republic of Ireland: the Council for the Status of Women", *Irish Political Studies* 6, pp. 37-51.

Gallagher, Michael, 1988. "Ireland: the increasing role of the centre", pp. 119-44 in Michael Gallagher and Michael Marsh (eds), *Candidate Selection in Comparative Perspective: the Secret Garden of Politics*. London: Sage.

Galligan, Yvonne, 1993a. "Gender and party politics in Ireland", in Joni Lovenduski and Pippa Norris (eds), *Gender and Party Politics*. London: Sage, forthcoming.

Galligan, Yvonne, 1993b. "The Report of the Second Commission on the Status of Women", *Irish Political Studies* 8, pp. 125-30.

Gardiner, Frances, 1992. "Political interest and participation of Irish women 1922-1992: the unfinished revolution", *Canadian Journal of Irish Studies* 18:1, pp. 15-39.

Girvin, Brian, 1986. "Social change and moral politics: the Irish constitutional referendum 1983", *Political Studies* 34:1, pp. 61-81.

Girvin, Brian, 1993. "The referendums on abortion 1992", *Irish Political Studies* 8, pp. 118-24.

Holmes, Michael, 1993. "The Maastricht Treaty referendum of June 1992", *Irish Political Studies* 8, pp. 105-10.

Inglehart, Margaret, 1981. "Political interest in west European women: an historical and empirical comparative analysis", *Comparative Political Studies* 14:3, pp. 299-326.

ICTU, 1992a. *Implementation of Equality Report "Programme for Progress"*. Dublin: Irish Congress of Trade Unions.

ICTU 1992b. "Women in the labour force", *Information Bulletin* 1/92. Dublin: Irish Congress of Trade Unions.

Joint Committee on Women's Rights, 1988. *Changing Attitudes to the Role of Women in Ireland: Attitudes Towards the Role and Status of Women 1975-1986*. Dublin: Stationery Office.

Joint Committee on Women's Rights, 1991. *Motherhood, Work and Equal Opportunity: a Case Study of Irish Civil Servants*. Dublin: Stationery Office.

Kelly, Mary, 1993. "Censorship of the media", pp. 185-211 in Connelly (1993).

Kennedy, Finola, 1989. *Family, Economy and Government in Ireland*. Dublin: Economic and Social Research Institute.

Kennelly, Brendan and Eilís Ward, 1993. "The abortion referendums", pp. 115-34 in Michael Gallagher and Michael Laver (eds), *How Ireland Voted 1992*. Dublin: Folens and Limerick: PSAI Press.

Manning, Maurice, 1987. "Women and the elections", pp. 156-66 in Howard R. Penniman and Brian Farrell (eds), *Ireland at the Polls 1981, 1982 and 1987: a Study of Four General Elections*. Durham NC: Duke University Press.

Marsh, Michael, 1987. "Electoral evaluations of candidates in Irish elections", *Irish Political Studies* 2, pp. 65-76.

Marsh, Michael, Rick Wilford, Paul Arthur and Rona Fitzgerald, 1993. "Irish political data 1992", *Irish Political Studies* 8, pp. 169-214.

MRBI, 1986. *Irish Times/MRBI Poll 3450/86*. Dun Laoghaire: Market Research Bureau of Ireland.

Nealon, Ted, 1977. *Guide to the 21st Dáil and Seanad*. Dublin: Platform Press.

Nealon, Ted, 1987. *Guide to the 25th Dáil and Seanad*. Dublin: Platform Press.

Nealon, Ted, 1989. *Guide to the 26st Dáil and Seanad*. Dublin: Platform Press.

Norris, Pippa, 1987. *Politics and Sexual Equality: the Comparative Position of Women in Western Democracies*. Brighton: Wheatsheaf.

Norris, Pippa, 1988. "The gender gap: a cross-national trend?", pp. 217-34 in Carol M. Mueller (ed.), *The Politics of the Gender Gap: the Social Construction of Political Influence*. London: Sage.

OECD, 1991. *Employment Outlook*. Paris: Organisation for Economic Cooperation and Development.

Randall, Vicky, 1987. *Women and Politics: an International Perspective*, 2nd ed. Basingstoke: Macmillan Education.

Randall, Vicky and Ailbhe Smyth, 1987. "Bishops and bailiwicks: obstacles to women's political participation in Ireland", *Economic and Social Review* 18:3, pp. 189-214.

Scannell, Yvonne, 1988. "The constitution and the role of women", pp. 123-36 in Brian Farrell (ed.), *De Valera's Constitution and Ours*. Dublin: Gill and Macmillan.

Sinkkonen, S. and E. Haavio-Mannila, 1981. "The impact of the women's movement and legislative activity of women MPs on social development", pp. 195-215 in Marguerite Rendel (ed.), *Women, Power and Political Systems*. London: Croom Helm.

Walker, Brian M., 1992. *Parliamentary Election Results in Ireland, 1918-92*. Dublin: Royal Irish Academy.

Wilcox, Clyde, 1991a. "Support for gender equality in west Europe—a longitudinal analysis", *European Journal of Political Research* 20:2, pp. 127-47.

Wilcox, Clyde, 1991b. "The causes and consequences of feminist consciousness among western European women", *Comparative Political Studies* 23:4, pp. 519-45.

1991). We do not have to go very far into their contending theories to appreciate the complexity of the external environment, but one of their basic distinctions provides a starting point for an analysis of Ireland's position in world politics.

Followers of what is often called the "realist" school stress the state as the focus of international politics, and look to "power" as a major explanatory factor. Given the anarchic nature of the international system—there is no authority above states—the ever present tendency to resort to force is seen as the most pressing problem of international life. In this view the foreign policy of a small state such as Ireland is above all a struggle for survival in a Hobbesian world of predatory great powers.

On the other hand, "interdependence" theorists have argued that economic forces are generally more important than the formal prerogatives of statehood. International actors other than states, such as international organisations and non-state ("transnational") bodies such as multinational corporations, may wield as much influence as states, if not more. In the eyes of these theorists, the politics of "security" is less significant than the characteristics of the international political economy. In this context, it is Ireland's small open economy that puts it at risk, rather than any lack of diplomatic or military power.

Ireland in a world of realpolitik, 1922-45

From the establishment of the Irish Free State as a member of the British Commonwealth until 1945, the international system approximated the realist model all too closely. The attempt to organise an international rule of law through the League of Nations failed dramatically, and international stability was eventually established only by force of arms. At first sight it seems paradoxical that Ireland's political independence was steadily consolidated during this period, but given that it was independence from British domination this result is not so surprising. British decline was a constant theme, giving Irish governments the leverage to obtain a somewhat ambiguous statehood in the first place, and then to remove most of the ambiguities by a variety of means.

These started with multilateral negotiations within the Commonwealth and the League, allowing for coalitions with the other dominions, and providing the basis for de Valera's unilateral revision of the 1921 Treaty in the form of the 1937 constitution. By this time the British government's policy of appeasement of Germany meant the appeasement of Ireland, in the handing over of the naval facilities at the ports, which in turn was a prerequisite of Irish neutrality throughout the second world war (Keatinge, 1986).

This achievement—and in Irish political culture neutrality acquired the status of a "core value", as the touchstone of independence—should not blind us to the limitations of Ireland's international position coming into the postwar era. Formal political independence had not been matched in economic terms; the economy remained almost wholly dependent on the fortunes (or more usually the misfortunes) of one of Europe's least successful economies. Partition was if anything consolidated, in spite of attempts to make it an international issue. Playing the (Irish-) American card was supposed to mobilise Washington against London, but that would always be a doubtful proposition when the exigencies of a great power alliance were at stake. Even wartime neutrality had not been played strictly according to the rules (Salmon, 1989; Fisk, 1983). It had been played quite skilfully, but in the end its viability owed more to geopolitical realities than to government policy. Irish neutrality was not tested to the extent experienced by, for example, Finland, which was located between the Soviet Union and the Third Reich—the least scrupulous of the great powers.

Ireland in an interdependent world, 1945-89

A very different international system existed between 1945 and 1989. This "bi-polar" system, although marked by a major international conflict (the cold war between the United States and the Soviet Union), came to acquire a much greater degree of stability than its predecessor. In the western world this permitted the development of a type of international politics that looks much more like the model of the interdependence theorists. Against a background of unprecedented economic growth, "international regimes" (a term that covers both formal organisations and looser arrangements) became the norm. Traditional distinctions between "foreign policy" and "domestic policy" tended to lose much of their meaning, especially among the countries forming the core of west European integration.

Ireland, like the other small peripheral states in western Europe, was slow to adapt to this process. In the late 1940s traditional concerns with Anglo-Irish relations and partition seemed at least as important as the new issues, such as the cold war, and geopolitical irrelevance again permitted the continuation of an even less clearly defined neutrality policy. Economic dependence on the United Kingdom inhibited a close involvement in the integration process, as British governments remained aloof from "Europe". However, a fundamental reappraisal of economic policy in the late 1950s led to a more active interest in European integration. This led to an application to join the EC in 1961, when the United Kingdom turned in this direction, only to be blocked by the veto on EC enlargement in 1963 imposed by French President Charles de Gaulle.

Nevertheless, the state's internationalisation did make some tentative progress. A founding member of the Organisation for European Economic Cooperation (OEEC) and the Council of Europe in the late 1940s, Ireland was at last admitted to the United Nations (UN) in 1955. The delay had more to do with cold war politics than with Irish policy, which had aimed at membership since 1946. Participation in the UN provided the basis of a peacekeeping role which became one of the constants of Irish foreign policy, and it also allowed the formation of policies towards the emerging third world countries.

"Europe"—that is, the EC—was, however, the focal point of government policy from the early 1960s onwards, mainly for economic reasons. When enlargement again became feasible in 1969 membership was negotiated and was approved in a referendum in 1972, by a majority of 83 per cent to 17 per cent in a turnout of over 70 per cent (see appendix 2h). Fianna Fáil and Fine Gael both supported entry, along with the employers' and farmers' organisations, while Labour and the trade unions opposed it, in a campaign dominated by economic issues. Although integration itself faltered in the 1970s and early 1980s, the reform of the EC in the Single European Act (SEA) was approved by a second referendum in 1987. However, the result—70 per cent to 30 per cent in a poll of only 44 per cent—reflected a measure of disillusionment, or at least of indifference. It may also indicate a degree of bewilderment concerning a very complex political system; what is certain is that none of the major parties came out of the ratification process of the SEA with any distinction (Gallagher, 1988).

Nevertheless, since EC entry the state's involvement in international affairs has been much more intensive, and the direct effects of EC membership have reached far into Irish public life (Keatinge, 1991). Between 1973 and 1991 the economy experienced a faster rate of growth than would otherwise have occurred. Financial support, initially mainly through the Common Agricultural Policy (CAP) and then more broadly through the structural funds (whose function is to promote development, especially in the less wealthy parts of the Community), now accounts for about 6 per cent of national income. It is a moot point whether Ireland's position as a net beneficiary has been exploited to maximum advantage through national economic policies. Community membership is not of itself a panacea, but at the very least it has provided a systematic way of influencing the collective EC response to global forces which are beyond the control of even the largest European economies.

The revival of west European integration in the late 1980s confirmed the significance of EC membership for Ireland. So too did a separate, and even more fundamental, change in world politics—the collapse of the Soviet Union as one of the world's two "superpowers" between 1989 and 1991. We shall deal with the implications of the consequent new world system in the final section of the chapter, after exploring the European dimension to Irish politics in some detail. First, however, a very distinctive element in the state's external environment merits further attention—the relationship between the governments in Dublin and London.

A special relationship: Ireland and Britain

As we have seen, Anglo-Irish relations were the predominant theme in Irish foreign policy from the founding of the state to the formative years of the cold war system in the late 1940s. In the critical period of 1948-49, while the western alliance system was being established under the North Atlantic Treaty, the Irish government was more concerned with the issues of constitutional status, Commonwealth membership and partition (McCabe, 1991).

Even when "Europe" assumed the central place in the state's external relations, Anglo-Irish relations retained an important place. Ireland's negotiations to join the European Community coincided with the collapse of political authority in Northern Ireland, and the subsequent conflict there has been a constant element in the state's external relations. While it goes against the grain of nationalist ideology to conceive of the North as "foreign policy", certain political and legal realities place this issue on the boundary between foreign and domestic politics. In attempting to influence political behaviour outside the jurisdiction of the state, Irish governments are inevitably brought into contact with the sovereign government in whose jurisdiction Northern Ireland actually lies.

Anglo-Irish relations therefore have an important diplomatic dimension, which led in the mid 1980s to an unusual experiment in bilateral relationships. For Dublin governments, northern policy was traditionally seen as the prerogative of the Taoiseach, but in operational terms the Department of Foreign Affairs deals with most of the business. Since 1969 that has been considerable (Keatinge, 1986). From a position of mutual incompetence on the part of Irish and

British governments, through often painful attempts to persuade London that an "Irish dimension" had any legitimacy or utility, Dublin's policy evolved to the point where a formal institutional basis was established in the Anglo-Irish Agreement of 1985.

For students of both Irish and international political processes, this bilateral "regime" possesses some interesting features. Following a period of acute adversarial party politics it was necessary to build a remarkably detailed consensus in the New Ireland Forum of 1983-84. This extra-parliamentary consultation between the Dáil parties and the SDLP produced a sufficient level of agreement and political will for the government of the day to engage in prolonged and intensive negotiations with its British counterpart. The commitment of the Taoiseach, Garret FitzGerald, and the involvement of a small group of senior civil servants contrasted with the rather marginal role of the government as a whole (Fitz-Gerald, 1991, pp. 460-575).

Once the agreement was signed a pattern of regular and quite frequent meetings of the Anglo-Irish Intergovernmental Conference took place, at which the Irish representative, the Minister for Foreign Affairs, could raise issues pertaining to the government of Northern Ireland with his counterpart, the British Secretary of State for Northern Ireland. This is not joint decision-making, but as an opportunity to influence policy in another jurisdiction, on matters of considerable sensitivity, it is an unusual form of international relationship.

Evaluations of the success of the process are, to say the least, mixed and to a large extent depend on the political eye of the beholder (McGarry and O'Leary, 1990; Cochrane, 1993). Irish governments, including those of Fianna Fáil (which originally opposed the agreement in 1985), have argued that it reduced the vulnerability of constitutional nationalists in Northern Ireland, and replaced "megaphone diplomacy" between Dublin and London by a more ordered, less tense and more sensitive relationship. The agreement's critics maintained that it did not achieve its primary aim of a lasting resolution of the conflict, and some of them—particularly the northern unionists—regarded it as part of the problem rather than as part of the solution.

Despite the generally dismal historical record, the search for a political rapprochement in Northern Ireland has remained high on the agenda of Anglo-Irish relations. Peter Brooke, the British Secretary of State for Northern Ireland from 1989 to 1992, tried to bring the northern political parties to the negotiating table. After a year's painstaking "talks about talks"—a process already attempted in 1987—the formal negotiations collapsed in July 1991, ostensibly over procedural differences but in reality because of the depth of distrust between the participants (Arthur, 1992). The resumed talks in 1992 under Brooke's successor, Sir Patrick Mayhew, met a similar fate (Arthur, 1993). In the absence of any real political accommodation in the north, Anglo-Irish relations will continue to be overshadowed by the need to contain the northern conflict.

In the early 1970s there were some expectations of possible ameliorative effects of European integration on the issue. It must be said that these expectations have not been met. The conflict was "internationalised" to some extent, but the basic antagonism remained impervious to external influences (Guelke, 1988). However, EC membership has had some positive effects; it brought the British and Irish governments into constant contact on less contentious issues, and at the same time helped the Irish government to mobilise international support. The EC itself has been a source of modest financial aid, in the form of cross-border projects and a contribution to the fund established alongside the Anglo-Irish Agreement. The hope that the weakening of the economic border in the European single market, together with moves towards political union, would make the Northern conflict more "anachronistic" than ever does not of itself suggest a resolution of the conflict. Being seen as anachronistic has rarely worried the extremes of Irish politics, and the borders to be crossed are psychological as well as economic. In any event, even if EC membership has had less impact than some anticipated on the Northern Ireland problem, it has undoubtedly had major ramifications for the Republic and its political life, as we shall now see.

THE EUROPEAN COMMUNITY

The European Community is a unique organisation, being much more than a traditional international organisation but much less than a fully fledged state. Within the Community, 12 sovereign states (Belgium, Denmark, France, Germany, Greece, Ireland, Italy, Luxembourg, the Netherlands, Portugal, Spain and the United Kingdom) agree to pool their sovereignty over a wide range of policy areas.

The EC differs from traditional forms of interstate cooperation in five main respects. First, the founders of the Community in the 1950s set out to lay the foundations of a federal Europe. After the war, there was a strong movement favouring European unity in Europe. Although the European Community has failed to live up to the expectations of the founding fathers, the notion of an "ever closer union among the peoples of Europe"—a phrase used in the preamble to the 1992 Treaty of Maastricht—is part of the rhetoric of EC policies and provides an ideological underpinning to European integration. Moreover, when a country decides to opt for EC membership, it is accepting an open-ended commitment to participate in an evolving political entity (Pinder, 1991).

Second, the Community has a constitution in the form of treaties. To date, the main treaties are the Paris Treaty (establishing the European Coal and Steel Community) of 1950, the Rome Treaties (European Economic Community and Euratom) of 1957, the Merger Treaty of 1965, the Budget Treaties of 1970 and 1975, the Single European Act of 1987 and the Treaty of Maastricht of 1992. The treaties deal with what the Community may do and how it goes about its business. Law plays a central role in the workings of the Community, and EC law in effect represents an "external constitution" for the Irish political system. Three characteristics of Community law are particularly important: direct effect, direct applicability and the supremacy of Community law over national law. The principle of direct effect means that Community law is not just a matter for public agencies but may be directed towards individuals and companies. Direct applicability, on the other hand, means that once a regulation is passed by the Community's legislative process it immediately becomes part of national law. The practical implication of these principles is that Community law involves not only governments and public agencies but also individual citizens or private bodies, and that Community law can override national law. When joining the Community, states must accept the entire *acquis communautaire*, a term used to describe the bundle of obligations that arise from Community law.

Third, the Community is endowed with a set of institutions to make and implement policy. There are four major institutions, which we shall look at in detail later on: the Commission, the Council of Ministers/European Council, the European Parliament, and the Court of Justice. The Community involves both traditional or orthodox *intergovernmental* cooperation (that is, cooperation between fully sovereign states) and, at the same time, elements of *supranational* authority, in the form of institutions that are largely independent of the member states (Nugent, 1991). Intergovernmental relations are formalised in the Council system, while supranational authority is represented by the Community's legal basis, the Commission, the Court and the European Parliament (EP). Other forms of policy cooperation, for example on foreign policy and on crime and immigration, have originated outside the strict confines of the treaties.

The treaty agreed in the Dutch town of Maastricht in December 19/1 provides for the consolidation of all forms of cooperation within a single treaty framework for the first time. It defines European Union as resting on three "pillars": first, the European Community (including economic and monetary union); second, common foreign and security policy; and third, cooperation in the spheres of justice and home affairs.

In practice, this means that there are three arenas of policy making. The roles and powers of the four institutions differ from one arena to another. The Commission, the Court of Justice and the Parliament have a far greater role in the first pillar (the EC) than in either of the other two. Put simply, the supranational element of the policy process is strongest in the Community pillar. Cooperation on foreign policy and judicial affairs takes place essentially within an intergovernmental format (Keatinge, 1992; see also pp. 243-4 below).

The fourth respect in which the EC differs from traditional forms of interstate cooperation is that it has an extremely wide policy reach. The treaties set out in considerable detail just what the Community should be doing, and the substance of much of what it does is economic. The EEC Treaty established the goal of integration as the creation of a customs union and a common market, in which there would be a free flow of goods, capital, workers and services. A large part of the Community's later policy developments flowed from the need to fulfil this goal. In addition, the treaty made provision for a common policy on agriculture and transport. Over time the Community's policy scope has widened to meet new problems such as the environment and regional development. The central thrust of the Single Act was the "1992 programme", whose aim was the creation by the end of 1992 of an internal market in which economic exchange between states would resemble economic exchange within a state. This involved nothing less than the abolition of border controls, the harmonisation of technical standards, the creation of a framework in which banks and insurance companies may set up in any member state, liberalising the rules governing air transport, and achieving a degree of convergence in rates of indirect taxation. In addition, the Treaty of Maastricht envisages the creation of an economic and monetary union (Laffan, 1992). There is now a "European" dimension to most areas of public policy.

Fifth, the Community has a presence in world politics. Some 140 states are accredited to the Community, with embassies in Brussels. The Community's international role has led to development cooperation with third countries, a number of association agreements with European and non-European states, the common commercial policy that makes the Community an important actor in the General Agreement on Tariffs and Trade (GATT), and the system of European Political Cooperation described below. In addition, the Treaty of Maastricht envisages the development of a common foreign and security policy among the member states.

EC INSTITUTIONS AND IRELAND

The treaties lay down a lengthy and complicated system of policy making in the Community. In this section we will give a brief overview of the role of the institutions and the Irish presence in each of them.

The Commission
The Commission, originally conceived of as the EC's embryonic government, has 17 members drawn from the member states. A commissioner holds office for a term of four years. Each of the seven smaller states (including Ireland) nominates one member of the Commission while each of the largest five states has two commissioners. Since 1973, there have been six Irish commissioners (see Table 12.1).

Table 12.1: Ireland's EC commissioners, 1973-93

	Appointing government	Period	Portfolio
Patrick Hillery	FF	1973-76	Social Affairs
Richard Burke	FG-Lab	1977-80	Transport, Consumer Affairs, Taxation, Relations with EP
Michael O'Kennedy	FF	1981-82	President's delegate, Administration
Richard Burke	FF	1982-84	Greek renegotiation
Peter Sutherland	FG-Lab	1985-88	Competition
Ray MacSharry	FF	1989-92	CAP
Pádraig Flynn	FF	1993-	Social Affairs/Justice

Although in principle the incoming president of the Commission should have a say over national nominees, in practice the government of the day decides who should get the Irish nomination. Apart from Peter Sutherland, who was the Attorney General prior to his appointment, all Irish commissioners have been former ministers and senior politicians within their political parties. A commissioner is assigned a "portfolio" in the Commission, much like a cabinet minister at national level, and there is considerable competition for the plum positions. Peter Sutherland was given Competition when he joined the first Delors Commission in 1985, an important portfolio because of its significance for the 1992 programme. Agriculture, for which his successor Ray MacSharry was given responsibility in the second Delors Commission in 1989, is also much sought after because the CAP commands a sizeable proportion of the Community budget. Pádraig Flynn's brief includes Social Affairs—regarded as a middle-ranking portfolio—and the new policy area of Justice, entailing responsibility for cooperation between member states on immigration and policing of international terrorism and drug trafficking.

The Commission's powers are established in the treaties, which state that it must act in the "general interest of the Community" and that commissioners must be "completely independent in the performance of their duties". This emphasises the (theoretically) European orientation of the Commission. In practice, though, commissioners are dependent on their national governments for their original appointment and for any reappointment. Hence, they maintain contact with their respective governments and bring their local knowledge to bear at Commission meetings, but, even so, they do not represent the views of the national governments. The Commission has three main responsibilities in the policy process: first, initiation and drafting of policy programmes and legislative acts; second, acting as guardian of the treaties; and third, implementation of Community policies.

The Commission is given the responsibility under the treaties of preparing draft legislation for consideration by the Council of Ministers and the European Parliament. It is also responsible for preparing policy documents on all major issues, since it is concerned not only with individual items of legislation but also with the broad outline of Community policy. For example, the programme on the completion of the internal market by the end of 1992 was launched by the Cockfield white paper in 1985, which outlined some 300 legislative acts that needed to be adopted. Because the Commission has an interest in seeing that its legislative proposals have a reasonable chance of success in the Council and in Parliament, it engages in extensive consultations with working groups, advisory committees and Brussels-based interest groups from an early stage in the policy process. The Commission frequently sends questionnaires to the 12 national civil services to find out the main lines of national policy before outlining specific legislative proposals. Hence, national civil servants are drawn into the process from a very early stage.

In its capacity as guardian of the treaties, the Commission is responsible for ensuring that the member states implement, observe and enforce Community laws and that private companies adhere to competition policy and to legislation on mergers. Because of its limited resources, it has to rely on the member states to notify it when they take steps to give domestic effect to EC law. In the absence of such notification, the Commission will ask member states to speed up the process of implementation. If this does not translate into action the Commission increases the pressure by issuing what is known as a "reasoned opinion", and ultimately it may take a case to the Court of Justice. The enforcement of competition policy depends very much on complaints from private companies concerning unfair trading of one kind or another.

The implementation and enforcement of Community law is seen by the Commission as a central part of the 1992 programme and it is taking a far more active role in monitoring the implementation of EC law than heretofore. Ireland, which had a reasonably good record on implementation in the mid 1980s, then fell behind in the incorporation of legislation on the internal market directives—a Commission report of December 1991 showed that only Italy and Luxembourg then had a higher rate of non-implementation (Commission of the EC, 1991, p. 57). The reasons for this included the absence of legal expertise within Irish government departments, reliance on the over-burdened parliamentary draftsman, staff shortages in some departments and the sheer weight of the Community's legislative programme in the run-up to 1992. With pressure from the Commission to complete the "single market" programme by the start of 1993, Ireland's performance improved to fifth in the league table of implementation by the end of 1992 (*European Report*, 5 December 1992).

The European Council and the Council of Ministers
The Council of Ministers is at the centre of the legislative process and is the juncture where the Community meets with the national political systems. Although the Council is legally just one body, in practice the appropriate national ministers (such as Agriculture or Transport) meet to negotiate on Commission proposals that fall within the ambit of their responsibilities at national level. The Council of Foreign Ministers has responsibility for coordinating the work of the other Councils, and national ministers for Finance, Agriculture, Economic Affairs, Trade and Industry meet frequently with their counterparts from other countries in the Council. The Council of Ministers has a vast and complicated substructure made up of some 200 working parties and committees. The most important of these is the Committee of Permanent Representatives, known as COREPER, which is responsible for channelling proposed laws from working parties up to the Council for decision. During a typical working week in Brussels, Irish civil servants and officials from state-sponsored bodies will be attending working-party meetings in the Commission or in the Council. The frequency of flights from Dublin to Brussels underlines the impact of this additional layer of government on Irish government and politics.

COREPER, a committee barely mentioned in the treaties, is made up of the ambassadors of the member states to the Community. Each country has a permanent representation centre or an embassy in Brussels. The head of the Irish delegation is always a senior ambassador from the diplomatic service, but the staff of the representation centre is drawn not just from Foreign Affairs but also from the main domestic departments involved in Community business. The representation centre in Brussels is Ireland's largest embassy, with 46 staff, of whom 23 have diplomatic rank. The size of the delegation is testimony to the perpetual negotiations that characterise the Community and to the importance of the Community to Irish public policy. The Irish delegation is responsible for representing the country in Council meetings and for channelling the views and negotiating stances of the other member states back to Dublin. A period working in the centre is seen as useful experience both for the diplomatic corps and for the domestic civil service.

When a Commission proposal comes into the Council system, it is sent in the first instance to the relevant working party composed of national civil servants. The bulk of Community work is carried out at official level, at which about 80 per cent of all agreements are worked out. Here, officials begin the tortuous process of accumulating agreement, ironing out differences, reaching compromises and building coalitions. The Commission and the presidency of the Council (see next paragraph) play an important role in mediating between the competing interests of the negotiators. When a working party has reached as much agreement as is possible, the proposal is sent up to COREPER and ultimately to the Council of

Ministers. There are three different ways in which the Council can reach a decision: on the basis of a simple majority of its members, a qualified majority or unanimity. Decision rules are laid down by the treaties, although considerable discretion is left to those chairing meetings. A qualified majority consists of 54 votes out of a total of 76, which are distributed on a weighted basis among the member states, with Ireland having three votes.[1] Following the Single Act, voting (as opposed to taking no decision until there was unanimous agreement) became more frequent in the Council, and so issues are moving up the Council hierarchy with greater speed than hitherto. As we shall see later, this has consequences for the management of EC business in Ireland.

The presidency, which was originally envisaged simply as a convenient mechanism to provide chairpersons for Council meetings, has become an important source of political direction within the Community. Member states hold the presidency on a rotating basis for a period of six months. Since joining the EC, Ireland has held it on four occasions: in 1975, 1979, 1984 and 1990. One of the merits of the presidency system is that it allows small states to play a central role in the Community and provides a limited check on the dominance of the larger states. During the 1990 Irish presidency, Ireland hosted two meetings of the European Council dealing with the momentous changes in eastern and central Europe and with German unification. During the presidency, a small state such as Ireland can enhance its status and involvement in international politics. Successive Irish governments have taken the presidency very seriously, seeing it as an opportunity to run the affairs of the Community in a businesslike fashion so as to build up a stock of goodwill in other member states.

The European Council (which comprises the heads of government of the 12 member states) evolved from the practice of holding periodic summit meetings of the heads of governments and has now become a permanent feature of the Community's institutional landscape. The European Council received its first treaty recognition in the Single Act of 1986 and is endowed with a pivotal role in the Treaty of Maastricht, which gives it responsibility for providing the necessary impetus for the development of the projected European Union and says that it "shall define the general political guidelines thereof". The European Council has in fact been exercising this role in political leadership since the establishment of the European Monetary System (EMS) in 1979 and is the centre of political authority within the whole Community. European Councils take place at least twice each year, with one meeting in each of the countries holding the presidency of the Council.

The European Parliament
The European Parliament is the Community's representative institution. It was conceived as a consultative body rather than a legislature by the Community's founding fathers, and so it could only give its views on legislative proposals, though it could dismiss the entire Commission by a two-thirds majority of its members. In 1975, the Parliament gained some budgetary powers. After 1979, when for the first time it was directly elected, its search for new powers was

---

1. The distribution of votes is as follows: each of the largest four countries (Germany, Italy, France and the UK) has 10 votes; Spain has 8 votes; Belgium, Greece, the Netherlands and Portugal have 5 votes each; Denmark and Ireland have 3 votes each; and Luxembourg has 2 votes.

underpinned by its democratic credentials. During the negotiations on both the Single Act and the Maastricht Treaty, the Parliament pressed for increased powers for itself, both in the legislative process and in relation to the Community's international role, and it was partially successful on each occasion, so the Council now has to take more heed of its views. The accountability of the Commission to the Parliament was reinforced at Maastricht, as the Parliament will henceforth vote on the appointment of the Commission, and the life of a Commission is scheduled to be coterminous with that of the Parliament from 1995.

The Parliament has 518 members (rising to 567 as from the 1994 election), of whom 15 represent the Republic and a further three Northern Ireland. While 15 seats might not appear that many, Ireland is generously represented in per capita terms: each of the Irish MEPs represents some 235,000 voters whereas their Italian counterparts represent some 709,000 voters (Gallagher, Laver and Mair, 1992, p. 276). MEPs do not sit in national delegations but as part of political groupings that are largely based on Europe's traditional party families.

Table 12.2: Irish party membership of EP groups, 1993

EP group	Total	Ireland
Socialist Group	180	1 (Labour)
European People's Party	162	4 (FG)
Liberal Democratic and Reformist Group	45	2 (PD, T. J. Maher)
European Unitary Left	29	1 (Democratic Left)
Greens	27	-
European Democratic Alliance	21	6 (FF)
Rainbow Group	15	1 (Neil Blaney)
European Right	14	-
Left Unity	13	-
Non-attached	12	-
Total	518	15

Irish MEPs are members of six of the Parliament's groups (see Table 12.2). When Ireland became a member of the Community in 1973, its political parties had to decide which EP groups to join. This was relatively straightforward for Labour, given its history of involvement in the Socialist International, so it joined the Socialist group. For Fianna Fáil and Fine Gael the decision was more difficult—for one thing, they could not join the same group because of electoral competition at national level. Fine Gael joined the largest of the conservative groups, the European People's Party (the Christian Democrats). Participation in the European christian democratic movement has widened the horizons of Fine Gael and has brought its senior members and some of its activists into contact with their counterparts in other countries. Fianna Fáil was left without a political grouping for its first six months in the Parliament. The advantages of belonging to a group—such as secretarial and research backup, speaking time and membership of committees—forced it to link up with the French Gaullists in the European Democratic Alliance. This has been an uneasy partnership, and Fianna Fáil has from time to time considered other options. The alliance with the Gaullists is limited to the Parliament—there are no party-to-party links of the sort

found in the christian democratic group or the Socialists. The Progressive Democrats joined the Liberal grouping in 1989. The Workers' Party MEP initially
joined Left Unity, the more hardline of the two Communist groups, but left in
December 1991 to join the more moderate group, the Unitary Left; shortly afterwards, most of the party's parliamentarians (including its MEP) left the Workers' Party to form Democratic Left (see Dunphy, 1992).

The five-yearly direct elections to the European Parliament have added a
sometimes unwelcome contest to the Irish electoral cycle. The Republic is divided
into four large constituencies for the purposes of European elections: Leinster (4
seats), Dublin (4 seats), Connacht-Ulster (3 seats) and Munster (4 seats). (At the
first three EP elections, of 1979, 1984 and 1989, Munster had 5 seats and Leinster
only 3.) Election is by STV, like Dáil elections (see chapter 4), though this could
well change in the future since the Treaty of Maastricht reiterates the objective
of a common electoral system for all member states laid down in the original
treaties. A uniform system would probably involve some type of list system of PR
(see p. 68 above) rather than STV or the single-member constituency system used
in the UK. In 1979 and 1984, elections to the European Parliament came at mid-
point in the governments' terms of office. Although the political parties paid lip
service to "European issues" at the hustings, on each occasion the election agenda
focused on the performance of the government in power and the government parties lost seats. The 1989 election (see Table 12.3) coincided with a national general election, which helped to increase the turnout from 47 per cent in 1984 to 68
per cent (Hainsworth, 1992; Keatinge and Marsh, 1990).

Table 12.3: European Parliament elections in Ireland, 1984 and 1989

Party	EP election 1989 Votes (%)	Seats	EP election 1984 Votes (%)	Seats	General election 1989 Votes (%)
Fianna Fáil	31.5	6	39.2	8	44.1
Fine Gael	21.6	4	32.2	6	29.3
Progressive Democrats	11.9	1	-	-	5.5
Labour	9.5	1	8.4	0	9.5
Workers' Party	7.5	1	4.3	0	5.0
Others	17.9	2	15.9	1	6.6

Irish MEPs inhabit a rather different world from that of their counterparts in
the Dáil. They must travel a lot and spend two or three weeks of every month
outside Ireland at plenary sessions of the Parliament, attending committee meetings and dealing with the work of their political grouping. This makes it difficult for them to maintain contact with their very large constituencies and to
maintain a profile in their political parties. The EP undertakes most of its work
in 18 standing committees, which examine Commission proposals and Council
positions. Here reports and resolutions to be put to the full parliament are drawn
up. Since direct elections began in 1979 only one Irish MEP, Eileen Lemass, has
chaired a committee, which underlines how difficult it is to get access to the
spoils without a major presence in the core political groups. Irish MEPs tend to
concentrate their efforts on a very narrow range of committees. In the 1989-94 Parliament, for example, both the Agricultural Committee and the Regional Policy

Committee contained four Irish MEPs, leaving Ireland without representation on six committees, including the powerful Budgets Committee. As the European Parliament becomes a central actor in the politics of the Community, Irish political parties will have to take it more seriously.

The Court of Justice

The Court of Justice consists of 13 judges and six advocates-general. The latter investigate cases and give opinions to the court. The Single Act made provision for an additional court, the Court of First Instance, which may be regarded as a lower court. Since its inception, the Court of Justice has played a key role in providing the legal cement for integration. It has interpreted the treaties in a dynamic fashion rather than in a static manner, and its legal activism has strengthened the federal character of the Community. The Irish judicial system now feeds into the Community's legal order because of the principles of Community law outlined above. Irish courts may seek rulings from the Court of Justice on the correct interpretation of Community law, and the Irish government and private citizens may find themselves before the court in Luxembourg.

THE EC AND THE IRISH POLITICAL SYSTEM

The management of Community policy in Ireland

The EC's complex policy process is but the tip of an iceberg that extends into the national political and administrative systems. Each member state must service the Brussels machine, the constant round of meetings held under the auspices of the Commission and the Council. Outside the formal legislative process, there are frequent informal meetings at various levels. During each set of negotiations and at all stages, Irish civil servants prepare briefing material and instructions for those going to Brussels to represent the Irish interest. The preparation of positions requires consultation and coordination both within and between departments. Moreover, Irish interest groups will seek to influence those formulating the Irish position. The farming organisations are active on all issues dealing with the CAP, and the employers and trade unions now debate labour law issues within a European framework.

The expanding scope of EC policy has an increasingly important impact on the political agenda in Ireland. Since 1989, the Irish government has had to deal with the MacSharry proposals for fundamental reform of the CAP, and these in turn impinged on trade talks, notably the GATT round. Internal EC policies such as the CAP are now an issue in relations between the Community and the rest of the world. An Irish government must seek to protect the interests of Irish agriculture not only within the Agricultural Council in Brussels but also in a wider international context. The government has also had to formulate policies and negotiating strategies for dealing with the most recent round of constitution-building in the Community, which led to the 1992 Maastricht Treaty. This involved an attempt to get increased resources for the poorer parts of the Community and to manage the delicate issue of neutrality. As the 1990s progress, Ireland's political agenda will be more and more influenced by developments in European integration.

Community membership placed a very heavy burden on the Irish civil service, one for which it was ill prepared. There had been little strategic thinking on the need to adapt administrative structures to deal with Brussels. The first three years of membership were thus a learning period as Irish civil servants found their way around the Community labyrinth. The Department of Foreign Affairs, being responsible for keeping a watching brief over the flow of legislation through the policy process and over the main lines of policy development, is the centre of day-to-day and week-to-week coordination. It has built up an extensive expertise on the Community, giving it a key role in the management of EC business in Ireland, and its responsibility for EC matters means that its importance within the administrative system has increased. In addition, the extensive nature of the Community's policy interests brings a European dimension to most issues of public policy, and the domestic departments are responsible for those areas of EC policy that fall within their normal duties. EC matters, then, have been internalised or added on to the process of public policy making.

All member states of the Community have set in place coordinating mechanisms to manage EC business, in order to ensure that the Brussels machinery is adequately serviced and that national priorities are highlighted. There are a number of different levels of coordination in Ireland. The cabinet, as the arena at which major policy issues are resolved and legislation is processed before it goes to the Oireachtas, deals with EC matters much as it deals with domestic policy. From time to time cabinet sub-committees have been set up to deal with particular areas of EC policy, but there is no standing committee on Europe. The European Communities Committee, which predates Ireland's membership of the Community, is the main centre of interdepartmental coordination and is responsible for formulating national strategy and for deciding on priorities.

This committee was chaired by the Department of Foreign Affairs from 1973 until 1987, when its composition changed somewhat. In 1987, Máire Geoghegan-Quinn was appointed Minister of State in the Department of the Taoiseach with responsibility for coordinating EC matters. She was given the task of chairing the EC Committee, which then became known as the Geoghegan-Quinn Committee. This added the authority of the Taoiseach's department to the committee and changed it from being purely administrative. During 1988 its work was somewhat overshadowed by a Committee of Ministers and Secretaries established by the Taoiseach, Charles Haughey, to prepare Ireland's national development plan for EC monies and to run the "EUROPEN" campaign (signalling that Europe was "open for business") on 1992. Whereas the European Communities Committee used to meet every month, the Haughey committee met once a week for a period of a year. This amounted to the most sustained high-level attention given to EC matters since 1973. This committee ceased to exist when the development plan was submitted to Brussels, and it was replaced in 1989 by a ministerial group to plan the 1990 Irish presidency. In the latter half of the Haughey administration, the Geoghegan-Quinn Committee lost its role in policy formation and concentrated on the logistics of the presidency. At the end of the presidency, the work of both committees fell into abeyance and they were not replaced by a new mechanism to ensure political and administrative coordination—Ireland's responses to the intergovernmental conferences on political union and economic and monetary union were worked out in two ad hoc committees. When Albert

Reynolds became Taoiseach in February 1992, he gave Tom Kitt responsibility for EC coordination and reactivated the European Communities Committee, an arrangement that was continued after the formation of the Fianna Fáil-Labour coalition government in 1993.

Since 1973, then, Irish policy makers have adopted a very pragmatic approach to the development of the EC and to the promotion of Irish interests. For many years there was little sustained thinking about the overall development of the Community and the needs of small states within it. The decision by the Taoiseach, Charles Haughey, to ask the National Economic and Social Council (NESC) to undertake an extensive review of Ireland's membership of the Community, and the subsequent publication of the NESC report (NESC, 1989), marked an important move away from the ad hoc approach of the past. A further attempt to develop a more considered approach was the establishment in 1991 of an Institute of European Affairs, a non-governmental organisation that promotes interdisciplinary Irish research on EC matters.

The role of the Oireachtas
Following membership of the Community, the Oireachtas lost the "sole and exclusive power of making laws" bestowed on it by Article 15.2.1 of the constitution. Like other parliaments in the member states, the Oireachtas sought to qualify its loss of law-making powers by establishing mechanisms to oversee the government's behaviour in the Community. Besides being to some extent accountable through the traditional mechanisms of parliamentary questions and debates (see chapter 7), the government is also committed to placing a report on developments in the EC before the Houses of the Oireachtas twice yearly. These reports generally arrive too late for parliament to give serious consideration to the issues they raise.

In addition, in 1973 the Oireachtas established the Joint Committee on the Secondary Legislation of the European Communities, as a watchdog committee on EC matters. Since Ireland does not have a strong tradition of parliamentary committees, as we saw in chapter 7, this committee was something of a novelty at the outset. It had 25 members (18 deputies and seven senators), with the political parties represented in proportion to their strength in the Oireachtas. Its terms of reference allowed it to examine and report to the Oireachtas on Commission policy proposals, legislative proposals, EC laws, regulations made in Ireland under the European Communities Act 1972, and all other legal instruments that flow from EC membership.

The Joint Committee suffered from a number of constraints that impede the work of all parliamentary committees. Its terms of reference were very restricted, so it concentrated most of its energies on secondary legislation and did not maintain a systematic overview of the flow of Community policies through the legislative process. Nor could it examine major changes in the European landscape, notably the collapse of communism and German unification, that were certain to shape the Community of the 1990s. In the work that it actually did, it was hampered by a weakness of both financial and human resources. Neither the members nor the secretariat of the committee had the legal or technical expertise to examine many of the complex issues involved in EC law and policies; the many time pressures on Irish politicians do not allow them to develop the kind of expertise required for a thorough examination of EC policies.

In response to these difficulties the Fianna Fáil-Labour government established a new Joint Oireachtas Committee on Foreign Affairs in the spring of 1993. This subsumes the work of the previous Committee on Secondary Legislation, and also covers a much broader agenda encompassing the state's foreign relations as a whole. Its capacity to scrutinise policy will depend even more on acquiring adequate research resources, as well as on fostering a satisfactory relationship with government departments. The Irish pattern is not so unusual—all national parliaments are faced with considerable difficulties when attempting to hold their executives accountable for what they do in Brussels.

The EC and Irish foreign policy
If membership of the EC impinges to such an extent on what is conventionally thought of as the internal policy process, it might be asked whether we can expect a member state, especially a small one such as Ireland, to conduct its own foreign policy. Not surprisingly, this activity does indeed largely take place in a collective setting, the process of foreign policy coordination known as European Political Cooperation (EPC). Yet although this involves intensive consultations with the other 11 EC states, EPC is a less closely integrated form of policy making than exists in many other areas of Community activity. To move beyond consultation to expressing a common view ("declaratory policy") or taking common action, such as imposing economic sanctions, requires a consensus of all the member governments.

National foreign policies have thus resisted the logic of integration to a considerable extent. Decisions on Irish foreign policy still rest with the government in Dublin, and the whole apparatus of national diplomacy—the Department of Foreign Affairs and its embassies abroad—grew in both size and political importance following Ireland's accession to the Community (Keatinge, 1978). When it takes its turn for six months every six years in the rotating EC presidency, the Irish government is actually responsible for the management of EPC, giving both the Foreign Minister and the Taoiseach an opportunity to play the "statesman's" role in public. Routine access to their counterparts in the major European states, on top of the vastly enhanced information available to the Department of Foreign Affairs, is arguably as much a national resource as it is a form of exposure to external influences. Moreover, in so far as EPC positions on major international issues are consistent with Ireland's interests and values, if they are advanced on behalf of 325 million people they are likely to bear more weight than statements on behalf of a society of 3.5 million (Keatinge, 1991).

At this level of generalisation it may seem that, so far, an acceptable balance has been found between the way in which Irish governments see their national foreign policies and the rather loosely framed obligations of EPC. This may not remain the case, though. Irish governments arrive at many foreign policy decisions with the minimum input from political parties, and enjoyed relatively large domestic freedom of manoeuvre so long as the Oireachtas was the only western European parliament without a standing foreign affairs committee. But the Treaty of Maastricht, by introducing the possibility of a European defence policy, may clash with a long standing element of Irish foreign policy—the stance of neutrality. We shall return to this question at the end of the chapter.

Nevertheless, Ireland's participation in EPC over the last 20 years does on the whole support the proposition that opportunities to pursue foreign policy objectives were enhanced by EC membership. Some examples may illustrate the point. So far as East-West relations were concerned, the EC states jointly were an important positive influence in the Conference on Security and Cooperation in Europe (the "Helsinki process"), which maintained a modicum of diplomatic engagement with the USSR during the tension of the "new cold war" of the early 1980s. In the Middle East, the Irish government's position on the Arab-Israeli conflict was mirrored in the EC's gradual receptiveness to the Palestinian case. For most of this period Ireland remained, as it had been before joining the EC, a consistent and credible contributor to United Nations peace-keeping operations, and governments developed a more substantial and systematic approach to relations with the third world (Holmes, Rees and Whelan, 1993).

This is not to suggest that Ireland's policy (or that of the EC as a whole) was an unequivocal success story. Trying to influence the unruly game of international politics is best approached in the Olympic spirit—"it is not to have won but to have taken part". Indeed, for a small state taking part may be what it really is all about. Ireland's activism on the question of sanctions against South Africa was resisted by other EC governments, but it answered at least some of the demands of the anti-apartheid lobby at home (Laffan, 1988).

IRELAND AND THE NEW INTERNATIONAL SYSTEM

Since the autumn of 1989, a new global political system has been taking shape in the wake of the implosion of the eastern bloc. This system is still in a state of unusual flux, even by the standards of international politics. The system is no longer bipolar, with a central pattern of antagonism between two military superpowers competing in ideological rhetoric and political influence on a global scale. That competition had been highly organised, and was conducive to a degree of stability that was easy to take for granted. The emerging system, on the other hand, is characterised by major uncertainties: the propensity of the former Soviet Union to fragment further, and possibly violently; the capacity and will of the USA to play the role of "global policeman"; and the proliferation of military technology of all sorts, especially weapons of mass destruction.

The extent of change in Ireland's external environment at this level has been greater than at any time since the immediate aftermath of the second world war. However, there is one important difference between these two transitional phases. In the late 1940s the complex networks of multilateral organisations— the UN and its agencies, alliance systems, and economic institutions—were at a formative stage, as were the conventions of modern multilateral diplomacy. Now they are mature, and while this maturity has eased the current transition there remains a major task of adaptation of institutions and attitudes alike.

The European Community is a central element in all this, and thus Ireland is much more directly involved in the making of this system than was the case in the late 1940s. One of the major decisions was even formally endorsed in Dublin, when Ireland held the presidency of the EC Council during the first six months of

1990. The context was the extraordinarily rapid reunification of Germany, itself marking a significant change in the distribution of power both in European and in global terms. Apprehensions about the re-emergence of the "German question" were met by the convening of an intergovernmental conference on political union, which in parallel with a similar conference on economic and monetary union negotiated the Maastricht Treaty.

Ratifying this required a change in the constitution, and was the subject of a referendum on 18 June 1992 (Holmes, 1993). This followed the unexpected rejection of the treaty by the Danish electorate two weeks earlier. The Danish vote called into question the ultimate fate of the treaty and further complicated what was already a confused Irish debate. The debate centred on two value issues—abortion and neutrality—as well as on economic issues. The government had inserted a protocol in the treaty, in order to protect Ireland's constitutional ban on abortion (Article 40.3.3), but the Supreme Court's subsequent interpretation of that Article in the "X" case (see p. 59 above) led to confusion about the meaning and remit of the protocol. Both feminist and anti-abortion lobbies opposed the treaty, alongside traditional nationalists and supporters of neutrality. On the other side was almost the whole political establishment (with the exception of Democratic Left, the Workers' Party and the Green Party) and the major economic interests.

The turnout of 57 per cent was noticeably higher than that in the SEA referendum, while the distribution of votes cast was similar, with 69 per cent in favour and 31 per cent against (see appendix 2h). In the circumstances this was a strong endorsement of Ireland's participation in the mainstream of European integration. In the event neither abortion nor neutrality proved to be decisive, but the difficulty for governments of making something as complicated as the Maastricht Treaty intelligible to the voters was plain to see.

A second Danish referendum in May 1993 reversed Denmark's initial rejection of the treaty, thus reviving the prospects for "European Union", albeit in circumstances where that rather ambiguous concept had lost much credibility. Against a background of worsening recession and civil war in Bosnia, the main points of substance in the Maastricht Treaty—economic and monetary union and a common foreign and security policy—seemed further away than ever. Even the existing arrangements for exchange rate stability were exposed in currency crises in the autumn of 1992 and the summer of 1993.

Nevertheless, the proposed transition from Community to Union raises three points of a speculative nature, which are likely to recur over the coming years. They derive from the prospect of further changes, whether contained in the treaty itself, in the enlargement of membership, or deriving from the evolution of the new global system; indeed, provision is made in the treaty for another intergovernmental conference to be convened in 1996.

The first question is a very general one, which up to now has been largely avoided in Irish debate on EC membership: is the European Union a decisive step closer to the creation of a single federal state? If it were, the prospect of a radical transformation of the Irish political system would be on the horizon. At present the Maastricht Treaty seems to fall well short of the federal mark, and it may be some years before its effects can be accurately gauged (Keatinge, 1992). Nevertheless, the long-running British controversy over the "f" word could well make an appearance on the Irish political agenda before long, with suitable adjustments to cater for the different political culture.

A second issue is the continuing impact of European integration on Irish politics. Even if Europe does not move in a federal direction, national and European politics are likely to become more intertwined in the 1990s. National budgetary policy will be greatly influenced by the goal of striving to meet the criteria established for membership of the Economic and Monetary Union. A major devaluation of the Irish pound at the end of January 1993 demonstrated the difficulty of sustaining a European orientation when British economic policy was moving in another direction. There is also the question of how a weak parliamentary system can hold Irish representatives in the Council accountable as Brussels becomes involved in a wider range of policies. Moreover, the use of the principle of "subsidiarity" (meaning that policy should be executed at the lowest effective level of government) in European politics will draw attention to the centralised nature of the Irish system of government. In the post-Maastricht era it is likely, therefore, that the Irish political system, or, to be more precise, the parties in parliament, will have to pay more attention to the state's external environment.

Although there are differences among the political parties in their attitudes towards European integration, a distinctive Irish approach is discernible. Ireland's experience as a small, peripheral, less developed economy, together with its traditional policy of neutrality, shapes attitudes towards integration. The defence of the CAP, the politics of redistribution and the need to ensure that EC laws are appropriate to Irish circumstances dominate Ireland's EC agenda. A recurring concern in Ireland's European policy is the need to ensure that political integration advances on the basis of balanced economic integration. Irish policy makers adopt a strongly federalist approach towards financial transfers from the richer to the poorer parts of the Community, favouring a much larger EC budget than exists at present.

Irish attitudes are less federalist concerning institutional development in the Community. Ireland has never lent its support to very significant increases in the powers of the European Parliament. The Council of Ministers is seen as the main arena for the protection of national interests; the presence of one Irish minister in the Council is regarded as a source of more influence than 15 MEPs in a parliament of 518 or 567. This said, Fine Gael and the Progressive Democrats tend to espouse more federalist policies than their counterparts in either Fianna Fáil or the Labour Party. Labour party activists and a number of TDs remain sceptical about the benefits of European integration for Ireland. Fianna Fáil, when in opposition, tends to be cautious about a deepening of integration. The smaller Dáil parties (other than the PDs) opposed ratification of the Maastricht Treaty, as we have mentioned, though this represented doubts about that particular treaty rather than opposition to Ireland's membership of the Community per se.

The Irish electorate has endorsed Ireland's membership of the Community and major developments in European integration on the three occasions when referendums were held to allow for constitutional change to accommodate Euro-politics. Acceptance of Ireland's involvement in European integration is now well rooted in the Irish body politic. Public support for the idea of European unity in principle has generally been higher in Ireland than in the EC as a whole—for example, in

12 / IRELAND IN INTERNATIONAL AFFAIRS

Patrick Keatinge and Brigid Laffan

Ireland is described in Article 5 of the constitution as a "sovereign, independent, democratic state". This reference to the state's legal right to conduct its own affairs without outside interference hardly stands up as an adequate description of the Irish state's political relationship with the rest of the world. For that purpose it makes more sense to adapt the terminology often used by economists, and to think of Ireland as a "small open polity".

Such an approach reminds us that the national political system is not self-contained, but is subject to complex influences from its external environment. In the first part of this chapter we identify the main characteristics of that environment, and show how changes at this "macro-political" level have affected Ireland's political development during the first 70 years of the state's existence. A significant example is the evolution of Ireland's single most important diplomatic relationship, that with the United Kingdom. This "special relationship" is now mediated partly through the European Community (EC) and partly through another unique international arrangement, set up under the Anglo-Irish Agreement of 1985.

One particular element in this international setting merits a more detailed analysis. The European Community, which Ireland joined in 1973, is a unique and complex political system in its own right. Its influence on its members is pervasive. EC membership is not just a "foreign policy" issue; in many respects it is an extension of national (or "domestic") politics. The second part of this chapter thus concentrates on the Community's impact on Irish political activity, and on the way in which Ireland's European policy is formed.

We also ask whether Ireland really has a "foreign policy", in the sense implied in the constitutional claim to independence quoted above. To what extent, and employing what means, do Irish governments pursue their values and interests in international politics in general? We shall see that much of this activity now takes place in conjunction with other EC states and through the complex web of multilateral networks that have been developed since the second world war. Finally, we look at the way in which recent changes in the external environment are affecting the European Community and are therefore impinging on Ireland. This raises questions about the viability of specific policies, such as neutrality, and even about the continued existence of the "sovereign, independent state".

THE EXTERNAL ENVIRONMENT

Any state's external environment consists of all other states together with the nature of the international system formed by their relationships. Writers in the field of international relations have disagreed when it comes to identifying the most important characteristics of the international system (Little and Smith,

the spring of 1993, 31 per cent of respondents in Ireland, compared with 25 per cent of all EC respondents, were "very much for efforts being made to unify western Europe" (*Eurobarometer* no. 39, June 1993, p. A15). However, the Irish public shares governmental reservations about increasing the power of the European Parliament; in the same poll, only 42 per cent of Irish respondents, compared with 50 per cent in the EC as a whole, wanted the EP to play a more important role within the EC (p. A42).

A third issue is the more sharply focused debate on neutrality. Not that Irish neutrality itself can be said to be a sharply focused concept (Keatinge, 1984); indeed, in the most detailed study made to date, applying rigorous criteria, it is interpreted as "non-belligerence" at best, and at worst an exercise in self-delusion (Salmon, 1989). Yet it clearly retains an important place in Irish political culture (Marsh, 1992), whether it is associated with quasi-pacifist or with nationalist values. In the emerging international system the basis of neutrality policy, like most other diplomatic orientations coloured by the cold war, is being subjected to reappraisal. This is true of those European neutrals, such as Austria, Finland, Sweden and Switzerland, which have had a more clearly defined (and more militarised) policy than Ireland; now they too are faced with the need to reconcile the forces of economic interdependence with a different set of security challenges and a multilateral approach to security commitments (Keatinge, 1993). This dilemma highlights the precarious grasp of small states on the substance, rather than the form, of independent statehood. Yet a Europe which is to an increasing extent composed of small states may prove to be less amenable to further integration than the familiar and more homogenous western Europe of the cold war era.

CONCLUSION: A SMALL OPEN POLITY

Ireland's external environment has been an important influence on the state's political development. In the turbulent international system up to the end of the second world war the British connection provided the main focus, in which the new state's political independence was demonstrated by the policy of neutrality during the war. After 1945 Ireland was gradually drawn into a broader, more stable and increasingly interdependent international system. The eruption of political violence in Northern Ireland ensured a continuing emphasis on Anglo-Irish relations, which entered a new phase with the Agreement of 1985. Nevertheless, involvement in west European integration now represents the most significant source of external influence on the Irish state.

Membership of the European Community since 1973 has had a major impact on the political life of Ireland. The EC differs from traditional interstate cooperation because its founders aspired to create a new political entity, a United States of Europe, and so member states agree to pool their sovereignty over a wide range of public policy within a system of law that interacts directly with national legal systems. Ireland, along with the other EC members, has representation in the main Community institutions: the Council of Ministers, the Commission, the European Parliament and the Court of Justice. Irish trade unions, employer groups, producer groups and many other representative organisations see Brussels as an important arena for politics. EC membership has made it even more difficult than before for the Oireachtas to hold the executive accountable for its actions.

Since 1989, there has been a major change in the state's external environment, with the unexpected end of the relatively stable bipolar system of the cold war era. So far this has led to a greater emphasis on the process of European integration, in the form of the Maastricht Treaty, which was endorsed by the Irish electorate in June 1992. Questions about the nature of European Union, the effects of integration on Irish politics, and the future of neutrality are being raised in the new, and much less stable, world system. In order to understand the future evolution of Irish politics, it will be essential to see the state as a "small open polity".

REFERENCES AND FURTHER READING

Arthur, Paul, 1992. "The Brooke initiative", *Irish Political Studies* 7, pp. 111-15.
Arthur, Paul, 1993. "The Mayhew talks 1992", *Irish Political Studies* 8, pp. 138-43.
Cochrane, Feargal, 1993. "Progressive or regressive? The Anglo-Irish Agreement as a dynamic in the Northern Ireland polity", *Irish Political Studies* 8, pp. 1-20.
Commission of the EC, 1991. *Report on the Implementation of Measures for Completing the Internal Market*, 2491 final, 19 December. Brussels: Commission of the European Communities.
Dunphy, Richard, 1992. "The Workers' Party and Europe: trajectory of an idea", *Irish Political Studies* 7, pp. 21-39.
Fisk, Robert, 1983. *In Time of War: Ireland, Ulster and the Price of Neutrality 1939-1945*. London: Andre Deutsch.
FitzGerald, Garret, 1991. *All in a Life: an Autobiography*. Dublin: Gill and Macmillan.
Gallagher, Michael, 1988. "The Single European Act referendum", *Irish Political Studies* 3, pp. 77-82.
Gallagher, Michael, Michael Laver and Peter Mair, 1992. *Representative Government in Western Europe*. New York: McGraw-Hill.
Guelke, Adrian, 1988. *Northern Ireland: the International Perspective*. Dublin: Gill and Macmillan.
Hainsworth, Paul (ed.), 1992. *Breaking and Preserving the Mould: the Third Direct Elections to the European Parliament (1989)—the Irish Republic and Northern Ireland*. Belfast and Jordanstown: Policy Research Institute.
Holmes, Michael, 1993. "The Maastricht Treaty referendum of June 1992", *Irish Political Studies* 8, pp. 105-10.
Holmes, Michael, Nicholas Rees and Bernadette Whelan, 1993. *The Poor Relation: Irish Foreign Policy and the Third World*. Dublin: Trócaire.
Keatinge, Patrick, 1978. *A Place Among the Nations: Issues of Irish Foreign Policy*. Dublin: Institute of Public Administration.
Keatinge, Patrick, 1984. *A Singular Stance: Irish Neutrality in the 1980s*. Dublin: Institute of Public Administration.
Keatinge, Patrick, 1986. "Unequal sovereigns: the diplomatic dimension of Anglo-Irish relations", pp. 139-60 in P. J. Drudy (ed.), *Ireland and Britain since 1922*. Cambridge: Cambridge University Press.
Keatinge, Patrick (ed.), 1991. *Ireland and EC Membership Evaluated*. London: Pinter.
Keatinge, Patrick (ed.), 1992. *Maastricht and Ireland: what the Treaty Means*. Dublin: Institute of European Affairs.
Keatinge, Patrick, 1993. "Ireland and European neutrality after the cold war", pp. 157-75 in Ronald J. Hill and Michael Marsh (eds), *Modern Irish Democracy*. Dublin: Irish Academic Press.
Keatinge, Patrick and Michael Marsh, 1990. "The European Parliament election", pp. 131-47 in Michael Gallagher and Richard Sinnott (eds), *How Ireland Voted 1989*. Galway: Centre for the Study of Irish Elections and PSAI Press.

Laffan, Brigid, 1988. *Ireland and South Africa: Irish Government Policy in the 1980s.* Dublin: Trócaire.

Laffan, Brigid, 1992. *Integration and Cooperation in Europe.* London: Routledge.

Little, Richard and Michael Smith (eds), 1991. *Perspectives on World Politics,* 2nd ed. London: Routledge.

McCabe, Ian, 1991. *A Diplomatic History of Ireland, 1948-49: the Republic, the Commonwealth, and NATO.* Dublin: Irish Academic Press.

McGarry, John and Brendan O'Leary (eds), 1990. *The Future of Northern Ireland.* Oxford: Clarendon Press.

Marsh, Michael, 1992. *Irish Public Opinion on Neutrality and European Union.* Dublin: Institute of European Affairs, Occasional Paper 1.

NESC, 1989. *Ireland in the European Community: Performance, Prospects and Strategy.* Dublin: National Economic and Social Council, Report no. 88.

Nugent, Neill, 1991. *The Government and Politics of the European Community,* 2nd ed. London: Macmillan.

Pinder, John, 1991. European Community: the Building of a Union. Oxford: Oxford University Press.

Salmon, Trevor, 1989. *Unneutral Ireland: an Ambivalent and Unique Security Policy.* Oxford: Oxford University Press.

13 / DEMOCRATIC POLITICS IN INDEPENDENT IRELAND

Tom Garvin

Having considered the mechanics of Irish politics in considerable detail, it is important for us to stand back and look critically at the achievements of the Irish state. To what extent was the promise of the new state fulfilled? What future lies in store in the new Europe for an Ireland in whose history a nationalist struggle played so important a part?

THE PURSUIT OF DEMOCRACY

Modern Irish democracy is the result of a long process of political agitation, argument and conflict. In this, it is typical of the democracies that have emerged, mainly in the west, in the past two hundred years. Irish democracy emerged as a result of a revolution which occurred between 1879 and 1923, the final, violent phase being in the last decade of this period. This revolution was a struggle for national independence rather than a classic social revolution as that of France after 1789 is often claimed to have been and as that of Russia between 1917 and 1921 certainly was. It was an attempt to assert, by a mixture of political agitation, propaganda and armed struggle, the national identity and political independence of an Ireland conceived of, often rather vaguely, as being both republican and democratic. The analogy commonly used by the Irish leaders themselves was the American Revolution of 1776-83. Other possible analogues are the Finnish campaign for national independence after the collapse of tsarism, the Baltic states' escape from Soviet rule in 1989-90 or the insurgencies against British, French and Portuguese power in Africa and Asia in the generation after the second world war.

The Irish civil war of 1922-23 had a profound impact on the form post-independence public life was to take. It was nominally fought over the issues of republicanism and democracy, and Irish politics for a generation after independence came to centre as much on a profound set of constitutional questions concerning the right relationships between the state and the citizenry as over questions of economic well-being, church versus state issues, or the interests of various sections of society. Nominally, the conflict was between a new British dominion, the Irish Free State, and a Republic of Ireland which had been formally brought into existence by the first Dáil in January 1919 (Curran, 1980; Thompson, 1969; Garvin, 1981; Garvin, 1988; Mair, 1987; Hopkinson, 1988).

Lloyd George and the Irish lawyers alike had spotted that the Irish-language rendering of the title "Republic of Ireland" used by the first Dáil was not the *Poblacht na hÉireann* of the 1916 Proclamation, but rather *Saorstát Éireann*, a newer coinage. The official notepaper used by de Valera in giving the 1921 plenipotentiaries their letters of credence during the treaty negotiations was headed *Saorstát Éireann/Respublica Hibernica*. In the Irish language, continuity of nomenclature survived the 1921-22 constitutional shift from Republic of Ireland to Irish Free State (Kennedy Papers, P4/196). Both sides in the civil war saw themselves as republican and democratic, yet they killed each other over different interpretations of these terms.

A brief survey of the two key words *democracy* and *republicanism*, so often invoked and so little examined in Irish public life, is appropriate before offering a general assessment of the Irish record of democratic and republican government two generations after independence.

Democracy

Democracy is a form of government that has been, historically, very rare. It is only in the past hundred years that a significant proportion of mankind has come to be governed by democratic or quasi-democratic regimes. Furthermore, democracy has commonly proved to be a fragile plant and has often failed. The destruction of the infant Russian democracy by Lenin in January 1918 and Hitler's murder of the Weimar democracy in 1933 are two of the better-known failures. Oligarchic government has been the norm for post-tribal mankind over millennia.

Formidable intellectual enemies have historically ranged themselves against the idea of popular government. The intellectual origins of modern fascism and authoritarian communism are in the heart of nineteenth century European culture. Anti-democratic thought has very old roots. Direct democracy, as tentatively experimented with in ancient Athens, was looked upon unfavourably by the founders of political theory. Plato and Thucydides saw the democracy of Athens, with much justification, as going hand in hand with greed and the imperialist aggression of the armed, land-hungry poor who manned the navy. Plato's condemnation of democracy as the rule of the unwise has echoed down the centuries, as has Aristotle's more measured and possibly more justified scepticism about the pure forms of democracy and aristocracy alike (Thucydides, 1910; Plato, 1960; Klosko, 1986; Aristotle, 1962).

The representative democracies that have evolved in western Europe and its new-world extensions since 1776 are intellectually related to, but structurally quite different from, the small-scale direct democracies of the classical era. The crucial difference is one of scale. Modern democracies have populations of millions, whereas in ancient Greece the privileged band of voting citizens was commonly less than 10,000. Large-scale representative democracy in our time has somewhat oligarchical tendencies and goes hand in hand with a private, commercialised economic order which also tends to favour the few over the many. However, it is relatively the most egalitarian and genuinely popular type of political system ever to evolve in the world, and is far more so than its most conspicuous recent challenger, Marxist-Leninist oligarchical communism, which has now largely disappeared.

Modern representative democracy has several historical roots. One is the medieval tradition of representative assemblies which survived the absolutist era to re-emerge in the late eighteenth century. Another important source was a tradition of political thought that can loosely, but usefully, be described as *republicanism*. A third source is the tradition of philosophical individualism sometimes labelled liberalism, but not quite coterminous with that word (Huntington, 1968, pp. 93-140; Montesquieu, 1989).

Republicanism

In Ireland, republicanism has come to refer not just to a particular form of political organisation but to a strongly nationalist political movement and ideology. This use of the term is rather parochial; it does, of course, have a broader meaning in the western intellectual tradition. Modern European and American republicanism was heavily influenced by the classical experience of Greece and Rome, by the writings of the Renaissance and by the English and French Enlightenments. It came to involve the idea of the law-bound polity, where both rulers and ruled were equally subject to the laws. Another central republican idea was the making of government policy in public, as distinct from behind closed doors: the creation of a public space in which citizens could engage in political participation, rather than being obedient and passive subjects and courtiers of an absolute monarch (Barker, 1951).

Republics need not be democratic. An aristocratic republic, such as that of eighteenth century Poland, where only the nobility or the rich have the vote, is perfectly feasible and has often occurred historically. A democratic republic, where the right of participation in political life is shared by all adults, is merely one of several possibilities. The aristocratic and democratic options can usefully be seen as "right" and "left" versions respectively of republicanism. Parenthetically, a state such as the modern United Kingdom or the Kingdom of Denmark, where the monarch reigns but does not rule, is best described, not as a monarchy, but as a "crowned republic".

"Left" or democratic republicanism has tended to win out in the last century in the west. Increasing democratisation and the development of large, popular electoral organisations such as political parties and single interest organisations have ensured this. A general move away from British-style plurality electoral systems to proportional representation and run-off ballot systems has also been part of this general long-term process (see chapter 4). The growing use of referendums to settle issues is an important democratic development.

Another central republican idea was that of the citizen as moral actor in the polity, an idea that has classical roots, and which has been put forward by political thinkers such as Hannah Arendt in the modern era. In practice, of course, the mundane activity of counting voters' heads in elections involving the suffrages of millions has become the norm in modern democracies. The older republican tradition has, however, survived, often as an inchoate, instinctive sense of the inadequacy of simple vote-counting as a basis for civic life. The concept of the fully participant citizen survives, for example, in the concept of trial by jury, in traditions of political activism and organisational agitation, in the institution of the referendum and in even the little thought-of but vital activity of discussing political events and what has been seen in the papers, heard on radio or seen on television with one's fellow citizens in a routine and daily fashion.

DEMOCRACY AND REPUBLICANISM IN INDEPENDENT IRELAND

For Ireland, the democratisation of the franchise coincided with the coming of independence for most of the island in 1922. The election of August 1923 was the first to be fought on the basis of a universal franchise in Ireland whose specific purpose was to decide which group of people was to form a government, as distinct from deciding which particular hundred mendicants would be sent to Westminster. As suggested earlier, the civil war of 1922-23 had divided the Sinn Féin movement into those who accepted and those who rejected a compromise agreement with London, involving a constitutional settlement for the 26 counties which was republican and democratic in essence but which retained much of the symbolism of monarchy in an uneasy blend with that of popular sovereignty (Kohn, 1932).

Although few admitted it publicly, neither side had any real idea what to do about Northern Ireland, whose existence predated the Irish Free State. Tacitly, it came to be set aside as unfinished business, or even to be written off until relatively recently. De Valera used it as a stick with which to beat the Cumann na nGaedheal government, but ended up conclusively demonstrating that he had no idea what to do about it either (Bowman, 1982). The party system came to divide republican moralists from crypto-republican pro-Treatyites, a general post-revolutionary pragmatism eventually winning an undeclared but overwhelming victory as the first generation of leaders died out and were replaced by younger and clearly post-revolutionary men and women (Cohan, 1972).

The new state had some oligarchical trappings, in particular the existence of special Dáil seats for graduates, but these were soon swept away in favour of formal electoral democracy. In local government, however, the trend was to some extent the other way; local democracy was seen as inefficient and corrupt, and a bureaucratisation of local government occurred, apparently with the acquiescence of local people. The introduction of the bureaucratic county manager system more or less coincided with the abolition of the property qualification for the local franchise in 1934. Irish political culture has commonly blended authoritarian and democratic forms in a characteristic way (see chapter 2), and the restructuring of local government illustrates this rather well (Mansergh, 1934).

The elimination, in 1928, of provisions for popular initiative and referendum illustrates another tendency for native governments to retreat shamefacedly to the more authoritarian traditions of pre-independence Ireland under pressure of party rivalries and fear of public disorder. The idealistic intentions which lay behind the extern ministry idea, by which the Dáil could have some input into government, were soon abandoned as power was centralised in the cabinet and the prime minister and party lines hardened. The referendum, but not the initiative, was restored in 1937 by de Valera's constitution. Power continued to be concentrated in the Taoiseach and the cabinet (see chapters 3 and 9).

In independent Ireland, fear of insurgency has, historically, discouraged moves towards truly republican, that is, open and law-bound, government. The activities of the IRA and similar anti-democratic organisations have given governments the excuse to step around the normal legal processes under both the 1922 and 1937 constitutions. The problem was recognised by government advisors at the very beginning. In July 1923, Senator J. G. Douglas begged the Attorney General to persuade the government, now that it had won its war, to move from the principle of militarily-enforced obedience to that of voluntary civic compliance as quickly as possible:

All the time that arrests and imprisonments, etc. were taking place as a result of the armed resistance to the Government it has been a source of great satisfaction to me, and I am sure to you also, that slowly and steadily the Government were building up a structure of order which was winning the respect of the people. The sending out of an unarmed police force was an act of courage and wisdom on the part of the

Government, and I believe did a good deal to add to public confidence and hope for the future. The promised creation of a new judiciary at an early date together with an unarmed police force with only the military in case of extreme disorder or organised violence, all pointed towards a speedy establishment of an Irish State ... My idea is that the aim of the Government should be to slowly and steadily withdraw the military rule with its abnormal powers and substitute the civil authority acting strictly in the spirit of the Constitution (Kennedy Papers, P4/1002).

Unfortunately, a certain tendency toward authoritarian law-enforcement and censorship in the name of keeping public order and also as a way of furthering state policy has persisted in Irish public life and detracts somewhat from the republican character of Irish political institutions even today, although the tradition has admittedly weakened as the judiciary has begun to flex its muscles and as Irish public opinion has become more articulate. By and large, the Republic's record on civil rights has been good.

The growing role of the judges has been important. Since the 1960s, the courts have shown an increased willingness to assert not only the human rights enshrined rather conditionally in the 1937 constitution but also unasserted rights which the judges have derived from them. A tradition of judicial review inspired by the American prototype has grown up to balance the older reliance on executive power, as we saw in chapter 3. The EC's Court of Justice has begun to perform a similar function in recent years. The Republic has gradually moved away from the British tradition of parliamentary supremacy and executive discretion and towards a more American and mainland European pattern of "judge-made law" which is more consonant with the principle of the supremacy of the constitution over parliament, executive and judiciary alike (see Chubb, 1991).

ELECTORAL DEMOCRACY IN IRELAND

The most important long-term general check on authoritarian tendencies in both state and church has, however, turned out to be the mechanism of electoral democracy. The founders of the state do not seem to have completely appreciated the importance of the new party organisations which were rising from the ruins of British rule. Certain provisions of both the 1922 and 1937 constitutions attempted to ignore the reality of party power. Highly disciplined organisations controlling the votes of substantial proportions of a newly enfranchised electorate installed themselves in local councils, took over the Dáil and penetrated the legal and teaching professions, the post office and other public and private organisations in the early decades.

The coming of the mass, voter-directed and disciplined political party, exemplified in particular by Fianna Fáil, surprised and dismayed some. The framers of the 1922 constitution had anticipated that PR-STV would generate a large number of small parties. However, Ireland was spared the fragmentation that plagued the parliaments of France, Germany and eastern Europe in the inter-war years. In turn, the new parties owed the adeptness of their activists at fighting elections to a tradition of public contestation which dated back to Daniel O'Connell (Carty, 1981; Garvin, 1981).

The securing of the adhesion of the bulk of the anti-Treaty forces to the institutions of the state in the form of Fianna Fáil in 1927 represented a real breakthrough in the process of legitimising the new system. It was an extraordinary triumph for William Cosgrave's statesmanship, and one that is frequently under-rated. Were it not for this tacit and sullen acceptance of Free State democracy by de Valera, the long-term viability of democratic rule in Ireland would have been seriously menaced, and authoritarian tendencies would have been greatly en-couraged. The years 1922-23, 1927, 1932 and 1937 are crucial in the evolution of Irish democracy. The armed defence of the majority's right to decide who was to govern, the acceptance of majoritarianism by the defeated minority in 1927, the transformation of that minority into a ruling majority, and the enactment of de Valera's non-Commonwealth constitution are all events that were not inevitable. The inexperienced politicians of the fledgling democracy managed to pass the test each time. Looked upon from a long historical perspective, the emergence and consolidation of what became the Republic of Ireland in 1949 is a formidable achievement; it constitutes the first regime ever to emerge in Ireland in which no significant group disputed its right to rule (Prager, 1986).

Fianna Fáil became the master of the applied science of winning elections very early in its history. Most of the vote-managing techniques which have fascinated observers of Irish politics were perfected by the party before 1932. A despairing private letter from a Cumann na nGaedheal activist in Waterford in 1932 mourned the defeat of the government party, but expressed admiration for the unrivalled efficiency of the Fianna Fáil electoral machine, against which Cumann na nGaedheal was helpless. The anti-Treatyites had lost the war but won the peace by means of a "wonderfully worked Organised Campaign", he said: "Outside the school wall [at Ballyduff] were two FF Cars and posters all over them, telling us to vote for Gould[ing], Little and Mansfield ... there were two FF cars plying to and from the booth laden with voters, most of them illiterate and well tutored how to vote" (Mulcahy Papers, P7B/89 (53)). Fianna Fáil, he re-ported, had systematic lists of voters, and had partitioned the constituency so as to maximise local loyalties and party preferences in a style that has now become a textbook classic (Sacks, 1976; Bax, 1976). Similar stories could have been told of most other counties, and the Fianna Fáil challenge forced other parties to imitate it; Fine Gael, Labour and other parties all had to take lessons from de Valera's party.

POLICY MAKING IN A SMALL DEMOCRACY

Party democracy in a country as small as the Republic of Ireland has always been liable to overwhelm the structures of impersonal bureaucratic administration in favour of a generalised spoils system, as happened in the United States in 1828 with the advent of Jacksonian democracy. In Ireland, the separation of function between politician and civil servant has been maintained, but it has often been en-dangered. A confusion of the two roles was evident in the minds of the early Sinn Féiners. The famous 1919 oath to the Republic itself refers to Dáil Éireann as the government (though it was in reality a parliament, not a government). In the Dáil government and in the first year of the Free State, members of parliament were commonly given administrative positions in defiance of the administra-tive/political distinction. The chief of staff of the army and the commissioner of the civic guards were, for example, Dáil deputies when appointed. This practice soon ceased, however. The formation of the Civil Service Commission and the

Local Appointments Commission in the mid-1920s reflected the government's sensitivity to the potential hazards of interpenetration of the political and administrative spheres. Civil servants came to be recruited on meritocratic and non-political grounds, a major achievement. By and large, the separation of function has been maintained. In some ways, the situation has improved; the growth of public service unions has, for example, made it more difficult for a politician to prevent a garda from doing his duty in enforcing the law. However, the Beef Tribunal that began its proceedings in 1991 has shown that civil servants are sometimes constrained to obey their political masters even when the legality of their instructions is in question.

Issues of this kind are rather difficult to explore in Ireland, partly because of a tradition of stifling secrecy in government. This tradition derives in part from the practices of the old British system), partly from the conspiratorial style of the first Irish Republican government and partly from a general secretive streak in the political culture. Most of the Irish governmental archives, for example, were kept closed to the public for 70 years after independence, a level of secretiveness that is almost Soviet in its intensity. Casual inspection suggests that many of the files that have been opened have been well weeded.

Policy-making, then, has proceeded in a rather indirect relationship to electoral politics, which tended to be fuelled by local economic, welfarist and nationalist passions. These then had to be translated or, rather, transformed into symbolic, constitutional and socio-economic policy outputs by an often secretive governmental process. The oligarchical relationships that evolved between the executive and parliament made this process irrational in many cases, subject not so much to an informed public opinion, as to veto from ecclesiastical and lay interest groups and local pressure in the context of a highly competitive electoral process. The growth of corporate collective bargaining structures since 1945 has further removed much policy making from both public opinion and the market, making for policies that are often not obviously in the public interest and are certainly arrived at by means that are not democratic (see chapter 10 and Hardiman, 1988).

An ideological preference for state monopoly and distrust for private enterprise in the 1930s acted together with the natural ease of monopoly formation in a small country to make Irish government big and interventionist in the economy. Electoral competition ensured that grants and hand-outs were spread around the country evenly even when it was obvious that this dissipation of resources did not make economic sense. Furthermore, the power of local interests ensured that such irrationalities long outlived their original purposes and arguably were contrary to the public interest.

A good example is afforded by the historical underdevelopment of the Irish road system. By the mid-1980s, the Republic of Ireland was said to have the worst main road system in western Europe, while having the greatest density of side roads. A preference for state transport systems and a dislike of the motor car as a vehicle of the rich combined with the natural inclination of the local councils to spread a labour-intensive type of road-mending activity evenly around their electoral areas. County engineers were forced to go along with this archaic system. A modern main road system could not be built by such methods nor with the kind of resources commanded by the local authorities. Small-town traders feared for the passing trade and blocked the making of bypasses. In 1948-49, a proposed dual carriageway bypass of Bray was blocked by the Taoiseach. The projected building of a new postwar road network was crushed to death between pressures from other departments on the Department of Finance to divert the money into more popular and apparently charitable areas such as social welfare and public housing (Department of Taoiseach, S12895, S13061, S13527, S14297).

It was not until the advent of European subventions in the 1980s that the blockages caused by Irish political structures started to be overcome, and a modern road system of international standard began to be put in place. It is impossible to say how much the generation's delay in supplying a modern transportation infrastructure has cost the Irish economy. It is certain that the price has been high. In other areas, political structures have not prevented successful reforms. A good example is the preventive medicine campaigns of the post-war period, which greatly improved the general health of the population in an efficient, humane and inexpensive way. Another example is the brilliant reconstruction of the primary school curriculum carried out during the 1970s.

TWO GENERATIONS OF SELF-GOVERNMENT

It is commonly said that independent Ireland started out life in 1922 with considerable advantages. Certainly this is true. Infrastructure was tolerably well-developed, the civil service was honest and fairly well-trained, and the agricultural economy had received a considerable fillip from the wartime boom in food prices. As argued above, the new state was also fortunate in that republican democratic institutions survived the bloody transition of 1921-23. An IRA victory in 1922 would have meant the eclipse of Dáil Éireann in favour of some kind of military directorate, and the ending of the principle of decision-making by the electorate, as it was exactly that principle that the IRA denied. Furthermore, the British would very probably have intervened, with horrendous consequences.

The legacy of British rule was, however, by no means as benign as it is sometimes permitted to appear. Irish slums were among the worst in Europe, and Irish agriculture was underdeveloped, at least a generation behind that of Denmark (Lee, 1989, pp. 513, 519). More subtly, the lack of a tradition of self-government and the experience of insurrection and revolution rendered many Irish people mentally unfit to think about the mundane but vital problems of self-government, and the civil war perpetuated a tradition of hate-filled and self-righteous rant which often drowned out any attempt at coherent and informed discussion of the new possibilities afforded by independence. As in other post-revolutionary societies, the culture developed an aspirational twist which prompted the noisy berating of the government for not immediately achieving the visions of the revolutionary martyrs.

The new party system, generated by a civil war that was itself a *lusus naturae*, was an oddity, in some ways a benign one. It forced the old Sinn Féiners to compete against each other and submit themselves and their often peculiar ideas to popular judgement. On the other hand, it may have encouraged much irrationality. For example, Fianna Fáil-led governments and Fine Gael-led governments have shown about the same aggregate propensity to spend public money; Fine Gael's more thrifty tradition has tended to be balanced by other, more spending-oriented allies in coalition governments.

Another long-term consequence of the split of 1922-23 was a chronic alienation between Fianna Fáil, because of its electoral prowess the natural governing party in the system, and the universities, which were quickly taken over in the early 1920s by Cumann na nGaedheal and its pro-Treaty clerical allies. The difficulties any government has with the media were compounded by the hostility between the anti-Treatyites and the overwhelmingly pro-Treaty press in 1922-23. Despite Fianna Fáil's developing a house newspaper, the *Irish Press*, the dislike of free journalism has persisted in a willingness to gag the electronic media, by-and-large controlled by the state at any rate.

Much of the opinion-forming process in Irish society is formed by third-level institutions in which the Fianna Fáil tradition is relatively weak and those of both Fine Gael and the left are relatively strong. The relative weakness of the usual left-right polarisation in the party system has encouraged a pragmatism that some-times veers into incoherence, opportunism or an intellectually and otherwise cor-rupt know-nothingness.

Irish political culture is just about post-peasant, and exhibits a tendency which I have labelled "communalism", or a propensity to fear the achievement by an-other individual of his interests on the ground that it might damage one's own interests and those of the collectivity; no one should be too successful. Opportun-ism can lurk behind "group-think". The party system communicates this general cultural propensity to the political system.

Despite structural and cultural problems of the kind I have outlined, policy does get made. Between 1922 and 1948, the new state experimented, at first ten-tatively and then boldly, with different economic and social policies. A low-tariff and non-*dirigiste* policy was followed in the 1920s. The government streamlined the local government system, imposed a puritan clean-up of prostitution and clamped down on literature and film. It also abolished the hated workhouses and replaced them by a more at-home relief system, started the electrification of the country and standardised quality and branding of exported agricultural goods.

Under Fianna Fáil, economic interventionism, state-led industrialisation, dis-couragement of foreign investment and import substitution industrialisation be-hind high tariff walls were given a determined trial between 1932 and 1959. It could be argued that the economic isolationists were unlucky because of the de-pression and the second world war, but it could be also argued that it was the depression that caused isolationism rather than isolationism curing the depres-sion. One's overall impression is of relatively little economic success between 1932 and 1948 (Lee, 1989, pp. 184-201).

The opening up of a new European order and the coming of Marshall Aid transformed the objective situation. What is important is how slow the Irish were to react to the new situation and get on the developmental bandwagon. Ireland missed out on the first 15 years of the post-war 30 year boom, the greatest such boom in history. Pre-war protectionism and discouragement of foreign invest-ment were clung to for a decade and a half too long. The country took a long time to "go developmental". Education, for example, which had been seen as a means of producing patriotic, pious and obedient citizens, only very slowly became also a means of producing skilled and competent workers who might contribute to the gross national product (GNP). The idea that Ireland might have an economy as well as be a country was routinely derided by journalists. The political system was seen primarily as a redistributive system and the Catholic church, as late as the early 1960s, had, in the minds of the many, a greater moral and even political legitimacy than did the elected leaders of the state.

Economic and social progress (and much regression) did occur in the first 30 years after independence, but progress was piecemeal and sluggish compared with the distance the country has covered since the mid-1950s. GNP per head has more than doubled, and this growth rate has approximated to that of the OECD countries during the last generation. Ireland has been damaged in this league table by its late start, due to the old revolutionaries passively and even actively preventing change between 1945 and 1960. Its relatively poor performance is, however, mainly due to the phenomenal economic growth rates of the defeated countries of 1939-45 (the Axis countries plus France and Finland). The success of these countries gives superficial credence to Olson's well-known thesis that defeat of a nation's ruling group unleashes energies that had previously been bottled up (Olson, 1982).

Clearly, Ireland's progress, although impressive in comparison with its own past, is not spectacular by the standards of the "top 24" economies. In part, this is an artefact of the figures. Irish people chose in the 1957-80 era to have a large number of children, and even the country's much lamented high emigration rate cannot reduce its dependency ratio, or proportion of the population who, because of youth or age, are out of the labour market, to average west European levels. On top of this, because of the baby boom, a generous unemployment relief scheme, obsolescence of many skills and economic sluggishness, unemployment is chronically high.

On the other hand, enormous progress has been made in many areas. In particular, a true revolution in public health has taken place since 1945. The life expectancy of women has increased by more than ten years, and diseases such as tuberculosis, polio, diphtheria and rickets have been stamped out (Garvin, 1989). In education, an equally sweeping transformation has occurred. Between 1922 and 1957, educational participation rates scarcely changed, a scandalous symptom of the hands-off posture enforced by jealous churches on a timid government which, in any case, saw education primarily as a means of cultural defence, much as did the churches themselves. Since 1957, Irish education has been revolutionised. In 1922, scarcely 4,000 privileged young people received third-level education. By 1957, the figure was not all that much higher. It nowadays approaches 60,000, a tripling since the mid-1960s. The proportion going to some kind of third-level education now surpasses its United Kingdom equivalent, an important historical landmark, but both countries lag well behind mainland European countries (Garvin, 1989).

Progress in many areas is associated with the elite generational change that occurred between 1957 and 1965, when old revolutionaries, often begrudgingly and with great foreboding, gave way to younger people. De Valera's last 15 years as leader of Fianna Fáil (1944-59) resemble faintly Brezhnev's last 15 as general secretary of the Communist Party of the Soviet Union (1968-83). In both cases the old leader had long outlived any usefulness he had had, and had succeeded in obstructing much-needed change. In the Irish case, turning things around was relatively easy, once the dead hand of the old revolutionaries was absent, because the Irish revolution was one of national separatism rather than one of social transformation. Old revolutionaries make the most implacable reactionaries, and with luck it takes only a generation to recover from a successful revolution. The fact of the matter is that the Irish revolution was an expensive business, and that expense was borne disproportionately by the poor. Given the fact of independence, the Irish state has some impressive achievements to its credit. The central achievement was, however, the establishment of a free political order, essentially republican and democratic, in a society with a long tradition of primitive hatred of government. Success in this has been so total that Irish people do not realise what an achievement it has been.

ENVOI

The passions that dominated the struggle for independence from the British Empire two generations ago are not quite dead. The coming of the European Union has led some to argue that Ireland is throwing away its much longed-for and dearly-bought sovereignty for a new version of the Act of Union of 1800. This is, actually, a poor analogy. The Act of Union ensured that Ireland would be perpetually in opposition within the joint Irish-British political system and would be perpetually an under-governed mendicant. The European Union gives Ireland, a tiny country, a veto over policy and preserves her domestic democracy (see chapter 12). Irish sovereignty is not being thrown away; it is being pooled with that of the largest and richest multinational commonwealth ever seen. European union may, however, mean that Ireland's separate history is coming to an end and is becoming part of the general history of Europe. In this sense, Irish independence may indeed be over.

REFERENCES AND FURTHER READING

Aristotle, 1962. *Politics*. Harmondsworth: Penguin.
Barker, Ernest, 1951. *Principles of Social and Political Theory*. Oxford: Clarendon Press.
Bax, Mart, 1976. *Harpstrings and Confessions: Machine-style Politics in the Irish Republic*. Assen: Van Gorcum.
Bowman, John, 1982. *De Valera and the Ulster Question*. Oxford: Clarendon Press.
Carty, R. K., 1981. *Party and Parish Pump: Electoral Politics in Ireland*. Waterloo, Ontario: Wilfrid Laurier Press.
Chubb, Basil, 1991. *The Politics of the Irish Constitution*. Dublin: Institute of Public Administration.
Cohan, Al, 1972. *The Irish Political Elite*. Dublin: Gill and Macmillan.
Curran, J. C., 1980. *The Birth of the Irish Free State, 1921-23*. Tuscaloosa, AL: University of Alabama Press.
Dahl, Robert, 1971. *Polyarchy*. New Haven: Yale University Press.
Dahl, Robert, 1989. *Democracy and its Critics*. New Haven: Yale University Press.
Department of Taoiseach. Papers, D/Taoiseach, National Archives, Bishop St, Dublin.
Garvin, Tom, 1981. *The Evolution of Irish Nationalist Politics*. Dublin: Gill and Macmillan.
Garvin, Tom, 1988. *Nationalist Revolutionaries in Ireland*. Oxford: Oxford University Press.
Garvin, Tom, 1989. "Wealth, poverty and development: reflections on current discontents", *Studies* 78:311, pp. 312-325.
Garvin, Tom, 1991. "Democracy in Ireland: collective somnambulance and public policy", *Administration* 39:1, pp. 42-54.
Hardiman, Niamh, 1988. *Pay, Politics and Economic Performance in Ireland 1970-1987*. Oxford: Oxford University Press.
Hopkinson, Michael, 1988. *Green against Green: the Irish Civil War*. Dublin: Gill and Macmillan.

Huntington, Samuel P., 1968. *Political Order in Changing Societies*. New Haven: Yale University Press.

Kennedy Papers. Archives Department, University College, Dublin.

Klosko, George, 1986. *The Development of Plato's Political Theory*. New York and London: Methuen.

Kohn, Leo, 1932. *The Constitution of the Irish Free State*. London: Allen and Unwin.

Lee, Joseph, 1989. *Ireland 1912-1985: Politics and Society*. Cambridge: Cambridge University Press.

Mair, Peter, 1987. *The Changing Irish Party System: Organisation, Ideology and Electoral Competition*. London: Pinter.

Mansergh, Nicholas, 1934. *The Irish Free State*. London: Allen and Unwin.

Montesquieu, 1989. *The Spirit of the Laws*. Cambridge: Cambridge University Press.

Mulcahy Papers. Archives Department, University College, Dublin.

Olson, Mancur, 1982. *The Rise and Decline of Nations*. New Haven and London: Yale University Press.

Plato, 1960. *Gorgias*. Harmondsworth: Penguin.

Prager, Jeffrey, 1986. *Building Democracy in Ireland: Political Order and Cultural Integration in a Newly Independent Nation*. Cambridge: Cambridge University Press.

Sacks, Paul, 1976. *The Donegal Mafia*. New Haven and London: Yale University Press.

Thompson, William, 1969. *The Imagination of an Insurrection*. Oxford: Oxford University Press.

Thucydides, 1910. *The History of the Pelopennesian War*. London: Dent.

Appendices

Appendix 1: Demographic data

Appendix 2: Electoral data

Appendix 3: Political office holders

Note: The data in these appendices refer to the territory of the Republic of Ireland, except where otherwise stated.

1a: Population and social indicators, 1841-1991

Year	Population	Urban population %	Dublin population %	Males in agriculture %	Catholics %	Other de-nominations %	Irish-speakers %
1841	6,528,799	16.7	3.7	74.3	.	.	.
1851	5,111,557	22.0	5.8	68.8	.	.	29.1
1861	4,402,111	22.2	6.7	64.6	89.3	10.7	24.5
1871	4,053,187	22.8	7.4	63.1	89.2	10.8	19.8
1881	3,870,020	23.9	8.4	62.6	89.5	10.5	23.9
1891	3,468,694	25.3	9.6	61.4	89.3	10.7	19.2
1901	3,221,823	28.0	11.2	61.7	89.3	10.7	19.2
1911	3,139,688	29.7	12.3	59.5	89.6	10.4	17.6
1926	2,971,992	31.8	13.7	58.9	92.6	7.4	19.3
1936	2,968,420	35.5	15.9	55.9	93.4	6.6	23.7
1946	2,955,107	39.3	17.1	54.1	94.3	5.7	21.2
1961	2,818,341	46.4	19.1	43.1	94.9	4.9	27.2
1971	2,978,248	52.2	26.9	31.9	93.9	4.3	28.3
1981	3,443,405	55.6	29.1	21.7	93.1	3.7	31.6
1991	3,523,401	57.0	29.1	19.0	.	.	(31.1)

Notes: All data refer to the present area of the Republic of Ireland. Urban areas are defined as those with a population of 1,500 or more, but figures for these and for Dublin are difficult to compare over time due to changes in boundary definition criteria. The data on involvement in agriculture are also difficult to compare over time due to varying classification criteria, and it has been possible to compute comparable data for men only. Data on religion are expressed as percentages of the total population (which includes those refusing to give information on this matter). Data on Irish speakers from 1926 onwards refer to the population aged over three years. The figure for Irish speakers in brackets in the bottom row refers to 1986.

Source: Calculated from *Census of Ireland* and *Statistical Yearbook of Ireland*, various dates, from *Labour Force Survey*, 1992, and from David Fitzpatrick, "The disappearance of the Irish agricultural labourer, 1841-1912", *Irish Economic and Social History* 7, 1980, pp. 66-92.

1b: Emigration, 1841-1991

Period	Total emigration	Annual average	Period	Net emigration	Annual average
1841-51	1,132,000	108,000	1911-26	405,029	27,002
1852-60	791,648	87,961	1926-36	166,751	16,675
1861-70	697,704	69,740	1936-46	187,111	18,711
1871-80	446,326	44,633	1946-61	528,334	35,222
1881-90	616,894	61,689	1961-71	134,511	13,451
1891-1900	377,017	37,702	1971-81	-104,000	-10,400
1901-10	266,311	26,631	1981-91	64,617	6,462

Note: The data for 1841-51 are estimates based on the assumption that the proportion of Irish emigrants coming from the present territory of the Republic was the same as in the 1852-60 period (the data begin in mid-year 1841). Net emigration refers to out-migration less in-migration, and the negative value in 1971-81 indicates a surplus of immigrants over emigrants in this period.

Source: computed from W. E. Vaughan and A. J. Fitzpatrick (eds), *Irish Historical Statistics: Population, 1821-1971* (Dublin: Royal Irish Academy, 1989), *Commission on Emigration and Other Population Problems 1948-1954, Reports* (Dublin: Stationery Office, [1956]) and *Census of Ireland*, 1981, 1986, 1991.

2a: Distribution of parliamentary seats by party, 1801-1918

Year	Southern Ireland					All Ireland				
	Tory/ Unionist	Whig/ Liberal	Nat. etc.	Other	Total	Tory/ Unionist	Whig/ Liberal	Nat. etc.	Other	Total
1801	23	16	0	39	78	34	16	0	50	100
1802	27	26	0	25	78	43	28	0	29	100
1806	34	34	0	10	78	50	36	0	14	100
1807	37	32	0	9	78	54	33	0	13	100
1812	43	28	0	7	78	59	30	0	11	100
1818	41	32	0	5	78	61	34	0	5	100
1820	44	29	0	5	78	63	32	0	5	100
1826	38	37	0	3	78	56	41	0	3	100
1830	34	41	0	3	78	49	48	0	3	100
1831	26	48	0	4	78	40	56	0	4	100
1832	14	26	42	0	82	30	33	42	0	105
1835	22	26	34	0	82	37	34	34	0	105
1837	14	38	30	0	82	32	43	30	0	105
1841	23	39	20	0	82	43	42	20	0	105
1847	20	21	36	5	82	31	25	36	13	105
1852	21	11	48	2	82	40	15	48	2	105
1857	26	43	13	0	82	44	48	13	0	105
1859	33	49	0	0	82	55	50	0	0	105
1865	24	58	0	0	82	47	58	0	0	105
1868	19	63	0	0	82	39	66	0	0	105
1874	16	4	60	0	80	33	10	60	0	103
1880	7	10	63	0	80	25	15	63	0	103
1885	2	0	76	0	78	18	0	85	0	103
1886	2	0	76	0	78	19	0	84	0	103
1892	4	0	74	0	78	23	0	80	0	103
1895	4	0	74	0	78	21	1	81	0	103
1900	3	0	75	0	78	21	1	81	0	103
1906	3	0	75	0	78	20	1	82	0	103
1910-1	3	0	75	0	78	21	1	81	0	103
1910-2	2	0	76	0	78	19	1	83	0	103
1918	3	0	2	70	75	26	0	6	73	105

Notes: "Southern Ireland" refers to the present territory of the Republic of Ireland. Before 1832 party affiliations are approximate only. "Tories/Unionists" includes Liberal Unionists; "Nationalists, etc." includes the Repeal Party (1832-47), the Independent Irish Party (1852-57) and the Home Rule or Nationalist Party, including breakaway factions and independent nationalists (1874-1918); "others" includes nonaligned MPs (1801-32), Peelites (1847-52) and two Irish Confederates in the South (1847); in 1918 it refers to Sinn Féin MPs.

Sources: Calculated from Henry Stooks Smith, *The Parliaments of England from 1715 to 1847*, 2nd ed, edited by F. W. S. Craig (Chichester: Political Reference Publications, 1973), and Brian M. Walker, *Parliamentary Election Results in Ireland, 1801-1922* (Dublin: Royal Irish Academy, 1978).

2b: Distribution of first preference votes in Dáil elections by party, 1922-92

Year	Fianna Fáil %	Fine Gael %	Labour Party %	Farmers' parties %	Republican parties %	Others %	Turnout %
1922	21.7	38.5	21.3	7.8	0.0	10.6	45.5
1923	27.4	39.0	10.6	12.1	0.0	10.9	61.2
1927-1	26.1	27.5	12.6	8.9	3.6	21.4	68.1
1927-2	35.2	38.7	9.1	6.4	0.0	10.7	69.0
1932	44.5	35.3	7.7	3.1	0.0	9.4	76.5
1933	49.7	30.5	5.7	9.2	0.0	5.0	81.3
1937	45.2	34.8	10.3	0.0	0.0	9.7	76.2
1938	51.9	33.3	10.0	0.0	0.0	4.7	76.7
1943	41.9	23.1	15.7	11.3	0.3	7.7	74.2
1944	48.9	20.5	8.8	11.6	0.0	10.2	67.7
1948	41.9	19.8	8.7	5.5	13.2	10.9	74.2
1951	46.3	25.8	11.4	2.9	4.1	9.6	75.3
1954	43.4	32.0	12.1	3.1	3.9	5.6	76.4
1957	48.3	26.6	9.1	2.4	7.0	6.6	71.3
1961	43.8	32.0	11.6	1.5	4.2	6.8	70.6
1965	47.7	34.1	15.4	0.0	0.8	2.1	75.1
1969	45.7	34.1	17.0	0.0	0.0	3.2	76.9
1973	46.2	35.1	13.7	0.0	2.0	3.0	76.6
1977	50.6	30.5	11.6	0.0	1.8	5.5	76.3
1981	45.3	36.5	9.9	0.0	2.5	5.9	76.2
1982-1	47.3	37.3	9.1	0.0	1.2	5.1	73.8
1982-2	45.2	39.2	9.4	0.0	0.0	6.3	72.9
1987	44.1	27.1	6.4	0.0	1.9	20.5	73.3
1989	44.1	29.3	9.5	0.0	1.2	15.9	68.5
1992	39.1	24.5	19.3	0.0	1.6	15.6	67.5

Notes: Fianna Fáil includes Anti-Treaty Sinn Féin (1922-23). Fine Gael includes Pro-Treaty Sinn Féin (1922) and Cumann na nGaedheal (1923-32). "Farmers' parties" includes the Farmers' Party (1922-32), the National Centre Party (1933), and Clann na Talmhan (1943-61). "Republican parties" refers to Sinn Féin, including the original party before 1970 (1927-1, 3.6%; 1954, 0.1%; 1957, 5.3%; 1961, 3.1%), "Official" Sinn Féin in the 1970s (1973, 1.1%; 1977, 1.7%), and "Sinn Féin" since 1981 (1982-1, 1.0%; 1987, 1.9%; 1989, 1.2%; 1992, 1.6%), and the following parties: Córas na Poblachta (1943, 0.3%), Clann na Poblachta (1948, 13.2%; 1951, 4.1%; 1954, 3.8%; 1957, 1.7%; 1961, 1.1%; 1965, 0.8%), Aontacht Éireann (1973, 0.9%), the Irish Republican Socialist Party (1977, 0.1%; 1982-1, 0.2%) and the National H-Block Committee (1981, 2.5%). "Others" includes the National League (1927-1, 7.3%; 1927-2, 1.6%), National Labour (1944, 2.7%; 1948, 2.6%), the National Progressive Democrats (1961, 1.0%), the Progressive Democrats (1987, 11.8%; 1989, 5.5%; 1992, 4.7%) and the Green Party (1987, 0.4%; 1989, 1.5%; 1992, 1.4%), as well as smaller groups and independents. From 1981, Sinn Féin the Workers' Party and its successor, the Workers' Party, have been grouped with "others" (1981, 1.7%; 1982-1, 2.2%; 1982-2, 3.1%; 1987, 3.8%; 1989, 5.0%; 1992, 0.7%), as has Democratic Left (1992, 2.8%).
The first Dáil was convened on the basis of the UK general election of 1918; at this election all seats in the north were contested, but only two thirds of those in the south (50); in the remaining 25, Sinn Féin candidates were returned unopposed, so vote totals do not give an accurate picture of party strengths. The second Dáil was convened on the basis of the elections in 1921 to the proposed Houses of Commons of Southern Ireland and Northern Ireland; at this, all seats were contested in the north, but none was in the south.
Source: Michael Gallagher (ed.), *Irish Elections 1922-44: Results and Analysis* (Limerick: PSAI Press, 1993); Brian M. Walker (ed.), *Parliamentary Election Results in Ireland 1918-92* (Dublin: Royal Irish Academy and Belfast: Institute of Irish Studies, 1992).

2c: Distribution of seats in Dáil by party, 1922-92

Year	Fianna Fáil	Fine Gael	Labour Party	Farmers' parties	Republican parties	Others	Total
1922	36	58	17	7	.	10	128
1923	44	63	14	15	.	17	153
1927-1	44	47	22	11	5	24	153
1927-2	57	62	13	6	.	15	153
1932	72	57	7	4	.	13	153
1933	77	48	8	11	.	9	153
1937	69	48	13	.	.	8	138
1938	77	45	9	.	.	7	138
1943	67	32	17	14	.	8	138
1944	76	30	8	11	.	13	138
1948	68	31	14	7	10	17	147
1951	69	40	16	6	2	14	147
1954	65	50	19	5	3	5	147
1957	78	40	12	3	5	9	147
1961	70	47	16	2	1	8	144
1965	72	47	22	.	1	2	144
1969	75	50	18	.	.	1	144
1973	69	54	19	.	.	2	144
1977	84	43	17	.	.	4	148
1981	78	65	15	.	2	6	166
1982-1	81	63	15	.	.	7	166
1982-2	75	70	16	.	.	5	166
1987	81	51	12	.	.	22	166
1989	77	55	15	.	.	19	166
1992	68	45	33	.	.	20	166

Notes: Fianna Fáil includes Anti-Treaty Sinn Féin (1922-23). Fine Gael includes Pro-Treaty Sinn Féin (1922) and Cumann na nGaedheal (1923-32). "Farmers' parties" includes the Farmers' Party (1922-32), the National Centre Party (1933), and Clann na Talmhan (1943-61). "Republican parties" refers mainly to Clann na Poblachta (1948-65) but includes also Sinn Féin (1927-1, 5 TDs; 1957, 4 TDs) and the National H-Block Committee (1981, 2 TDs). "Others" includes the National League (1927-1, 8 TDs; 1927-2, 2 TDs), National Labour (1944, 4 TDs; 1948, 5 TDs), the National Progressive Democrats (1961, 2 TDs), Sinn Féin the Workers' Party and its successor, the Workers' Party (1981, 1 TD; 1982-1, 3 TDs; 1982-2, 2 TDs; 1987, 4 TDs; 1989, 7 TDs), the Progressive Democrats (1987, 14 TDs; 1989, 6 TDs; 1992, 10 TDs), the Green Party (1989 and 1992, 1 TD) and Democratic Left (1992, 4 TDs), as well as smaller groups and independents.
The first Dáil was convened on the basis of the British general election of 1918; at this election Sinn Féin won 73 seats (all except three of these in the south; two of the northern seats were won by candidates who were also successful in the south and one candidate was returned for two constituencies in the south, leaving Sinn Féin with 70 MPs), the Unionists 26 (all except three in the north) and the Nationalists won six (four in the north and two in the south). The second Dáil was convened on the basis of the elections in 1921 to the proposed Houses of Commons of Southern Ireland and Northern Ireland; at this, Sinn Féin won 130 seats (all except six of these in the south; five of the northern seats were won by candidates who were also successful in the south, leaving Sinn Féin with 125 MPs), the Unionists 40 (all in the north), the Nationalists six (all in the north) and independents won four (all in the south).
Source: Michael Gallagher (ed.), *Irish Elections 1922-44: Results and Analysis* (Limerick: PSAI Press, 1993); Brian M. Walker (ed.), *Parliamentary Election Results in Ireland 1918-92* (Dublin: Royal Irish Academy and Belfast: Institute of Irish Studies, 1992).

2d: Distribution of men and women in the Oireachtas, 1922-93

	Dáil Éireann				Seanad Éireann		
Year	*Men*	*Women*	*Total*	*Year*	*Men*	*Women*	*Total*
1922	126	2	128	-	.	.	.
1923	148	5	153	1922	56	4	60
1927-1	149	4	153	1925	56	4	60
1927-2	152	1	153	1928	55	5	60
1932	151	2	153	1931	55	5	60
1933	150	3	153	1934	57	3	60
1937	136	2	138	1938-1	56	4	60
1938	135	3	138	1938-2	57	3	60
1943	135	3	138	1943	57	3	60
1944	134	4	138	1944	57	3	60
1948	142	5	147	1948	57	3	60
1951	142	5	147	1951	57	3	60
1954	142	5	147	1954	57	3	60
1957	142	5	147	1957	56	4	60
1961	141	3	144	1961	57	3	60
1965	139	5	144	1965	56	4	60
1969	141	3	144	1969	55	5	60
1973	140	4	144	1973	56	4	60
1977	142	6	148	1977	54	6	60
1981	155	11	166	1981	51	9	60
1982-1	158	8	166	1982	52	8	60
1982-2	152	14	166	1983	54	6	60
1987	152	14	166	1987	55	5	60
1989	153	13	166	1989	54	6	60
1992	146	20	166	1993	52	8	60

Notes: The data refer to the position immediately after general elections to Dáil Éireann (1922-92) and Seanad Éireann (1938-93). The earlier data on Seanad Éireann refer to the position immediately after the initial installation of the first Seanad under the Free State constitution (1922) and after the triennial elections which renewed a portion of its membership (1925-34).

Oniy one woman was returned from the 105 Irish seats in the British general election of 1918; of the 73 Sinn Féin seats, 72 were occupied by men (since three of these seats were double returns, the full potential membership of the first Dáil was 69 men and one woman). Eight women were returned from the 180 seats to the Houses of Commons of Southern Ireland and Northern Ireland in 1921, two Unionists in the north and six Sinn Féin members in the south (since the 130 Sinn Féin seats were occupied by only 125 people due to double returns, the full potential membership of the second Dáil was 119 men and six women).

2e: Distribution of first preference votes in European Parliament elections, 1979-89

Year	Fianna Fáil %	Fine Gael %	Labour Party %	Workers' Party %	Progressive Democrats %	Others %	Turnout %
1979	34.7	33.1	14.5	3.3	.	14.4	63.6
1984	39.2	32.2	8.4	4.3	.	15.9	47.6
1989	31.5	21.6	9.5	7.5	11.9	17.9	68.3

Notes: "Workers' Party" includes Sinn Féin The Workers' Party; "Others" includes Sinn Féin (1984, 4.9%; 1989, 2.3%) and the Green Party (1989, 3.7%).

2f: Distribution of first preference votes in local elections, 1967-91

Year	Fianna Fáil %	Fine Gael %	Labour Party %	Workers' Party %	Progressive Democrats %	Others %	Turnout %
1967	40.2	32.5	14.8	.	.	12.5	69.0
1974	40.1	33.7	12.8	1.5	.	11.9	61.1
1979	39.2	34.9	11.8	2.3	.	11.8	63.6
1985	45.5	29.8	7.7	3.0	.	14.0	58.2
1991	37.9	26.4	10.6	3.7	5.0	16.4	55.1

Notes: These figures relate to the results in county and county borough elections only. "Workers' Party" includes Sinn Féin (1974) and Sinn Féin the Workers' Party (1979); "Others" includes Sinn Féin (1979, 2.2%; 1985, 3.3%; 1991, 1.7%) and the Green Party (1991, 2.0%).

2g: Distribution of votes in presidential elections, 1945-90

Year	Candidate	Count 1 No. (%)	Count 2 Transfers	Result (%)	Comment
1945	McCartan, Patrick	212,834 (19.6)	-212,834	-	Ó Ceallaigh elected;
	MacEoin, Seán	335,539 (30.9)	+117,886	453,425 (44.5)	turnout: 63.0%
	Ó Ceallaigh, Seán T.	537,965 (49.5)	+27,200	565,165 (55.5)	non-transferable: 67,748
1959	de Valera, Eamon	538,003 (56.3)			de Valera elected;
	MacEoin, Seán	417,536 (43.7)			turnout: 58.4%
1966	de Valera, Eamon	558,861 (50.5)			de Valera elected;
	O'Higgins, Thomas F.	548,144 (49.5)			turnout: 65.4%
1973	Childers, Erskine	635,867 (52.0)			Childers elected;
	O'Higgins, Thomas F.	587,771 (48.0)			turnout: 62.2%
1990	Currie, Austin	267,902 (17.0)	-267,902	-	Robinson elected;
	Lenihan, Brian	694,484 (44.1)	+36,789	731,273 (47.2)	turnout: 64.1%
	Robinson, Mary	612,265 (38.9)	+205,565	817,830 (52.8)	non-transferable: 25,548

Note: In 1938, 1952, 1974, 1976 and 1983 no contests took place as only one candidate was nominated.

2h: Results of referendums, 1937-92

Date	Subject (article altered)	For %	Against %	Turnout %	Spoiled %
1.7.37	Approve new constitution	56.5	43.5	75.8	10.0
17.6.59	Replace proportional representation by plurality system (*3rd amendment; 16*)	48.2	51.8	58.4	4.0
16.10.68	Permit flexibility in deputy-population ratio (*3rd amendment; 16*)	39.2	60.8	65.8	4.3
16.10.68	Replace proportional representation by plurality system (*4th amendment; 16*)	39.2	60.8	65.8	4.3
10.5.72	Permit EC membership (3rd amendment; 29)	83.1	16.9	70.9	0.8
7.12.72	Lower voting age to 18 (4th amendment; 16)	84.6	15.4	50.7	5.2
7.12.72	Remove "special position" of Catholic church (5th amendment; 44)	84.4	15.6	50.7	5.5
5.7.79	Protect adoption system (6th amendment; 37)	99.0	1.0	28.6	2.5
5.7.79	Permit alteration of university representation in Senate (7th amendment; 18)	92.4	7.6	28.6	3.9
7.9.83	Prohibit legalisation of abortion (8th amendment; 40)	66.9	33.1	53.7	0.7
14.6.84	Permit extension of voting rights to non-citizens (9th amendment; 16)	75.4	24.6	47.5	3.5
26.6.86	Permit legalisation of divorce (*10th amendment; 41*)	36.5	63.5	60.5	0.6
26.5.87	Permit signing of Single European Act (10th amendment; 29)	69.9	30.1	43.9	0.5
18.6.92	Permit ratification of Maastricht Treaty on European union (11th amendment; 29)	69.1	30.9	57.3	0.5
25.11.92	Restrict availability of abortion (*12th amendment; 40*)	34.6	65.4	68.2	4.7
25.11.92	Guarantee right to travel (13th amendment; 40)	62.4	37.6	68.2	4.3
25.11.92	Guarantee right to information (14th amendment; 40)	59.9	40.1	68.1	4.3

Notes: Amendment numbers in italics refer to constitutional amendment bills rejected at a referendum. The first amendment bill (state of emergency, affecting article 28) and the second amendment bill (emergency provisions and various matters, affecting articles 11-15, 18, 20, 24-28, 34, 40, 47 and 56) were passed by the Oireachtas without a referendum in 1939 and 1941 respectively (see pp. 55-6, 63-4 above).

2j: Opinion poll support for parties by social group, 1969-93

Party	Year	All	Middle class	Working class	Large farmers	Small farmers
Fianna Fáil	1969	43	45	42	38	53
	1977	49	46	50	48	48
	1981	44	39	43	42	53
	1985	42	37	45	41	46
	1989	38	35	38	39	47
	1993	36	35	34	40	44
Fine Gael	1969	25	28	16	46	26
	1977	28	30	21	42	38
	1981	32	41	28	43	32
	1985	28	37	21	38	23
	1989	23	25	17	43	21
	1993	16	14	15	29	15
Labour Party	1969	18	14	28	2	5
	1977	9	7	15	1	5
	1981	10	4	14	1	4
	1985	5	6	5	0	2
	1989	6	5	9	3	2
	1993	15	16	18	3	8
Workers' Party	1985	2	1	4	0	0
	1989	4	4	6	0	0
Progressive Democrats	1989	5	6	5	3	3
	1993	9	12	8	8	5

Notes: The figures relate to the percentage of each occupational group that expressed an intention to vote for the party in question. The occupational groups are defined as follows: middle class, ABC1 (professional, managerial and clerical); working class, C2DE (skilled and unskilled manual workers); large farmers, F1 (farmers with 50 acres or more, except in 1969, when the cutoff was 30 acres); small farmers, F2 (farmers with less than 50 acres, except in 1969, when the cutoff was 30 acres). Poll dates were April 1969 (Gallup), May-June 1977 (IMS), May 1981 (IMS), February 1985 (MRBI), June 1989 (MRBI) and July 1993 (MRBI). Percentages for a given occupational group will not necessarily total 100 across parties due to the omission of supporters of other parties or of none.

3a: Heads of state, 1922-93

Dates of office	Name
	Governor-General
6.12.22 - 1.2.28	Timothy Healy
1.2.28 - 1.11.32	James MacNeill
26.11.32 - 12.12.36	Dónal Ó Buachalla
	President
25.6.38 - 25.6.45	Douglas Hyde
25.6.45 - 25.6.59	Seán T. Ó Ceallaigh
25.6.59 - 25.6.73	Eamon de Valera
25.6.73 - 17.11.74	Erskine Childers
19.12.74 - 22.10.76	Cearbhall Ó Dálaigh
3.12.76 - 3.12.90	Patrick Hillery
3.12.90 -	Mary Robinson

Note: The Governor-General was officially the Representative of the Crown: Kings George V (1910-36), Edward VIII (1936) and George VI (1936-52).

3b: Heads and deputy heads of government, 1922-93

Date	Head of government	Deputy head of government
	President of the Executive Council	*Vice President of the Executive Council*
6.12.22	William T. Cosgrave	Kevin O'Higgins
		Ernest Blythe (10.7.27)
9.3.32	Eamon de Valera	Seán T. Ó Ceallaigh
	Taoiseach	*Tánaiste*
29.12.37	Eamon de Valera	Seán T. Ó Ceallaigh
		Seán Lemass (14.6.45)
18.2.48	John A. Costello	William Norton
13.6.51	Eamon de Valera	Seán Lemass
2.6.54	John A. Costello	William Norton
20.3.57	Eamon de Valera	Seán Lemass
23.6.59	Seán Lemass	Seán MacEntee
		Frank Aiken (21.4.65)
10.11.66	Jack Lynch	Frank Aiken
		Erskine Childers (2.7.69)
14.3.73	Liam Cosgrave	Brendan Corish
5.7.77	Jack Lynch	George Colley
11.12.79	Charles Haughey	George Colley
20.6.81	Garret FitzGerald	Michael O'Leary
9.3.82	Charles Haughey	Ray MacSharry
14.12.82	Garret FitzGerald	Dick Spring
		Peter Barry (20.1.87)
10.3.87	Charles Haughey	Brian Lenihan
		John Wilson (13.11.90)
11.2.92	Albert Reynolds	John Wilson
		Dick Spring (12.1.93)

3c: Composition of governments, 1922-93

Date	Government	Fianna Fáil	Fine Gael	Labour	Other	Total	Dáil support
14. 1.22	Collins	.	8	.	.	8	49.0
22. 8.22	Cosgrave 1	.	9	.	.	9	49.0
9. 9.22	Cosgrave 2	.	11	.	.	11	45.3
6.12.22	Cosgrave 3	.	10	.	.	10	45.3
19. 9.23	Cosgrave 4	.	11	.	.	11	41.2
23. 6.27	Cosgrave 5	.	10	.	.	10	30.7
11.10.27	Cosgrave 6	.	9	.	.	9	40.5
2.4.30	Cosgrave 7	.	9	.	.	9	40.5
9.3.32	de Valera 1	10	.	.	.	10	47.1
8.2.33	de Valera 2	10	.	.	.	10	50.3
21. 7.37	de Valera 3	10	.	.	.	10	50.0
30. 6.38	de Valera 4	10	.	.	.	10	55.8
1.7.43	de Valera 5	11	.	.	.	11	48.5
9.6.44	de Valera 6	11	.	.	.	11	55.1
18. 2.48	Costello 1	.	6	2	5	13	45.6
13. 6.51	de Valera 7	12	.	.	.	12	46.9
2.6.54	Costello 2	.	8	4	1	13	50.3
20. 3.57	de Valera 8	12	.	.	.	12	53.1
23. 6.59	Lemass 1	13	.	.	.	13	53.1
11.10.61	Lemass 2	14	.	.	.	14	48.6
21. 4.65	Lemass 3	14	.	.	.	14	50.0
10.11.66	Lynch 1	14	.	.	.	14	50.0
2.7.69	Lynch 2	14	.	.	.	14	52.1
14. 3.73	Cosgrave	.	10	5	.	15	50.7
5.7.77	Lynch 3	15	.	.	.	15	56.8
12.12.79	Haughey 1	15	.	.	.	15	56.8
30. 6.81	FitzGerald 1	.	11	4	.	15	48.2
9.3.82	Haughey 2	15	.	.	.	15	48.8
14.12.82	FitzGerald 2	.	11	4	.	15	51.8
10.3.87	Haughey 3	15	.	.	.	15	48.8
12.7.89	Haughey 4	13	.	.	2	15	50.0
11.2.92	Reynolds 1	13	.	.	2	15	50.0
12.1.93	Reynolds 2	9	.	6	.	15	60.8

Notes: The first three governments were provisional governments. "Fine Gael" includes also the Pro-Treaty party or Cumann na nGaedheal (1922-33). "Others" include two Clann na Poblachta, one Clann na Talmhan, one National Labour and one independent in 1948, one Clann na Talmhan in 1954, and two Progressive Democrats in 1989 and 1992. "Dáil support" refers to Dáil seats held by parties participating in government as percentage of total Dáil membership immediately after the formation of the government; independent deputies committed to supporting the government (as in 1948) are not included; the first two figures in this column are estimates.

3d: Ceann Comhairle of Dáil and Cathaoirleach of Seanad, 1922-93

Date	Ceann Comhairle	Date	Cathaoirleach
9.9.22	Michael Hayes (CnG)	12.12.22	Lord Glenavy (Ind)
9.3.32	Frank Fahy (FF)	12.12.28	Thomas Westropp Bennett (CnG)
		27.4.38	Seán Gibbons (FF)
		8.9.43	Seán Goulding (FF)
		21.4.48	T. J. O'Donovan (FG)
13.6.51	Patrick Hogan (Lab)	14.8.51	Liam Ó Buachalla (FF)
		22.7.54	Patrick Baxter (FG)
		22.5.57	Liam Ó Buachalla (FF)
7.11.67	Cormac Breslin (FF)	5.11.69	Michael Yeats (FF)
		3.1.73	Micheál Cranitch (FF)
14.3.73	Seán Treacy (Lab)	1.6.73	James Dooge (FG)
5.7.77	Joseph Brennan (FF)	27.10.77	Séamus Dolan (FF)
16.10.80	Pádraig Faulkner (FF)	8.10.81	Charlie McDonald (FG)
30.6.81	John O'Connell (Ind)	13.5.82	Tras Honan (FF)
14.12.82	Tom Fitzpatrick (FG)	23.2.83	Pat Joe Reynolds (FG)
10.3.87	Seán Treacy (Ind)	25.4.87	Tras Honan (FF)
		1.11.89	Seán Doherty (FF)
		23.1.92	Seán Fallon (FF)

3e: Leaders of political parties, 1922-93

Fianna Fáil
Eamon de Valera (1926-59)
Seán Lemass (1959-66)
Jack Lynch (1966-79)
Charles Haughey (1979-92)
Albert Reynolds (1992-)

Fine Gael
Eoin O'Duffy (1933-34)
William T. Cosgrave (1935-44)
Richard Mulcahy (1944-59)
James Dillon (1959-65)
Liam Cosgrave (1965-77)
Garret FitzGerald (1977-87)
Alan Dukes (1987-90)
John Bruton (1990-)

Labour Party
Thomas Johnson (1918-27)
T. J. O'Connell (1927-32)
William Norton (1932-60)
Brendan Corish (1960-77)
Frank Cluskey (1977-81)
Michael O'Leary (1981-82)
Dick Spring (1982-)

Progressive Democrats
Desmond O'Malley (1985-)

Cumann na nGaedheal
William T. Cosgrave (1922-33)

Democratic Left
Proinsias de Rossa (1992-)

Note: The party to which the Democratic Left deputies belonged was originally Sinn Féin, after 1970 known as "Official" Sinn Féin; it became Sinn Féin the Workers' Party in 1977 and The Workers' Party in 1982. Six of its seven deputies left in 1992 to form Democratic Left. The original party had been led by Tomás Mac Giolla (1962-88) and Proinsias de Rossa (1988-92).

4: Biographical notes on major political figures

Note: The following notes give basic information on all those who have held the post of Governor-General, President, President of the Executive Council, Taoiseach, Vice President of the Executive Council or Tánaiste. For further information on most of these, see Henry Boylan, *A Dictionary of Irish Biography*, 2nd ed. (Dublin: Gill and Macmillan, 1988), Ted Nealon's *Guides* to the Dáil and Seanad, various years, and *Who's Who, What's What and Where in Ireland* (London: Geoffrey Chapman, in association with *The Irish Times*, 1973).

Aiken, Frank. Born Camlough, Co Armagh, 13 February 1898; educated Christian Brothers, Newry; worked as a farmer; active in Gaelic League and in Irish Volunteers; leading figure in IRA during war of independence and civil war; anti-Treaty Sinn Féin and Fianna Fáil TD, 1923-73; government minister, 1932-48, 1951-54, 1975-69; Tánaiste, 1959-69; died 18 May 1983. One of the last IRA divisional commanders to take sides in the civil war, was associated with the pursuit of neutrality also in international affairs; as Minister for External Affairs, guided Ireland along an independent line in the United Nations.

Barry, Peter. Born Cork, 6 August 1928; educated Christian Brothers, Cork; worked as a tea importer and wholesaler; Fine Gael TD since 1969; government minister, 1973-77, 1981-82, 1982-87; Tánaiste, 1987. A popular and respected elder statesman in Fine Gael, built up a positive image as foreign minister; nevertheless, did not succeed to the party leadership in a context where youth appeared to take precedence over experience; Tánaiste only for a few weeks after the collapse of the Fine Gael-Labour coalition in 1987.

Blythe, Ernest. Born Lisburn, Co Antrim, 13 April 1889; educated locally; worked as a clerk in the Department of Agriculture; active in the Gaelic League, IRB and Irish Volunteers; Sinn Féin MP/TD, 1918-22; pro-Treaty Sinn Féin and Cumann na nGaedheal TD, 1922-33; lost his seat, 1933; minister in Dáil government, 1919-22; government minister, 1922-32; Vice President of the Executive Council, 1927-32; died 23 February 1975. A northern Protestant, was strongly associated with the Irish language movement and with Irish cultural activities, going on after his retirement from politics to become managing director of the Abbey Theatre; as Minister for Finance, won notoriety for reducing the old age pension from ten to nine shillings (from 50 pence to 45 pence!).

Childers, Erskine. Born London, 11 December 1905; educated Norfolk and Cambridge University; worked in Paris for an American travel organisation; advertising manager, *Irish Press*; Fianna Fáil TD, 1938-73; government minister 1951-54, 1957-73; Tánaiste, 1969-73; President of Ireland, 1973-74; died 17 November 1974. Was a son of Robert Erskine Childers (1870-1922), a Clerk in the House of Commons who had Irish connections, became involved in the Irish nationalist movement, took the anti-Treaty side during the civil war and was executed in 1922.

Colley, George. Born Dublin, 18 October 1925; educated Christian Brothers, Dublin, and University College, Dublin; worked as a solicitor; Fianna Fáil TD, 1961-83; parliamentary secretary, 1964-65; government minister, 1965-73, 1977-81; Tánaiste, 1977-81; died 17 September 1983. Contested the leadership of Fianna Fáil against Jack Lynch in 1966 and against his long-time rival and former school classmate, Charles Haughey, in 1979; intensely suspicious of Haughey since the arms crisis of 1970, insisted during Haughey's first government on being given a veto on appointments to the security ministries (Defence and Justice).

Collins, Michael. Born Clonakilty, Co Cork, 16 October 1890; educated local national school; worked in London as a clerk in the post office and for a firm of stockbrokers; participated in 1916 rising as IRB member; Sinn Féin TD/MP, 1918-22; minister in Dáil government, 1919-22; Chairman of Provisional Government and Commander-in-Chief of the new national army, 1922; killed in an ambush at Béal na mBláth, Co Cork, by anti-Treaty forces during the civil war on 22 August 1922. Was a charismatic leader during the Anglo-Irish war of 1919-21 and a very effective director of intelligence for the IRA; his influence helped to swing the IRB (of whose Supreme Council he was President) and many members of the IRA into support for the Anglo-Irish Treaty, which he had negotiated as one of the representatives of the Irish side.

Corish, Brendan. Born Wexford, 19 November 1918; educated Christian Brothers, Wexford; worked as a local government official; Labour TD, 1945-82; leader of the Labour Party, 1960-77; parliamentary secretary, 1948-51; government minister, 1954-57; Tánaiste, 1973-77; died 17 February 1990. Though a popular party leader, was relatively unassertive in his later years and allowed strong-willed colleagues considerable latitude when the party was in government, 1973-77.

Cosgrave, Liam. Born Dublin, 13 April 1920; educated Christian Brothers, Castleknock College and King's Inns; called to bar, 1943; Fine Gael TD, 1943-81; leader of Fine Gael, 1965-77; parliamentary secretary, 1948-51; government minister, 1954-57; Taoiseach 1973-77. A son of William T. Cosgrave; his period as Taoiseach was marked by a strong emphasis on the maintenance of law and order.

Cosgrave, William T. Born Dublin, 6 June 1880; educated Christian Brothers, Dublin; joined the early Sinn Féin movement and the Irish Volunteers and participated in 1916 rising; Sinn Féin MP/TD, 1917-22; pro-Treaty Sinn Féin, Cumann na nGaedheal and Fine Gael TD, 1922-44; leader of Cumann na nGaedheal, 1923-33 and of Fine Gael, 1935-44; minister in Dáil government, 1919-22; President of Executive Council, 1922-32; died 16 November 1965. Despite his background as a revolutionary in 1916, was associated with conservative policies during the first decade of the new state.

Costello, John A. Born Dublin, 20 June 1891; educated University College, Dublin; called to bar, 1914; worked in Attorney General's office, 1922-26; Attorney General, 1926-32; Cumann na nGaedheal and Fine Gael TD, 1933-43, 1944-69; head of first and second Inter-Party governments and Taoiseach, 1948-51 and 1954-57; died 5 January 1976. Associated with a striking about-face in Fine Gael when he moved in 1948 to sever Ireland's links with the Commonwealth and declare the state a republic; did not support his Minister for Health, Noel Browne, whose "Mother and Child" health care proposals in 1950 were strongly opposed by the Catholic church and led ultimately to the collapse of Costello's first government.

de Valera, Eamon. Born New York city, 14 October 1882; brought up Bruree, Co Limerick; educated Christian Brothers, Charleville, Blackrock College, Dublin, and Royal University; teacher of mathematics; involved in early Gaelic League and Irish Volunteers and participated in 1916 rising; senior surviving commandant of rising; leader of Sinn Féin, 1917-22, of anti-Treaty Sinn Féin, 1922-26 and of Fianna Fáil, which he founded, 1926-59; Sinn Féin TD/MP, 1917-22; anti-Treaty Sinn Féin and Fianna Fáil TD, 1922-59; President of Dáil government, 1919-22, President of Executive Council, 1932-37, Taoiseach, 1937-48, 1951-54 and 1957-59; President of Ireland, 1959-73; died 29 August 1975. An enigmatic figure who played a leading role in Irish politics from 1916 to 1973, and a controversial one at certain times, such as 1921-23 and 1926-27; was largely responsible for leading the bulk of the anti-Treaty side into operating within a constitutional framework in the 1920s; though committed to Irish unity and the Irish language, made little progress on the former and saw the latter weaken further; was more successful in the area of foreign relations, where he succeeded in greatly enhancing Ireland's independence.

FitzGerald, Garret. Born Dublin, 9 February 1926; educated Belvedere College, University College, Dublin and King's Inns; worked as a research and schedules manager in Aer Lingus and later as lecturer in Political Economy, University College, Dublin; Fine Gael senator, 1965-69 and TD 1969-92; leader of Fine Gael, 1977-87; government minister, 1973-77; Taoiseach 1981-82 and 1982-87. Led his party to its largest ever share of electoral support in 1982; his liberal agenda was undermined by conservative outcomes in referendums on abortion (1983) and divorce (1986), but his Northern Ireland policy was significantly advanced by the signing of the Anglo-Irish Agreement (1985).

Griffith, Arthur. Born Dublin, 31 March 1871; educated Christian Brothers, Dublin; worked as a printer and then as a journalist; editor of a number of nationalist periodicals and pamphlets; founder of Sinn Féin party and member of Irish Volunteers, but did not participate in 1916 rising; Sinn Féin MP/TD, 1918-22; minister in Dáil government, 1919-22; President of Dáil government, 1922; died 12 August 1922. Was responsible for popularising the Sinn Féin policy of economic self-reliance after 1905; this also envisaged following the Hungarian model of 1867, by which an independent Irish state would be established as part of a dual monarchy, linked to Britain only by the crown.

Haughey, Charles J. Born Castlebar, Co Mayo, 16 September 1925; educated Christian Brothers, Dublin, University College, Dublin, and King's Inns; worked as an accountant; Fianna Fáil TD, 1957-92; leader of Fianna Fáil, 1979-92; parliamentary secretary, 1960-61; government minister, 1961-70 and 1977-79; Taoiseach 1979-81, 1982, 1987-92. A son-in-law of Seán Lemass; was dismissed as Minister for Finance by Jack Lynch in 1970 in the course of the "Arms Crisis", but was acquitted in court of all charges; fought his way back to emerge as party leader in 1979 with the support of the party's backbenchers; led his party into its first ever coalition government in 1989.

Healy, Timothy. Born Bantry, Co Cork, 17 May 1855; educated local Christian Brothers; worked in England as a railway clerk and later as a nationalist journalist; Nationalist MP 1880-86, 1887-1910 and 1911-18 (anti-Parnellite, 1890-1900, then an independent Nationalist); Governor-General, 1922-28; died 26 March 1931. Noted as a lively and witty debater, but divisive as a political figure.

Hillery, Patrick. Born Miltown Malbay, Co Clare, 2 May 1923; educated Rockwell College and University College, Dublin; practised as a medical doctor; Fianna Fáil TD, 1951-72; government minister, 1959-72; Irish member of EC Commission, 1973-76; President of Ireland, 1976-90, a post for which he was an unopposed nominee. As Minister for External Affairs, was responsible for handling Irish foreign policy in the difficult period coinciding with the outbreak of the Northern Ireland troubles and with the negotiation of EC membership.

Hyde, Douglas. Born Castlerea, Co Roscommon, 17 January 1860; educated Trinity College, Dublin; collector of Irish folklore, of which he published many volumes; professor of Modern Irish, University College, Dublin; founder member of Gaelic League, of which he was first president (1893-1915); maintained a non-political role, and resigned as president of the League when it began to follow a more political path; independent member in Senate of Irish Free State, 1925, but failed to secure election in 1925 Senate general election; senator (Taoiseach's nominee), 1938; President of Ireland, 1938-45, a post for which he was an all-party choice; died 12 July 1949. Son of a Protestant rector in Co Roscommon, was much loved by language revivalists for his work for their movement, and was the author of the first play in Irish ever to appear on a professional stage (1901).

Lemass, Seán. Born Dublin, 15 July 1899; educated Christian Brothers; worked in his father's drapery shop; joined Irish Volunteers and participated in 1916 rising; active in IRA, 1919-23; anti-Treaty Sinn Féin and Fianna Fáil TD, 1924-69; government minister, 1932-48, 1951-54, 1957-59; Tánaiste, 1945-48, 1951-54, 1957-59; Taoiseach 1959-66; died 11 May 1971. Associated with the shift in Fianna Fáil, of which he was a founder member, from traditional nationalist policies to support for rapid economic development and normalisation of relations with Britain and Northern Ireland.

Lenihan, Brian. Born Dundalk, Co Louth, 17 November 1930; educated Marist Brothers, Athlone, University College, Dublin and King's Inns; worked as a barrister; Fianna Fáil TD, 1961-73, and since 1977; lost his seat, 1973; Fianna Fáil senator, 1973-77; parliamentary secretary, 1961-64; government minister, 1964-73, 1977-81, 1982, 1987-90; Tánaiste, 1987-90. An enormously popular politician, was a casualty of an incident during the 1990 presidential election campaign in which he appeared to be giving contradictory versions of an event in 1982 involving an alleged attempt to bring undue pressure to bear on the President; though he sought to explain the incident away in terms of his medical condition (he was seriously ill at the time and under heavy medication), it is believed to have cost him the presidency and it brought about his dismissal as Tánaiste.

Lynch, John (Jack). Born Cork, 15 August 1917; educated Christian Brothers, Cork, University College, Cork, King's Inns; worked in civil service and later as a barrister; Fianna Fáil TD, 1948-81; parliamentary secretary, 1951-54; government minister, 1957-66; Taoiseach, 1966-73 and 1977-79. His sporting background (in Gaelic football and hurling) and personable character won him immense popularity; his qualities as a leader were severely tested in the early years of the Northern Ireland troubles (1969-70), as his party sought to come to terms with the state's impotence in the face of attacks on nationalists in the North;

in 1977, led his party to its greatest ever size in the Dáil and largest share of the vote since 1938, but ironically was forced to step down as leader two years later.

MacEntee, Seán. Born Belfast, 22 August 1889; educated St Malachy's College, Belfast, and Belfast Municipal College of Technology; worked as a consulting electrical engineer and registered patent agent; active in Irish Volunteers; participated in 1916 rising, sentenced to death but reprieved; active in IRA; Sinn Féin MP/TD, 1918-22; Fianna Fáil TD, 1927-69; government minister, 1932-48, 1951-54, 1957-65; Tánaiste, 1959-65; died 10 January 1984. Noted as a poet in his early life, later devoted himself fully to politics.

MacNeill, James. Born Glenarm, Co Antrim, 27 or 29 March 1869; educated Belvedere College, Dublin, and Cambridge University; worked in Indian civil service; on early retirement joined Sinn Féin; Irish high commissioner in London, 1923-28; Governor-General, 1928-32; died 12 December 1938. Though with a less political past than his elder brother, Eoin (Professor of History at University College, Dublin, leader of the Irish Volunteers and government minister, 1922-25), became fully immersed in political conflict in 1932 following the change of government; de Valera forced his resignation as Governor-General within a few months.

MacSharry, Ray. Born Sligo, 29 April 1938; educated locally and Summerhill College, Sligo; worked as a haulier, auctioneer and farm owner; Fianna Fáil TD, 1969-89; minister of state, 1977-79; government minister, 1979-81, 1982, 1987-89; Tánaiste, 1982. Rated very highly as minister for finance, went on to become an extremely successful EC commissioner for agriculture, a position from which he retired in 1992.

Norton, William. Born Dublin, 1900; educated locally; worked in the post office and as a trade union official; Labour TD, 1926-27, 1932-63; lost his seat, 1927; leader of the Labour Party, 1932-60; Tánaiste 1948-51, 1954-57; died 4 December 1963. Though he built up the support base of his party until 1943 and led it into government for the first time ever in 1948, in his later years was more preoccupied with trade union affairs and with his own constituency than with the leadership of the party.

Ó Buachalla, Dónal (also known by the English form of his name, **Daniel Buckley**). Born Maynooth, Co Kildare, 3 February 1866; educated Belvedere College and Catholic University School, Dublin; owner of a shop in Maynooth; member of the Gaelic League and IRB; participated in 1916 rising; Sinn Féin MP 1918-22; Fianna Fáil TD, 1927-32 (lost his seat in 1922 and again in 1932); Governor-General, 1932-36; died 31 October 1963. Achieved early prominence when prosecuted for painting his name in Irish on his cart; as Governor-General avoided meeting the King, never left the state and resided in a house in Dun Laoghaire rather than in the Viceregal Lodge in the Phoenix Park.

Ó Ceallaigh, Seán T. (also known by the English form of his name, **Seán T. O'Kelly**). Born Dublin, 25 August 1882; educated Christian Brothers; active in Gaelic League, Celtic Literary Society, IRB and Sinn Féin; participated in 1916 rising; Sinn Féin MP/TD, 1918-22; anti-Treaty Sinn Féin and Fianna Fáil TD, 1922-45; Ceann Comhairle of first Dáil; government minister, 1932-45; Vice President of Executive Council, 1932-37; Tánaiste, 1937-45; President of Ireland, 1945-59; died 23 November 1966. Though personally popular, was in effect "pushed upstairs" to the presidency in 1945, making way for Seán Lemass, 17 years his junior, to take over as Tánaiste and heir apparent to de Valera.

Ó Dálaigh, Cearbhall. Born Bray, Co Wicklow, 12 February 1911; educated Christian Brothers and University College, Dublin; called to the bar, 1944; active in Fianna Fáil; Attorney General 1946-48, 1951-53; Supreme Court judge, 1953; Chief Justice, 1961; Irish member of European Court of Justice, 1972; President of Ireland, 1974-76, a post for which he was an unopposed nominee; died 21 March 1978. A lover of the Irish language; his resignation from the presidency was precipitated by a chain of events that began when the Minister for Defence, speaking at a military function, described him as "a thundering disgrace" for referring an Emergency Powers Bill to the Supreme Court to test its constitutionality.

O'Higgins, Kevin. Born Stradbally, Co Laois, 7 June 1892; educated Clongowes Wood and University College, Dublin; early member of Sinn Féin; Sinn Féin MP/TD, 1918-22; pro-Treaty Sinn Féin and Cumann na nGaedheal TD, 1922-27; government minister, 1922-27; Vice President of the Executive Council, 1923-27; assassinated on 10 July 1927 while walking to mass by a group of anti-Treaty IRA members of the 1922-23 period who came upon him by accident. As Minister for Home Affairs during the civil war, was associated with the strong measures taken by the government to ensure victory, including the execution of 77 of the anti-Treaty side.

O'Leary, Michael. Born Cork, 8 May 1936; educated Presentation College, Cork and University College, Cork; worked as a trade union official; Labour TD, 1965-82; Fine Gael TD, 1982-87; leader of the Labour Party, 1981-82; government minister, 1973-77, 1981-82; Tánaiste, 1981-82. Associated with his party's move to the left in the late 1960s and initially an opponent of coalition, his switch of allegiance to Fine Gael in 1982 was one of the more spectacular somersaults in Irish politics.

Reynolds, Albert. Born Rooskey, Co Roscommon, 3 November 1932; educated Summerhill College, Sligo; worked as director of his own petfood company; Fianna Fáil TD since 1977; government minister 1979-81, 1982, 1987-92; Taoiseach since 1992. Though regarded as one of the more conservative members of his party, negotiated a coalition agreement with Labour following his defeat in the 1992 general election.

Robinson, Mary. Born Ballina, Co Mayo, 21 May 1944; educated Mount Anville, Paris, Trinity College, Dublin, and Harvard University; Reid Professor of Constitutional and Criminal Law, Trinity College, Dublin; independent senator, 1969-76, 1985-89; Labour party senator, 1976-85; President of Ireland since 1990. Resigned the Labour whip in 1985 over the party's support for the Anglo-Irish Agreement, but was nominated and supported by Labour in her successful presidential election campaign in 1990.

Spring, Dick. Born Tralee, Co Kerry, 29 August 1950; educated Christian Brothers, Tralee, St Joseph's, Roscrea, Trinity College, Dublin and King's Inns; worked as a barrister; Labour TD since 1981; leader of the Labour Party since 1982; Tánaiste 1982-87 and since 1993. Enjoying an enormously high rating with the voters as leader of his party, his victory in 1992 placed him in a much stronger position than any previous Labour leader in hammering out a coalition deal and in giving Labour a more powerful position in cabinet than ever previously.

Wilson, John. Born Kilcogy, Co Cavan, 8 July 1923; educated St Mel's College, Longford, University of London and University College, Dublin; worked as a teacher and university lecturer; Fianna Fáil TD, 1973-92; government minister, 1977-81, 1982, 1987-92; Tánaiste, 1990-92. One of the more popular elder statesmen within Fianna Fáil, took over as Tánaiste when the politically wounded Brian Lenihan was dismissed during the presidential election campaign; a witty contributor in the Dáil, and a Latin scholar.

Glossary

Áras an Uachtaráin (*aw*-rus un *ook*-ta-rawn) - Residence of the President

ard-fheis (ord-*esh*) - national convention [of a political party]

Bunreacht na hÉireann (*bun*-rokt ne *hay*run) - constitution of Ireland

Cathaoirleach (ka-*heer*-luck) - chairman [of the Senate]

Ceann Comhairle (kyon *kohr*-le) - speaker or chairman [of the Dáil]

Clann na Poblachta (clon ne *pub*-lak-ta) - "party of the republic" [party name, 1946-65]

Clann na Talmhan (clon ne *tal*-oon) - "party of the land" [party name, 1939-65]

comhairle ceantair (*koh*-er-le *kyon*-ter) - district council [in Fianna Fáil]

comhairle dáilcheantair (*koh*-er-le *dawl*-kyon-ter) - constituency council [in Fianna Fáil]

cumann (*kum*-man) - branch [of a political party or other organisation]; plural **cumainn**

Cumann na nGaedheal (*kum*-man ne *ngale*) - "party of the Irish" [party name, 1923-33]

Dáil Éireann (dawl *ay*-run) - national assembly of Ireland; plural **Dála**

Éire (*ay*-reh) - Ireland

Fianna Fáil (*fee*-an-a *fawl*) - "soldiers of Ireland" [party name]

Fine Gael (*fin*-a *gale*) - "Irish race" [party name]

Gaeltacht (*gale*-tuckt) - Irish-speaking districts

garda [síochána] (*gawr*-da shee-*kaw*-ne) - [civic] guard, policeman; plural **gardaí**

Oireachtas (*ih*-rock-tus) - parliament

Saorstát Éireann (*sayr*-stawt *ay*-run) - Irish Free State

Seanad Éireann (*sha*-nad *ay*-run) - senate of Ireland

Sinn Féin (shin *fayn*) - "ourselves" [party name]

Tánaiste (*taw*-nish-deh) - deputy prime minister

Taoiseach (*tee*-shuck) - prime minister; plural **Taoisigh**

Teachta Dála (*tak*-tuh *dawl*-uh) - Dáil deputy, TD

Uachtarán (*ook*-ta-rawn) - president

Note: A number of the party names above have a range of alternative translations; see John Coakley, "The significance of names: the evolution of Irish party labels", *Études Irlandaises*, 5, 1980, pp. 171-81. The pronunciation system indicated above is approximate only, and follows in part that in Howard Penniman and Brian Farrell (eds), *Ireland at the Polls: a Study of Four General Elections* (Durham, NC: Duke University Press, 1987), pp. 265-6. Italics indicate stressed syllables.

Notes on contributors

John Coakley is Lecturer in Politics at University College Dublin and Secretary General of the International Political Science Association. He has published extensively on Irish and comparative politics, and has edited *The Social Origins of Nationalist Movements* (London, 1992) and *The Territorial Management of Ethnic Conflict* (London, 1993), as well as a special issue of the *International Political Science Review* on the resolution of ethnic conflict.

Brian Farrell is former Associate Professor of Government at University College, Dublin. His extensive writings on Irish politics include: *Chairman or Chief?* (Dublin, 1971), *Seán Lemass* (Dublin, 1983) and the edited collections *The Irish Parliamentary Tradition* (Dublin, 1973), *Communications and Community* (Dublin, 1984), and *De Valera's Constitution and Ours* (Dublin, 1988). He is also senior presenter on RTE current affairs television and, in that capacity, has interviewed all leading politicians of the last 30 years.

Michael Gallagher is a lecturer in the Department of Political Science at Trinity College Dublin. He is author of *The Irish Labour Party in Transition* (Manchester, 1982), *Political Parties in the Republic of Ireland* (Manchester, 1985), co-author of *Representative Government in Modern Europe* (New York, 1995), and co-editor of *Candidate Selection in Comparative Perspective* (London, 1988), *How Ireland Voted 1989* (Galway, 1990), *How Ireland Voted 1992* (Dublin and Limerick, 1993) and *The Referendum Experience in Europe* (Basingstoke, 1996). He was co-editor of *Irish Political Studies* 1992–94.

Yvonne Galligan is a lecturer in the Department of Political Science at Trinity College Dublin. She is author of a number of articles on women and politics and has contributed to *Irish Political Studies, West European Politics, Gender and the Law in Ireland* (edited by Alpha Connelly, Dublin, 1992), and *Gender and Party Politics* (edited by Joni Lovenduski and Pippa Norris, London, 1993).

Tom Garvin is Professor of Politics and Head of the Department of Politics at University College, Dublin. He is the author of many publications on Irish politics, including *The Evolution of Irish Nationalist Politics* (Dublin, 1981) and *Nationalist Revolutionaries in Ireland 1858-1928* (Oxford, 1988).

Patrick Keatinge is Jean Monnet Professor in European Integration at Trinity College, Dublin. His publications include *The Formulation of Irish Foreign Policy* (Dublin, 1974), *A Place Among the Nations: Issues of Irish Foreign Policy* (Dublin, 1978), *A Singular Stance: Irish Neutrality in the 1980s* (Dublin, 1984), and many articles on Irish foreign policy. He edited *Ireland and EC Membership Evaluated* (London, 1991) and *Ireland and Maastricht: what the Treaty means* (Dublin, 1992).

Lee Komito is a lecturer in the Department of Library and Information Studies at University College Dublin. He is an anthropologist, whose main research interests are urban politics, social networks, and information technology and culture. He has published extensively in these areas, and has contributed to *Ireland from*

Below: Social Change and Local Communities (Galway, 1989) and *Environment and Development in Ireland* (1992).

Brigid Laffan is Jean Monnet Professor in European Politics at University College Dublin. She is author of numerous articles on European integration and has contributed to *Making European Policies Work* (edited by H. Siedentopf and J. Ziller, London, 1988) and to *Ireland and EC Membership Evaluated* (edited by P. Keatinge, London, 1991). She wrote a book on *Ireland and South Africa: Government Policy in the 1980s* (Dublin, 1988), and her *Cooperation and Integration in Europe* (London) was published in 1992.

Michael Laver is Professor of Political Science at Trinity College Dublin. Before that he held the Chair in Political Science and Sociology at University College Galway. He has also taught at Queen's University Belfast, the University of Liverpool, the University of Texas at Austin, Harvard University and Duke University. Recent books include the co-authored *Representative Government in Modern Europe* (1995), and *Making and Breaking Governments* (1996). He also coedits the *European Journal of Political Research*.

Peter Mair is Professor of Politics at the University of Leiden. He has published widely in the fields of Irish and comparative European politics, is author of *The Changing Irish Party System* (1987) and coauthor of *Representative Government in Modern Europe* (1995) and *Identity, Competition and Electoral Availability* (1990), which was awarded the Stein Rokkan Prize in Comparative Social Research.

Michael Marsh is a Senior Lecturer in Political Science at Trinity College Dublin. He coedited *Candidate Selection in Comparative Perspective* (London, 1988) and *Modern Irish Democracy* (Dublin, 1993), and has been co-editor of *Irish Political Studies*. He edited a special issue of the *European Journal of Political Research*, dealing with the selection of party leaders, and has written a range of articles on electoral behaviour and political parties.

Eunan O'Halpin is Associate Professor in Government and Public Administration at Dublin City University. He is the author of *The Decline of the Union: British Government in Ireland, 1892-1920* (Dublin, 1987) and *Head of the Civil Service: a Study of Sir Warren Fisher* (London, 1989). He is preparing books on the Irish administrative system and on *The State and its Enemies: Defence, Security and Subversion in Ireland, 1922-92*.

Richard Sinnott is a lecturer in the Department of Politics at University College Dublin. He has written extensively on Irish electoral behaviour and public opinion. He is a contributing co-editor of *How Ireland Voted 1987* (Swords, 1987) and *How Ireland Voted 1989* (Galway, 1990), and his *Irish Voters Decide: Voting Behaviour in Elections and Referendums since 1918* was published by Manchester University Press in 1995.

Index